Proportional Representation on Trial

Proportional Representation on Trial

Jack Vowles, Peter Aimer, Jeffrey Karp, Susan Banducci, Raymond Miller, Ann Sullivan

Auckland University Press

First published 2002
Auckland University Press
University of Auckland
Private Bag 92019
Auckland, New Zealand
http://www.auckland.ac.nz/aup

ISBN 1 86940 265 0

Typeset by Amy Tansell
Printed by Publishing Press, Auckland

CONTENTS

Tables and Figures   vii

Preface   xi

Part I: The 1999 Election

1. New Zealand Politics in the 1990s   1
   Peter Aimer and Raymond Miller

2. Did the Campaign Matter?   16
   Jack Vowles

3. Elections, Citizens, and the Media   34
   Susan Banducci and Jack Vowles

4. Gender and Leadership   50
   Susan Banducci

5. Coming Home? Maori Voting in 1999   66
   Ann Sullivan and Dimitri Margaritis

6. What Happened at the 1999 Election?   83
   Jack Vowles

Part II: The Impact of Electoral System Change

7. The Puzzle of Turnout   99
   Jack Vowles

8. Coalition Government: The Labour–Alliance Pact   114
   Raymond Miller

9. Members of Parliament and Representation   130
   Jeffrey Karp

10. Direct Democracy on Trial: The Citizens-Initiated
    Referendums   146
    Jeffrey Karp and Peter Aimer

Part III: Evaluating MMP

11. Public Opinion, Public Knowledge and the Electoral System   160
    Jack Vowles, Jeffrey Karp, Susan Banducci, Peter Aimer

12. Reviewing MMP   175
    Jack Vowles, Jeffrey Karp, Susan Banducci, Peter Aimer, Raymond Miller

Appendixes
A. The New Zealand Election Study   192
B. Questionnaires   196
C. Statistical Methods and Supplementary Tables   220
D. Section 264 of the Electoral Act 1993   230
E. Summary of NZES Recommendations for the MMP
    Review, July 2000   231

Notes   233

References   239

Notes on Authors   249

Index   251

TABLES AND FIGURES

Tables

Table 2.1   Flow of Vote Intentions 18 October–6 November to Party Vote
27 November

Table 2.2   Per Cent Most Popular Leader Ratings, Comparing First Half of
Campaign to Post-Election (Panel)

Table 2.3   Most Important Issue by Party Closest on Most Important Issue,
Campaign Panel Respondents

Table 2.4   Most Preferred Party on the Issues, Pre- and Post-Election,
Comparing First Half of Campaign to Election Day

Table 2.5   Opinion Polls Released during the 1999 Campaign: Countrywide, Coromandel and Tauranga

Table 2.6   Party Most Preferred and Party Vote

Table 2.7   Significant Effects of Party Identification, Campaign Intention,
Issue and Leader Preference Change on Election Day Vote
(Percentage Probabilities)

Table 3.1   During the election campaign, how often did you follow the
election news and advertising on the television and in the
newspapers?

Table 3.2   Rankings of Issues and the 1999 Election Agenda: Parties, One
News, and the Voters

Table 4.1   How Leadership Traits Affect Party Vote Choice: Change in
Probability of Party Vote

Table 4.2   How Traits Affected National and Labour Party Switches:
Estimating Probability of Switching to Labour or National

Table 5.1   Voting in the 1996 and 1999 Elections, Change, and Split Voting
by Party

Table 5.2   Flow of the Maori Electorate Votes from 1996 to 1999

Table 5.3   Voting, Vote Change from 1996, and Split Voting in the Maori
Electorates, 1999

Table 5.4   Party and Electorate Votes: Defections from the Party Vote in the
             Maori Electorates, 1999 Election
Table 5.5   Party Vote Preferences and Social Groups
Table 5.6   Maori Attitudes on Economic, Social and Maori Issues

Table 6.1   Seats, Votes and Hypothetical FPP Vote at the 1999 Election
Table 6.2   Party and Electorate Votes: Defections from the Party Vote, 1999
             Election
Table 6.3   Flow of the Party Votes from 1996 to 1999
Table 6.4   Turnout and Party Membership, 1990–1999
Table 6.5   The National/Labour Gender Gap in New Zealand Elections,
             1963–1999

Table 7.1   Campaign Expenditures in 1999 and Percentage Changes from
             1996
Table 7.2   1996 and 1999: Did Anyone from the Following Political Parties
             Contact You during the Campaign?
Table 7.3   Campaign Contacts, Percentages by Number, 1996 and 1999
Table 7.4   Types of Contacts by Party, 1999 Election and (1996) Election,
             Percentages Contacted
Table 7.5   Attitudes, Perceptions and Non-voting

Table 8.1   Single-Party versus Coalition Government, 1999 Campaign,
             by Intending Voters
Table 8.2   Campaign Opinion: MMP Gives Too Much Power to Small
             Parties
Table 8.3   Parties Should Announce Their Coalition Intentions in Advance

Table 9.1   Attitudes Toward Descriptive Representation (1993–99)
Table 9.2   Opinions About Maori Seats Over Time and by Enrolment
             Status
Table 9.3   Changes in Political Attitudes Over Time (% in agreement)
Table 9.4   Opinions about Electorate and List MPs, 1999
Table 9.5   Opinions about Open Lists and Approval of List MPs, 1999
Table 9.6   Importance of Representative Activities by Candidate Type
Table 9.7   Time Spent by Incumbent MPs
Table 9.8   Number of Constituents Problems per Week

Table 10.1   Mass Opinion about Direct Democracy (%)
Table 10.2   Elite Opinion about Direct Democracy (%)

Table 11.1   Would You Vote to Retain or Replace MMP? (%)
Table 11.2   Vote to Retain MMP 1993–2001: Voters/Intending Voters and
             Party Candidates
Table 11.3   MMP Disaster, Too Soon To Tell, or Success? Opinion 1998–
             2001
Table 11.4   Preferences for Coalition or Single-Party Government, 1998–
             2001

Table 11.5   Generally speaking, do you think that a government formed by one party, or one formed by more than one party, is better at doing the following things?

Table 11.6   MMP versus FPP, Core and Soft Support by Knowledge of PR and Electoral Systems

Table 11.7   Attitudes to Proportionality

Table 11.8   Attitudes Toward Proportionality: Manufactured Majority

Table 11.9   Proportionality vs. Single-Party Governments, Voters and Candidates Post-Election 1999

Table 12.1   Knowledge by Opinion on the Size of the House

Table 12.2   Women and Minorities in Parliament 1990, 1993, 1996 and 1999 Elections

Table 12.3   Opinions on Changes to MMP, June–July 2001

Table 12.4   Referendums and Time to decide, 2000–2001

Table 12.5   An MMP Scorecard

Supplementary Tables (Appendix C)

Chapter 3:
Estimated coefficients for Figure 3.2: Probability of Voting Labour: Logistic Regression Coefficients
Estimated coefficients used in Figure 3.4: Media Tone, Gender and Preferred Prime Minister

Chapter 4:
Full model for Table 4.1: How Leadership Traits Affect Party Vote Choice: Change in Probability of Party Vote
Full model for Table 4.2: How Traits Affected National and Labour Party Switches: Estimating Probability of Switching to Labour or National
Full Model for Figure 4.4: The Impact of Trait Ratings on Preferred Prime Minister

Chapter 6:
Vote by Social Structure, 1999 Election (Percentages)
Social Structure and Voting Choices, 1999 (Regression Coefficients)

Chapter 10:
Explaining Voting to Reduce the Number of MPs (Logistic Regression Coefficients)
Explaining Voting to Get Tough on Crime (Logistic Regression Coefficients)

Figures

Figure 1.1   One News/Colmar Brunton Polls, 1997–October 1999

Figure 1.2   Preferred Prime Minister, 1997–October 1999

Figure 1.3   Support for National, Economic Optimism and Economic Growth, 1995–99

x *Proportional Representation on Trial*

Figure 2.1   Campaign Trends in Voting Intentions to Election Day Vote, 1999 Election
Figure 2.2   Percentage of Respondents with a Different Pre-Election Vote Intention Than Their Reported Vote by Day of Campaign (Five-Day Rolling Averages)
Figure 2.3   Did the Polls Underpin the Green Surge in the Party Vote?
Figure 2.4   A Model of Campaign Effects

Figure 3.1   A Comparison of News Coverage: TV One and TV3 18 October –6 November (first eight stories only)
Figure 3.2   Media Exposure, Leader Evaluation and Issues
Figure 3.3   Evaluation of Party Leaders — One News
Figure 3.4   Media Tone, Gender and Preferred Prime Minister

Figure 4.1   Preferred Prime Minister during the Campaign
Figure 4.2   Gender Differences on Preferred Prime Minister: Shipley and Clark
Figure 4.3   Shipley and Clark: Leadership Traits during the Campaign
Figure 4.4   Effect of Traits on Preferred Prime Minister
Figure 4.5   Gender Differences in Leadership Traits: Post-Election

Figure 6.1   Respondents' Placements on the Left–Right Scale and the Average Placements for Parties by Respondents
Figure 6.2   Party Identification Trends in New Zealand, 1975–1999
Figure 6.3   Class Voting in New Zealand, 1963–1999
Figures 6.4–6.9   Age, Non-Voting, and Party Voting

Figure 7.1   Comparing Turnout by Electorate Safety/Marginality, 1990 and 1999 (Electorate Vote)
Figure 7.2.   Accounting for Turnout Decline, 1996–1999

Figure 8.1   Support for MMP and Support for Government Parties
Figure 8.2   Preference for Single-Party or Coalition Outcome: National and Labour Voters, 1999 Campaign
Figure 8.3   Campaign Coalition Expectations
Figure 8.4   Campaign Coalition Preferences
Figure 8.5   Labour–Alliance–Green Coalition Preferences

Figure 9.1   Party Positions under FPP and MMP

Figure 10.1   Factors Influencing Likelihood of Voting to Reduce the Number of MPs
Figure 10.2   Factors Influencing Likelihood of Voting to Get Tough on Crime

PREFACE

Proportional Representation on Trial is the fourth in a series of studies of New Zealanders as they go to the polls every three years, exercising their democratic right to choose their elected parliamentary representatives. The series, published by Auckland University Press, arises out of the New Zealand Election Study (NZES) programme (see Appendix A). The core of the programme is a nationwide survey of citizens qualified to vote, conducted immediately after each election. From the many thousands of respondents to our questionnaires, we can present a unique picture of the way individual voters' responses to events and people in politics produce a collective decision — an election result. Together, the four election studies are a record of an extraordinary decade of political and constitutional change.

The first book in the series, *Voters' Vengeance*, described how the Lange–Palmer–Moore Labour government was swept aside in the 1990 election. *Proportional Representation on Trial* sees Labour return to office in 1999, but in the unfamiliar role of partner in a minority coalition government. Never in the party's long history had it shared power in this way. This was not because it had won a smaller share of the votes than ever before, but because the votes were tallied up in a different way. The 1999 election was New Zealand's second election under proportional representation (PR). Under PR more parties could win more seats in Parliament than under the former first-past-the-post (FPP) voting system. No party could now confidently expect to govern alone with a manufactured majority as in the past.

The campaign for electoral reform in the second half of the 1980s, the decisive referendum in 1993, and the introduction of the mixed-member proportional (MMP) system in 1996 marked a historic process that few developed democracies have experienced in the last half-century. There could be no clean switch from 'classic' first-past-the-post electoral politics to proportional representation. Rather, the referendum of 1993 initiated a period of transition. The process of adaptation to the new electoral environment was complex and slow. Opponents of MMP maintained their rage. Legally also the process was not over by 1999. The 1993 Electoral Act required the incoming government to undertake a parliamentary review of MMP to be completed by June 2002.

In and after the 1999 election, therefore, proportional representation was still on trial, as the book's title asserts. The book has a dual focus. It continues the catalogue of voting behaviour of ordinary citizens, election by election, begun in 1990; and it identifies, analyses and evaluates the major effects of MMP up to and since the 1999 election.

The chapters in Section 1 of *Proportional Representation on Trial* are primarily concerned with the conduct, events and outcome of the election. The first chapter places the 1999 contest in the context of the turbulent political events of the decade. For most people an election begins and ends with the few weeks of intense campaign activities before polling day. Yet many have been forming their political impressions and making up their minds for a long time before the campaign. Chapter 2 therefore asks the question: 'Did the Campaign Matter?'. Before the campaign, but even more during it, voters rely on the media for political information, opinions and impressions. This vital process is examined in Chapter 3. One election outcome was certain before the campaign even began, namely that after polling day New Zealand would have its second woman Prime Minister. The rivalry between Jenny Shipley, the incumbent, and Helen Clark, the challenger, attracted international attention. How people saw and responded to the two women contestants and to the leaders of the smaller parties is the subject of Chapter 4. As Dover Samuels, MP for Te Tai Tokerau, avows, 'Maori politics is never boring'. One of the most dramatic results in the 1996 election had been Labour's loss of all five Maori electorates. This result was overturned in 1999, when Maori voters 'came home' again to Labour, as Chapter 5 explains. The return of Maori voters to Labour was a significant factor in the election outcome, but by no means the only one. The final chapter in Section 1 demonstrates that indeed many factors contribute to an election result, some working directly toward the result, others having contradictory effects.

Chapters 7–10 in Section 2 discuss the impact of MMP on several fundamental aspects of a functioning democracy. Proportional voting systems worldwide are associated with higher levels of citizen participation than plurality (FPP) systems. Advocates of MMP had used this fact in support of their case for electoral reform. In 1996, turnout for the first MMP election in New Zealand rose; at the second election in 1999 it declined again. Why? Chapter 7 searches for an answer. Perhaps the most significant effect of MMP has been the destruction of the 'manufactured' parliamentary majorities that had underpinned 60 years of one-party governments in New Zealand. Until 1996, governments were determined on election night. Under proportional representation the process of government-building begins (or ought to begin) before the election with the search by parties for potential parliamentary allies, and continues after the election in negotiations for a possible coalition. Parties and politicians nurtured in the old ways have struggled to adjust to the demands of the more multi-party setting under MMP. Chapter 8 backgrounds and describes the formation of the Labour–Alliance minority coalition government, and presents the stark contrast with the previous National–New Zealand First government. One effect of MMP that even its opponents acknowledge (not always approvingly) has been the election of more diversely representative Parliaments. This is explored in Chapter 9. Besides their voting papers, people were confronted with two referendum questions in 1999. Originating as citizens' initiatives under the process laid down in the Citizens

Initiated Referenda Act (1993), the referendums were another constitutional innovation 'on trial', only one CIR having been held since the Act was passed. This experiment in 'direct democracy' is examined in Chapter 10.

The final two chapters in *Proportional Representation on Trial* begin the process of evaluating the new electoral system. It is only a beginning, because as reported in Chapter 11, many people acknowledge that the transition to the new politics of proportional representation is still under way, and that it is 'too soon to tell' whether MMP is working as intended or not. MMP has experienced a rocky path to date, and for busy people, preoccupied with other things in life, impressions of politics since the advent of PR have often been unfavourable. At the same time, many can see that changes of this magnitude take time, and are prepared to withhold definitive judgement for a while longer. Others are more willing to write off the new system. But there is much in MMP that appeals to many people who do not want the proverbial baby to be sacrificed with the bathwater. Chapter 11 explores the structure and trends of public opinion toward MMP. Finally, Chapter 12 presents an overall evaluation of electoral system change. It takes account of the parliamentary select committee's review of MMP in July 2001, but concludes that neither politicians' committees nor citizens' initiatives provide the best means of determining important constitutional issues.

Full acknowledgements of the various sources of funding and institutional support of this research can be found in Appendix A. All authors are either contracted under the Foundation for Research, Science, and Technology to deliver the NZES (Vowles, Aimer, Miller, and Sullivan), or served as Research Fellows in the programme (Banducci and Karp). Information about the NZES programme can be found on its web page at <http://www.nzes.org>. Susan Banducci and Jeffrey Karp's continued participation has been with the support of their current employers at the University of Amsterdam, for which we are all most grateful. Peter Aimer deserves the thanks of all the other authors for taking on a large part of the editorial task. His hand is visible throughout the entire book, and it is much the better for it. He was also responsible for the candidate survey. Aside from the Maori Election Study, which was contracted to A. C. Neilsen (NZ) Ltd, Jack Vowles, Jeff Karp and Susan Banducci oversaw the collection of the other data sets, assisted in the editorial process, and drew the figures. Of course, the success of a study like this one requires the participation of many people beyond the group of authors listed here. They warmly acknowledge the wisdom of the Auckland University Press committee, and the director, Elizabeth Caffin, for again undertaking publication of our research. They acknowledge also the contributions of Katrina Duncan, Christine O'Brien and Annie Irving, at Auckland University Press, and Amy Tansell, for her skill in turning a disk into a book. Simon Cauchi as copy-editor found and repaired blemishes and inconsistencies in the text and tables. Research assistants over the period of the study made a great contribution: they were Matthew Gibbons, Philippa Miskelly, and most of all Clare Williams, who bore the brunt of the campaign study and the immediate post-election process of data preparation. We owe thanks to numerous other people, too many to name, who have helped us in significant ways. Above all, we owe a huge debt to the thousands of people who participated as respondents in the various stages of the study. Without them, the project would have been impossible.

Jack Vowles, Peter Aimer, Jeffrey Karp, Susan Banducci,
Raymond Miller, Ann Sullivan
August 2001

CHAPTER 1

NEW ZEALAND POLITICS
IN THE 1990s

Peter Aimer and Raymond Miller

The 1990s belonged to National after Jim Bolger led the party back into government in 1990. It was then another nine years until National finally lost its place on the Treasury benches in the last election of the decade. Yet the appearance of political stability and one-party dominance given by National's three consecutive terms in office was deceptive. The 1990s were the most electorally unsettled decade for more than fifty years. People were cynical about politicians, distrustful of the major parties, and volatile in their party choices (Vowles and Aimer 1993; Vowles, Aimer, Catt, Lamare, Miller 1995). The historic outcome of this was radical electoral reform. The introduction of the mixed-member proportional (MMP) form of proportional representation in 1996 was undoubtedly the pivotal political event of the decade. With MMP came major changes at all levels of politics, from the grassroots to the top floor of the 'Beehive' (the distinctively shaped building housing the cabinet and executive offices of New Zealand government).

Voter Volatility and MMP: 1990–93

Early in the decade, the fluctuating electoral fortunes of the two major parties were a clear measure of the public's political disquietude. On election day in 1990, legions of angry and disillusioned former Labour voters abandoned the party. Many simply stayed at home, while others fled in every political direction, most switching to National, or to one of the two prominent new parties, the Greens, or NewLabour, led by Labour's former President and the sitting MP for Sydenham, Jim Anderton (Vowles and Aimer 1993, 9–15). Together, NewLabour and the Greens siphoned off 12 per cent of the votes, both crossing the future 5 per cent threshold for parliamentary representation under MMP. But under first-past-the-post (FPP), their voters were too thinly spread across the country to be effective in the 97 separate electorate contests. Only Anderton beat off his opponents in Sydenham to sit in Parliament as the sole MP outside the ranks of National or Labour. Not for the first time, the House of Representatives was conspicuously unrepresentative of the wider

1

electorate, a result that advocates of voting reform were quick to exploit. Nearly 220,000 people had voted for the two new parties, with only one MP to show for it. After 1990, most of these voters would be eager recruits to the cause of electoral reform.

The issue of electoral reform had surfaced during the term of the Labour government (1984–90), which had appointed a Royal Commission on the electoral system. In December 1986, the commission startled many people and delighted others by recommending a radical change from the traditional first-past-the-post voting system to MMP — a form of proportional representation closely modelled on German practices. The political climate was right for change, even if the Labour and National leaderships were resistant, and the idea of electoral reform took hold. Electoral instability, with its source in the declining strength of voters' party allegiances, had been growing for some time (Vowles, Aimer, Catt, Lamare, Miller 1995, 43–4). There was increasing un-ease over the 'elective dictatorship' of one-party governments. Beginning as a reaction to the authoritarian style of the Muldoon years (1975–84), the mood was now swollen by widespread public anger and disillusion with the pace of Labour's radical free-market reforms (1984–90) and with the parliamentary process more generally. In recommending electoral reform, the Royal Commission had provided a tangible focal point for a host of generalised dissatisfactions. Neither major party could ignore the issue in the approach to the 1990 election. Seeking tactical advantage, both Labour and National offered competing promises of referendums on electoral reform. The 'genie' of proportional representation was well and truly out of the bottle (Jackson and McRobie 1998, 125).

Even before the 1990 election, the electoral reform movement had been gathering pace, driven by growing distrust of traditional two-party politics. By 1990 only 11 per cent of electors were prepared to say that Labour was 'trustworthy', and only 19 per cent expressed trust in National (Vowles, Aimer, Banducci, Karp 1998, 164). In other words, most people were voting for parties they were either unsure of, or believed to be untrustworthy. Cynicism had become deeply embedded in New Zealand's democratic process. Three years later, the picture was even slightly bleaker. By 1993, the National government had lost the trust of electors just as decisively as Labour had in 1990. The organised advocates of change led by the Electoral Reform Coalition gratefully exploited the mood.

Back in government after its sweeping victory in 1990, National might have regretted its promise of a binding referendum on the electoral issue, but the commitment having been made, the Prime Minister was not prepared to back away, having already reneged on the party's undertaking to remove Labour's surtax on superannuation (Jackson and McRobie 1998, 130). The government's decision to implement its promise by means of a two-stage referendum process guaranteed continued debate and media commentary, and a surprisingly high level of public interest in the issue.

The first, non-binding referendum, held in September 1992, confirmed that the public was indeed of a mind to change the electoral system, and that its greatly preferred option was MMP. Fifty-three per cent of registered electors voted, a high turnout for a stand-alone referendum. Of these, 84.7 per cent declared for change, and 70.5 per cent selected MMP against other options. The result obliged the government to hold a second, binding referendum at the same time as the 1993 general election, in which the choice was between FPP and MMP. Despite a short but well-funded and hard-hitting campaign in support of FPP, a majority of 54 per cent of voters authorised the government to introduce MMP in time for the 1996 election. Both major parties now faced the transition to MMP. Over the next three years, the implementation of electoral reform then became the catalyst for further political changes (Boston, Levine, McLeay, Roberts 1996).

At the 1993 general election it was National's turn to experience the wrath of the voters. The euphoria in National's ranks after its landslide victory in 1990 had been short-lived. Within months of its return to office, public support for National had plunged from a commanding 47.8 per cent on election night to a mere 22 per cent in opinion polls (Vowles, Aimer, Catt, Lamare, Miller 1995, 9). The National party's cohesion, like Labour's before it, crumbled under the radical neo-liberal policies driven by a dominating Minister of Finance. In that respect, National's Ruth Richardson and Labour's Roger Douglas were Tweedledum and Tweedledee to successive governments. Only an unsteady electoral recovery by National over the next two years enabled Jim Bolger to lead his party to the narrowest of election wins in 1993. While the mechanics of the first-past-the-post voting system delivered National another victory, it was on a slightly smaller share of the vote than the party's previous electoral nadir in 1984, which had seen it swept from office. After shedding 13 per cent of its 1990 support, National, with a little more than one-third of the votes, clung to office in 1993 with 50 seats out of 99. Most — nearly two-thirds — of the voters had not wanted a National government, yet such were the vagaries of the FPP electoral system, that is what they got. On the other hand even fewer voters wanted a Labour government. But a majority clearly did want a change of political direction, for together Labour and the Alliance took 53 per cent of the votes.

The Transition to MMP: 1993–96

Bolger was shaken by the closeness of the result, and chided the opinion polls in memorable terms ('What I might have said was: bugger the pollsters'). The polls had predicted a comfortable election win. Bolger later gave a more conciliatory and measured response. Temperamentally adaptable, and more politically pragmatic than MPs in the extreme free-market wing of his party, Bolger accepted the twin verdicts of the election and the referendum with a laudable if necessary equanimity. Bolger's priority was to repair the electoral damage of the preceding three years. As a first step, he replaced his Finance Minister. Ruth Richardson relinquished the portfolio reluctantly to Bill Birch. Refusing to accept any other cabinet position, Richardson resigned from Parliament in July 1994. Her departure was the first of a series of ructions in the National caucus during the lead-up to the first MMP election. The parliamentary Labour party, however, fared little better.

Some reconfiguration of the party system was to be expected during the transition from FPP, with its strong two-party tendency, to proportional representation, conducive to a more multi-party format. The process had begun even before the 1993 referendum, with the formation of the left-leaning Alliance (the umbrella for the NewLabour, Green, Democrat, Liberal, and Mana Motuhake parties) and of the centrist New Zealand First party. Between 1993 and 1996, however, the established parties experienced a further shake-up in anticipation of the new electoral era.

The prospect of MMP greatly enhanced the political opportunities for small parties, giving representation to all those crossing the threshold of 5 per cent of the overall vote or winning an electorate seat. With representation came the potential to influence the shaping of policy, and even the construction of governments. There was an incentive, therefore, for aggrieved or ambitious MPs to hive off from existing parties and establish a new niche party. The incentive was all the stronger because of the radical revision of electorate boundaries following the reduction of electoral districts from 99 in 1993 to 65 for the forthcoming MMP election. Although, with the addition of 55 list seats, the overall size of Parliament was increased to 120, the radical reshaping of the electoral districts altered the career prospects of many MPs. Not all sitting MPs could rely on their parties to allocate them a safe list placing. Exit from their existing parties thus became a rational if somewhat desperate strategy for a number of MPs from both major parties. Bolger, responding to the inevitable and seeking to manage the process, openly invited National MPs to form new parties, as long as they continued to support his government (Vowles, Aimer, Banducci, Karp 1998, 13).

Politicians who sat uneasily within the broad coalitions of National or Labour soon began to make their moves, setting in train a process of party fragmentation and party building in anticipation of the introduction of proportional representation. A diffuse constituency attracted to conservative Christian values was amenable to mobilisation through church-based networks. In mid-1995, the strongly Christian National MP, Graeme Lee, a minister in Bolger's first government, but omitted from cabinet after the 1993 election, left National to launch the Christian Democrats. The potential for such a party had already been demonstrated by the more fundamentalist (and less appealing) Christian Heritage party, which had won 2 per cent of the vote in 1993. In March 1996, the two Christian parties agreed to combine their electoral efforts by campaigning as a single Christian Coalition, and only narrowly failed to surmount the 5 per cent threshold in the 1996 election.

Meanwhile, a more financially and organisationally well-resourced party to the economic right of the government, ACT New Zealand, was being formed outside Parliament. Initially it took shape around Roger Douglas, Labour's former Finance Minister (1984–88). ACT took its place in the party system at the opposite end of the ideological spectrum to the Alliance, as the advocate of small government, private enterprise, and market liberalism. It was the centre of the political spectrum, however, which generated the most activity. As is commonly the case in broad-spectrum ('catch-all') parties, there were incipient factional divisions in both National and Labour. There were politicians in both parties whose political outlooks were almost indistinguishable from those across the party divide. Only a strong Westminster tradition of strict party discipline preserved the clarity of the parliamentary line between the major parties. With National and Labour bound to continue as the two pillars of the new MMP party system, a pivotal centre party, amenable to coalition agreements with either side, was therefore a strategically attractive prospect to MPs of both parties.

In June 1995, seven MPs (four from National, and three from Labour, including Peter Dunne, who had earlier left Labour to form the Future New Zealand party), combined to set up the centrist United New Zealand party. The centre ground, however, was already being staked out by New Zealand First, launched in July 1993 by the sacked National Minister of Maori Affairs, Winston Peters. Under the banner of his new party, Peters had successfully defended his Tauranga seat in the 1993 election, and in a more dramatic coup the party's candidate for Northern Maori, Tau Henare, had won that seat, breaking Labour's long monopoly of the Maori electorates. While on the one hand New Zealand First's emerging appeal to Maori voters, and Peters' vigorous campaign in 1996 against immigration, diminished the party's centrist credentials, on the other they were strengthened when politicians from both National (Michael Laws and Peter McCardle) and Labour (Jack Elder) joined the party in 1996. Although Laws did not contest the 1996 election, both McCardle and Elder were to be elected as New Zealand First list MPs, earning cabinet places in the first coalition government under MMP.

For National after 1993, the transition to MMP meant above all maintaining the government's parliamentary base as politicians on both sides manoeuvred for position in anticipation of the new electoral system. This was a challenge which the Prime Minister, Jim Bolger, managed with skill and adaptability. The site of Labour's challenge was electoral — the battle to maintain its place as the dominant party of the centre-left. Labour's electoral prospects were still under the cloud of its recent past. An internal party debate over how it should reconcile its social democratic tradition with a reputation gained in the 1980s for radical free-market reform was unresolved. The issue of leadership aggravated the tensions. After Labour's loss in the 1993 election, Helen Clark replaced Mike Moore as leader, a move designed to signal a repositioning of Labour on the centre-left of the political spectrum. Yet this put the party in direct competition with the Alliance, a movement that had laid claim to Labour's ideological tradition, as well as part of its electoral constituency. By late 1995 the Alliance had begun to overtake Labour, and in the opinion polls Clark trailed well behind Anderton as preferred Prime Minister. In turn both Labour and the Alliance were subsequently hurt in mid-1996 by the dramatic surge in popular support for Winston Peters and New Zealand First. Labour trod an uphill electoral path to the 1996 election, the first in the country's history to be held under the rules of proportional representation, and therefore crucial to the status of all parties in the evolving multi-party composition of Parliament.

Coalition Collapse and the Recovery of the Left: 1996–99

The 1996 election and its aftermath clarified both the shape of the future multi-party system and the potential relationships between the parties. Despite the politicians' flurry of party-building activity between 1993 and 1996, the net electoral changes were surprisingly modest. The parties' vote shares in the 1996 election were not greatly different from those in 1993. National, Labour, New Zealand First, and Alliance — all four parties that had won seats in 1993 — retained their parliamentary presence after 1996. ACT was the only new party to cross the 5 per cent threshold, while United was represented when Peter Dunne secured his seat after National, acknowledging a potential parliamentary ally, refrained from contesting it. The greatest impact of MMP, however, was not the small increase in the number of elected parties, but the proportional allocation of parliamentary seats. In that respect, the 1996 election result was very different indeed from that in 1993. In 1993, under FPP, National's 35 per cent of the vote had given it a narrow parliamentary majority; in 1996, under MMP, its 34 per cent of the party vote left it 16 seats short of a majority. Labour, still climbing out of its electoral trough, was 23 seats short of a majority on a historic low of 28 per cent of the party vote. The electorate and the politicians now faced the fact that proportional representation meant that the make-up of the next government was not always clear at the end of vote-counting on election night. Rather, governments would henceforth be formed on the basis of the parties' pre-election pacts and their relative parliamentary strength and strategic position after the election.

Counting the parties' shares of the votes (and seats) in 1996 from either the left or the right gave New Zealand First the vital median position. Save for an unlikely grand coalition between National and Labour, neither could command a majority of seats without including New Zealand First. As Peters had foreshadowed, the party therefore assigned to itself the role of pivotal centrist party, entering into prolonged negotiations with both National and Labour over the terms of its possible participation in a coalition government. Coalition theory favoured an accord with National, as together National and New Zealand First could form a majority government. For Labour to lead a government, on the other hand, required a potentially less stable accord with both New Zealand First and the Alliance to establish the necessary parliamentary base for governing. Thus, the eventual outcome, a National–New Zealand First coalition, was both theoretically sound, and in some respects the more politically tenable option.

Yet it was still a deeply flawed solution. While it may have been a rational outcome in the eyes of the party elites, to many voters and grass-roots party workers the coalition agreement was an anathema. The party leadership had certainly not prepared the public for the coalition. There had been few if any convincing displays of coalition-type behaviour between the parties before the election, which would have provided cues for their prospective voters, in marked contrast with the explicitly stated intentions of Labour and the Alliance in 1999 (see Chapter 8). In 1996, few voters choosing National or New Zealand First expected them to become coalition partners. During the five weeks of the campaign period, intending National voters consistently placed New Zealand First last in their ranking of preferred coalition partners, lower even than the Alliance, and intending New Zealand First voters reciprocated, placing National well below either Labour or the Alliance as a potential coalition partner (Vowles, Aimer, Banducci, Karp 1998, 126–30).

Most electors giving New Zealand First their party vote in 1996 did so in the belief (which the party's leadership had promoted) that they were voting for a change of government. Peters subsequently claimed that the coalition amounted to a change of government, but this, although obviously correct, was not how most people saw it. Clinging to the assumptions of FPP politics, people still interpreted a change of government to mean 'throwing the rascals out' — right out.

The unfamiliarity of party leaders and strategists with the practice of multi-party politics was partly to blame for the inauspicious start to the MMP electoral era. To go into government at all was a tactical error by Peters. It betrayed the expectations of the bulk of New Zealand First voters. It subjected members of his caucus, who had no prior experience even as MPs, to the work pressures, frustrations, and media exposure of cabinet office, alongside fellow ministers from an experienced but resentful coalition partner. Bolger's error was to forgo the opportunity to continue in government as a one-party minority administration, with assured support on supply and confidence from ACT and United. There would have been risks in such a strategy, in which responsibility for maintaining the government in office would ultimately rest with New Zealand First. But the minority option would have played to Bolger's strengths of political experience, negotiating ability, and pragmatic flexibility. Moreover it was closer to the preference of National voters for a one-party National government, albeit a majority one (Vowles, Aimer, Banducci, Karp 1998, 127–9). Faced with the options, National's membership and the party's wider voting constituency would probably have found the necessary compromises of minority government easier to accept than the humiliation of working with a party and a leader disliked by many National voters (Vowles, Aimer, Catt, Lamare, Miller 1995, 157).

It was nine weeks before the post-election coalition process reached its conclusion in an Agreement signed by Bolger and Peters. It was a 74-page document, which set out the government's policies in rigid detail, and allocated New Zealand First five seats in the 20-member cabinet, including Peters in the powerful post of Treasurer, plus another four ministers outside cabinet, with the promise of three additional cabinet positions by October 1998. While there was initial relief among National's supporters that there would be a centre-right government, jubilation was subdued by the apparent generosity of the deal offered to New Zealand First and the policy concessions and compromises it entailed.

The operating culture of the National–New Zealand First coalition was scarred from the outset by feelings of resentment and suspicion at all levels of both parties. New Zealand First's inexperience, poor management structures and lack of internal party discipline contributed much to this. Only Peters had any background in government, while five of the nine New Zealand First ministers were new to Parliament, and unprepared for the intense parliamentary pressures and media scrutiny. National politicians for their part were irritated by their enforced association with MPs and ministers some of whom quickly attracted damaging publicity. Early in the new government's term, a New Zealand First Maori MP, Tukoroirangi Morgan, attracted wide derision for his lavish expenditure on clothing and other personal items in his previous role as a director of the failed Aotearoa Television Network. Shortly after, the Minister of Consumer Affairs, Robyn McDonald, was severely criticised for an expensive and allegedly unnecessary trip to a meeting in France. Peters himself was accused of assaulting the National MP and former Minister of Police, John Banks, and though later cleared of contempt by Parliament's Privileges Committee, rejected the committee's request for an apology. Policy differences then surfaced in a series of public attacks by the Associate Minister of Health, Neil Kirton, on his senior minister, National's Bill English. Refusing to be silenced, Kirton was dismissed from all his ministerial responsibilities.

The main crack in the coalition's unity was widest between National's free-market MPs and the more free-spending members of New Zealand First. While National was reluctantly prepared to accede to the junior partner's key policy initiatives, notably free doctor's visits for those under the age of six, a work-for-the-dole scheme, and removal of the vilified superannuation surtax, party members were more openly critical of the decision to increase fiscal spending by a further five billion dollars. In addition to endangering future surpluses, the coalition's spending commitments meant deferring National's promised tax cuts, which were strongly backed by the party's right wing, and endorsed by ACT, with which National was competing for votes in its heartland rural and city electorates. The fears of National's pro-market MPs were realised when the party's earlier prediction of a fiscal surplus reaching $6.4 billion by 1999–2000 was trimmed back to only $3 billion in Peters' first Budget (*Sunday Star Times*, 7 December 1997).

Although the binding nature of the coalition Agreement acted as a brake on the debate over the level of fiscal spending, the same constraint did not apply to Peters' compulsory superannuation proposal. Known as the Retirement Saving Scheme, a main element of which was a 3 per cent contribution per individual, rising to 8 per cent at a later stage, the proposal enjoyed the qualified support of Bolger and his deputy leader, Don McKinnon. In contrast, a number of prominent National ministers and backbench MPs became outspoken critics. Under the terms of the Agreement, the superannuation proposal was put to a binding referendum in September 1997. As the critics of the scheme had anticipated, the level of public rejection (91.8 per cent) was overwhelming. As well as helping to quantify the unpopularity of the coalition government, and in particular that of the scheme's chief architect, Winston Peters, the referendum further exposed the cracks within the coalition and dealt a severe blow to Bolger's leadership.

The formation of an unpopular coalition, and its shaky start, had an immediate effect on the electoral standing of the coalition parties. Figure 1.1 shows support for New Zealand First draining steadily away, and National's plunging through 1997, while Labour's support level soared, in a continuation of the party's recovery during the 1996 election campaign. Volatile voting intentions were not the only effect of a fractious government. Public regard for coalition government, and for the first MMP Parliament, also suffered (Vowles, Aimer, Banducci, Karp 1998, 207). Disillusion with MMP focused on the behaviour of individual MPs, a few of whom would have been unlikely to have entered Parliament under the old voting system. It was largely a transitional problem, however, rather than systemic. Parties had not yet perfected their selection procedures to take account of both the electorate and list components of candidacy under MMP, and the reduced number of electorates had further complicated the process, leading, as we have seen, to considerable 'party hopping' by MPs. The glue of party loyalty had been temporarily weakened in the volatile transition to MMP.

Figure 1.1: One News/Colmar Brunton Polls, 1997–October 1999

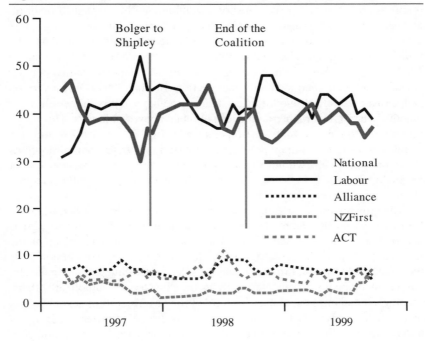

Disillusion with MMP was premature, but it is perceptions that count, and disillusionment was deepened by the controversy over the first case of 'party hopping' after the election. In July 1997, Alamein Kopu, an Alliance list MP, resigned from the party and declared herself to be an Independent, on the ground that the Alliance had failed to offer 'practical and real support' in her role as a Maori MP (*New Zealand Herald,* 17 July 1997). Despite having signed a pledge of loyalty to her party, Kopu rejected any ethical obligation to continue as an Alliance MP. Her decision raised doubts about the legitimacy of her role as an Independent list member, especially when it became known that, as a constituency candidate in the Maori seat of Te Tai Rawhiti in 1996, she had won a mere 5.7 per cent of the vote. The public's scorn was further kindled by the fact that, despite drawing a $74,500 salary, the previously unemployed grandmother had until then attended only 16 of Parliament's 47 sitting days (*Evening Post,* 22 July 1997).

Kopu's move raised several issues of principle and practice under MMP. Since list MPs were allocated to ensure that parties were represented in Parliament according to their overall vote, the defection of a list MP threatened to distort the proportionality of Parliament. Because list MPs owed their seats in Parliament to their party's list ranking, questions were raised over the legitimacy of Independent list MPs. Who did they represent; and to whom were they accountable? Kopu's defection reinforced the difficulty many people had in accepting the calibre and role of list MPs. This and the issues of party loyalty and discipline surfaced again a year later amid the drama of New Zealand First's collapse and the defection of nine of its MPs.

Meanwhile, there was growing unrest in National too. There is a loose relationship between a party's electoral standing and the perceived qualities and performance of its leader (see Chapter 4). An unpopular leader can depress a party's electoral standing, while effective leadership augments it. This relationship began to hurt National in 1997. During the 1996 election campaign Clark had fought her way into contention as a leader with substantial popular appeal. The trend continued after the election. In May 1997, Clark overtook Bolger as 'preferred Prime Minister', and soared beyond him in the following months, when Labour's party vote also climbed above National's. This was a major blow to the credibility of Bolger's leadership. By late 1997, National's dismal results in the opinion polls, and the coalition's 95 per cent disapproval rating prompted calls within National for a new and more aggressive style of leadership, especially in the party's relationship with its junior coalition partner (*Dominion*, 4 November 1997).

The growing crisis for Bolger came to a head in November 1997, when his fifth-ranked minister, Jenny Shipley, marshalled the numbers to topple him as leader and Prime Minister. Figure 1.2 charts the immediate effect of the leadership coup on the 'preferred Prime Minister' rankings. In opinion polls reporting the 'preferred Prime Minister', the leader holding that office usually has an incumbent's advantage, and can be expected to outpoll all others. Shipley's initial meteoric rise as 'preferred Prime Minister' thus acknowledges in the first instance that she had become the Prime Minister (as Bolger's descent records his loss of office). More importantly for National, however, Shipley's leadership change was accompanied by a rapid rise in National's electoral standing (Figure 1.1). This neutralised the appeal of Helen Clark, whose ratings along with Labour's began to fall. The signs were that the leadership coup had been a success.

Of equal relief for National, after initial hesitancy on Peters' part, the coalition government remained intact on the basis of the original Agreement. But there were at least two potential sources of conflict in the relationship: the expectation within the National party that Shipley would assert the senior coalition partner's dominance more forthrightly, and the need for New Zealand First to emerge from National's shadow in order to recover electoral support. Besides tension between the coalition partners, there was also by 1998 serious friction within New Zealand First. Rumours that Tau Henare and four other Maori MPs were considering forming a new Maori party led to Peters' dismissing Henare as deputy leader. The growing schisms within New Zealand First, another steep downturn in the opinion polls for National after a promising recovery following the leadership change and the near-loss of the safe rural seat of Taranaki-King Country in a by-election strengthened Shipley's resolve to reclaim National's control of government.

The coalition finally collapsed, along with New Zealand First's fragile

Figure 1.2: Preferred Prime Minister, 1997–October 1999

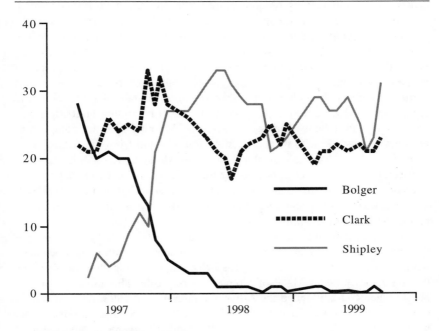

SOURCE: One News/Colmar Brunton Polls

unity, in August 1998, when Peters and three of his New Zealand First min-
isterial colleagues walked out of the weekly cabinet meeting in protest at
National's decision to sell the Crown's 66 per cent shareholding in Wellington
Airport. Peters' action reflected his need to reassert his party's separate identity
as much as the magnitude of the issue, but the consequences for him and his
party were major. In response the Prime Minister dismissed Peters as Deputy
Prime Minister and Treasurer, but offered the seven remaining New Zealand
First ministers the option of keeping their ministerial warrants. Four of them,
Tau Henare, Peter McCardle, Jack Elder and Tuariki Delamere promptly
resigned from New Zealand First and retained their ministerial posts, while a
fifth, Deborah Morris, decided to resign from both the ministry and her party.
The defectors were joined by three other New Zealand First MPs, Rana Waitai,
Tukoroirangi Morgan, and Ann Batten. They, together with the former Alliance
MP, Alamein Kopu, United's Peter Dunne, and the eight ACT MPs, provided
National with sufficient parliamentary numbers to continue in government.
Irretrievably lost, however, was any remaining image of the administration's
stability and cohesion.

The collapse of the National–New Zealand First coalition left National
vulnerable in the MMP multi-party arena as the 1999 election approached.
Perhaps preoccupied with continual difficulties within the coalition up to 1998,
and distracted by post-coalition problems after that, National appeared to make
no effort to develop a culture of political accommodation and compromise with
its potential strategic ally, ACT. Yet the notion of two competing electoral blocs

— National and ACT on the centre-right and Labour and the Alliance on the centre-left — was gaining obvious currency as New Zealand First declined, and Labour and the Alliance adjusted to the logic of the new party system.

Following New Zealand First's decision to coalesce with National on the centre-right, the Labour and Alliance parties took advantage of the growing unpopularity of the coalition government to build a strategic foundation for the next electoral contest (see Chapter 8). A stable coalition between the centre-left parties offered the best chance not only to win government but to restore the credibility of MMP before a parliamentary review beginning in 2000. It was not an easy course considering the recent background of bitter antagonism between the parties, with its source in Anderton's split from the Labour government in 1987. NewLabour, the core of the Alliance after 1992, had been formed in order to replace Labour as the true voice of social democracy in New Zealand. Many Alliance activists, formerly stalwart Labourites, were still hostile toward Labour and deeply cynical of its motives, attitudes that were reciprocated by some within Labour.

Yet mindful of the electoral damage suffered by both Labour and the Alliance by their rigid stand-off in 1996, the leaders of both parties began to work toward a joint approach to the 1999 election, preparing their members for the inevitability under MMP of a power-sharing role. This move was made public when Clark attended the Alliance conference in 1998. Delegates then discussed the relative merits of 'binding' and 'loose' coalition arrangements with Labour. While some preferred a 'fully fledged' agreement, others argued that the Alliance's support should be limited to matters of confidence and supply. Opponents of a binding agreement expressed concern that the Alliance could become marginalised to a point where it had minimal influence over policy. Anderton, on the other hand, cautioned that Labour was unlikely to be sympathetic to a partnership with a party 'that refused to take the brickbats of power along with the bouquets' (Trotter 1999). One way around the seeming impasse was to avoid New Zealand First's mistake of insisting on a highly detailed and inflexible coalition agreement (*National Business Review*, 27 August 1999). By avoiding specific policy commitments in advance, it was argued, the Alliance would be free both to distance itself from unpalatable Labour initiatives and to seek parliamentary support for policies of its own.

By the time the election campaign began, the Alliance had moved a long way from its rigid stance in 1996. Then, after failing to secure Labour's agreement to negotiate a pre-election coalition agreement, it had proposed twelve non-negotiable policy goals, most of which Labour would have found impossible to meet. In 1999, by contrast, it adopted a surprisingly pragmatic approach to policy compromises with Labour, perhaps the most prominent of which was the decision to flatten out its income tax rates to make them more consistent with Labour's. From a party opposed to economic liberalism, this was a major concession to Labour's commitment to a free market, and was reassuring to those Labour voters who feared that the Alliance was incapable of significant compromise.

There was no precedent for such coalition-type behaviour between parties in New Zealand's traditionally adversarial political culture, and some mutual tensions and suspicions inevitably remained. Some in Labour continued to advocate either a stand-alone Labour government, or alternatively a coalition with the Greens in preference to the more ideologically rigid Alliance. To appease the anti-Alliance faction in Labour, as well as to reassure conservative voters, Helen Clark suggested a 'ratio-based' approach to policy and the allocation of ministerial positions. In her opinion, the six-to-sevenfold poll margin now enjoyed by Labour entitled it to a dominant role in any centre-left government. To protect Labour's post-election bargaining position and to prevent the Alliance from frightening potential voters, Clark called for a commanding party vote on election day. In response, the Alliance's Laila Harré challenged Clark to agree that 'neither party in a coalition would be subsumed by the other's agenda' (*New Zealand Herald*, 15 October 1999).

By 1999, despite lingering distrust between them, Labour and the Alliance had far outpaced the centre-right parties in developing the bloc-based accommodative strategies appropriate for the new MMP electoral system. Compared to this, the composition and even feasibility of a centre-right government were obscure. Considering National's own diminished level of support, there was inadequate electoral compensation among its potential coalition partners, ACT, United and Mauri Pacific (a new party formed by the former New Zealand First deputy, Tau Henare). If the Prime Minister therefore would not rule out the possibility of a deal with New Zealand First, Peters' hostility to National, and the refusal of the ACT leader, Richard Prebble, to 'support a government in which New Zealand First is present', appeared to preclude such an option (*New Zealand Herald*, 2–3 October 1999). ACT and New Zealand First further compounded the impression of a dysfunctional centre-right bloc by adopting non-negotiable polices, as had the Alliance three years before.

Apart from the showpiece APEC conference held in Auckland, the months leading up to the election campaign did not go well for the government. Early in the year it was in trouble over the deregulation of the electricity industry, with higher prices resulting rather than the promised reductions. There were continuing problems with the restructuring of the Fire Service, allegations of excessive salary payments to public officials, examples of bureaucratic inefficiency and extravagance at Work and Income New Zealand, and several contentious public sector scandals. One, involving 'golden handshakes' to departing Tourism Board members, led to the resignation of the minister concerned, and over another issue — a large payment by Television New Zealand to the sacked newsreader John Hawkesby — the Prime Minister found herself apologising for having 'made up' the sum she had mentioned during a television interview. The incident caused the government considerable embarrassment and reflected badly on the credibility of its leader at a crucial time for National's electoral recovery.

Although Jenny Shipley outpolled other leaders as 'preferred Prime Minister' for most of her term after taking over the office, the size and fragility of her lead over Clark were a bad sign for the government. It suggested that the hoped-for leadership effect in National's favour was insufficient to undo the electoral attrition of nine years in government and the damage it had suffered by entering into an unpopular alliance with New Zealand First, by the coalition's subsequent performance and spectacular collapse, and by National's troubled final year of office. Clark's ratings remained high for an opposition leader, and twice Shipley's lead melted, first in the aftermath of the coalition's collapse, and again, closer to the election campaign, in the wake of the Tourism Board episode.

The cumulative effect of the government's problems appeared also to cancel out any electoral benefit it might have expected from favourable economic conditions in its final year. Figure 1.3 tracks National's poll support against economic optimism, as defined by the percentage sampled by Colmar Brunton who said they expected the economy to improve over the coming year. The generalised trend lines (shown as dotted lines) for both variables are superimposed on the more detailed data. Economic growth on a quarterly basis is presented in the lower portion of the table. As GDP growth slackened through 1996–97, economic optimism also declined, but began to recover even before growth reached its lowest point late in 1998, during the Asian economic crisis. Through 1999, election year, the economy was again buoyant, and economic confidence growing. Yet National's electoral support not only failed to respond, but as the smoothed trend line in the grey dots shows, National was losing ground.

Figure 1.3: Support for National, Economic Optimism and Economic Growth, 1995–99

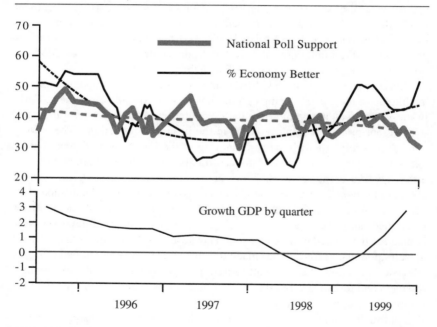

SOURCES: One News/Colmar Brunton Polls, Statistics New Zealand

Although Labour's support was also falling in tandem with National's throughout most of 1999, it still led National by varying margins in the polls (Figure 1.1). In February and March the two parties were close, but Labour had drawn ahead again by mid-year, and the trend after that was ominous for National, as its share of the intended vote slipped back almost to its level when

Shipley replaced Bolger. Nevertheless, the gap between the two parties was never great, and narrowed in the final weeks before the election campaign. Despite the government's troubled, and at times crisis-ridden term, the centre-left could never be assured of victory. Indeed, in the last One News/Colmar Brunton opinion poll on the eve of the campaign, in mid-October, Labour's margin over National fell to only two percentage points. National was down, but not out, and four weeks from polling day as the campaign commenced the result of the 1999 election was anything but a foregone conclusion.

CHAPTER 2

DID THE CAMPAIGN MATTER?

Jack Vowles

The main parties opened their campaigns on 29 October. The election was held four weeks later on 27 November. While all parties received attention, the main focus of the campaign was on the two major rivals, National and Labour, one of which was certain to form the core of the next government. National's campaign strategy was to portray itself as a party of 'common sense, not ideology' (*New Zealand Herald*, 27 September 1999). By conjuring up an image of pragmatism and moderation, the party hoped to both distance itself from any reputation for extremism and project an image of Labour as a party of doctrine and social division. As part of this plan, National singled out Labour's promised tax increases on those earning above $60,000, as well as its proposals to restore accident insurance to a state corporation monopoly and to repeal the Employment Contracts Act. According to National, the latter would result in a reassertion of trade union influence and power. In contrast, National offered tax cuts for those on middle and upper incomes.

Sensing victory this time, Labour conducted a cautious and tightly managed campaign. In mid-year, the party had released a credit-card list of policy pledges guaranteed to arouse neither excitement nor hostility.[1] Its official campaign launch and media campaign were built around Clark's leadership qualities, including a sound grasp of policy and a claimed ability to construct a stable and effective coalition government. Part way through the campaign it became clear that Labour's approach had become too predictable. The 1999 campaign was Labour's to lose, and for a while it looked as if it might do so.

Under MMP the success of smaller parties may contribute decisively to an election's outcome. Which ones have crossed the threshold for representation, and by how much, may make much difference. The success and failure of the smaller parties during the campaign can determine not only their own future political roles, but also that of one or another of the major parties. MMP is sensitive to all changes in party support. The importance of the campaign period is therefore potentially greater under the new voting system than under the old. Yet attention to campaigns is not confined to proportional electoral systems. There is now considerable interest worldwide in campaign practices and their effects on elections (Farrell 1996), in part because of common trends in voting behaviour in many countries. The campaign period is now more critical as people's voting choices have become more volatile from one election to the next. Moreover, New Zealanders, like citizens elsewhere, tend increasingly to defer making up their minds how they will vote until close to the election.

Tracking the Voters' Intentions

This chapter, building on earlier research conducted for the 1996 NZES (Johnston 1998), shows how the campaign made a difference in New Zealand in 1999, and why.

The 1999 NZES again included a sample of people interviewed on a daily basis throughout the campaign. The same people were then invited to participate in the post-election survey, forming a panel, or two-wave pre- and post-election study. By the end of the campaign, about 2400 people had provided information about their campaign vote intentions and indicated, after the election, how they actually voted.

Using data from the pre- and post-election panel, Figure 2.1 displays estimates of the trends in party support during the campaign.[2] National, Labour, and New Zealand First kicked off their campaigns on 29 October, and that day can be taken as the start of the campaign proper. There was a close race between Labour and National until the end of the first week of the campaign (5 November), and thereafter an increasing trend to Labour. The last estimates centre on the nine days around 22 November (N=675), five days before the election. They indicate that Labour may have peaked somewhat before election day, and National may have made a slight recovery over the last days of the campaign. The most crucial period in the campaign was from about 6 November to 10 November. Until 6 November, both Labour and National were in decline and their respective potential coalition partners, the Alliance and ACT, were gaining ground. By 10 November, however, Labour was drawing ahead, New Zealand First was in decline, and the Green party was beginning its rise toward the 5 per cent party vote threshold of parliamentary representation. National recovered briefly, peaking on 13 November, probably thanks to its successful focusing of public attention on economic issues. However, that recovery was temporary, and after shifting focus to the menace of the Green party in the Coromandel electorate National lost momentum in the third week of the campaign (Vowles 2000a).

While these trends are clear, there are limits to their day-by-day interpretation. Statistical uncertainty makes it impossible to definitively connect changes in vote intention to specific campaign events. At most, one can suggest plausible associations. In addition, effects on daily vote intentions may be short-term and not carry through into choice on election day. To better assess campaign effects one needs to compare people's stated campaign intentions with their vote. The panel of respondents makes this possible.

The importance of the campaign depends in part on the number of voters who report deciding how they will vote during the campaign. The effect of the campaign will be less if most voters have already made up their minds before it starts. In 1999, the potential for campaign change was considerable. After the election, almost half (48 per cent) of those who voted indicated that they had

Figure 2.1: Campaign Trends in Voting Intentions to Election Day Vote, 1999 Election

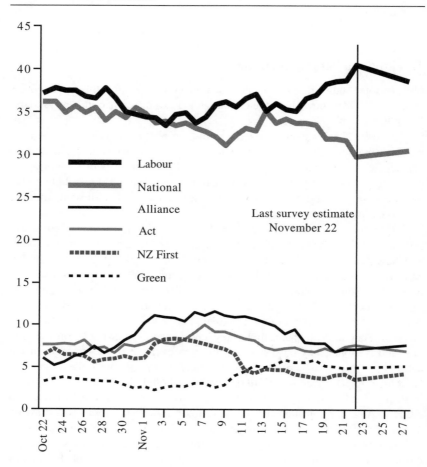

Nine-day Rolling averages, N=2210 (average daily N: days 1–34, 56; days 35–40, 81.) Weighted by household size, age and gender across the whole sample, and by 1999 party vote on a daily basis. For further details see Appendix A.

made up their minds during the campaign, including 14 per cent who said they had decided during the last week, and another 12 per cent on election day itself. Of course, some or even many of these people may have made up their minds to continue with an earlier tentative preference. Nevertheless, weighted to reflect equal sampling across the whole campaign, pre-election intentions when compared with post-election reports of vote show that 31 per cent of the respondents cast a vote that was inconsistent with their intention when interviewed during the campaign.[3]

Because these intentions were spread throughout the campaign, this figure underestimates the extent of campaign movement. Figure 2.2 shows that people questioned early in the campaign were more likely to change than those

Figure 2.2: Percentage of Respondents with a Different Pre-Election Vote Intention than Their Reported Vote by Day of Campaign (Five-Day Rolling Averages)

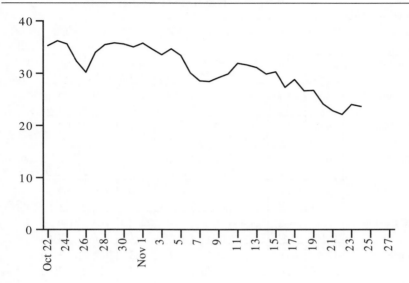

surveyed closer to the election. There was approximately a 35 per cent probability that people sampled at the beginning of the campaign would vote differently from their earlier intention. By the day before the election, this probability had lessened to a little more than 20 per cent, still a substantial rate. As most polls closest to the election predicted the election result, the effects of people moving in one direction were apparently offset by movements in the other. There is no guarantee that late-campaign volatility will always be even-handed.

Table 2.1 indicates how people who reported their intentions in the first half of the campaign voted on the day. The total figures for campaign vote intentions up to 6 November in the bottom margin of the table show how close the race was between National and Labour during the first half of the campaign, when we can also see that Green support was at about 2 per cent on average, less than half of its share on election day. The totals in the right-hand margin show the election-day breakdown, including non-vote. Comparing these figures with those in the bottom margin shows which parties gained or lost favour as the campaign went on. The left-hand top of each cell in the table shows the percentage of election day votes that came from the sets of campaign intentions in each column. For example, 77.4 per cent of National's votes on election day came from those with National voting intentions in the first half of the campaign, and 5 per cent of National's election day votes came from people who had intended to vote Labour in the first half of the campaign (1.3 per cent of all possible voters, as indicated in the figure in the bottom right of the cell). Labour was relatively successful at converting people who were intending to vote National in the first half of the campaign. They made up 9.4

Table 2.1   Flow of Vote Intentions (18 October–6 November) to Party Vote 27 November

Row % *Cell %*	First Half of Campaign								
Election Day	DK/NV	Lab	Natl	All	NZF	ACT	Grn	Oth	N vote total %
Nonvote	20.3 *3.3*	25.1 *4.1*	30.7 *5.0*	0.7 *0.1*	12.8 *2.1*	4.7 *0.8*	0.0 *0.0*	5.7 *0.9*	172 16.2
Labour	8.8 *2.9*	69.7 *22.8*	9.4 *3.2*	5.5 *1.8*	3.2 *1.0*	1.1 *0.4*	1.0 *0.3*	1.3 *0.4*	348 32.7
National	5.9 *1.5*	5.0 *1.3*	77.4 *20.0*	2.3 *0.6*	1.7 *0.4*	5.2 *1.3*	1.3 *0.3*	1.2 *0.3*	275 25.8
Alliance	10.8 *0.7*	29.6 *1.9*	4.7 *0.3*	52.8 *3.4*	0.0 *0.0*	0.0 *0.0*	2.1 *0.1*	0.0 *0.0*	69 6.5
NZ First	5.1 *0.1*	9.9 *0.3*	7.9 *0.2*	0.0 *0.0*	75.9 *2.0*	0.0 *0.0*	0.0 *0.0*	1.3 *0.0*	28 2.6
ACT	5.5 *0.3*	4.2 *0.2*	21.4 *1.3*	0.0 *0.0*	0.0 *0.0*	68.2 *4.1*	0.7 *0.0*	0.0 *0.0*	64 6.0
Green	12.4 *0.5*	23.6 *1.0*	9.6 *0.4*	10.9 *0.4*	4.6 *0.2*	4.3 *0.2*	30.9 *1.3*	4.3 *0.2*	43 4.1
Other	10.3 *0.7*	12.5 *0.8*	17.5 *1.2*	11.1 *0.7*	5.6 *0.4*	4.4 *0.2*	0.0 *0.0*	68.2 *4.1*	66 6.2
N Campaign total %	109 10.2	342 32.1	334 31.3	75 7.1	64 6.0	74 6.9	22 2.1	45 4.2	1065

per cent of Labour's election-day voters (3.2 per cent of all possible voters). National and ACT competed for 2.6 per cent of the votes, exchanging about half of this group between them. Labour and the Alliance exchanged intentions and votes similarly, among a somewhat larger group of about 4 per cent. Labour was the main beneficiary of New Zealand First's campaign decline over the campaign. On the other hand, the Greens' rise during the later stages of the campaign owed most to respondents whose early voting intentions were Labour, followed by those in the 'don't know' and non-vote categories, and next by those who had intended voting Alliance. During the campaign, Alliance lost most to Labour, followed by non-vote, then National, and somewhat less to the Greens. Campaign 'don't knows' split two to one in favour of Labour over National, but the largest group ended up as non-voters. Our measurement of campaign effects is conservative, because almost certainly some post–18 October change is absorbed in the 'constant' group, made up of the diagonal shaded cells.

What distinguishes people who changed their intentions? Those with high hopes in democracy might expect that people most prone to making up their minds during the campaign would be those most attentive to the campaign, particularly through the media. On the other hand, evidence from many election studies indicates that, if anything, the opposite is the case, those being most fluid in their choices tending to be those with least media exposure. Data from the 1999 NZES offers support to neither side. In 1999 there were no significant differences between campaign changers and campaign constants in television exposure or newspaper readership. However, this does not exclude media effects entirely, particularly where they might have influence through changes in leadership perceptions and issue salience. We explore more fully the possible effects of the media in chapters 3 and 4.

Party identification is a traditional stabiliser of voting behaviour and party systems. It refers to the tendency of people to develop a continuing preference for one party over others, and to express this by varying degrees of commitment to the party — approval of its policies and politicians and, more importantly, a likelihood of voting for the party. This element of partisan loyalty that exists in all democracies is measured as the proportion of electors who agree that they 'usually think of themselves' (in New Zealand) as Labour, or National, or Green, or any other party they name, and also indicate how strong this sense of affiliation is. 'Identifiers' are the most stable and predictable voters, while volatility is associated with weak or no party identifications. Thus party identification is a good predictor of propensity to change during the campaign: of those with no post-election party identification (nearly half the voters), 55 per cent were campaign changers. Of those with a very strong party identification (9 per cent of the voters), the odds of campaign change were greatly reduced, although a still significant 6 per cent did so between the first half the of campaign and election day.

Leaders and Issues

There are two major potential explanations of voting intention change: changes in perceptions of party leaders, and a change of intended vote because one party rather than another became the most favoured on an issue or issues of concern to particular voters. People's intentions may change, either through what one might call a 'true conversion', or otherwise because the campaign has provided information and cues needed to return to a past loyalty, or one that was still possessed in latent form. Thus campaigns clarify and update preferences, and may change uncertain early campaign intentions toward a vote more consistent with people's basic loyalties and prior attachments (Gelman and King 1993; Stevenson and Vavreck 2000).

Chapter 4 investigates the effects of leadership in greater detail and depth. Here Table 2.2 addresses the leadership issue by comparing first-half campaign and post-election leader preferences among the same group of respondents. Jenny Shipley had taken over as Prime Minister toward the end of 1997 and, from the beginning of 1998, had led Clark as preferred Prime Minister. One News/Colmar Brunton polls reported Shipley's average support at about 27 per cent from December 1997 through to November 1999 (see Chapter 1). Helen Clark had not been far behind, averaging about 23 per cent, and had twice briefly edged ahead of Shipley. Early in the campaign, preferences for the two leaders mirrored this pattern, but post-election, Clark's support had increased significantly, and Shipley's had dropped slightly. Because our post-election estimate of leader support was taken when the outcome of the election was

Table 2.2: Per Cent Most Popular Leader Ratings, Comparing First Half of Campaign to Post-Election (Panel)

	To Nov 6	Post-election
Clark	19	32
Shipley	29	25
Anderton	6	10
Prebble	3	4
Peters	5	4
Fitzsimons	0.3	5
N	1095	1095

NOTE: Because of question format differences between pre- and post-election questionnaires, leadership ratings are estimated differently but in a way designed to make them as consistent as possible. Pre-election, respondents were asked which candidate for Prime Minister they most liked. Those most liking a candidate scored 1 for the pre-election rating, others scored 0. Post-election, a most preferred Prime Minister estimate again scoring 1 for the most preferred candidate was constructed by taking the most popular leader from the questions in B8 and, if there was a tie, supplementing this with the leader deemed most popular from questions B9–B12 (see Appendix B).

known, it is possible that it is contaminated by that knowledge. But it is more likely that the data are evidence of Clark's effectiveness on the campaign, a reaffirmation of her success in 1996 (Aimer 1997a). Meanwhile, during the campaign, Prebble (ACT) slightly increased his support, Anderton (Alliance) somewhat more so, while Green co-leader Jeanette Fitzsimons made a rapid ascent as the Greens became a contender for parliamentary seats over the second half of the campaign period. More detailed analysis of these changes over the campaign can be found in Chapter 4.

During an election campaign, political parties work in two ways on 'the issues'. They attempt to convert voters to their position on particular issues but, more importantly, they try to set the agenda of the campaign. They talk most about the issues on which they have good reason to believe they have the greatest support. Other parties will try to move the debate onto other issues that favour them, but if concern about a particular issue is strong, a party may be forced to defend its policies even if it knows that it is at a disadvantage.

The two most important issues were health and education (40 per cent together). Table 2.3 shows that in the 1999 campaign Labour clearly had the advantage on these two, as well as on five others which were each deemed important by smaller numbers of voters. Many New Zealanders believed that during the 1990s under National governments health and education had been underfunded. Health, in particular, had been under pressure because of attempts to make its administration more efficient — attempts that, many believed, had been spectacularly unsuccessful. Accordingly, many more people had come to favour Labour's policies on health and education more than National's.

Table 2.3: Most Important Issue by Party Closest on Most Important Issue, Campaign Panel Respondents

Column % Row %	Most Impt	Lab	Nat	All	ACT	NZ First	Green
Health	*23*	**46**	18	11	3	3	0
Education	*17*	**50**	13	16	1	0	1
Economy	*10*	17	**52**	6	12	2	0
Unemployment	*9*	**42**	16	7	3	5	0
Taxes	*9*	19	**53**	1	20	1	2
Government Honesty	*6*	17	**21**	7	4	5	3
Superannuation	*5*	**58**	10	11	3	14	0
Welfare/Poverty	*5*	**39**	18	19	2	0	3
Law and Order	*5*	13	26	3	**30**	4	0
Student Loans	*2*	**51**	29	11	0	2	0
Labour Relations	*1*	**70**	18	9	0	0	0
Environment	*1*	27	8	1	0	5	**56**
N	2117						

Table 2.4: Most Preferred Party on the Issues, Pre- and Post-Election, Comparing First Half of Campaign to Election Day

	To Nov 6	Post-election
Labour	24	43
National	18	24
Alliance	6	6
ACT	5	6
NZ First	3	1
Greens	1	nm
None/Don't know	43	20
N	875	875

NOTE: Because of question format differences between pre- and post-election questionnaires, most preferred party on issue preferences was estimated differently, but in a way designed to make them as consistent as possible. Pre-election, respondents were asked which issue was most important to them, and then what party's position was closest to theirs on that issue. Post-election, party most favoured on issues was constructed by summing the number of times each party was mentioned in the questions in A6, and taking the party chosen the most frequently.

National's best issues were the economy and taxes. It was given credit for some economic success for New Zealand during the 1990s, and, as we saw in Chapter 1, economic recovery in the second half of 1999 should have given the government a boost. Meanwhile National was promising tax cuts, whereas

Labour planned to increase taxes for the highest 5 per cent of income earners. Together, however, only about 19 per cent thought one or the other of these issues was the most important. There was little variation in issue importance over the campaign. Health and education remained dominant, but unemployment, a Labour issue, fell back, and the economy and taxes became slightly more important in the latter half of the campaign. National's issue momentum waned after about 16 November, whereas Labour's continued upward. The pattern of party preference on issues among panel respondents closely corresponded to the trend in party voting intentions over the remainder of the campaign (Vowles 2000a, 157–8).

Effective election campaigns have an educative role. Between elections, many people do not pay much attention to politics or political issues. During the campaign, voters gain knowledge or, at least, receive cues that certain issue positions are consistent with their values and preferences. Both National and Labour proved effective in reaching voters with their messages, but Labour was the more effective. It started out with an advantage on the issues, and as the campaign unfolded Labour was able to further widen the gap. In most explanations of elections, preferences for leaders and issue identification with particular parties form the largest part of the explanation of electoral change. At the margins, however, there may be other influences. Parties seek to generate support by projecting images of confidence and of 'winning'. However, such efforts can be compromised by the release of poll information that tells a different story. This can be particularly uncomfortable for parties that appear to be losing in the race, as was the case for New Zealand First.

Polls

The possible influence of opinion polls raised important issues about their publication and interpretation. Some members of the New Zealand First and National parties believed that public responses to the reporting of polls had the effect of discouraging voters from supporting them. National feared that some potential National voters had become convinced that Labour would be able to govern, and cast a tactical vote for Labour to enhance its power relative to its more left-leaning prospective coalition partner, the Alliance. Some National politicians also believed that poll results released before the election and indicating almost certain National defeat might have created a more general bandwagon effect in favour of Labour, while discouraging National supporters from casting their votes. For its part, New Zealand First declined in support according to the published polls, but did better in the election than most had predicted. Despite this, New Zealand First members presumably felt that had the polls told a different story, or if no polls at all had been published during the campaign, the party might have done better still.

In their analysis of the 1996 election in New Zealand, Johnston and Vowles (1997) found small but significant effects of polls on people's expectations of the outcome of the election, particularly with respect to parties close to the 5 per cent or one-electorate thresholds for seats in Parliament. Thus, in 1996 poor national polling for the Christian Coalition diminished expectations that it

**Table 2.5: Opinion Polls Released during the 1999 Campaign:
Countrywide, Coromandel and Tauranga**

Where	Field	Release	Nat	Lab	Diff*	All	NZF	ACT	Green
Countrywide									
TV1	11–14 Oct	17–Oct	37	39	2	4.5	6	7	1
TV3	14–20 Oct	21–Oct	33	37	4	7	6	9	2.5
NBR	14–17 Oct	22–Oct	32	37	5	7	7	8	3.6
NZH	29 Oct–3 Nov	5–Nov	33.6	35.2	1.6	8.7	5.5	9.2	2.9
SST	29 Oct–4 Nov	7–Nov	32.8	37.6	4.8	11.9	5	7.7	
TV3	1–7 Nov	8–Nov	28	41	13	7	6	10	2.9
NZH	4–10 Nov	12–Nov	31.7	33.4	1.7	7.8	6.5	10.5	4.6
TV1	8–11 Nov	13–Nov	33	34	1	9	6	11	2.4
SST	5–11 Nov	14–Nov	26.8	44.5	17.7				
TV3	11–17 Nov	18–Nov	30	37	7	9	6	9	2.8
NBR	11–16 Nov	19–Nov	30	35.6	5.6	10.4	4.6	8.2	4.6
NZH	11–17 Nov	19–Nov	29.1	37.8	8.7	8.6	4.8	10	5.2
SST	12–19 Nov	21–Nov	27.7	39.3	11.6				
TV1	22–24 Nov	25–Nov	31	39	8	8	3.2	7	6
TV3	18–24 Nov	25–Nov	29	34	5	9	5.5	11	6
NZH	18–24 Nov	26–Nov	29.8	39.8	10	7.7	3.6	8.5	5.4
Coromandel									
SST		24–Oct	37		–3				34
TV1		10–Nov	36		3				39
Dom		15–Nov	35		8				43
TV1		24–Nov	39		5				44
Tauranga									
BOP		28–Aug	26	18	19		45		
NBR		9–Sep	23	24	16		40		
TV1		12–Nov	32		–1		31		
BOP		13–Nov	33		–2		31		
TV1		24–Nov	30	29	–3		27		

NOTES: TV One polls were conducted for One News by Colmar-Brunton; TV3 polls were
conducted by CM Research; NZH polls were conducted for the *New Zealand Herald*
(Auckland) by DigiPoll; countrywide polls for the *Sunday Star Times* by the NZES, and
in Coromandel by UMR-Insight; *NBR* polls were conducted by UMR-Insight;
Dominion (Wellington) polling by UMR-Insight; BOP for the *Bay of Plenty Times* by
Key Research. Polls in electorates other than Coromandel and Tauranga are excluded.

*   'Diff' column is Labour minus National for the countrywide polls and Green or NZ
First minus their major competitor. in the electorate section.

would win a seat, whereas electorate polls produced the opposite positive
effects for ACT and United. Those expectations may have influenced vote
intentions, particularly for ACT, by reassuring supporters that a party vote for
it would not be wasted.

Table 2.5 indicates the timing of fieldwork and release and the findings of significant published polls during the 1999 campaign. Polls tended to be released with little emphasis on the time of fieldwork: the average difference between the midpoint of the fieldwork period and the time of release was about five days, giving those paying attention a somewhat lagged impression of opinion trends. Media attention to the polls was high, most of the countrywide polls featuring as a lead item on television news programmes and as front-page news in the newspaper that commissioned them. One News/Colmar Brunton polls got the most publicity, as One News has the widest audience, but TV3–CM Research polls also got national exposure. The *New Zealand Herald* has the highest circulation of New Zealand's newspapers, and includes the north of the North Island, which contains about 50 per cent of the population. Higher exposure polls are lightly shaded in the table.

Countrywide polls clearly indicated declining support for National and New Zealand First. The two most highly publicised countrywide polls put New Zealand First above the 5 per cent threshold throughout most of the campaign, dipping below it in the final days. For both New Zealand First and the Greens, electorate contests were also significant. Winning even a single electorate qualifies a party for proportional representation, thus potentially delivering a few extra list seats, even if its party vote is less than 5 per cent. In the Tauranga electorate vote intentions, the margin between New Zealand First party leader Winston Peters and the National candidate, Katherine O'Regan, shifted from a strong advantage to Peters at the outset of the campaign to a substantial disadvantage by its end, matching the trend of New Zealand First's nationwide support. As it turned out, Peters narrowly won Tauranga and the New Zealand First Party vote was significantly higher at 4.3 per cent than the last published poll for New Zealand First, which put it at only 3.6 per cent.

It is easy to understand why Winston Peters and New Zealand First did not appreciate the message that the polls were delivering to them. However, New Zealand First had a difficult campaign, and the polls and media coverage simply reflected that. Controversy on the choices and rankings of its list candidates had plagued the party from the beginning of the campaign. Yet both in Tauranga and in its nationwide vote New Zealand First did better on election day than the polls predicted, weakening the case that their bad news had adverse effects.

Turning to the Green party, there is good prima facie evidence for a positive effect on its party vote as the result of electorate polls in Coromandel, the seat contested and narrowly won by Green co-leader Jeanette Fitzsimons. Figure 2.3 presents the graphic evidence. Polls are reported by their day of release, plotted against the preliminary NZES day-by-day campaign estimates of Green support, ending up with the election day result.[4] As depicted in the figure, polls are assumed to shape perceptions until the next poll in the series. Two sets of polls are shown. Coromandel electorate polls are indicated by the margin favouring the Greens, which was negative until 8 November. The countrywide polls simply report the percentage support reported for the Greens. Both are represented by continuous lines that run between the reports of each poll in the series. The closest links between polls and voting intentions are evident in the trends described by the party vote intentions measured by the NZES, and the Coromandel electorate polls reported on 23 October, and 10, 15, and 24

Figure 2.3: Did the Polls Underpin the Green Surge in the Party Vote?

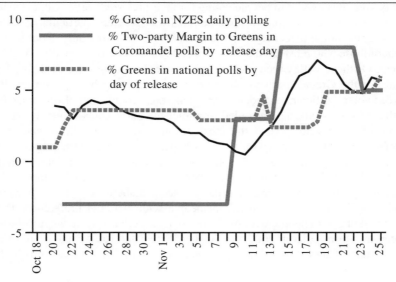

November. Polling across the country in general, on the other hand, seems to have followed rather than prompted the Green surge in Coromandel, although some reported results may have helped consolidate the process as potential Green voters began to realise that the party was getting closer to both vital thresholds.

When people change their vote intentions, one normally interprets this either as evidence of conversion to a new party choice or a return to an older choice from an uncertain commitment elsewhere. One can also identify a small minority of people who are voting 'strategically', less for a particular party, and more for a preferred outcome. If there is a poll effect it may be found among this group. Before asking respondents how they intended to vote, the NZES questionnaire gave them the opportunity to express a party preference independent of vote, based on the question 'which party do you like the most?'. Using this question, we can divide voters into two kinds: those apparently expressing a sincere preference (that is, those who voted for the party they 'most liked') and those who may have voted strategically (that is, they cast their party vote for a party other than the one they most preferred).

Why would people vote in this apparently perverse way? The label 'strategic' covers this group, although not all within it necessarily had strategy in mind. Nevertheless, some would have done so for a variety of strategic reasons. Some may have voted for a party other than the one they most liked to assist a small allied party over the threshold, or because they wanted a smaller party allied to their favourite party to have greater ability to 'keep it honest'. Or, anticipating the result of the election, as some National strategists have suggested, people may have wished to give a larger party they were certain would form a government (i.e. Labour) more strength to exert leadership in a coalition government (containing the Alliance), even though they might have preferred a different (National-led) government altogether.

Table 2.6 indicates the association between 'party most liked' and actual party vote. It shows most people voting for their preferred party, with evidence of votes being transferred to potential coalition partners, particularly junior ones. The column percentages in the first section show that only about 83 per cent of those who most liked the Labour and National parties actually voted for them. Of those with Green preferences, about three-quarters cast their party vote for the Greens, perhaps an indication that polling had given potential Green voters sufficient confidence that their votes would count. In contrast, the Alliance stands out, having failed to attract the party votes of nearly one in three of those who liked it the most. About a quarter of those who most preferred the Alliance voted for Labour (20 per cent) or the Greens (4 per cent). However, as a percentage of all voters (given in italics), Alliance gained more people with Labour preferences (2.3 per cent) than it lost among those with Alliance preferences casting their party vote for Labour (1.4 per cent). Similarly, ACT gained more votes from people with National preferences than National did from people with ACT preferences. Perhaps while languishing in some mid-term polls in 2000 and 2001, Alliance and ACT could draw some reassurance that the flow of strategic voters on election day seems to favour the smaller parties.

Table 2.6: Party Most Preferred and Party Vote

Section A	Party Preferred, Column %, *Total %*					
Party voted	Nat	Lab	All	ACT	Grn	NZF
National	83.1	2.6	2.2	15.5	1.3	2.5
	27.7	*1.0*	*0.1*	*0.8*	*0.0*	*0.1*
Labour	3.0	83.5	19.8	2.1	14.0	8.0
	1.0	*33.8*	*1.4*	*0.1*	*0.5*	*0.3*
Alliance	0.5	5.6	68.6	0.4	4.1	3.0
	0.2	*2.3*	*4.7*	*0*	*0.1*	*0.1*
ACT	8.0	0.4	0.4	74.1	1.5	0.0
	2.7	*0.0*	*0.0*	*4.1*	*0.1*	*0.0*
Green	0.7	3.2	4.0	1.0	74.0	0.0
	0.2	*1.3*	*0.3*	*0.1*	*2.6*	*0.0*
NZ First	0.9	2.2	0.7	0.3	2.3	79.5
	0.3	*0.9*	*0.1*	*0.0*	*0.1*	*2.6*
Other	3.8	2.4	4.3	6.6	2.8	7.0
	1.2	*1.3*	*0.3*	*0.4*	*0.2*	*0.2*
Preferences by party (row %)	33.3	40.6	6.8	5.5	3.6	3.3

Section B	Party Votes (Total %)					
Vote type by party as % all votes	Nat	Lab	All	ACT	Grn	NZF
Preference vote	27.7	33.8	4.7	4.1	2.6	2.6
Strategic vote	2.9	4.7	3.1	3.0	2.5	1.7
Total vote (row %)	30.6	38.5	7.8	7.1	5.1	4.3

The second section of the table divides each group of party voters into those who voted for the party they most liked (preference voters) and those who did not (strategic voters). The table shows that strategic voters made up about 10 per cent of National voters, 12 per cent of Labour voters, but between 40 per cent and a half of voters for the smaller parties.[5] This reflects the greater stability of support for the major parties, and the greater reliance of smaller parties on the votes of those whose preferences are weak or uncertain.

Weighing Up the Variables

So far the analysis has treated the main variables — party identification, leaders, issues, and polls — one by one, as though each acted in isolation to influence and possibly change people's vote intentions during the campaign. The next step is to estimate the effects of all together on vote, and of each variable taking into account the effects of the others. For many voters, campaign vote intention and actual vote will be the same; for many others they will differ. Either way, people's earlier campaign intentions will themselves influence election-day choices as well as being subject to change in response to other variables. Campaign vote intention is thus entered into our model separately, where it acts as a control on the effects of the other variables, so that we measure their contribution only after campaign vote intention has been taken into account. Figure 2.4 displays diagrammatically the assumed relationships between the variables, with all arrows ending finally at vote. In the centre of the diagram, campaign vote intention is itself assumed to be influenced by a selection of the more fundamental background factors that shape voting choices among New Zealanders in the longer term. Among these, the most important is party identification. We expect people's party identifications and other social background characteristics not only to directly influence their campaign vote intentions, as the arrow shows, but also to identify a possible 'homing tendency'. As noted earlier, the campaign may serve not so much to change preferences as to reinforce or revive earlier ones, turning latent preferences into active intentions, or shifting people back to old preferences from new ones only tentatively adopted either before the campaign or early in its progress.

The other variables shown in the diagram are entered into the model in such a way as to reflect the timing of leaders' debates, change in people's preferences for party leaders, change in their preferred party on issues, and reported poll results between the time our respondents were interviewed and election day. Table 2.7 reports general conclusions from the data, with reference to vote and to the two forms of voting — 'preference' and 'strategic' voting — introduced earlier into the discussion.[6] There were no significant effects for the timing of leadership debates.

For each party, the figures in the table show, in the first row, the average for each significant variable. Over the campaign, intended Green voters averaged about 3 per cent, and Green party identifiers about 1 per cent. For measurement of issue and leadership influences, in the model itself 0 indicated no change in preference, −1 a change away, and +1 a change toward the party's leader or to the party as one most preferred on the major issue. In the table these figures are

Figure 2.4: A Model of Campaign Effects

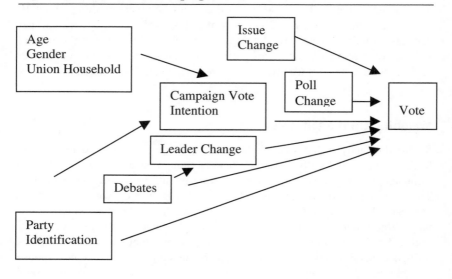

multiplied by 100 to make the average more understandable in percentage terms. On average, there was a small shift toward the Greens as the party preferred for its leadership: 5 points, when 100 would have indicated all voters shifted to the Greens from another preference, and –100 that all voters shifted away from a Green preference to another. The figures measuring the effects of these variables indicate the shift in per cent probability for each type of voting from one value of the independent variable to another. For example, under polls, during the campaign the average poll margin to the Greens in Coromandel was just over 3 per cent. We have measured the effects of the shift from –3 against the Greens to +5 in their favour. Similarly, we have measured the percentage probability effects of a campaign intention (1) versus the lack of one (0), and a party identification (1) versus the lack of one (0).

Overall, as one might expect, respondents' campaign intentions had the largest influence on their vote. The table indicates that a person intending to vote Green during the campaign was 41 per cent more likely to vote for the Greens on election day than a person not intending to do so, after controlling for the effects of all the other variables. However, campaign intentions were most strongly associated with preference voting for the two main parties and Alliance, that is, with voting by people who also said the parties were their 'most liked' choices. By comparison, the minor parties, with the exception of New Zealand First, which was losing support during the campaign, were more likely to be the target of strategic voters, choosing a party on the day which attracted their support, but which was not the one they 'most liked'. Strategic voting for ACT was notably strong, relative to preference voting, and marginally so for the Greens.

Again as one would expect, pre-election party identification was a strong influence among Labour and National voters, especially preference voters. Party identification also indicates a 'homing tendency', as campaign vote in-

Table 2.7: Significant Effects of Party Identification, Campaign Intention, Issue and Leader Preference Change on Election Day Vote (Percentage Probabilities)

		Campaign Intent	Party ID	Issue	Leader	Polls (E)
	Range of Prob	0–1	0–1	−1 to +1 (*100)	−1 to +1 (*100)	−3 to 5
	Mean	3	1		5	3.01
	Vote	41**	33**	nm	11**	
Green	Strategic	20**	10**	nm	5**	
	Preference	19**	17**	nm	4**	1**
	Mean	08	1	−1	1	
	Vote	21**	3**	1*		
NZF	Strategic	08**			1*	
	Preference	10**	2**			
	Mean	7	1	2	1	
	Vote	48**				
ACT	Strategic	24**				
	Preference	19**	2*	1**		
	Mean	8	2	0	3	
	Vote	49**		4*	5**	
Alliance	Strategic	21**				
	Preference	35**		2*	3**	
	Mean	34	23	17	12	
	Vote	54**	25**	24**	22**	
Labour	Strategic	12**				
	Preference	49**	22**	23**	22**	
	Mean	30	26	6	−2	
	Vote	53**	29**	24**	18**	
National	Strategic	06**	03*			
	Preference	51**	15**	20**	.17**	

**significant at p< 0.01   *significant at p< 0.05

SOURCE: Vowles 2001c. Green issue effects could not be measured due to missing data.

tention is included in the model. National had a slightly higher level of party identification than Labour (26 per cent to 23 per cent), and reaped slightly more advantage from it than Labour. A person with a National party identification was 29 per cent more likely to vote National on election day, compared to the Labour figure of 25 per cent. Party identification also had a significant effect on Green voting, but as only very few voters reported a Green identification (a little less than 1 per cent), the influence of this variable, though strong when present, was limited. Similarly ACT, New Zealand First, and Alliance voting received little reinforcement from party identification, although the Alliance, at just over 2 per cent, had the highest identification rate of the small parties. This is further evidence that small parties' vote shares are unstable, as vote volatility is greater among those without a party identification.

Compared to campaign voting intentions and party identification, changes in the respondents' perception of issues and leadership had modest effects on how they finally voted. The Alliance made gains when voters came to believe that its issue stance was closest to their own most important issue, and made losses when voters moved away from an Alliance issue preference. Thus a person shifting toward an Alliance issue preference was 4 per cent more likely to vote Alliance than a person shifting away from one. However, as the issue preference change mean for the Alliance was 0, the combined effects of these preference shifts were neutral. While the effects of issue preference shifts were about the same for the two main parties (24 per cent), Labour benefited from a much stronger positive issue movement, with a mean of 17 compared to only 5 for National. Respondents were more likely to vote for a party if, during the campaign, they acquired a preference for the party's leader. A three-point move toward preference for Anderton's leadership during the campaign and a small positive effect on this variable gave the Alliance vote a significant boost. A leadership preference effect among strategic New Zealand First voters helped to stem its losses, although an issue shift against the party had negative effects of a similar order. Evaluations of Clark's leadership pulled ahead of Shipley's, and Labour accordingly reaped more benefits than National from a stronger leadership effect on its vote, as Chapter 4 explores in greater detail.

The only statistically significant polling effect was for the Green party. Changes in the reported poll margin between the Greens and National in the Coromandel electorate between the first poll taken in the electorate and election day were worth 1 per cent to the Greens, one-fifth of the Green party vote. Reports of polling in the Coromandel electorate therefore almost certainly propelled the Greens into Parliament. While detailed analysis of Coromandel electorate polling data would be needed to confirm an electorate-level bandwagon effect for the party, that data is not available, but it seems almost certain that there was one, and that it mobilised preference voters. Unexpectedly, its effect on the countrywide party vote did not mobilise a significant strategic vote. Instead, reports of Coromandel polling influenced people with Green preferences who had intended to cast their votes elsewhere when polls looked bad for the Greens. After later polls predicted a win for the Greens' co-leader, Jeanette Fitzsimons, in her Coromandel electorate, people with Green preferences gained the confidence to express them in their party vote.

There was no equivalent Tauranga poll effect for New Zealand First, where the party's leader, Winston Peters, was the candidate and the sitting MP. An attempt at explanation of this can only be speculative. New Zealand First had crossed the threshold for seats in 1996 and, although depleted, remained a force in the outgoing Parliament. Its polling nationally had remained above the 5 per cent threshold for most of the campaign, and it was easy for supporters of an embattled party to discount or ignore the bad news in the final polls. By contrast, the Greens had not yet entered Parliament in their own right, and they appeared highly unlikely to do so until well into the campaign. They received greater publicity in the last two weeks of the campaign, much of it generated by the National party.

With the exception of the Greens in Coromandel, there is no evidence that polling information had significant effects on New Zealanders' vote choices in 1999, either to the benefit or detriment of any other parties. If there were such effects, they were too small for our models to detect and therefore too small to have had significant political consequences. The absence of stronger polling effects in New Zealand in 1999 is surprising, as research based on similar models has found quite substantial polling effects in successive elections in Canada (Blais, Gidengil, and Nevitte 1997). MMP possibly provides the explanation for the difference. There are much smaller incentives for such poll-generated voting in New Zealand under MMP than in Canada or in any other country with an FPP system. Under MMP, because the party vote counts proportionally, all who favour a major party which, according to the polls, is expected to 'lose', still have an incentive to maximise its vote so that it gains as many seats in the House as possible, and can therefore form a stronger Opposition. In addition, because proportional representation has opened up the political marketplace, people wishing to vote for small parties are less discouraged from doing so. When polls reveal that a party is close to a threshold of representation under MMP, one most expects to find voters responding to this information.

Changes in voting intentions over the campaign to the election were not large or dramatic, but in the end they altered the balance of party representation decisively. Labour had the advantage of voter disillusion with nine years of National or National-led government. Yet National entered the campaign in a far more competitive position than many had anticipated. Only as the campaign took hold did Labour recoup its advantage on the issues, remind sufficient voters of Helen Clark's abilities as a leader, and bring home voters who tended toward Labour but had not finally committed themselves to its support. Labour consolidated over the second half of the campaign, making gains on both issues and leadership. Topped off by the Greens' late surge, the campaign laid the electoral basis for the formation of a Labour-Alliance coalition government, with support from the Greens. In short, the campaign mattered a lot.

CHAPTER 3

ELECTIONS, CITIZENS
AND THE MEDIA

Susan Banducci and Jack Vowles

Jenny Shipley took time out from attacking the Greens to
discuss the future of the Kopu Bridge
— Photo caption, *New Zealand Herald*, 18 November 2000

As in most Western democracies, a citizen's experience of an election
campaign is mediated by newspaper and, mostly, television coverage of the
campaign events and issues. A significant part of the parties' campaign budgets
was spent on television and, to a lesser extent, radio broadcasting (see Chapter
7). Therefore, to understand whether or not an election campaign influences
voters, one cannot ignore campaign media coverage. There are two broad
questions to address in considering media coverage of election campaigns.
First, what is its content? Under this broad question, the amount of coverage
devoted to issues, strategy and party leaders is considered as well as the tone
of that coverage. Two trends noted by media analysts are the increasing focus
on party strategy and the 'horse race' (which party is ahead), at the expense
of issues, and the increasing focus on party leaders ('presidentialisation').
Overall, there is a concern that campaign reporting, and political coverage in
general, has become increasingly negative and dominated by the American
model of reporting.

The second question about the media is the influence it has on public
opinion and voting behaviour. Initial examinations of the influence of the
media assumed that campaign propaganda would sway unwitting voters. After
examining data from large-scale surveys, this assumption was replaced by the
notion that media coverage, in particular television news coverage, had a
minimal effect on the opinions of voters. More recent research has shown that
while news coverage may not tell voters what to think, it can influence what
voters think about and the issues upon which candidate evaluations are based.
More recently, there is also concern that the negative tone of political coverage
turns citizens off and keeps them at home on election day.

In this chapter, we examine news coverage of the 1999 election campaign
and its influence on voters. Our conclusions about the content of campaign
news coverage are based on analysis of TV One and TV3 nightly news from

18 October until 26 November (the five week campaign period). According to the post-election wave of the NZES, close to 90 per cent of the electorate followed political news on TV One and TV3 'always' or 'sometimes' (see Table 3.1). Limited resources prevented coding of the entire broadcast of the nightly news on TV3. Therefore, when we make comparisons between TV One and TV3, we rely on the first eight stories on each broadcast. Based on an analysis of the entire TV One broadcast, we found that 64 per cent of the election-related stories appeared within the first eight stories of the broadcast, and 71 per cent of the time devoted to election news was in the first eight stories. Also, the top news stories occur in the first part of the broadcast and are more likely to be remembered by viewers. Therefore, we are fairly confident that in analysing the top eight stories we are capturing what a large share of the New Zealand electorate experienced in terms of campaign media coverage. The content of the newspaper campaign coverage has been analysed elsewhere (Hayward and Rudd 2000).

We start by looking at the sources of campaign news. Post-election respondents were asked how much attention they paid to each of the sources of campaign news. Respondents placed themselves along a four-point scale from 'not at all' to 'often'. The average for each medium is given at the bottom of the table. The average person said they followed campaign news on TV One very close to 'sometimes', and campaign news in the newspapers slightly less than 'sometimes'. More people followed the campaign news on TV One and in newspapers than on TV3 as the average respondent watched TV3 only a little more often than 'rarely'. Comparing the averages for each medium in 1996 with those in 1999, there was little change to where New Zealanders turned for election information.[1]

Table 3.1: During the election campaign, how often did you follow the election news and advertising on the television and in the newspapers?

	TV One	TV3	Newspapers
Often (1)	31	13	28
Sometimes (.66)	38	29	32
Rarely (.33)	16	18	17
Not at all (0)	14	40	23
Average 1999	0.62	0.39	0.55
Average 1996	0.64	0.41	0.56

Party Messages

Political parties had only a certain amount of control over the way that their messages were communicated during the campaign because most were mediated indirectly through television, newspapers and radio. Parties can only directly influence voters through their advertising and allocated television time, and by contacting voters personally by door-knocking, mail or telephone.

Parties must seek to set the agenda of the campaign, emphasising the issues on which they can attract the strongest support, and doing their best to sideline the issues on which their opponents have the advantage. One of the parties' key tasks is to project a positive image of their own confidence and competence, while painting alternative parties in as bad a light as possible.

For example, National used a series of television advertisements which featured Prime Minister Jenny Shipley and other senior cabinet ministers, projecting them as experienced managers of the country's affairs, whose mistakes and misjudgements had been minor compared to their achievements. On the negative side, and particularly in the latter stages of the campaign, National sought to promote an image of a future Labour-led government unable to work with its allies, the Alliance and the Greens. Labour's positive images centred on leader Helen Clark. Its negative advertising highlighted the record of the previous government, and its history of excessive public sector pay-outs which Labour said it would bring to an end.[2]

However, the parties' own presentations of their messages tend to be sidelined and filtered by the media. Campaign events reported in the media may not always be planned or favourable to the party concerned. Television and newspapers may publish negative material that subverts a party's carefully packaged positive images and gives support to the negative images promoted by its opponents. Journalists may focus on issues to which parties would prefer little or no attention to be given. This does not necessarily reflect 'media bias' or an intention to give one or more parties negative publicity. Journalists and news editors simply want stories that will capture people's attention. The 1999 campaign was widely perceived to be dull, or boring. Editors and journalists wishing to attract the biggest possible audience for their product had to look for stories of interest. As Church puts it succinctly, during the 1999 campaign 'a sore lesson learnt was that bad news for a party could guarantee much coverage, but not of the good kind' (Church 2000, 125–6).

Consequently, when a party's leaders and candidates performed badly, or, even worse, when they began to fight or bicker with politicians from an allied party, that party got media attention. For example, when ACT released its economic policy on 14 November, it was attacked by National's Minister of Finance, Bill English, as 'unrealistic'. Media coverage focused on the divergence between the two parties more than the content of the policies. A few days earlier, Labour and Alliance spending plans were released, with Labour's Michael Cullen describing those of the Alliance as 'heroic'. Alliance leader Jim Anderton's response to reports of the comment were interpreted on the most widely watched television news programme, One News, as a falling out between the two potential coalition partners. Labour and the Alliance both later maintained that the episode had been blown up out of proportion by the One News report. When, for the second election in a row, conflict broke out within New Zealand First over the ordering of candidates on its party list, negative publicity for that party was more newsworthy than anything else it did or had to say.

On top of such coverage, as we saw in Chapter 2, media organisations commission and publish polls that indicate how parties are losing or gaining support. Such polls may occasionally have electoral effects. Much of the election coverage is concerned with the 'horse race', rather than with the messages the politicians are trying to deliver. Indeed, one of the most notable trends in news coverage of elections campaigns is an increasing focus on the 'horse race' and the strategy of election campaigns. As pre-election polls become more of a part of the election landscape, there is an increasing focus by the news on which party is ahead in the polls, and on party strategies to overcome weaknesses in polling numbers. This focus reflects the desire of news organisations to capture the conflict of the campaign. The increasing focus on strategy and conflict in political campaign has been blamed for the electorate's increasing cynicism (Patterson 1993). Moreover, coverage of party strategy and who is ahead displaces important coverage of issues and party issue positions. Therefore, voters are presented with little information on which to base electoral decisions.[3]

Even when the messages are being discussed, journalists tend to frame their coverage around matters of style, delivery and effectiveness, rather than the content of the messages. Those politicians reported to be losing in the race face even more trials and tribulations as their credibility suffers. Both National and New Zealand First received somewhat more than their share of bad news from polls during the campaign. What, then, was the content of the 'media messages'?

In order to answer the question about the focus of campaign coverage, we coded the first eight stories on the evening news broadcasts on TV One and TV3.[4] Besides looking at the nature of the coverage during the campaign, we were also interested in looking at differences between the two types of television stations. The division between public and private broadcast organisations is important when examining both the content of programming and the effect it has on viewers (Norris 2000). For example, public broadcasting tends to produce a more highly informed electorate (Holtz-Bacha and Norris 2000). However, most consider that traditional public broadcasting on television has not existed for at least ten years in New Zealand and the focus over the past years has been on profit not quality local programming (Harcourt 2000). The content on the TV One news programme, One News, is produced by TV New Zealand (TVNZ), a state-owned enterprise that relies for most of its revenue on advertising. Although a state-owned enterprise, TVNZ had no strict charter on its mission or broadcast content in 1999, as did, for example, Radio New Zealand. On the other hand, TV3 is a completely commercial venture and is almost entirely owned by CanWest, a Canadian company. Both TVNZ and TV3 receive funding from New Zealand On Air (NZOA), a government agency that distributes public funds to broadcasters. Given the commercial or profit motivation of both TV3 and TVNZ, we may see little difference in content as both news programmes are driven by a need to attract audiences.

Figure 3.1 compares news coverage during the election on the two different news programmes. In the top two pie charts, the top eight stories of each news broadcast on TV3 and TV One are divided between three categories according to the focus of the news story: (1) election news, (2) coverage of issues such as unemployment, health or the economy, that were not mentioned in the context of election news and (3) other stories such as crimes being committed, natural disasters and human interest stories. The amount of time spent on stories in each of these categories is then calculated. In the bottom pie charts, all election stories are further classified by the topic of the election story. Because most stories will contain multiple topics, we coded only the main topic (the topic to which the most time was devoted). Stories were coded as mainly being about (1) campaign events such as rallies or speeches by candidates, (2) which party or candidate is ahead, behind, expected to win or lose, i.e. the 'horse race', (3) the issue positions of the parties, (4) possible coalition partners or the formation of a coalition government, (5) the MMP electoral system, (6) the list of candidates put forward by the party, (7) the bases of support for the parties such as which groups tend to support a particular party, and (8) the leaders of the parties.

News on both programmes was dominated by non-issue and non-election related stories, the 'other' category. Crime, car accidents and human interest stories dominate this category. We see little difference between the two TV channels in terms of election and issue coverage. Indeed the distribution of the type of coverage on each is strikingly similar. Some differences do emerge when we look specifically at the election coverage. One News devoted twice as much time to stories about party positions. However, One News spent less time on campaign events than TV3 News. Surprisingly, One News also devoted more time to stories about who was ahead in the polls — the 'horse race'. The difference in time devoted to party positions may be important for it suggests that those viewers who were paying attention to One News received more information about issues and where the parties stood on the issues than those who tuned in to the news on TV3.

Overall, during the five weeks leading up to the election, 26 per cent of domestic stories on the evening news on each station were devoted to election-related stories. Of these election stories, only 6.1 per cent of the time (or 19.5 per cent of the election coverage) was devoted to the 'horse race'. The proportion of 'horse race' stories is somewhat lower than might be expected in the light of media critics who complain that too much election coverage tends to be focused on the contest itself at the expense of issues. Comparatively, campaign events were the focus of one-third of the election stories on TV One and almost one-half of the stories on TV3. Party positions and coalitions were the focus of 27 per cent of election stories on TV One and 23 per cent on TV3. Therefore, more time was devoted to party positions, activities and possible coalition partners than on strategy and the 'horse race'. Additionally, over 10 per cent of domestic coverage was devoted to issues. Even though these issues were not necessarily presented in the context of the election (hence they are coded into a separate category), they still may play a role in informing voters. In sum, electors, if they paid attention to television news coverage during the campaign, were exposed to a substantial amount of issue-based coverage.

In examining all of the domestic news stories on TV One (not just the first eight stories), we found that 85 per cent of the election-related stories featured one or more party leaders, even though they may have not been the main focus of the story. In contrast, only 33 per cent of the election-related stories mentioned the parties' positions on issues. This difference in coverage between leaders and party positions may be a reflection of a party strategy that puts leaders at the centre, and not simply a matter of the news media finding it easier

**Figure 3.1. A Comparison of News Coverage: TV One and TV3
18 October–6 November (first eight stories only)**

to focus on a handful of personalities as the symbols for parties (see Chapter 4). The media's attention to personalities during the election may put party leaders rather than issues at the top of the list of voters' considerations when making a vote choice (Mendelsohn 1996). This effect is termed 'priming' and refers to the influence of the media's agenda priorities on the weight individuals give to various considerations in their political evaluations or choices (see Iyengar, Peters and Kinder 1982). For example, if the news media are giving priority to economic issues, citizens' opinions of the economy will weigh more heavily than their opinions about foreign policy when they are asked to evaluate how the prime minister is handling her job. A similar priming effect can apply to election campaigns. If the media focus more on leaders than on the parties' positions on issues, voters' evaluations of party leaders will have greater influence on their vote choice than issue positions. In other words, the news coverage of the campaign will 'prime' leadership evaluations rather than issues or partisanship in the vote decision. Therefore, we might expect those who pay a great deal of attention to campaign news in the media to rely more heavily on leadership evaluations than on issues when making their vote decision.

In order to test the proposition that campaign news primes leadership evaluations, we compare the relative effect of leaders, issues and partisanship in predicting party vote choice. Using the post-election survey data, we predict vote for Labour using a variety of measures: an issue scale, rating of Clark, ideology, education, gender, and attention to the various media seen in Table 3.1. In order to determine whether attention to news about the campaign primes leadership or issues, we combine attention to the various news outlets with issues and leadership evaluations in an interaction term. An interaction term is the product of two quantitative variables. For our purposes, therefore, we multiply attention to the news by leadership evaluation and attention to news by issues. If these interaction terms are statistically significant, it suggests that the effects of issues and leadership evaluations on vote choice depend on how much a voter is paying attention to the news. If television news primes leadership, we would expect the interaction term multiplying leadership evaluations and attention to television news to be positive and significant, suggesting that those who pay a great deal of attention to television news are more likely to rely on how much they like party leaders in their vote decisions.

After analysing the data, we do find evidence that campaign news primes leadership. However, we also find that campaign news primes issues as well. The difference between priming leadership evaluations or issues depends on the news outlets. Attention to newspapers primed leadership evaluations. On the other hand, attention to National Radio failed to prime leadership and attention to TV3 failed to prime issues. In other words, those paying a great deal of attention to newspapers during the campaign were more likely to rely on leadership evaluations than those who paid little attention to newspapers; those paying a great deal of attention to National Radio were less likely to rely on leadership evaluations than those who paid little attention to National Radio, and those who paid a great deal of attention to TV3 were less likely to rely on issues than those who paid little attention to TV3.

To illustrate these differences, controlling for the effects of other relevant variables, we have plotted the effect that issues and leadership evaluations have on those who pay attention to National Radio and TV3. Details of the method used can be found in Appendix C. Looking at Figure 3.2a, we see the effects of issues on the probability of casting a party vote for Labour. The dotted line

Figure 3.2: Media Exposure, Leader Evaluations and Issues

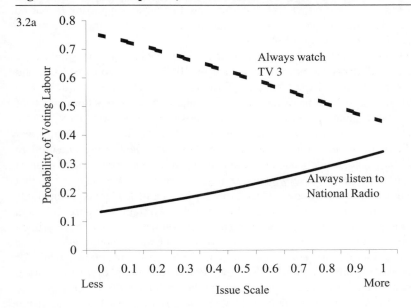

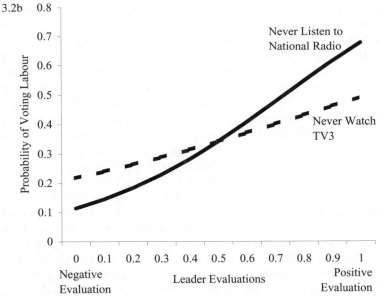

represents the effect of issues for those who always watch TV3 while the solid line represents the effect of issues on vote choice for those who always listen to National Radio. As is evident from the graph, the direction of the relationship for National Radio listeners indicates that there is a positive relationship between more spending on government programmes which is consistent with party campaign promises and support for Labour. However, for frequent watchers of TV3 news, there is a negative relationship between more spending on government programmes and support for Labour suggesting that those who watched TV3 were either less likely to view Labour as supporting increased government spending or less able to match preferences for more government spending with support for Labour.

Figure 3.2b shows the effect of leadership evaluations on support for Labour and shows the priming effects of the different news outlets. The solid line represents the effect of leadership evaluations on vote choice for those who never tune in to National Radio while the dotted line represents the effects of leadership evaluations on vote choice for those who never watch TV3. From Figure 3.2b, we can see that leadership evaluations are a much stronger predictor of support for Labour among those who *never* pay attention to National Radio, while leadership evaluations are a weak predictor of support for Labour among those who *never* pay attention to TV3, suggesting that listening to National Radio reduced the importance of leadership evaluations in the voting decisions of citizens. If we take the two figures (Figures 3.2a and 3.2b) together, we see that the different media outlets appear to have primed different considerations in the voters' minds. For those paying attention to National Radio, issues tend to be important predictors of vote choice, while for those not paying attention to National Radio leadership evaluations were primed. Likewise, there is an inconsistent relationship between issues and vote choice for those paying attention to TV3 and a more consistent relationship between issues and vote choice for those paying attention to National Radio.

The data presented in Figure 3.1 suggests that content may contribute to these differences in priming. The news on TV3 had discussed party positions half as often as One News, suggesting that there were fewer mentions of where the parties stood on issues. Data collected by Hayward and Rudd (2000) shows that party leaders account for over 18 per cent of the campaign coverage. While the television content we have coded and the newspaper content they have coded may not be strictly comparable, we do see that newspapers seemed to focus more on party leaders. On the broadcast news 6 per cent or fewer of the stories focused on the party leaders (see Figure 3.1). This difference in focus on the leaders suggests a possible explanation why attention to newspapers is more likely to prime leadership evaluations. While we have no comparable data for National Radio, there are two possible reasons why leadership evaluations may not be primed. First, radio, of course, does not rely on visual images and may rely less on the party leaders as representative images of the parties. Therefore, party leaders will not feature as prominently in radio coverage. Second, Radio New Zealand is the only true public broadcaster in New Zealand and its content is regulated by a strict charter stating that the programmes must contribute toward, among other things, intellectual development and informed public debate. Therefore, we suggest, the actual content of the news stories may be focused more on parties, their positions and issues than on leader images.

Issues and Agenda Setting

Election coverage may influence what voters rely on to make decisions in the polling booth and the coverage may also influence what voters see as the

Table 3.2: Rankings of Issues and the 1999 Election Agenda: Parties, One News and the Voters

	Voters*	One News**	ACT***	Labour***	Alliance***	National***
Immigration	16	12		14.5		
Privatisation	13.5	15.5		12.5	4.5	
Law and order	8.5	7.5	7.5	8.5		13.5
Student loans	10	11		10.5	11.5	13.5
Superannuation	6.5	12		8.5	11.5	13.5
Environment	11.5	7.5		6.5	9.5	13.5
Health	1	4		3	7	13.5
Unemployment	3.5	3		14.5	4.5	13.5
Labour relations	11.5	5		12.5	7	9
Maori	13.5	7.5	4.5	5	9.5	8
Defence	15	10				7
Education	2	12	6	6.5	7	6
Welfare/Poverty	8.5	15.5	4.5	4	2	5
Other			2			
Taxes	5	7.5	7.5	10.5	13	3
Economy	3.5	2	3	2	3	2
Politicians	6.5	1	1	1	1	1
Correlation:						
With voters		.42	.33	.50	.47	.47
With one news	.42		.23	.37	.27	.36

*   Most important issue, % of campaign respondents naming an issue

**   Minutes of coverage, % of total issue content of campaign coverage

***   % of opening and closing speeches

NOTE: correlation coefficients are Spearman's rank order, excluding the 'other' category.

important issues facing New Zealand. One of the main themes about the role of the media in politics centres on 'agenda setting'. Agenda setting refers to the correspondence between the importance given in the media to specific issues and the order of significance attached to the same issues by the public (McQuail 1994). Research into the effects of political communication indicates that it is much easier for politicians to influence what issues people are thinking about than what people may think on a particular issue. Early research in the U.S. indicated that the media played an influential role in setting the public agenda — influencing what people considered to be the important issues of the day (McCombs and Shaw 1972).

In order to examine the question of agenda setting during the 1999 New Zealand election, we compare the agendas of the public, the parties and the media. Table 3.2 compares issue priorities from three distinct sources: a content analysis of party leaders' speeches given at their campaign openings, our content analysis of One News issue coverage during the campaign, and the issues prospective voters thought most important during the campaign.[5] On a simple agenda-setting hypothesis, we might expect that parties would influence voters through the media, so media issue priorities would correlate more strongly with those of voters than with those of parties. However, the issue priorities of the Labour, National and Alliance opening campaign speeches were closer to those of voters than those presented on One News during the campaign. Either those parties were able to directly influence voters' issue priorities, independently of the news (an unlikely prospect), or they were largely responding to what they thought voters wanted to hear, contrary to the agenda-setting hypothesis.

While ACT, Labour, National, and One News made much mention of Maori issues, only 0.4 per cent of voters named those as the most important issue when they thought about voting, and hence its low ranking by voters in Table 3.2. One News almost failed completely to take up education as an issue, despite all the four main parties giving it modest attention and its status as the second most important issue among voters. Only on the specific matter of student loans did One News pay significant attention somewhat beyond that of parties and voters. Of the parties, only Labour emphasised health relatively strongly. One News did feature health issues to some degree, but not nearly as much as one would have expected, given the importance of the issue among voters.

We saw in Chapter 2 that that health and education were strong Labour issues, and more attention to them might have boosted Labour, but Labour itself did not perhaps give health as much priority in its campaign as it could have done. The relatively strong focus on the economy given by One News may have slightly advantaged National. The economy did become a more important issue among voters as the campaign progressed. Yet One News gave less relative attention to taxation than National or ACT, or voters themselves. Reducing taxes had promise as an issue for the centre-right, but fell back in salience among voters in the week before the election (Vowles 2000a, 158). There may have been opportunities for greater agenda setting during the 1999 campaign, but there is little obvious evidence of strong effects in our data. The lack of clear findings on agenda setting in New Zealand is consistent also with recent research in other countries on the effects of election media coverage on what people see as the most important problem.[6]

Opinion Formation and Leader Evaluations

Besides the media's influence on what voters saw as the most important issue, the media could potentially influence voters in other important ways during the campaign. Among these are the processes of opinion formation and opinion change. Most campaign research points to the importance of campaigns in mobilising or reigniting latent partisan tendencies rather than in converting voters from one partisan camp to another. The campaign also plays an important role in guiding those voters who have not yet made up their minds. In the following section, we investigate the role of the media in opinion formation and opinion change. In doing so, we address questions raised in the introduction to the chapter. First, can the media influence the process of opinion formation and opinion conversion? Second, if the media focus on party leaders what influence does this have on voters?

To examine the role of the media in opinion formation we examine how the tone of coverage may influence voters. In order to do this, we examined news coverage from the perspective of the party leaders, coding news stories that mentioned the party leaders as favourable, neutral, or unfavourable with respect to the leader mentioned. A rating of 1.0 indicates report of a major accomplishment: none attained this. Ratings of 0.5 indicate success or achievement at more modest levels, 0.0 signifies neutral or mixed evaluations, –0.5 unfavourable coverage (problems in the campaign, or in the style of the campaign), and –1.0 represents extremely unfavourable coverage. These have been averaged across the campaign period for the stories on One News and are displayed in Figure 3.3. The total number of mentions during the campaign on One News are also given in Figure 3.3.

Figure 3.3: Evaluations of Party Leaders — One News

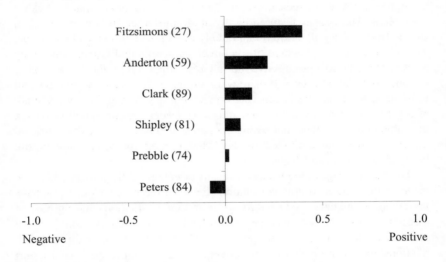

NOTE: Total number of mentions is given in ( ).
SOURCE: Content analysis of One News's 6 p.m. news broadcasts.

Overall, Clark was evaluated positively only slightly more than Shipley. But correlation coefficients derived from running leader evaluations against day of the campaign show that Clark's coverage became more favourable as the campaign went on, and Shipley's more negative.[7] Jenny Shipley spear-headed an aggressive campaign against the Green party over much of the second-to-last week of the campaign. During that period, support for Shipley as preferred Prime Minister fell sharply. Evaluations of her performance on One News turned negative (dropping from 0.4 to –0.1), although they quickly became more positive. Turning her attention back to Labour in the last week of the campaign, she made a significant recovery in public preferences and media evaluations.

The New Zealand First party leader, Winston Peters, gained the least favourable evaluation. Overall, assessments of Peters were the only ones to be marginally negative with an average of −.08. The range of evaluations for Peters was also greater: he received high rankings but also lower rankings than any other leader. Jeanette Fitzsimons had the most favourable coverage, most of it coming in the latter weeks of the campaign. Of the leaders of the smaller parties, Peters also attracted the most attention, averaging about two stories per day over the 40-day campaign period. The ACT leader, Richard Prebble, had less coverage than Clark, Shipley and Peters, but it was also more mixed and only marginally positive on average. Peters and Prebble gained more coverage not because they were favoured by One News, but because they were more controversial and newsworthy. This explanation is evident when we look at both the amount of coverage and the less than positive tone of coverage. The Green and Alliance leaders received less coverage, but what they got was more uniformly positive.

Coverage of all leaders increased over the campaign, but most for National and the Greens. In the case of Shipley and National, this reflected a peak in the second-to-last week of the campaign, the period of National's main attack on the Greens. The Greens featured hardly at all until after 10 November, when for the first time a poll showed them likely to win the Coromandel electorate. The relative lack of coverage of the Green campaign and Green issues may have contributed to a progressive fall in Green support until the 10 November Coromandel poll. However, if there were any such effects they were too small to be measurable on the Green vote on election day. While there were small effects for coverage of Green issues and Green leaders on Green polling during the campaign, these were not strong enough in themselves to have significant effects on vote choice on election day. Media reports of polls, however, did have effects, shown in Chapter 2.

Did the coverage of the leaders have any effect on public perceptions of the leaders? Looking at simple correlations between the number of respondents preferring each leader as Prime Minister and the evaluations and number of mentions in One News coverage, for all leaders except Clark more positive evaluations led to greater support. For Clark there is a slight negative relationship, meaning that as the coverage became more positive support declined. All of these relationships are fairly weak. Day-by-day correlations of the amount of media coverage to the leaders against preferred Prime Minister responses tell a clearer story. The number of mentions of Shipley had a very small negative effect on preference for her as Prime Minister, and coverage for both Prebble and Peters had stronger negative effects. Effects were positive for all leaders of the centre-left parties, but most of all for Clark, although hers is the only relationship that approaches statistical significance. The positive effect for leaders on the left reflects their increased standing in the polls as the campaign progressed.

These evaluations and the changes in them over the campaign essentially reflected the performance of the leaders as evaluated by editors and journalists and other campaign commentators. It is impossible to separate the effect of the evaluations from the effect of the events themselves. Moreover, while it is highly probable that Shipley's performance from 16 to 21 November was counterproductive, she recovered the following week, and its effects on voter choices on election day, if there were any, are too small to estimate.

While we see only weak relationships between the tone and amount of coverage for the leaders and their support in the polls, the media may influence certain segments of the population more than others. Communication theorists have long noted that particular groups are more likely than others to be persuaded by certain messages. For example, when considering campaign communications, electors are less likely to be persuaded by negative messages about their preferred candidate (Zaller 1992). Given the considerable gender gap in support for the parties and party leaders (see Chapter 4), one could construct an alternative version of this communication model. If certain groups of voters are more predisposed to accept or reject particular messages, we might hypothesise that women are less likely to accept negative messages about women party leaders (Gidengil and Everitt 2001). Therefore, with two women in contention for the position of Prime Minister, the reason we see little effect from the tone of coverage on preferences for Prime Minister is that the tone of coverage tends to influence only male voters.

In order to ascertain whether or not this was the case, we looked more closely at how the tone of coverage and the amount of coverage influenced support for Clark and Shipley for men and for women. Once we controlled for Labour or National support and the amount of coverage, we found two explanations for why we saw only weak correlations between the leader tone and support for the leaders (see Appendix C for the full estimation model). First, rather than the tone of coverage of the leader influencing support for that leader, the tone influenced support for the other leader. So, as the tone of coverage became more positive about Clark, support for Shipley declined, and when coverage became more negative about Shipley, support for Clark grew. For example, among the average Labour supporter, the probability of preferring Clark for Prime Minister among all other party leaders was .46 when coverage of Shipley was most positive. But the probability of support increased to .69 when coverage of Shipley was at its most negative. Among the average National supporters, the predicted probability of supporting Shipley when Clark's coverage was at its most positive was .67 (much higher than in the case of Clark), but the probability of support increased to .76 when coverage of Clark was at its most negative. Therefore, we saw no effects in the bivariate correlations because we were looking at coverage of the leader and support for that same leader when we should instead focus on how coverage of one major party leader influences support for the other major party leader. We do not suggest that people switched from Shipley to Clark as the most preferred Prime Minister, but that as the tone of coverage became more negative about Shipley, support most likely solidified among the left and those who were undecided. The reverse is also true for Clark: support among the right solidified as coverage about Clark became more negative.

Second, we found that, contrary to our expectations, women were more likely to be influenced by the media evaluations of Clark than were men. Figure 3.4 shows the relationship between the tone of coverage, support for Clark and gender. As the coverage of Clark became more negative, women were less likely to support Clark. When coverage was most positive the probability of a women preferring Clark as Prime Minister was 0.45, whereas when coverage was most negative the probability fell to 0.35. This is a statistically

Figure 3.4: Media Tone, Gender and Preferred Prime Minister

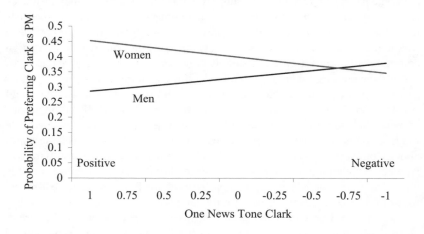

significant difference. Figure 3.4 also shows that as coverage became more negative men became more supportive, but this is not a statistically significant effect. We should note that we did not find a similar gender effect in the relationship between media evaluations and support for Shipley. It appears as if the gender dynamic was much more evident in support of Clark.

Conclusion

In this chapter, we addressed the content of television news coverage during the 1999 election and its effect on voters. We know that most voters experience the election campaign indirectly through the media. Only a very limited number of the electorate has direct experience of the leaders, parties and campaigns. Therefore, how news coverage mediates the election experience and influences voters is important. The content of the news on television offered voters issues and party positions which are important for making voting decisions. A substantial part of the coverage was spent on the 'horse race' aspects of the campaign — who is ahead and who is gaining in the polls. This is understandable, as it is a way for the media to present the election in terms of conflict among players, and conflict attracts attention.

Our look at agenda setting yielded little to show that the agenda of One News influenced what voters saw as the most important problem. We also saw only a weak relationship between what the parties focused on and what the news covered. But media coverage did have some influence on voters in two other areas. First, the evaluations of leaders in the media influenced support during the campaign for preferred Prime Minister. We should be careful though in concluding that the evaluations by One News influenced the outcome of the election. Rather, some events or statements covered by the news simply reflected poorly on the leaders, such as hecklers at Shipley's appearances or her attack on the Greens in the Coromandel. It is the reporting of these unfavourable or favourable events that influenced preferences.

Second, the concern that campaign coverage has become too focused on the personalities of party leaders at the expense of issues does not apply when we look at either the content of the news coverage or at the decision-making processes of voters. There were fewer stories focused on party leaders than on party positions on both One News and TV3 news, though the coverage of party leaders on TV3 was only slightly lower (2 per cent) than the number of stories on party positions. When we look at the factors voters rely on to make their decisions, we see that these depend, to some extent, on which media they were paying attention to. The personalities of party leaders were more important to those who were not paying attention to a more serious outlet for news, National Radio.

This chapter began with a newspaper photo caption. It points to the importance of campaigns and the media coverage of them. In this instance National's 'attack' on Jeanette Fitzsimons and the Greens in the Coromandel electorate temporarily damaged the poll standings of National and Shipley. It was thus a strategy that backfired. For even when Shipley attempted to turn her attention elsewhere, such as the Kopu bridge, readers of the newspaper were reminded that she was only 'taking time out from her attack on the Greens'.

CHAPTER 4

GENDER AND LEADERSHIP

Susan Banducci

I'm a politician . . . but I'm also a Mum.
— Prime Minister, Jenny Shipley, National Party
Election Broadcast, 31 October 1999

From an international perspective, the story of the 1999 New Zealand election
was about the contest between two leaders of major parties who happened to
both be women. Women party leaders and women Prime Ministers are rare.
According to the Stockholm-based International Institute for Democracy and
Electoral Assistance, women make up less than 11 per cent of party leaders
worldwide. The proportion of women Prime Ministers is even smaller and
there had never before been an election for national government where women
headed both major parties contesting the election. Indeed, much international
coverage of the 1999 New Zealand election focused on the presence of the two
women leaders.

Put into the context of New Zealand's history of women in politics, the fact
that both major parties were led by women may not be so very surprising.
Women in New Zealand were the first to gain suffrage in 1893, more women
were represented in New Zealand's Parliament than in any other country
employing first-past-the-post elections and even than in most proportional
representation countries, and women have regularly served as government
ministers since the 1970s. Perhaps this explains the lack of local media focus
on the novelty of the election being contested by two women.

The campaigns, however, did revolve around the party leaders as all parties
build their campaigns around their leaders. After her strong performance in,
and since, the 1996 campaign, putting Clark at the centre of the campaign in
1999 was not as risky for Labour as it had been then. Shipley, however, was
campaigning for the first time as party leader in 1999, although in that role
she was also the Prime Minister. Both women featured prominently in their
respective parties' opening broadcasts. Shipley appeared in various locations
around New Zealand discussing the preservation of the gains of the National
government and investing in the future. The broadcast also included plenty of
footage of Shipley hosting world leaders during the APEC meetings. Clark was
seen holding discussions with everyday New Zealanders about the lack of
support under current government policies for those in need of assistance.

50

Families also featured prominently in these broadcasts. Clark tried to portray herself as understanding the plight of New Zealand families, despite not having children herself, while Shipley focused on the issue of making families more self-sufficient.

The increasing focus on party leaders in parliamentary systems can be seen as the result of at least two trends: the decline in deeply held attachments to political parties (Katz and Mair 1994), and the changing role of the electronic media (Mughan 1995). If people have weak attachments to political parties, greater demand is placed on leaders to mobilise their voters. Additionally, it is much easier for the media to focus on a handful of leaders as the symbols of the parties (McAllister 1996, 287) and there is some evidence that leaders are gaining more media coverage than issues (Butler and Ranney 1992). Previous analysis of New Zealand elections has examined the relative influence of leadership, local candidates, and partisanship on voting (Bean 1992; Vowles, Aimer, Catt, Lamare, Miller 1995). Since the 1960s there has been a noticeable decline in the influence of partisanship and an increase in the influence of party leaders and local candidates (Bean 1992, 149). With the advent of MMP and the importance of the overall party vote for electoral success, party leaders are possibly even more at the centre of the campaigns than under the FPP voting system. The five televised leaders' debates during the 1999 election campaign certainly served to bolster the role of leaders in the campaign, the media coverage given them, and their place in voters' minds. Three of the five televised debates were between the leaders of the two main parties only, which further enhanced the focus on Clark and Shipley. Because party leaders are central to election campaigns, and the two major parties were headed by women, for the first time in New Zealand politics women were at the centre of a campaign.

Yet despite the historic novelty of two women competing for the position of Prime Minister, we should be cautious in concluding that this changed the nature of the political agenda or the style of the campaigns. Although paid parental leave was raised as an issue ten months prior to the election when an Alliance MP, Laila Harré, sponsored a bill for employer-paid parental leave, other prominent women's issues, such as childcare or even gender equity issues, were not debated during the campaign. Indeed, very little of either party's rhetoric focused on women. Instead, each party presented policies as being 'family friendly'.

Little symbolic attention also was paid to the party leaders being women. The party leaders did not attempt to differentiate themselves in terms of who would be a greater champion of women's causes. Instead, Shipley tried to steer the debate toward motherhood. She attempted to distinguish herself from the childless Clark during the National party broadcast with her often quoted line: 'I'm a politician . . . but I'm also a mum'. Even though there is overlap between family and women's concerns, the symbolic rhetoric was focused on family issues rather than on gender equity issues.

Though both women would consider themselves feminists, Shipley's version of feminism differs from Clark's; each is consistent with her ideological leanings. Clark's leanings were more consistent with the left-wing ideology of the early women's movement, while Shipley's views can be described as fitting in the tradition of liberal feminism. As Shipley explains, 'feminism means that I want people to have an equal opportunity to be who they are' (quoted in Cohen 1997). Indeed, comparisons have been made between Shipley and Margaret Thatcher, and certainly Shipley's policies have been more consistent with Thatcher's than with any other female party leader's. As minister of social welfare and of health, Shipley oversaw drastic cuts in welfare payments and in the restructuring of the health care system. Her economic policies and support of privatisation were also consistent with Thatcher's.

Preferred Prime Minister

One measure of a leader's performance in that role is the occupant's standing in the regular opinion polls that are now a normal part of the media's presentation of politics. Early in the campaign, Shipley's status as the incumbent Prime Minister helped her standings in the polls for 'preferred Prime Minister'. However, we see a substantial amount of variation in electors' preferences over the course of the campaign. As shown in Chapter 1, these preferences were linked to support for the parties. Figure 4.1 shows the five-day moving averages of electors' responses when asked to identify their 'preferred Prime Minister'. As the campaign advanced, Shipley's initial lead in the polls was overcome by Clark two weeks prior to the election. This increase for Clark built on a substantial base of prior support (Chapter 1), and came after the first head-to-head debate between Clark and Shipley on 8 November. Having served two years in the role, Shipley had already shown the voters that she was Prime Minister material. This debate was the first opportunity for Clark to show she was the equal of Shipley. Assessments of neither leader were stable, however. Clark's support declined around 15 November, but then Shipley's support also declined noticeably after her attack on the Greens in Coromandel. Both leaders then recovered support to be evenly placed as the 'preferred Prime Minister' in the final days of the campaign.

Despite the centrality of the party leaders in the campaign, and in particular the focus on Clark and Shipley, many electors were disinclined to regard either as their 'preferred Prime Minister'. Among electors' responses, the category 'none' received the third highest rating for 'preferred Prime Minister' and 'don't know' was not far behind. In Figure 4.1, these two groups have been combined into a single 'no preference' category, which accounted for nearly one-third of electors throughout the campaign. We would expect the number of 'don't knows' to decline as the campaign wore on and voters were exposed to more information about the party leaders and candidates. While there is variation during the campaign in the number of those not knowing their preference, the number at the end of the campaign is roughly equivalent to the number at the beginning. This may explain some of the fluctuation in support for both leaders during the campaign. People may respond to the cue 'preferred Prime Minister' on the basis of very short-term, media-sourced information. Such essentially superficial assessments were also unstable. Thus, one of the notable dips in the numbers of 'don't knows' occurred when Clark's support surged after the first head-to-head debate, suggesting that Clark mobilised a considerable number of voters to her side during this period, but that the effects were short-lived.

Besides the two women leaders of the major parties, the leaders of the smaller parties played significant roles in the election campaign. There were two televised debates early in the campaign where five party leaders (Clark, Shipley, Anderton, Peters and Prebble) appeared together. In these, the performance of the minor party leaders won mixed reviews from most journalists, with Anderton receiving the most favourable comments. Shipley and Clark were seen as stiff and their performances scripted, while the men were described as hogging the limelight in a story titled 'Support acts outshine big two' (*New Zealand Herald*, 28 November 1999). We see in Figure 4.1 that minor party leaders were also helped in the polls by their debate performances, most notably Anderton. He was seen as one of the winners of the first debate held on 27 October on TV 3. His support surged after this debate, as it did again after the debate on 1 November. Peters' performance in the first all-leaders debate was also generally viewed favourably and we can see a slight jump in his support after the first debate. However, his support hit a low point after the second all-leaders debate and at the time of the controversy surrounding the New Zealand First party list, where two incumbent women were placed so far down the list as to be assured they would not be serving in Parliament after the election. As we will also see, Peters also began to be perceived as the most 'arrogant' of the leaders.

Figure 4.1   Preferred Prime Minister during the Campaign

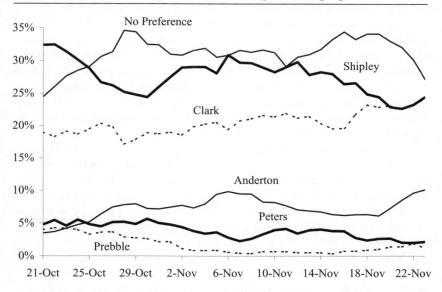

Since two women were the featured leaders of the two largest parties and the gender gap was a significant feature in the 1996 campaign, we might expect that gender played a role in channelling support for the leaders (Banducci and Karp 2000). The history of the gender gap in New Zealand follows a pattern similar to that in many Western democracies in which women moved from support for parties on the right to support for parties on the left. Survey data from the 1963 election in New Zealand show an advantage for the right-of-centre National party among women when appropriate control variables are added; however, this advantage had disappeared by 1981 (Vowles 1993). In 1993 a gender gap reappeared, but this time more women were supporting the Labour party on the left. Following Labour's defeat in 1993, the party's caucus selected Helen Clark to lead the party. There was therefore no alternative for Labour strategists than to put Clark at the centre of their 1996 campaign (Levine and Roberts 1997). Although early campaign polls suggested lack-lustre support for Clark, her performance in the two debates (in which she was identified as 'the winner') helped Labour immensely, bringing the party within reach of National (Johnston 1998). Labour's recovery was accompanied by a widening gender gap among electors. In the 1996 election, the party enjoyed an advantage of almost 10 per cent among women, the widest gap observed in New Zealand elections (Vowles 1998a, 33; see also Chapter 6). However, the gender gap does not appear to have been simply a drift to the left among women. For it is not evident in support for the Alliance, a party to the left of Labour, suggesting that it was as a woman leader that Helen Clark may have attracted a disproportionate share of women on the left.

Moving the analysis forward to 1999, Figure 4.2 shows support for Shipley (4.2a) and Clark (4.2b) among women and men separately. At the beginning of the campaign, women were more supportive of Clark than were men, whereas support for Shipley showed little difference between men and women. There is little divergence between men and women in support for Shipley until after the first head-to-head debate on 8 November. Support among men then in-creased and reached a peak around 16 November, while support for Shipley among women declined. At the same time we also noted in Figure 4.1 a general shift in support for Clark. As we can now see from Figure 4.2b, a lot of this increase in support came from women. Also during this period, around 10 November, the first poll showing that Jeanette Fitzsimons was ahead of the National MP, Murray McLean, in the Coromandel electorate was published. Bad economic news about the growing trade deficit and the continued weaken-ing of the New Zealand dollar also dominated news coverage during this week.

We might conclude that this bad news for the incumbent Prime Minister seemed to resonate more with women than men, as her support plummeted among women but remained steady among men. However, a later period of divergent gender patterns suggests a different relationship. During National's attack on the Greens in the Coromandel electorate, most of the drop in support for Shipley was due to loss of support among men. In Chapter 3, we examined whether women or men were more affected by adverse news coverage of the two leaders. While we did not find a significant effect on support for Shipley, Figure 4.2 does suggest that at least during the week in which National was attacking the Greens, men responded more adversely to the events. Therefore, the drop in support among women for Shipley during the earlier period may reflect instead Clark's strength coming off the first head-to-head debate, rather than a response to adverse news. We also saw in Chapter 3 that as the tone of news coverage grew more negative about Shipley, support for Clark increased. However, the evidence also again suggests that such campaign events have

**Figure 4.2   Gender Differences on Preferred Prime Minister:
Shipley and Clark**

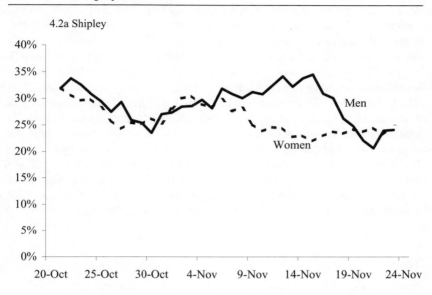

4.2a Shipley

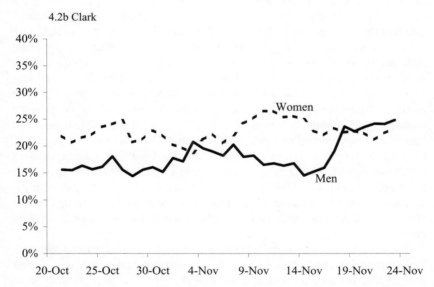

4.2b Clark

somewhat superficial and short-term leadership effects. Shipley recovered
quickly from the negative fallout from the attack on the Greens, and the gap
between men and women in support for her as 'preferred Prime Minister'
disappeared prior to the election.

Nevertheless, strong gender gaps were evident in the 1999 party vote (as
distinct from expressions of 'preferred Prime Minister'). The advantage for
Labour among women was a substantial 9 per cent (meaning that 9 per cent
more women than men voted Labour). There was also a very slight advantage

for National among women of about 1.5 per cent. There were no noticeable gender differences in the votes for Alliance or New Zealand First. However, ACT had an almost 7 per cent advantage among men. The Greens also enjoyed a slight advantage among men. Part of the gender gap is due to women voters being to the centre-left and men being to the right. The gender gap is also partly due to men supporting more extreme parties, being more likely to vote for ACT and the Greens, while women stayed with the major parties of the centre. This is further borne out by comparing voters' choices in 1996 with choices in 1999, which shows that women were less likely to switch from National and Labour than were men. Looking at our panel respondents who participated in both the 1996 and 1999 surveys, we see that of women who voted Labour in 1996, 88 per cent voted Labour again in 1999. Of male Labour voters in 1996, 84 per cent returned to Labour. National had much lower retention rates overall, but like Labour, they kept more women voters than men. Of men who voted National in 1996, 65 voted National again in 1999. On the other hand, of women National voters in 1996, 73 per cent again voted National in 1999.

Traits

Besides noting how the leaders fared in terms of 'preferred Prime Minister', we can also look at how voters ascribed traits of the different leaders. During the campaign period we asked how traits such as 'strong leader', 'compassionate', 'trustworthy' and 'arrogant' described Clark and Shipley. In the post-election survey, we asked these trait questions also about the five leaders who appeared in the televised debates. The questions were asked in order to ascertain whether or not voters assigned traits to the leaders on the basis of gender stereotypes. Experiments have demonstrated that women candidates are more likely to be ascribed stereotypical feminine traits such as 'compassion', while men are more likely to be seen as 'strong leaders' (Kahn 1994). 'Compassionate' and 'trustworthy' are viewed as positive female traits while 'arrogant' is a negative trait, particularly for women in politics. Because politics is traditionally a man's job, women who enter the electoral arena may be viewed as 'arrogant'. Stereotypes commonly serve as a short cut when making judgements in the absence of other information. Therefore, they are more likely to be used by voters who have little information or when a candidate or leader is not well known.

Most of the experimental evidence is based on comparisons between female and male candidates. Little is known about the prominence of gender stereotyping when both candidates are women. However, there are reasons to expect that gender stereotyping will be less prominent in races where both candidates or (as in our case) both party leaders are women. We might also expect less gender stereotyping because both women were leaders of the major parties and had played prominent roles in politics for some time.

However, a distinction did emerge between the two leaders along lines of stereotypical gender traits. In this case, however, the ascription of gender traits may not have grown out of gender stereotypes held by voters, but rather, taking their cues from the leaders, the voters were responding to campaign strategies employed to bring attention to particular leadership traits. Thus, Shipley tried to portray herself as the compassionate mother to distinguish herself from the childless Clark. Tacitly reinforcing this distinction, the Prime Minister's husband and children accompanied her on many campaign outings. It was not until late in the campaign that Clark successfully neutralised the issue by commenting during a debate that while she had no children of her own she was not without children in her life.

The gender differences in leadership trait ascription during the campaign are shown in Figure 4.3. In order to determine if there are any gender differences in the use of traits, the figure separates the ascription of traits to Shipley and Clark by women and men. The largest differences on the leader traits appear for the most part on the characteristically 'feminine' traits — 'compassion' and 'trustworthiness'. Even though Shipley attempted to portray herself as the compassionate mother, Clark scored ahead of her on the 'compassion' trait. Estimates of Clark's 'compassion' picked up in the fourth week while those for Shipley dropped in the final week. That Clark was more often thought of as 'compassionate' than Shipley may be due to a transfer to the Labour leader of stereotypes about left parties being more caring of people than parties on the right. On the negative trait of 'arrogance', Shipley was disadvantaged throughout the campaign, being consistently viewed as more arrogant than Clark. This negative stereotype, which in some ways presents itself as the opposite of 'compassionate', may have resulted from her high profile in the traditionally male role of Prime Minister. In addition, during the campaign, public rallies were kept to a minimum and all public appearances were well scripted in order to reduce the likelihood of the hecklers and crashers that had plagued Shipley's early appearances (Harris 2000). The closed rallies may have given voters the impression that Shipley was aloof. It was a judgement, however, that was consistent with TV3/CM Research polls between April and November 1999, which reported an average of 63 per cent of respondents agreeing that Shipley 'tends to talk down to people', and 61 per cent who agreed that she 'is out of touch with ordinary people'. By comparison, Clark's ratings on these unfavourable cues were much lower at 25 per cent and 24 per cent, respectively (CM Research (NZ) Ltd., 18 November 1999). This was also consistent with Clark's lower ratings on the negative trait of 'arrogant' .The estimates of Shipley's 'arrogance', which had been declining, also increased again during National's attacks on the Greens, between the third and fourth weeks of the campaign.

In Figure 4.3, all trait evaluations are averaged over the campaign; therefore, the figure does not show how the ascription of traits varied over the campaign. However, the ascription of traits showed little variation over the course of the campaign with one exception. Of all the traits, 'strong leadership' — a prerequisite for a Prime Minister — showed the most movement, particularly for Clark. Clearly, her performance in the debates and during the campaign assured voters that she was capable Prime Ministerial material. By the final week of the campaign she had pulled slightly ahead of Shipley in the number of people agreeing that 'strong leader' described her.

Let us now turn to the question of whether men or women were more likely to see the women leaders in gender-stereotypical ways by focusing on the

Figure 4.3 Shipley and Clark: Leadership Traits during the Campaign

■ Trait fits Shipley (among Men)   ▨ Trait fits Shipley (among Women)
▣ Trait fits Clark (among Men)   ■ Trait fits Clark (among Women)

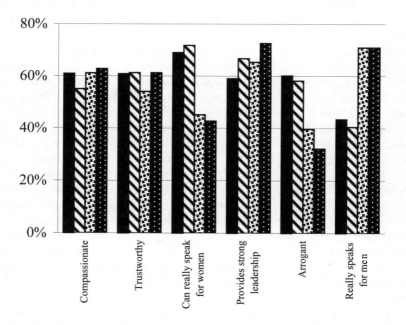

NOTE: The lines represent the percentage of people who agreed that the trait fitted the leader.

differences in the lines for women and men. There is little evidence in Figure 4.3 that women systematically evaluated leadership traits differently than men. One exception is that the favourable traits ascribed to Shipley declined among men in the first week of the campaign. The percentage of men agreeing that Shipley 'speaks for women', 'speaks for men', and is trustworthy declines in the fifth week among men. A similar decline is not evident among the women who were asked the same questions. This decline in the evaluations of Shipley among men reflects the drop in support for her as preferred Prime Minister that was evident among men during the same period of time (Figure 4.2a). A second exception is the attribution of 'arrogance' to Shipley. Whereas the estimation of Shipley's arrogance among the women asked seems to reach a high point in the second week and then decline throughout the rest of the campaign, the trend for men appears to be the opposite reaching a low point in the second week, and then increasing, before slightly decreasing in the fifth week. Other than these two exceptions, the traits track fairly consistently for Clark and Shipley among both men and women.

By ascribing particular traits to party leaders, people may also be developing a perception of how suitable the different candidates are for office. For example, evaluations of 'strength of leadership' and 'trustworthiness' may serve as short cuts to judgements about a leader's ability to fulfil promises once in office. In order to examine this question, we look to see whether the ascription of certain leader traits influenced people's choice of 'preferred Prime Minister' during the campaign period. We use the respondents' evaluations of Shipley and Clark on the six leadership traits to predict whether or not the respondent preferred Shipley or Clark as Prime Minister. Because such evaluations are likely to be coloured by respondents' prior party preferences, often related to social influences, we have also added controls for such potentially confounding variables as party attachment and socio-demographic factors. This allows us to measure the net effect of leadership traits separately from these influences. The full model is given in Appendix C.

The result of this procedure suggests that some traits are strongly linked to 'preferred Prime Minister' while others are not. Overall, the traits that were linked to 'preferred Prime Minister' for both Clark and Shipley are 'speaks for women', 'strong leadership', and 'arrogant'. The strongest trait for Clark is 'speaks for women'. Those who thought that she was able to 'speak for women' were four-and-a-half times more likely to prefer her as Prime Minister than those who did not, whereas those who thought Shipley 'speaks for women' were only slightly over one-and-a-half times as likely to prefer her. 'Strong leadership' is also an important trait in the models. It is the strongest trait predicting support for Shipley, and the second strongest for Clark. While there is thus some evidence that the stereotypical feminine trait of 'speaks for women' and the negative feminine trait of 'arrogance' have a role in predicting leader support, 'strong leadership', a stereotypical male trait, also plays a role.

The least important trait for both leaders was 'speaks for men'. The two feminine traits of 'compassionate' and 'trustworthy' were not significant in the model predicting preference for Clark, though they were important in predicting support for Shipley. That 'trustworthiness' and 'compassion' were important for Shipley and not for Clark reflects Shipley's focus on her role as a mother in the campaign. Although we saw that voters overall did not think Shipley was more compassionate than Clark, for those who did, the campaign had primed them to evaluate Shipley in terms of the qualities associated with motherhood — such as compassion and trustworthiness.

All traits except 'compassion' were significant in distinguishing between Clark and Shipley. Using the difference between the trait rating for Clark and the rating for Shipley, we see that these traits have a substantial impact on 'preference for Prime Minister'. When comparing only Shipley and Clark (eliminating the other leaders from the analysis), 'speaks for women' and 'trustworthiness' are the two strongest predictors. Those who thought that Clark 'speaks for women' while Shipley did not were over seven times more likely to prefer Clark as Prime Minister. Those who thought Clark was trustworthy and Shipley not were also over seven times as likely to prefer Clark to Shipley. Thus, two of the stereotypical feminine traits were the most important in distinguishing between Shipley and Clark as 'preferred Prime Minister'. 'Strong leadership' and 'speaks for men' were also significant in distinguishing between Clark and Shipley but not as important as the stereotypical feminine traits. Additionally, those who thought Clark was arrogant but not Shipley were less than half as likely to prefer Clark. We do therefore see

Figure 4.4 Effect of Traits on Preferred Prime Minister

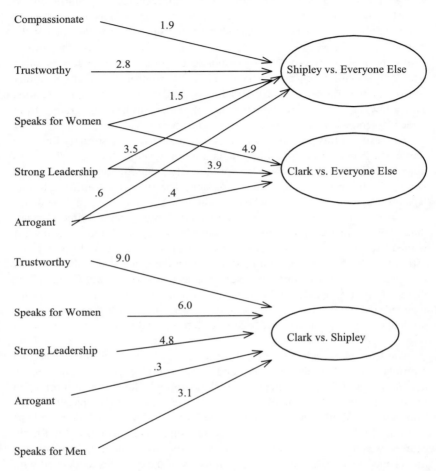

NOTE: Only the significant coefficients are shown. In the top figure, the numbers represent the change in the likelihood of preferring Clark or Shipley as Prime Minister compared to all other possible leaders. For example, those who thought 'strong leader' applied to Clark were three times more likely to prefer her as Prime Minister. In the bottom figure, the numbers represent the change in likelihood of preferring Clark over Shipley as Prime Minister. The full models are given in Appendix C.

some evidence that the female party leaders could be distinguished on the basis of feminine traits.

Our pre-election data do not allow comparisons with the male party leaders during the campaign. However, the post-election survey enables us to extend the analysis to them. Although the item 'can speak for men' was excluded from the list of traits in this phase of the study, in other respects it allowed for a more detailed analysis. The response categories in the post-election survey were extended to allow respondents not only to 'agree' or 'disagree' that the trait fitted the leader, as in the campaign survey, but also say whether they thought it fitted 'very well', 'fairly well', 'not very well' or 'not at all'. With the male party leaders included, there is still little evidence of gender differences in the evaluations of leader traits. However, there is some evidence that partisan stereotypes are at play.

Figure 4.5 shows the average ranking on the traits for five party leaders among the parties' supporters. For example, the figure displays how National voters ranked Shipley, and how Labour voters viewed Clark. By controlling for party support, we can see how evaluations of the leaders differed on the traits even without the influence of partisanship. For 'compassion' and 'trustworthiness', we see more partisan effects in the pattern of responses than gender stereotyping. Thus, the highest ratings on the feminine trait 'compassion' were shared, not by Clark and Shipley, but by the Labour and Alliance leaders (Clark and Anderton). The party leaders on the political left were also rated more 'trustworthy', although the differences between them and other leaders were not as large. In comparison, however, the two women party leaders scored highest on 'speaks for women'. Parties of the centre-right and right (National, New Zealand First, ACT) scored highest on the negative trait of 'arrogance', even though we have controlled for partisan support. In other words, even those sympathetic to these parties perceived 'arrogance' in their leaders, regardless of gender. The leaders of the major parties and Anderton scored highest on 'strong leadership'. Again, we see less evidence of gender stereotyping than of trait attribution due to party standing and election performance. We also see that party supporters were more likely to ascribe the positive traits of 'trustworthy' and 'strong leadership' to the leaders of their preferred parties. This finding supports the notion that 'trustworthiness' and 'strong leadership' have more influence on voters' assessment of the leaders than the other traits.

There has been considerable debate over the role of party leaders in vote choice. The debate focuses on whether leaders have become more important in campaigns, and why they might have. Weakening partisan attachments have certainly allowed the importance of leadership evaluations to grow in voters' decision-making. In order to see how evaluations of leadership traits affected vote choice in the 1999 election, we have used the trait evaluations of each leader to predict his or her party's vote. For example, to predict vote for Labour, we have used the trait evaluations of Clark, and for National's vote we have used Shipley's trait evaluations, and so on for the rest of the parties. We have also again controlled for factors such as party identification and socio-demographic factors that may confound the results. Table 4.1 presents the data. The numbers in the table represent the change in probability that someone will vote for the party listed if their evaluation of how well the given trait fits the leader changes from the bottom of the scale ('not at all') to the top of the scale ('very well'). For example, a voter responding that 'trustworthy' fits Clark 'very well' is 24 per cent more likely to vote for Labour than another party.

Ideal leaders have been characterised as competent and intelligent, sociable and good-natured, aggressive and bold, and as possessing conviction and integrity (Hellweg 1979, Kinder et al. 1980). Some traits, however, are more important than others when forming an overall evaluation of a leader. While personal attributes such as warmth or approachability may make candidates

Figure 4.5 Gender Differences in Leadership Traits: Post-Election

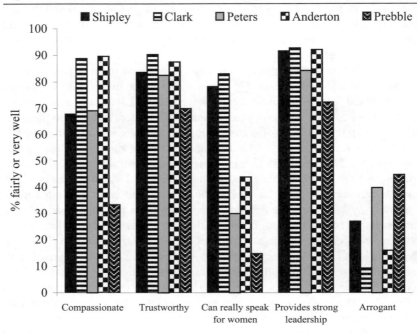

Table 4.1 How Leadership Traits Affect Party Vote Choice: Change in Probability of Party Vote

| | Vote for: | | | | |
	Labour	National	Alliance	ACT	NZ First
Trait Describing Party Leader:					
Compassion	0.08	0.14*	0.21*	0.05	0.20
Trustworthy	0.24*	0.37*	0.36*	0.40*	0.33*
Speaks for Women	–0.07	0.06	–0.12	0.01	0.09
Strong Leader	0.33*	0.16*	0.22*	0.23*	0.40*
Arrogant	–0.20*	–0.22*	–0.14	–0.15	–0.34*

* Effect is significant at p < .05
NOTE: See Appendix C for full model.

more likeable, they are not likely to influence vote choice (Kinder et al. 1980). A similar variance emerges from our data. In Table 4.1, two leader traits in particular stand out because they consistently predict party vote across all party leaders: 'trustworthy' and 'strong leader'. These clearly serve as important evaluations of New Zealand leaders that influence vote choice. The trait of 'trustworthiness' also may have been cued in voters' minds by Clark's statement during the first head-to-head debate with Shipley that 'you can trust me', an assertion which, of course, implies the opposite for Clark's opponent.

The trait 'speaks for women' is not significant in any of the models and 'compassion' is only significant in the model predicting vote for National and for Alliance. In this, we again see evidence that Shipley's tactic of portraying herself as the traditional mother seems to have primed 'compassion' as one of the traits people used to evaluate her overall performance as Prime Minister and which they relied on in the' vote decision-making process. However, this focus on her role as a mother did not raise her overall rating on the trait of 'compassion'. As we have seen, voters found her to be much less compassionate than Clark and Anderton (see Figure 4.5).

Interestingly, 'arrogance' is only significant in predicting votes for the two major parties and for New Zealand First. As the negative signs show, perceptions of Shipley's and Clark's 'arrogance' reduced the likelihood of voting for National or Labour. Similarly, those who found Peters 'arrogant' were less likely to vote for New Zealand First. Peters' 'arrogance' became the subject of the coverage of the two debates that featured all party leaders. Peters interrupted the other leaders, called them 'Klingons' and suggested Labour and National were 'two old grey parties' while New Zealand First was 'an exciting new party'. Indeed, Peters came to be seen as one of the most 'arrogant' of the party leaders (see Figure 4.5); thus it is not difficult to see why this trait weighed significantly on voters' minds when deciding whether or not to vote for New Zealand First. Obviously, Peters' perceived 'arrogance' turned away voters from New Zealand First. Shipley's perceived aloofness seems to have hurt National as well. Stereotypes are generally applied in the absence of other information about the leaders. As such, it is unclear whether the importance of 'arrogance' in voting for Labour and National results from negative stereotypes about women leaders or from evaluations that voters developed during the campaign.

A more difficult test of the electoral significance of the leader traits is to determine whether they helped to switch voters from one party to another. Did the trait evaluations of Clark and Shipley lead voters to their respective parties? In order to answer this question, we look at only a subsample of voters. We compare voters who switched to Labour in 1999 from voting for another party in 1996, to those who switched away from Labour in 1996 to another party in 1999. We then do the same for those switching to and from National. In order to have a big enough sample of party 'switchers', we rely on the respondents' recall of their vote in 1996, rather than using the 1996–99 panel.

The results are reported in Table 4.2. As in Table 4.1, we have reported the change in probability of switching to Labour or National if a respondent moved from the lowest trait ranking for the relevant party leader to the highest. In this more difficult test of persuading voters away from, or driving them to, other parties we see that some leadership traits still have an effect. Most notably, 'strong leadership' is a defining trait. Those who felt 'strong leader' described Clark 'very well' were 33 per cent more likely to switch to Labour than away from Labour when compared to a respondent who thought that 'strong leader' did not describe Clark at all. Also, those who thought Shipley was a 'strong leader' were 25 per cent more likely to switch to National than away from National. The reverse is also true: those who thought that 'strong leader' did not describe Shipley at all were 25 per cent more likely to move away from

National. The only other leadership trait that helped distinguish party 'switchers' to and from National is 'trustworthiness'. Those who saw Shipley as 'trustworthy' were 32 per cent more likely to switch to National in 1999 from a different party in 1996.

Table 4.2. How Traits Affected National and Labour Party Switches: Estimating Probability of Switching to Labour or National

	Switch to:	
	Labour	National
Trait Describing Party Leader:		
Compassionate	−0.17	−0.09
Trustworthy	0.14	0.32*
Speaks for Women	−0.12	0.05
Strong Leader	0.33*	0.25*
Arrogant	−0.12	−0.17

* Effect is significant at p < .05

NOTE: See Appendix C for full model.

Conclusion

In this historic campaign between two women we see that they were neither hampered nor favoured by stereotyped responses to leadership traits. Ironically, the campaign seemed to be absent of gender stereotyping by the voters, or any unique focus on women's issues, or even much focus on the two leaders as women. Having women leaders competing for the role of Prime Minister evidently does not push women's issues onto the agenda. Clark and Shipley were both well-known leaders, and voters did not need to rely on stereotypes to evaluate them. Also, a great number of New Zealanders do not see women in politics as a novelty, given women's high numbers in Parliament. If stereo-typing occurred, it was based on the parliamentary status of their respective parties and partisan ideology. Shipley benefited in terms of evaluations of leadership ability from her status as leader of the governing party and in-cumbent Prime Minister. However, to the extent that her status as incumbent increased perceptions of her arrogance, her status seems to have negatively affected National's performance at the polls. Evaluations of Clark's leadership ability caught up to those of Shipley due to her strong performance in the debates, and building on her high ratings since the previous election. The measures of post-election traits (Figure 4.5) are to some extent influenced by the election outcome — the defeat of Shipley's National government by the Labour-Alliance combination — as Clark was ranked higher than Shipley, and Anderton almost as highly, on 'leadership'.

Evaluations of leadership traits weigh heavily in the minds of voters when they make their party vote decision. Overall, perceptions of 'strong leadership' seem to be the most influential in vote choice, but other traits, notably 'trust-worthiness', are also important. These traits are important because they are probably the best indicators of how a party and leader will perform once in office. For Shipley, 'compassion' stood out as a particularly influential trait. Rather than suggesting gender stereotyping, however, the effect is most likely due to her attempts to portray herself as the compassionate mother during the campaign.

In this chapter, we have examined how voters responded to the leaders, particularly the two women leaders. Party leaders are at the centre of election campaigns, and the spotlight on them is intensified by televised leaders' debates, and the reporting of other leader activities. Party leaders consequently influence the decisions of voters, and thus the fortunes of their parties. In our case, the evidence points to Clark's and Shipley's perceived leadership abilities drawing votes for Labour and National, while Peters' perceived arrogance was losing votes for New Zealand First. From the evidence presented in this chapter and Chapter 3, Anderton's positive evaluations, outweighing the negative, also bolstered the prospects of Alliance. The lack of similar favourable ratings for Prebble, however, appears to have led to a lack of mobilisation of ACT voters.

CHAPTER 5

COMING HOME?
MAORI VOTING IN 1999

Ann Sullivan and Dimitri Margaritis

In 1999 the Labour party recaptured all six of the Maori electorates that New Zealand's electoral system reserves for those of Maori descent who choose to enrol in them.[1] Those Maori voters, it seemed, had 'come home'. For half a century from 1944 until 1993 Labour had monopolised all of the Maori electorates, of which there were then only four. Along with the poorer city electorates, they were the safest of Labour's seats (Chapman 1986). Maori support for Labour developed from the party's commitment to equalise welfare support between Maori and other New Zealanders in the 1930s. Class voting patterns during the Maori urbanisation period of the 1950s and 1960s helped consolidate Maori support for Labour. The passing of the Treaty of Waitangi Act 1975 and the inclusion of reference to the principles of the Treaty of Waitangi in various pieces of legislation by Labour governments in the 1980s further helped maintain Labour's Maori support

By the end of the 1980s, however, traditional Maori support for Labour was eroding (Sullivan and Vowles 1998, 173). The social and economic reforms of the 1984–90 Labour government impacted heavily on Maori, and resulted in high Maori unemployment (Dalziel and Fox 1996). In 1993 one of Labour's once-solid electoral foundations collapsed. Tau Henare, standing as the candidate for the newly formed New Zealand First party, gained a surprise victory in the electorate of Te Tai Tokerau. New Zealand First was led by Winston Peters, a prominent politician of northern Maori (Nga Puhi) descent, and a former National party Member of Parliament who had also served briefly as Minister of Maori Affairs. In the new party, Maori began to see an alternative, more assertive agency of Maori political influence. Three years later, New Zealand First swept up all five of the Maori electorates established for the 1996 election. Had an historic realignment of Maori political preferences taken place? Such were the portents in 1996, and the evidence was consistent with that scenario (Sullivan and Vowles 1998). But the performance and achievements of the new team of Maori leaders in Parliament failed to meet Maori expectations. What had appeared as a possible realignment of the Maori vote proved instead to be a fleeting experiment. In reverting to traditional voting behaviour in 1999, Maori had also demonstrated for the second time a distinctive and very non-traditional degree of electoral volatility. Maori voters were back 'home', but was it for good, or were they merely visiting?

Other questions about Maori politics emerge from the 1999 election. Was the return to Labour as evident in the electorate vote as it was in the party vote, or were Maori using their two votes under MMP for different purposes? How strategic is Maori voting? How much support do Maori voters give to minor Maori parties, and are Maori voters willing to support a clearly identifiable Maori party? Why were Maori disillusioned with their parliamentary representatives and why was New Zealand First unable to retain its party support? Are there any characteristics that identify the type of party a Maori voter is likely to support? Are the Greens likely to have an impact in the Maori electorates? Finally, after the first comprehensive survey of Maori political behaviour and opinion, what does the data indicate about Maori political attitudes at the end of the 1990s?

Patterns of Voting

In all six electorates, Maori moved to Labour in almost equal proportions, the party's overall vote rising from 32 per cent in 1996 to 55 per cent in 1999. But Maori candidates gained less than their party as Maori voters made full use of the strategic potential of MMP's two votes 'to maximise the effectiveness of their vote' (Vowles, Aimer, Banducci, Karp 1998, 101). Under MMP, political parties emphasise the importance of capturing the party vote rather than the electorate vote, because it is the nationwide party vote that determines the number of seats a party wins. Maori on the other hand demonstrated that they consider the electorate vote to be worthy of equal consideration. Personal factors played a major role in electorate voting patterns in both the 1996 and 1999 elections (Sullivan and Margaritis 2000, 179–80).

Table 5.1   Voting in the 1996 and 1999 Elections, Change, and Split Voting by Party

	Electorate Vote			Party Vote			Split Votes	
	1996	1999	Change	1996	1999	Change	elect	party
Labour	28.9	48.9	20.0	31.9	55.1	23.2	17.9	31.4
NZ First	48.8	14.4	–34.4	42.3	13.2	–29.1	37.7	37.5
Alliance	7.4	8.5	1.1	8.5	6.7	–1.8	60.5	54.9
National	4.5	3.9	–0.6	6.1	5.7	–0.4	23.9	52.3
Green	–	–	–	–	5.0	5.0	–	100
Mana Maori	4.6	5.1	0.5	3.3	4.4	1.1	19.7	82.9
Mauri Pacific	–	6.3	6.3	–	2.8	2.8	62.3	41.6
ACT	1.4	0.6	–0.8	1.1	0.8	–0.3	58.9	75.4
Independent		7.5	7.5	–	–		100.0	–
Turnout*	72.7	–7.0	65.7					
Aggregate Volatility**			35.6		31.85			

*   Turnout is defined as valid votes as a percentage of those on the roll.

**   Aggregate Volatility is the sum of the absolute differences between vote shares for each party between the two elections.

In 1996 New Zealand First won all five Maori electorates, and gained 48.8 per cent of the total Maori electorate vote. In 1999 it won no Maori seats at all and was reduced to 14.4 per cent of the total Maori electorate vote. The outcome for Labour was a mirror image of this erratic result. Labour in 1996 won no Maori seats, and sank to 28.9 per cent of the Maori electorate vote, then rebounded in 1999 to 48.9 per cent, when it won all six seats. However, Labour's gains were somewhat lower than New Zealand First's losses.

Total vote splitting in the Maori electorates was 41.1 per cent, as compared to 34.9 per cent in the General electorates (New Zealand Electoral Commission 2000). The figures in the split-voting columns are supplied by the Chief Electoral Office, and indicate split votes cast as a percentage of electorate and party votes cast for all parties. They can be understood as 'defection rates' from each: thus of those who cast Labour party votes, 31.4 per cent defected to another party or candidate with their electorate vote.

The aggregate volatility rate for the electorate vote between 1996 and 1999 was 35.6 per cent; while for the party vote, it was 32 per cent. For the electorate vote, this was about twice that among voters as a whole (17.3 per cent). This measurement of volatility of course underestimates its full extent.[2] Table 5.2 displays the flow of the Maori electorate vote from 1996 to 1999 based on a sample of 647 Maori voters. The figures at the top of each cell in the table record the make-up of the 1999 Maori electorate vote in terms of the votes cast in the 1996 election. The bottom figures in italics show the percentage of all respondents represented by that cell. For example, the top figure of the fifth cell indicates that of those who did not vote in 1999, 23.9 per cent had voted for New Zealand First in 1996; and the bottom figure in this cell shows that they accounted for 8.5 per cent of all respondents. The shaded diagonal cells in the table indicate the 'straight' or 'loyal' electors who did not switch from one election to the next. Interestingly, the largest group in this category, and indeed the largest in the whole table, are the 15 per cent of enrolled electors who did not vote in either election. The next largest group, comprising 13 per cent of Maori electors, were those who voted for Labour candidates both times, followed by the 6.5 per cent who were loyal to New Zealand First candidates.

Movement by voters into and out of non-voting is part of the wider pattern of volatility among Maori electors. The bottom figures in the shaded diagonal cells of Table 5.2 show, however, that when straight non-voters are excluded, only 22 per cent of Maori voters chose candidates from the same party in both elections. In 1996 only 20 per cent had made the same choice (Sullivan and Vowles 1998, 183). The advent of MMP and coalition politics has thus coincided with, and doubtless contributed to, a period of very high voting volatility among Maori. The table shows that, overall, in a unique demonstration of electoral volatility, nearly two-thirds (63 per cent) of Maori electors eligible to vote in both elections made a different choice of party candidate in 1999 compared to 1996.

The fluctuating fortunes of the New Zealand First and Labour candidates, respectively, account for much of this volatility. It was, as we would expect from the overall result of the election, a very uneven traffic. Of those who cast a Labour electorate vote in 1999, Table 5.2 ('Labour' row, 'NZF' column) shows that 27 per cent (or 8.5 per cent of all respondents) had given their

Table 5.2 Flow of the Maori Electorate Votes from 1996 to 1999

Row % *Cell %* 1999	1996								N 99 total %
	Non- vote	Nat	Lab	All	NZF	ACT	MM	Oth	
Non-vote	42.3	3.8	14.4	4.3	23.9	1.9	4.5	5.0	234
	15.1	*1.3*	*5.1*	*1.5*	*8.5*	*0.7*	*1.6*	*1.8*	*35.7*
National	11.4	29.6	23.0	6.8	29.2	0.0	0.0	0.0	15
	0.3	*0.7*	*0.5*	*0.2*	*0.7*	*0.0*	*0.0*	*0.0*	*2.3*
Labour	14.9	5.2	41.5	6.9	27.0	1.4	1.7	1.5	206
	4.7	*1.6*	*13.0*	*2.2*	*8.5*	*0.4*	*0.5*	*0.5*	*31.4*
Alliance	23.4	8.0	15.1	26.8	26.6	0.0	0.0	0.0	36
	1.3	*0.4*	*0.8*	*1.5*	*1.5*	*0.0*	*0.0*	*0.0*	*5.5*
NZ First	15.7	4.7	5.8	0.0	70.1	0.0	0.0	3.7	61
	1.5	*0.4*	*0.5*	*0.0*	*6.5*	*0.0*	*0.0*	*0.3*	*9.3*
Mana Maori	42.3	18.3	0.0	0.0	39.4	0.0	0.0	0.0	23
	1.5	*0.7*	*0.0*	*0.0*	*1.4*	*0.0*	*0.0*	*0.0*	*3.6*
Mauri Pacific	13.3	0.0	15.8	0.0	44.3	0.0	0.0	0.0	26
	1.6	*0.0*	*0.6*	*0.0*	*1.7*	*0.0*	*0.0*	*0.0*	*3.9*
Ind	26.8	11.1	19.4	0.0	14.5	0.0	28.2	0.0	31
	1.3	*0.5*	*0.9*	*0.0*	*0.7*	*0.0*	*1.3*	*0.0*	*4.7*
Other	7.5	0.0	17.7	13.6	22.0	0.0	24.3	14.9	24
	0.4	*0.0*	*0.7*	*0.5*	*0.7*	*0.0*	*0.8*	*0.5*	*3.7*
N 96 total %	180	37	146	38	198	7	28	20	647
	27.5	5.7	22.3	5.8	30.2	1.1	4.3	3.1	

electorate vote to a New Zealand First candidate in 1996. A mere half a per cent of Maori voters switched the other way, that is, from a Labour to a New Zealand First candidate ('NZ First' row, 'Lab' column).

The failure of New Zealand First Maori candidates in 1999 to retain the loyalty of those who had voted for the party's candidates in 1996 was a hallmark of the election. Our survey data shows that only about one in five of all Maori voters who gave New Zealand First candidates their electorate vote in 1996 felt inclined to use it the same way in 1999. Where did the rest of those many disillusioned New Zealand First voters move to in 1999? More than a quarter of them (28 per cent) did not bother to cast a vote in 1999. A similar proportion went to Labour candidates. The rest were distributed fairly evenly among Alliance (5 per cent), Mana Maori (5 per cent) and Mauri Pacific (6 per cent) candidates, with National, Independents and others all receiving around 2 per cent each of the former New Zealand First vote. Yet while losing votes to candidates across the party spectrum, New Zealand First candidates also attracted small numbers of new supporters, as the 'NZ First' row in Table 5.2 shows. The largest group (making up 16 per cent of the party's total candidate vote) came from those who had not voted in 1996, with much smaller numbers from those who had previously voted for Labour and National candidates. These, however, could not compensate for the large numbers of voters turning away from New Zealand First candidates. Because they were unable to attract many new voters in the 1999 election, nearly three quarters (70 per cent) of New Zealand First candidates' votes came from 1996 supporters.

Table 5.3: Voting, Vote Change from 1996, and Split Voting in the Maori Electorates, 1999

	Electorate Vote			Party Vote			Split Votes	
	1996	1999	Change	1996	1999	Change	Elect	Party
Hauraki								
Labour	28.5	60.3	31.8	32.3	56.1	23.8	24.0	19.4
NZ First	51.3	14.5	−36.8	42.0	13.3	−28.7	34.0	29.2
Alliance	8.2	9.4	1.2	8.0	6.5	−1.5	65.7	51.4
National	4.8	4.2	−0.6	6.3	5.7	−0.6	27.1	46.4
Green	−	−	−	−	6.0	6.0	−	100.0
Mana Maori	−	2.5	−	3.1	−	58.2	66.7	
Mauri Pacific	−	3.0	3.0	−	2.5	2.5	55.0	47.1
Te Tawharau		3.0	3.0	−	−			−
Total Split Voting								35.0
Ikaroa-Rawhiti								
Labour	32.8	41.0	8.2	34.8	59.0	24.2	14.7	41.0
NZ First	42.2	6.0	−36.2	39.7	12.0	−27.7	26.8	63.7
Alliance	8.4	5.3	−3.1	8.7	6.7	−2.0	57.5	66.7
National	3.3	2.1	−1.2	4.9	4.5	−0.4	16.8	61.5
Green	−	−	−	−	4.0	4.0	−	100.0
Mana Maori	−	−	−	−	4.1	−	−	100.0
Mauri Pacific	−	3.2	3.2	−	2.0	2.0	79.5	67.2
Independent		37.2	37.2		−	−	100.0	−
Total Split Voting								54.2
Te Tai Hauauru								
Labour	27.3	52.2	24.9	31.0	55.4	24.4	19.4	24.8
NZ First	48.1	12.3	−35.8	44.0	12.5	−31.5	29.5	31.2
Alliance	6.5	6.8	0.3	8.7	6.2	−2.5	60.5	57.1
National	5.3	3.5	−1.8	5.0	4.4	−0.6	28.3	43.0
Green	−	−	−	−	4.1	4.1	−	100.0
Mana Maori	−	9.0	−	−	6.1	−	57.7	38.4
Mauri Pacific	−	10.4	10.4	−	4.9	4.9	64.9	25.1
Total Split Voting								35.3
Te Tai Tokerau								
Labour	19.0	47.3	28.3	28.1	51.6	23.5	16.2	46.3
NZ First	62.7	15.9	−46.8	47.2	15.7	−31.5	25.4	50.0
Alliance	6.3	7.1	0.8	7.9	6.7	−1.2	42.4	68.0
National	4.1	4.5	0.4	6.7	6.5	−0.2	26.6	68.4
Green	−	−	−	−	5.7	5.7	−	100.0
Mana Maori	−	−	−	−	2.7	−	−	100.0
Mauri Pacific	−	15.3	15.3	−	4.1	4.1	56.1	37.8
Independent		3.1	3.1			0.0		
Total Split Voting								41.9

Te Tai Tonga

Labour	36.4	49.3	12.9	35.1	53.8	18.7	16.3	24.0
NZ First	37.4	25.0	−12.4	32.2	10.4	−21.8	59.4	3.1
Alliance	9.8	9.9	0.1	11.4	7.8	−3.6	56.4	45.2
National	5.8	5.3	−0.5	8.9	8.4	−0.5	13.4	45.6
Green	−	−	−	−	6.1	6.1	−	100.0
Mana Maori	−	−	−	−	2.0	−	−	100.0
Mauri Pacific	−	4.2	4.2	−	1.8	1.8	70.8	32.9
Total Split Voting								34.3

Waiariki

Labour	28.6	45.1	16.5	30.0	54.9	24.9	15.4	31.3
NZ First	51.8	12.3	−39.5	49.0	15.2	−33.8	23.9	39.2
Alliance	5.4	12.7	7.3	6.3	5.9	−0.4	72.4	40.9
National	3.5	3,7	0.2	4.5	4.6	0.1	33.6	47.2
Green	−	−	−	−	3.7	3.7		100.0
Mana Maori	−	20.0	−	−	8.3	−	0.0	98.8
Mauri Pacific	−	1.7	1.7	−	1.7	1.7	60.6	61.9
Total Split Voting								44.8

NOTE: 1996 voting figures are reallocated into the new 1998 boundaries for purposes of comparison (McRobie 1998).

Since five of the six New Zealand First candidates in 1999 had not been candidates in the 1996 election, it can be reasonably assumed that their electoral support was strongly influenced by the party vote. Yet the emphatic rejection of the five former New Zealand First parliamentary representatives demonstrates that the electorate vote is a very significant variable in Maori political choice. The 'mana' (authority, prestige) and performance of candidates, including loyalty to their parties, are important criteria by which candidates are judged. Four of the five former New Zealand First Members of Parliament had resigned from their party mid-way through their parliamentary term. Voters were not impressed with either their performance or their lack of respect for the will of the people who had voted them into office as representatives of New Zealand First. Incurring voter displeasure, while also lacking the New Zealand First party label, the four former representatives managed to accumulate a total of only 12 per cent of the Maori electorate vote. By contrast, in the southern Maori electorate of Te Tai Tonga, New Zealand First's loyal candidate, Tutekawa Wylie, won 25 per cent of the electorate vote. While this represented a loss of 12.4 percentage points as compared to votes cast in 1996, it was much less than the decline of between 34.4 and 46.8 percentage points experienced by other New Zealand First candidates. Yet New Zealand First's party vote (10.4 per cent) in Te Tai Tonga was the lowest of all the Maori electorates. Clearly, personal factors, not the party label, had lifted Wylie's support to more than double the average for the party's five other Maori candidates. He was the only New Zealand First Maori electorate member who remained with the political party that had taken him into Parliament in the 1996 election. This support would have been considerably reduced if he too had chosen to defect from New Zealand First (Sullivan and Margaritis 2000, 180).

As it was, only 12 per cent of his 1996 supporters changed their allegiance in 1999.

Labour's recovery was the second defining feature of the 1999 election. In 1996, voters had deserted the Labour candidates in large numbers, many turning instead toward New Zealand First candidates (Sullivan and Vowles 1998). In 1999, Labour candidates reclaimed much of their support. As the bottom figures in the Labour row in Table 5.2 indicate, Labour's candidates attracted larger numbers of voters from all other parties than their candidates took from Labour. Yet against the drift of voters to Labour's candidates, 5 per cent of Maori who had voted Labour in 1996 chose not to vote in 1999, and the same source contributed one-fifth of the votes won by Independent candidates, nearly all of which went to Derek Fox, in the Ikaroa-Rawhiti electorate, who only narrowly trailed the Labour candidate by 695 votes. Notwithstanding its recovery, Labour had some problems in mobilising its own 1996 supporters to go to the polls, and then to favour a Labour candidate. Overall, only 58 per cent of those who voted for a Labour candidate in 1996 did so again in 1999. Together, the loss of former Labour voters into non-voting, and in smaller but cumulatively significant numbers to other rival candidates, along with the large number of disillusioned New Zealand First voters who bypassed Labour candidates by not voting, clouded Labour's recovery. Although Labour candidates achieved a spectacular reversal of the 1996 results in the first-past-the-post elections in the six Maori electorates, only two — John Tamihere (Hauraki) and Nanaia Mahuta (Te Tai Hauauru) — attracted an outright majority of voters. Sobering also for Labour's comeback was the 7 per cent decline in turnout of Maori electors, from 77.6 per cent in 1996 to 70.6 in 1999.[3]

Split Voting

The separate party and electorate (candidate) votes under MMP provided Maori voters with two paths leading 'home' to Labour: a vote for their Maori Labour electorate candidate, and a party vote for Labour. In the following analysis of split voting, Table 5.4 uses information compiled from the combined sample used in Table 5.2, less those who did not vote. Table 5.4 is set out in the same way as Table 5.2. The figures at the top of each cell indicate how the party votes cast were divided among the various options for the electorate vote and the figures at the bottom of each cell are the percentages of all the respondents represented by that combination of party and electorate vote. The shaded diagonal cells identify the 'straight' voters for each party, those who did not split their votes, while all other cells represent different combinations of split voting. Because the cell sizes for many groups are very small, the figures should be interpreted cautiously, and with reference to the official split voting data reported in Table 5.1.

There is a distinctive split-voting pattern in the Maori electorates for the Labour, New Zealand First and Alliance parties (Sullivan and Margaritis 2000). Apart from the electorate of Hauraki, Labour's party vote was higher than the votes received by Labour candidates. For Maori voters, coming

Table 5.4   Party and Electorate Votes: Defections from the Party Vote in the Maori Electorates, 1999 Election

Row % *Cell %* Party Vote	Electorate Vote								
	Lab	NZF	All	Nat	MM	MP	Ind	Other	
Labour	67.5 *39.2*	6.5 *3.8*	6.8 *3.9*	1.3 *0.8*	3.7 *2.1*	4.5 *2.6*	7.1 *4.1*	2.1 *1.2*	284 *58.0*
NZ First	1.8 *0.3*	64.9 *9.0*	4.6 *0.6*	1.8 *0.3*	0.0 *0.0*	2.1 *0.3*	7.3 *1.0*	1.9 *0.3*	68 *13.9*
Alliance	31.4 *2.2*	10.2 *0.7*	44.0 *3.1*	2.9 *0.2*	0.0 *0.0*	0.0 *0.0*	5.1 *0.4*	3.3 *0.2*	34 *7.1*
National	27.1 *1.6*	16.9 *1.0*	0.0 *0.0*	47.6 *2.9*	0.0 *0.0*	0.0 *0.0*	4.8 *0.3*	0.0 *0.0*	29 *6.0*
Mana Maori	0.0 *0.0*	0.0 *0.0*	12.7 *0.6*	0.0 *0.0*	51.9 *2.4*	0.0 *0.0*	20.2 *0.9*	15.2 *0.7*	22 *4.6*
Mauri Pacific	24.8 *0.7*	0.0 *0.0*	0.0 *0.0*	0.0 *0.0*	0.0 *0.0*	75.2 *2.2*	0.0 *0.0*	0.0 *0.0*	14 *2.9*
Other**	19.3 *1.3*	10.4 *0.7*	2.9 *0.2*	0.0 *0.0*	7.1 *0.5*	15.5 *1.0*	11.7 *0.8*	33.1 *2.2*	33 *6.7*
	48.3	*15.2*	*8.4*	*4.1*	*5.0*	*6.1*	*7.5*	*4.6*	489

NOTE: Figures in the top left of each cell are row percentages, and those italicised in the bottom right of each cell are percentages of the total N of respondents. Marginals add the italicised figures by row and column, with row Ns.

**   The 'other' category includes: ACT, Christian Heritage. Aotearoa Legalise Cannabis, Future New Zealand, McGillicuddy Serious, One New Zealand, South Island Party, Animal Liberation, Libertiarianz, NMP, and the Natural Law Party.

SOURCE: Combined Maori Electorate Sample, NZES.

'home' meant turning to the Labour party more than it meant supporting Labour candidates. Thus, as the marginal figure (58 per cent) in the top row of Table 5.4 shows, even though Labour dominated the party vote in the Maori electorates, one Labour Maori voter in every three gave their electorate vote to a non-Labour candidate. By contrast, although New Zealand First was the conspicuous loser in the election, there was variable lingering support for some of its candidates. As we have seen in Table 5.3, while the party received more votes than its candidates in three electorates, in two others the shares were even, while in Te Tai Tonga, the candidate vote was far in excess of the party vote.

Patterns of split voting can be most easily understood by looking at candidate factors in the Maori electorates. Over 6 per cent of Labour party supporters gave their electorate vote to a New Zealand First candidate. They mainly went to the New Zealand First candidate in Te Tai Tonga, who, as we have already noted, received twice as many votes as any other New Zealand First Maori candidate, and twice as many votes as his party was able to capture in any Maori electorate. Another 7 per cent of Labour party voters gave their electorate vote to an Alliance candidate. One effect of this was that in all electorates Alliance candidates received more votes than did their party. Among them, however, the highest polling candidate in Waiariki doubled the party support in his electorate (12.7 per cent vs 5.9 per cent). The highest percentage of split voting in the Maori electorates took place in Ikaroa-Rawhiti where 54.2 per cent of the voters (the third highest in all sixty-six General and Maori electorates) divided their party and candidate vote. Among them were the largest group of Labour split voters. The incentive to split in this case was the presence of Derek Fox, a well-known Maori broadcaster and mayor of Wairoa, who, standing as an Independent candidate, took 37.2 per cent of the electorate vote, the largest group of which were Maori who had given Labour their party vote. The effect was to reduce the Labour candidate's net gain in Ikaroa-Rawhiti to only 8.2 percentage points, compared to a net gain for Labour candidates in all Maori electorates of 20 percentage points. In Hauraki, by contrast, only 35 per cent of electors split their vote. There, party and candidate factors pulled in the same direction, and there was minimal incentive for Labour party voters to split their vote. The Labour candidate — the high-profile former chief executive officer of the urban Maori authority, Te Waipareira Trust — received 60.3 per cent of the votes, compared to the 28.5 per cent which had gone to the Labour candidate in 1996.

The dominant split-voting patterns clearly show Maori electors using their electorate votes to discriminate among candidates (as was the intention of MMP). Electors, however, also split their votes for strategic purposes. Candidates put up by supporters of the minor parties (including National in the Maori electorates) had little or no likelihood of winning a plurality of votes. As the shaded diagonal cells in Table 5.4 show and the official data in Table 5.1 confirm, minor parties recorded the highest percentages of split votes, with Labour candidates probably prime beneficiaries. Only 44 per cent of Alliance party voters gave their electorate vote to an Alliance candidate (N=34). Instead, nearly one-third of them preferred Labour candidates, another 10 per cent went to New Zealand First candidates, and a smaller group added to Derek Fox's mixture of party supporters. A little more than half of National party voters (N=29) followed the same pattern of split voting, with proportions choosing the Labour and New Zealand First candidates, and Derek Fox, ahead of National candidates. Fox, the Independent candidate in Ikaroa-Rawhiti, clearly had considerable personal appeal that surpassed traditional party-loyalty voting patterns. While the table suggests that the Mauri Pacific party's tiny following were the least likely group to split their votes, this is an artefact of a small cell size of only fourteen. Table 5.1 provides a better indication of the high levels of vote splitting among the smaller parties.

Of more significance are the almost equal levels of 'straight' voting for the two largest parties vying for the support of Maori electors. Given the long history of incumbency of Labour MPs in the Maori electorates up to 1996, and the party's resurgence in 1999, a relatively high level of loyalty to Labour candidates among party voters is to be expected. More surprising, perhaps, is the almost equally high rate of loyalty (65 per cent) to their party's candidates among New Zealand First party voters, even though only one of the party's five original MPs was standing for New Zealand First in 1999. This evidence of a strong core of loyal supporters implies that the New Zealand First party had considerable influence on levels of support for the New Zealand First candidates, assisting them to be within one per cent of their party's vote in four of the six electorates, and to surpass it in Te Tai Tonga. Only in Ikaroa-Rawhiti did the candidate vote fall well short of the New Zealand First party vote. This exceptional pattern occurred because, in the absence of a 'Derek Fox party', Fox's supporters assigned their party votes to other parties, including New Zealand First.

Minor Maori Parties

As a separate Maori party Mana Motuhake had gradually built its support from 15 per cent in 1981 to a high of 22 per cent in 1990. This was at the expense of the Labour vote. When Mana Motuhake joined the Alliance in 1993 its voter support dropped to 18 per cent. New Zealand First benefited from that decline rather than Labour (Sullivan and Vowles 1978, 173). The same pattern was evident in 1996 except that the voter decline was much steeper. Table 5.1 shows that in 1996 Alliance/Mana Motuhake could manage only 7.4 per cent of the vote in the Maori electorates, and 8.5 per cent of the party vote. In 1999, when there was a change back to more traditional Labour voting behaviour among Maori electors, only 8.5 per cent gave their electorate vote to Alliance/ Mana Motuhake candidates, and even fewer gave their party vote (6.7 per cent) to Alliance/Mana Motuhake. Formed in 1980, Mana Motuhake is now a marginal Maori party, supported as we will see below by voters occupying a very narrow range of social groupings.

One of the newest vehicles for predominantly Maori aspirations, Mauri Pacific, was launched on 28 October 1998. It was established by five former New Zealand First Members of Parliament: Tau Henare, Tukoroirangi Morgan, Rana Waitai, Ann Batten, and Jack Elder. They had resigned from their party but not Parliament after the collapse of the National–New Zealand First coalition (Chapter 1). Mauri Pacific professed to represent peoples of the Pacific, but was essentially viewed as a Maori party. Few policies were articulated. Its high-profile leader, Tau Henare, remained Minister of Maori Affairs in spite of his desertion from New Zealand First, thereby ensuring the new political party received media attention. He had been the outspoken deputy leader of New Zealand First until 1998, a member of the 1996–99 National–New Zealand First coalition government, and Minister of Maori Affairs. Henare had received considerable endorsement from his northern Maori electorate of Te Tai Tokerau. He had won a surprise victory in 1993, capturing the parliamentary seat from an incumbent Labour representative. Henare consolidated his position in 1996 when he won nearly 61 per cent of the electorate vote, with a majority of 8,418 votes — by far the highest of the five Maori electorate MPs. This was an increase of his 1993 support by more than 25 percentage points. However when he defected from the political party that had provided him with the profile, the avenue to Parliament, and a ministerial position, even incumbency could not save his electorate support from disintegrating. As Table 5.3 shows, in 1999 he retained only 15.3 per cent of the electorate vote, a resounding vote of no confidence. A similar pattern can be seen for Tukoroirangi Morgan in Te Tai Hauauru and Rana Waitai in Ikaroa-Rawhiti. Morgan managed to retain only 10.4 per cent of his electorate vote and Waitai a dismal 3.2 per cent. At the 1999 election nearly half of Mauri Pacific's electorate support came from those who in the 1996 election had voted for New Zealand First. Overall, Mauri Pacific candidates polled only 6.3 per cent of the total Maori electorate vote. The party vote was smaller still at a mere 2.8 per cent of the total party vote. Clearly, Maori voters were not persuaded that Henare and the other Mauri Pacific candidates could provide a credible political party. Even their discredited former party, New Zealand First, retained 13 per cent of the overall Maori party vote (16 per cent in Tau Henare's electorate, the party's original Maori stronghold).

MP for Waiariki and cabinet minister, John Tuariki Delamere, also failed to find a viable new party base to sustain his short-lived parliamentary career. His lack of partisan consistency would not have helped. Before joining New Zealand First he had been a National party member. As a first-term New Zealand First MP in 1996 he was immediately promoted to the Executive and became Minister of Customs, and later of Immigration. However he abandoned New Zealand First in August 1998, though he remained in office as an Independent MP. Only a few months before the election he declared himself to be the parliamentary representative of the Maori political party, Te Tawharau, which had been formed in 1996, and was closely aligned to the Ringatu church (*New Zealand Herald*, 6 October 2000). Just weeks before the election, Te Tawharau became a component of the Mana Maori Movement three-party alliance (Mana Maori, Te Tawharau, Piri Wiri Tua Movement).[4] Even though this last-minute alliance was designed to prevent competition among themselves, support for Mana Maori candidates was limited. Delamere and other Te Tawharau candidates were unable to mobilise the Ringatu vote. As Table 5.5 below shows, Ringatu voters heavily favoured Labour (38 per cent), while Alliance, New Zealand First, and Mana Maori each received around 6 per cent of the Ringatu vote. Delamere, as the prominent incumbent in Waiariki, while retaining 20 per cent of the electorate vote, still trailed the Labour candidate by 25 per cent. Delamere's lack of loyalty to New Zealand First, his subsequent political manoeuvres, his removal as Minister of Immigration within days of the election, and his attachment to an insignificant party grouping, all combined to end his parliamentary career.[5]

Alamein Kopu was another Maori MP who left her party, lost credibility among Maori voters, and failed to find an effective vehicle for re-election. Having entered parliament in 1996 by way of the Alliance party list as a Mana Motuhake nominee, Kopu became disillusioned with Alliance, defected, and spent most of her parliamentary term as an Independent. She formed her own Maori women's political party (Mana Wahine Te Ira Tangata), but failed to register a party list with the Electoral Commission. This meant her party was not on the party vote ballot. In addition, Mana Wahine candidates contested only four of the six Maori electorates where they received a combined total of 756 votes. It is not difficult to understand why Maori may support the idea of a Maori party, but fail to cast their votes for Maori parties. The actions of some former representatives have created an important problem of credibility.

The People and their Choices

The 1999 New Zealand Election study includes a separate survey of people who identified as Maori. This comprehensive survey provides us with fairly representative data concerning Maori political opinions, choices and behaviour (see Appendix A for further details).

Table 5.5 presents a comprehensive array of data arranged by party vote support in the 1999 election. Taken together the rows of variables enable us to build up a profile of each party's 1999 voters, although caution is needed when cell sizes fall to small numbers. For example, the data indicate that, largely as a consequence of Labour's high overall level of support in 1999, Maori Labour party voters did not come from any one obvious social or economic group. Nevertheless, Labour did receive considerable support from voters who were over 45 years old and union members. Of those who stated their religious preference, Labour secured the majority of the Mormon vote (56 per cent), and was still strong among Ratana voters. Voters who had degrees, however, were disproportionately under-represented in Labour, compared to people without a degree. Like their pakeha (European) counterparts, Maori voters with high personal incomes do not favour Labour, but are more likely to be National party supporters.

Table 5.5: Party Vote Preferences and Social Groups

Row % ages		Nonv	Nat	Lab	All	NZF	ACT	MM	MP	Grn	Oth	N	%
All		24	6	46	5	7	1	1	2	4	4	1000	
Gender	Male	26	5	45	5	9	1	1	2	4	4	400	40
	Female	23	6	48	5	6	0	1	2	4	5	600	60
Roll	Maori	17	4	52	6	8	1	3	3	3	5	514	56
	General	20	9	47	5	8	1	0	0	6	4	405	44
Age	18–24	40	5	36	3	1	1	1	3	8	4	180	18
	25–34	31	8	35	6	5	2	3	1	4	5	258	26
	35–44	21	9	48	6	7	0	2	2	4	2	259	26
	45–54	11	3	57	6	13	0	0	2	1	6	143	14
	55–64	13	1	67	4	8	0	0	1	1	5	85	9
	65+	10	1	63	1	19	0	0	0	3	3	72	7
Education	Incomplete	29	5	46	4	8	0	1	1	3	4	512	51
	Non-Degree	20	7	48	5	7	1	1	1	5	4	431	43
	Degree	9	5	34	13	4	2	7	11	4	13	56	6
Union	Union	13	6	58	6	5	0	2	3	3	4	187	19
	Non-Union	27	6	44	5	8	1	1	1	4	4	813	81
Occupation	Non-Manual	19	7	44	6	10	1	2	2	4	5	455	47
	Manual	28	4	49	4	5	1	1	1	4	3	503	52
	Farmer	27	20	33	0	7	0	0	0	0	13	15	2
Benefits	Benfiits	28	3	48	5	7	0	1	2	3	5	522	52
	No Benefit	20	9	44	5	8	1	2	2	5	4	478	49
Housing	Mortgage Free	11	2	63	3	11	1	1	1	1	6	149	15
	Mortgage	17	9	47	5	9	1	2	1	5	4	286	29
	Rental-Private	33	4	40	6	5	1	1	2	5	5	348	35

	Rental-State	23	6	52	6	6	0	1	0	4	2	142	14
	Whanau	42	7	31	4	5	0	1	4	3	3	74	7
Income													
Household \$	<13,900	22	2	54	6	10	0	0	1	3	3	143	14
	13,900–19,899	30	3	47	3	7	0	2	1	3	4	155	16
	19,900–31,399	30	5	46	7	3	0	0	1	4	4	140	14
	31,400–48,099	23	6	45	6	7	0	1	3	6	4	146	15
	48,100–71,599	10	10	45	3	18	1	1	3	6	3	126	13
	71,600–93,099	23	9	43	4	6	2	4	2	2	6	53	5
	>93,100	19	11	40	6	9	4	4	2	2	2	47	5
Personal \$	<\$13,900	27	5	47	4	8	1	1	1	4	3	428	43
	13,900–19,899	29	1	50	5	3	1	1	2	3	6	159	16
	19,900–31,399	20	8	47	8	5	0	1	0	5	5	155	16
	31,400–48,099	16	6	49	2	12	1	3	4	6	2	126	13
	48,100–71,599	13	9	38	11	13	4	2	2	4	2	45	5
	71,600–93,099	20	20	40	20	0	0	0	0	0	0	5	5
	>93,100	25	25	17	0	8	8	0	0	8	8	12	1
Religion	None	28	7	42	6	5	1	2	2	6	3	192	19
	Christian	21	5	50	5	9	1	1	1	3	4	452	45
	Fundamentalist	38	6	30	2	6	2	0	2	4	10	50	5
	Latterday Saints	13	8	56	4	13	0	1	3	1	0	75	8
	Ratana	29	5	51	4	3	0	0	0	4	3	93	9
	Ringatu	24	9	38	7	7	0	5	1	3	7	92	9
	Others	25	5	35	0	5	0	0	15	0	15	20	2
Unemployed	21	9	46	6	8	1	2	2	5	1	463	56	
Tribal Area	Yes	21	5	50	5	8	1	2	2	3	5	343	34
	No	26	6	45	5	7	1	1	2	4	4	654	66
Urban	Big Cities	26	6	46	5	7	0	2	1	4	3	373	38
	Cities	21	6	49	4	9	1	1	2	4	3	238	24
	Towns	27	5	45	6	7	1	1	3	2	3	273	28
	Rural	21	7	48	5	7	1	1	1	8	2	102	10

Older people, reluctant to relinquish their traditional Labour loyalties, did not support Alliance, though New Zealand First found support among the elderly (over 65). In general, the profile of New Zealand First party voters lacked clear distinguishing features. The 1999 data shows a continuing slight male bias although it is not as high as in the 1996 sample (Sullivan and Vowles 1998, 180). The party appealed more to middle-aged and elderly voters than to those under the age of 45 years. The age profile, with a high proportion of retired voters, also means that they were less likely to be union members. The slight overall influence of religion in Maori voting patterns can also be seen in the disproportionate appeal of New Zealand First to members of the Latter Day Saints. Overall, around 7 per cent of the Maori population belong to the Church of Latter Day Saints (Statistics New Zealand 1997, 75). Very close to this figure, our data show that 8 per cent of respondents identified as Mormon, and New Zealand First polled well (13 per cent) among these voters, compared to its overall support among Maori of 7.2 per cent.

It is also possible to give a preliminary outline of the potential Maori Green supporter. While the sample size of the Green voters is small (38 respondents) there are some noticeable characteristics. For example a Green supporter was twice as likely to be registered on the General electoral roll than on the Maori roll, and was more likely to be living outside their tribal area. Most of the Green support came from people under the age of 34 years, and especially among those aged 18–24 years. They were more likely to be in comfortable economic circumstances, living in households with incomes between $30,000 and $70,000, but, consistent with their relative youth, their personal incomes were more widely spread, from $20,000 to $70,000. Also linked to age, they tended not to be union members, and in religion were slightly over-represented among the non-religious group.

National has never polled well among Maori voters and 1999 was no exception. In our sample, they received less than 6 per cent of the total Maori vote, and their supporters were twice as likely to be on the General electoral roll, rather than the Maori roll. As expected, National polled especially well among Maori farmers, and among the small number of voters who reported incomes in excess of $71,600, although cell sizes are very small. Support for ACT was even sparser. However, the small numbers in the sample identify a tendency for ACT voters to have been young, male, educated, and economically secure, nearly all living in households with incomes over $71,600, and personal incomes of $48,100 to $71,600.

Table 5.6   Maori Attitudes on Economic, Social and Maori Issues

Row % ages (N=1000)	Strongly Agree	Agree	Neutral	Disagree	Strong Disagree	Don't Know
ECONOMIC ISSUES						
State of Economy	1	21	40	24	11	4
Household Finance	9	19	45	17	9	1
Lower Taxes	14	21	26	25	12	2
Import Controls	16	43	18	14	4	6
Privatisation	4	13	13	33	32	6
Scrap ECA	19	29	18	23	5	7
Unions too Powerful	4	25	27	30	7	7
Unions Necessary	21	57	13	6	1	2
Work for Benefits	17	46	19	13	4	0
SOCIAL ISSUES						
Death Penalty	27	30	18	14	9	2
Pro-immigration	3	5	36	19	33	4
Protect Environment	22	36	25	10	5	1
MAORI ISSUES						
Women equal to men	8	25	12	41	12	3
General Roll	6	20	11	45	15	3
Maori Roll	9	27	12	40	11	2
Treaty in law	4	11	18	36	26	5
General Roll	6	15	19	34	19	6
Maori Roll	2	6	15	38	33	5

Pro-compensation	28	37	18	12	4	2
General Roll	20	35	22	16	5	2
Maori Roll	35	39	14	8	3	1
Government Appointees out of Touch	14	46	19	15	3	4
General Roll	14	49	17	14	2	4
Maori Roll	14	44	20	15	3	3

State of Economy: What do you think of the state of the economy these days in New Zealand? Would you say that it is very good, good, neither good nor bad, bad, or very bad? 'Very good'=strongly agree, 'good'=agree, neither=neutral, 'bad'=disagree and 'very bad'= strongly disagree.

House Finances: How does the financial situation of your household now compare with what it was 12 months ago? Is it a lot better, a little better, about the same, a little worse, or a lot worse. 'A lot better'=strongly agree ,'better'=agree, 'about the same'=neutral, and 'a little worse'=disagree and 'a lot worse'=strongly disagree.

Lower Taxes: Do you think taxes should be reduced, or do you think they should be increased so that government can spend more on things like health and education? Whereabouts on the scale on this card (from 1 to 7) would you place your view? 1= strongly agree, 2–3=agree, 4=neutral, 5=disagree and 6–7=strongly disagree.

Import Controls: To solve New Zealand's economic problems the government should introduce import controls.

Privatisation: To solve New Zealand's economic problems the government should privatise more state assets.

The Employment Contracts Act should be scrapped.

Trade unions in New Zealand have too much power.

Trade unions are necessary to protect workers.

People who are unemployed should have to work for their benefits.

The death penalty for murder should be reintroduced.

Do you think the number of immigrants allowed into New Zealand nowadays should be increased a lot, increased a little, remain the same, reduced a little, reduced a lot? Increased a lot=strongly agree, Increase=agree, the same=neutral, reduce a little=disagree, reduce a lot=disagree strongly.

Protect Environment: How far do you think we should go to protect the environment? Position 1 on this card means that we should concentrate more on protecting the environment, even if it leads to considerably lower incomes, while position 7 means we should safeguard our income levels before we seek to protect the environment. Whereabouts on this scale would you place your view? 1–3=agree, 4=neutral, 5–7=disagree.

In Maori society, women are equal to men.

Treaty in law: The Treaty of Waitangi should be removed from the law.

Maori should be compensated for land confiscated in the past.

Maori who are appointed to government bodies are out of touch with people like me.

Table 5.6 presents data on Maori attitudes to a variety of issues. Generally, the range of responses reveals that while there was a diversity of opinion among Maori electors, they were not radical in their attitudes or outlook. Rather, as with other New Zealanders, opinions tended to cluster around the middle of the political spectrum. The resurgence among Maori of Labour voting in 1999, rather than pursuing more radical minor party options, can therefore be seen as broadly consistent with Maori conservatism in a number of economic, social and environmental issues, underpinned at the same time by traditional Labour attitudes.

In 1999 Maori voting was not driven by a perception of economic deterioration. The largest groups had neutral assessments of the state of the economy (40 per cent) and their household finances (45 per cent). Respondents were evenly divided about having lower taxes as opposed to raising taxes to pay for better social services. However, there was a powerful consensus in favour of trade unions. Similarly, there was overwhelming support for reintroducing import controls, despite their removal having in many cases assisted people on low incomes, by reducing the cost of basic consumer goods such as shoes, clothing, appliances and used cars. On the other hand, Maori responses to this item may reflect the fact that freeing imports has impacted on the unskilled or semi-skilled workforce. Many employed Maori became redundant as local firms were forced to exit the market or move offshore. Similarly there was not much Maori support for privatisation, many Maori having been employed in former state-owned enterprises such as railways, forestry or energy and communication industries. Such attitudes — in favour of import controls, and against privatisation, which invoked Labour's past rather than its contemporary position — might indeed have been expected to lead Maori in greater numbers toward the Alliance.

Even more contrary to the trend of Maori voting in 1999, four out of five Maori believed that individuals on benefits should have to work for their benefit. This was an attitude that New Zealand First had exploited with its 'work for the dole' policy, and the policy was promoted by the National party as recently as its 2001 conference. That 60 per cent of Maori supported the introduction of the death penalty, and more than 50 per cent thought that the number of immigrants allowed into New Zealand should be reduced, was equally incompatible with the dominant voting trend among Maori. Another powerful, distinctive, and in many respects conservative, consensus emerged over protection of the environment. Nearly 60 per cent agreed (and only 15 per cent disagreed) that the environment should receive more protection, even if that meant lower incomes.

On certain 'Maori issues' a strong consensus aligned Maori with the historical role of Labour and the actions of past Labour governments. Above all, over 60 per cent of respondents opposed the removal from law of references to the Treaty of Waitangi, and only 15 per cent thought they should be removed. Maori who had chosen to be on the Maori electorate rolls were more adamant about preserving the place of the Treaty (72 per cent) than Maori respondents on the General roll (53 per cent). A similar overall consensus, with a similar division between respondents on the different rolls, is evident on the issue of whether Maori should be compensated for land confiscated in the past. Overall, two-thirds of Maori agreed that there should be compensation, made up of 55 per cent of those on the General roll, and 74 per cent of respondents on the Maori roll. Twice as many on the General roll disagreed with the practice of compensation compared to the Maori roll. On the other hand the division disappeared into general agreement with the proposition that Maori who were appointed to government bodies were 'out of touch with the average Maori'.

Conclusion

The upsurge in support for New Zealand First in the Maori electorates in 1996 evaporated just as quickly three years later. There had been no realignment of the Maori vote, quite the reverse. Rather than consolidating the dramatic 1996 vote shift, 1999 was a reinstating election. This was not because Maori disillusionment with Labour had been fully resolved, but because the alternative had failed. New Zealand First, a populist minor party with a charismatic Maori leader, had been manifestly unable to provide the leadership desired by Maori. New Zealand First's coalition with National, and the performance of the Maori representatives, were more disillusioning for Maori electors than Labour's perceived shortcomings. As a result Maori reverted to more traditional voting patterns in 1999. Yet it is unlikely that Labour will be able to take future Maori support for granted, especially with the additional electoral levers of influence provided Maori by MMP. Maori are more likely to split their two votes than are general electors, and they place considerable importance on their electorate vote. The support given to the Independent candidate in Ikaroa-Rawhiti is indicative that Maori voters are making conscious and strategic choices about candidates and the political parties. Personalities and strategic voting patterns are clearly discernible among Maori voters.

Nevertheless, the 1999 election has given Labour another chance to consolidate its broad base of support among Maori voters, especially those on the Maori roll. This will not be easy, considering the demonstrable volatility of recent Maori voting behaviour, and given also that Maori policy preferences certainly do not always align with Labour's. On the other hand, there is no evidence of any other party at present able to appeal to as broad a cross-section of Maori electors as Labour. National is still a minor party in the Maori electorates. New Zealand First's claim on Maori allegiance was badly damaged by the events of 1996–99, and the age profile of New Zealand First Maori voters also identifies a significant demographic problem for the party. In contrast, although the Greens in 1999 were starting to have an impact on younger Maori voters, it tended to be among those who have reasonable incomes, and are also most likely to be on the General electoral roll. At present the Greens have made no significant inroads into the Maori electorates, despite the evidence of strong pro-environment attitudes among Maori. Other minor parties, including the Mana Maori Movement and Mauri Pacific, appeared in 1999 as little more than names on the party ballot paper, none receiving more than a quarter of 1 per cent of the vote.

Despite Labour's setback in 1996, history and the breadth of the party's social base among Maori electors therefore place it in a strategic position to maintain its recovered dominance. One further challenge, however, will be to mobilise support among younger electors, who form a very large pool of non-voters.

CHAPTER 6

WHAT HAPPENED AT THE
1999 ELECTION?

Jack Vowles

The 1999 general election may become a landmark in New Zealand politics. First, it resulted in the replacement of one government by another, made up of completely different parties and personnel, an outcome apparently consistent with majority opinion, and sometimes claimed to be unusual under proportional representation (Pinto-Duschinsky 1999). In general, such replacement or 'dismissal' elections enter into political history as more notable than others. New governments mean new policies and, sometimes, significant changes of direction. Secondly, the election might be expected to mark a stage in an adaptive or transitional process from FPP to proportional representation. In the second MMP election we might expect to identify the beginning of some predictable patterns under the new system, in the wake of the changes wrought by the 1993 electoral reform referendum.

The reasons for supposing this are to be found in theories of electoral stability. For example, theorists in the social psychology of politics tradition originating at the University of Michigan propose that there are stabilising trends in mass electorates in the absence of externally created disturbances (for an extended discussion of these theories in the New Zealand context see Vowles 1997). They argue that stability is generated by people's social group identities, and by the transmission of loyalties (including politically partisan loyalties) between generations. This theory finds some empirical support in New Zealand political history (Leithner 1997; Leithner and Vowles 1997).

Meanwhile institutional theories of electoral systems propose that during electoral system change, such as that experienced in New Zealand in the 1990s, instability will increase in the short term (Lijphart 1994). Over the longer term, however, electoral volatility or instability is likely to be less under PR than FPP systems. This is because FPP systems reduce the effectiveness of small parties, thus restricting voters' choices and encouraging both strategic and protest voting, neither of which is a stable expression of political preference. In PR systems, by contrast, there is much more incentive for electors to cast sincere votes on a consistent basis, knowing that their votes even for small parties are much more likely to see the parties represented in Parliament. Thus under MMP, all other things being equal, electoral behaviour should become more stable. Evidence of increased stability would be a decline in the proportion of electors switching their vote from one election to the next. Offsetting this, however, is the likelihood that the higher the number of parties able to elect candidates to choose between, the more the opportunity for volatile behaviour (Bartolini and Mair 1990). Institutional theories also predict that voter turnout should increase under MMP (Blais and Dobrzynska 1998). Higher turnout would therefore be another sign that a stabilisation process was under way.

It would be misleading to assume that all the electoral patterns and trends evident at the 1999 election were necessarily a consequence of the shift to MMP. Many political issues and controversies to which the voters were responding after 1996 might also have occurred under FPP. To control for this, we therefore construct counterfactual or hypothetical election outcomes showing what might have been the results of the 1996 and 1999 elections if they had been held under FPP. Table 6.1 compares the party votes, electorate votes, and hypothetical FPP vote for the 1999 election. The information for the FPP vote is available from one of our questions, which asked respondents how they would have voted had the election been held under the old FPP system, in which they would have had one vote only for a candidate in their electorate. This provides a better indication of what the hypothetical FPP vote might have been than extrapolating from the MMP electorate vote. For, as columns 3 and 4 in the table show, significantly more hypothetical FPP votes were transferred from smaller parties to National and Labour when respondents were asked to imagine how they would have voted under the old system, than were cast for National or Labour in the electorate vote.

The table shows that under FPP Labour would have won the 1999 election with a convincing electoral mandate — probably by a landslide. With over ten percentage points separating the two main parties, Labour on its own would almost certainly have had a substantial parliamentary majority. There are thus two strands to the question 'what happened at the 1999 election?'. The first connects voters to the political events of the previous three years. This strand is seen in the changes in the parties' electoral fortunes during that time, and principally in Labour's rise from 28.2 per cent of the party vote in 1996 to 38.7 per cent in 1999. The second strand, as a comparison of columns 2 and 4 shows, connects the electoral system with people's decisions on which party they would vote for, as distinct from which one they most preferred at the time. We can see that under either FPP or MMP, most people would keep to their primary decisions. But under FPP some, disinclined to waste their vote on an unelectable small party, would have reallocated their vote to one of the two main parties.

Political parties in New Zealand line up along a continuum or spectrum of policy and political proximity usually summarised as 'left' and 'right'. Table 6.1 organises the parties from 'left' to 'right' down the columns. While the meaning of these terms is not precise, 'left' usually means a preference for state intervention to redistribute income, while 'right' means a preference to allow the market a free hand in the allocation of resources and rewards. Under the multi-party politics characteristic of MMP, these terms are more useful for classifying parties and their policies than under FPP. Theory has it that under FPP two parties tend to compete very closely for the centre, seeking to attract

Table 6.1: Seats, Votes and Hypothetical FPP Vote at the 1999 Election

	Seats Won	Party Vote %	Electorate Vote %	FPP Vote %
Green	7	5.2	4.2	2.1
Alliance	10	7.7	6.9	5.3
Labour	49	38.7	41.2	46.1
NZ First	5	4.3	4.2	3.7
United	1	0.5	1.1	0.4
National	39	30.5	31.3	35.4
ACT	9	7.0	4.5	3.5
Christian Heritage		2.4	2.2	0.8
Independent			1.1	0.0
Other		3.7	3.3	2.7
Combined Left	66	51.6	52.3	53.5
Combined Right	48	37.5	35.8	38.9
N				5110

the 'median voter' (Downs 1957). Under the multi-party politics of MMP, where parties are more widely spread in 'ideological space', it is assumed that parties are more likely to compete for voters away from the centre. We can also assume that party cooperation (perhaps leading to coalition) is easier the closer the parties are to each other on the left–right spectrum: that is, in the terms used by coalition theorists, where parties are ideologically 'connected', or at least proximate, to each other. Thus, in the New Zealand party spectrum, National is more likely to be able to work with ACT, immediately to its right, and United, immediately to its left, than with other parties. However, in 1996 the United party, National's preferred centrist ally, only had one seat. The 'pivot' of the new system was therefore New Zealand First, because in 1996 it would have been very difficult to form a government without its support. In 1999, however, it would have been even more difficult to form a government without Labour, which had captured the strategically vital pivotal position in the MMP party system (Kaiser and Brechtel 1999). There was no need, however, for Labour to behave in a pivotal way by contemplating a coalition with a party to its political right, when, as Table 6.1 shows, the parties of the combined left held a clear electoral (as well as parliamentary) majority. Our survey data enables us to fill in the details of this general picture.

Figure 6.1 shows how New Zealanders distributed themselves on the left–right scale when asked to do so after the election, and, also, the averages for their placements of the parties on the same scale. The figure 0 marks the most extreme left, 10 the most extreme right, and 5 the centre, where the 'median voter' is expected to be found. From this figure, we can assess the proximity and distance between the parties as voters perceived them, and line up these perceived party positions against the distribution of voters on the left–right scale. The 'average' respondent was slightly to the right of centre (at 5.3). The middle position for those on the left is a 2 and the middle position for the right is an 8. The main cluster of voters on the left was smaller and more moderate,

**Figure 6.1: Respondents' Placements on the Left–Right Scale and the
Average Placements for Parties by Respondents**

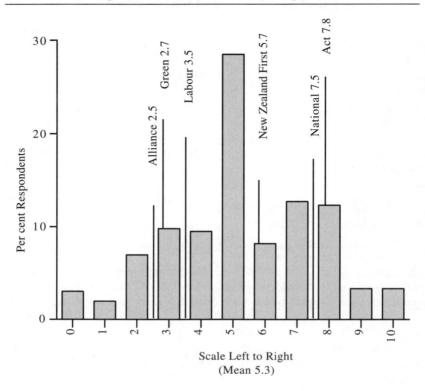

Scale Left to Right
(Mean 5.3)

that is, closer to the centre (on 3 and 4) than the main groupings of support for
the right (on 7 and 8). Labour's placing on the spectrum by respondents was
more moderate than National's, and closer to the average voter (separated by
1.8 points, compared to National's 2.2).

Figure 6.1 thus identifies Labour's ability to win centrist voters (30 per cent
of those who classified themselves on the scale) as one of the key reasons why
it 'won' the 1999 election. While centrist voters were the least likely to vote (20
per cent failed to do so), by far the largest group voted Labour (35 per cent,
compared to 20 per cent National). Although both Labour and National were
perceived to be in the middle of their core areas of ideological support, the
main concentration of left support was closer to the centre, as we have seen.
Yet if National had moved closer to the centre in voters' perceptions, it would
have run a greater risk than Labour of losing support to its right, particularly
to ACT. Labour risked loss of support to its left, too, but there was less support
there to lose, and there were much better pickings in the centre.

Another feature of the 1999 general election was a significant new player
on the left of the spectrum, the Green party. The Greens emerged out of the
remains of the Values party in 1989. Values, formed in 1972, had gained 5 per
cent of the vote in 1975, but no seats. It subsequently fell into the political

margins after faction-fighting between its left and its right. Re-launched, the Green party gained 6.9 per cent of the vote in 1990, again receiving no seats. It joined the Alliance in 1992, and under that bigger umbrella, three of its members became MPs with the introduction of MMP in 1996. The Greens' decision to leave the Alliance in 1997 was courageous, and only two of the three Green members took the plunge. To remain true to their mandate in 1996, however, the departing Green MPs remained part of the Alliance caucus until September 1999. Most observers and commentators wrote off the Greens, and their achievement of parliamentary representation in 1999 was one of the main surprises of the election.

With the arrival of the Greens as a separate party in the House, the number of elected parties increased from six in 1996 to seven in 1999. Yet there was also something of a reversion to greater support for the two major parties, mainly due to Labour's continued electoral recovery, a trend begun during the 1996 campaign. Together National and Labour accounted for 62 per cent of the votes in 1996, rising to 69 per cent in 1999, and the trend has strengthened since the election, if opinion polls are any indication. As another measure of this trend, a distinction can be usefully made between the number of actual parties contesting elections or in the House, and the number of 'effective' parties. The effective party calculation weights the number of parties by their proportions of party votes or parliamentary representation.[1] As a result of the redistribution of votes between 1996 and 1999, the number of actual parties went up by one, as we have seen. The number of 'effective' parties went down, however. Effective parties seeking election were 4.38 in 1996, and 3.86 in 1999, and effective parliamentary parties 3.76 and 3.45 respectively, the differences signifying the trend in 1999 toward a greater degree of two-party dominance (Aimer 2001).

Yet such summary statistics, based only on the party vote, conceal the extent to which people spread their votes under MMP. MMP provides for two votes, enabling people to cast votes for more than one party, a practice that has been dubbed 'split voting'. The extent of split voting gives an indication of how much voters used their options under MMP. Those who split their votes between a party vote cast for one party and an electorate vote cast for a candidate from another party formed 37 per cent of all who used their two votes in 1996 and an only slightly lower 35.2 per cent in 1999 (New Zealand Electoral Commission 1997, 2000).

Table 6.2 shows the relationship between the party and electorate votes as indicated by our surveyed electors in 1999. Voters who did not split their votes (straight voters) are in the diagonal shaded cells. Both Labour and National had by far the largest groups of such voters. In each case they retained about 77 per cent of their party voters at the electorate level. Of the smaller parties, New Zealand First and Christian Heritage returned the most straight votes, followed by the Alliance. Slightly more than one-third of those who gave the Alliance their party vote also chose an Alliance candidate, but half of the Alliance party voters cast an electorate vote for Labour. Only about a quarter of ACT supporters cast 'straight' ACT votes, with another 60 per cent giving their electorate vote to a National candidate. However, our figure showing straight voting for the Greens at only 23.3 per cent may be too low. Other evidence suggests that it was 30.7 per cent.[2] Nevertheless, probably at least 40 per cent of Green party voters cast their electorate vote for Labour.

As in 1996, the split vote pairings suggest that most voters were using their two votes in ways that were rational and consistent. Only rarely are the candidates of small parties likely to be in a competitive position in the electorate contests, the three exceptions in 1999 being the leaders of the Alliance (Jim Anderton) and New Zealand First (Winston Peters), and the Greens' co-leader (Jeanette Fitzsimons). Those giving their party vote to a small party have good reason therefore to attempt to influence the outcome in their electorates by choosing between the rival candidates of the main parties, rather than waste a vote on a candidate who has no chance of winning. In so doing, they are also often expressing their preference for a proximate party. Far fewer ACT party voters chose a Labour candidate than a National one; similarly Alliance party voters preferred Labour candidates many times more than National candidates. The data on split voting thus echo that in Table 6.1, showing small party voters tending to desert to one of the major parties in a hypothetical FPP election.

Table 6.2   Party and Electorate Votes: Defections from the Party Vote, 1999 Election

Row % *Cell %* Party Vote	Electorate Vote								
	Lab	Nat	All	NZF	ACT	Grn	CHP	Other	
Labour	77.1 *29.8*	4.3 *1.6*	8.9 *3.4*	2.0 *0.8*	0.8 *0.3*	3.5 *1.4*	0.3 *0.1*	3.1 *1.2*	1984 *38.6*
National	9.2 *2.8*	76.8 *23.5*	1.2 *0.4*	1.3 *0.4*	6.8 *2.1*	1.0 *10.3*	0.7 *0.2*	3.0 *0.9*	1575 *30.6*
Alliance	50.2 *3.9*	4.0 *0.3*	34.4 *2.7*	3.7 *0.3*	0.7 *0.1*	4.1 *0.3*	0.8 *0.1*	2.5 *0.2*	402 *7.8*
NZ First	21.3 *0.9*	10.4 *0.4*	2.8 *0.1*	58.1 *2.4*	0.6 *0.0*	2.4 *0.1*	0.9 *0.0*	4.5 *0.2*	215 *4.1*
ACT	8.2 *0.6*	59.5 *4.3*	1.0 *0.1*	0.3 *0.0*	23.9 *1.7*	1.6 *0.1*	0.8 *0.1*	4.7 *0.3*	369 *7.2*
Green	47.8 *2.4*	8.4 *0.4*	8.4 *0.4*	3.2 *0.2*	4.2 *0.2*	22.7 *1.2*	0.4 *0.0*	5.0 *0.2*	261 *5.1*
CHP	17.3 *0.4*	23.9 *0.6*	0.8 *0.0*	0.8 *0.0*	1.5 *0.0*	0.8 *0.0*	46.8 *1.2*	8.7 *0.2*	127 *2.5*
Other	24.2 *1.0*	19.2 *0.8*	3.2 *0.1*	2.0 *0.1*	6.6 *0.3*	7.7 *0.3*	4.1 *0.2*	17.8 *0.7*	209 *4.1*
Other/Other**							15.2 *0.6*		
	41.8	*32.0*	*7.3*	*4.1*	*4.7*	*3.7*	*1.8*	*4.7*	5142

The most significant changes in voting behaviour, however, are not the hypothetical ones, but the real movements from one election to the next. Of course, some change between elections comes about because the voting population is not exactly the same in any two elections. Young people reach voting age, while old people die, and patterns of voting among new voters can be expected to be somewhat different from those who have just died. Nevertheless, most change is caused by people choosing a different party from the one they chose at the previous election. It is the volume and direction of change that provides the fascination of election night, and the material for the TV graphics. What were the voter movements among the parties in 1999? From where did parties gain votes, and to which others did they lose them?

Table 6.3 displays the flows of the party votes between 1996 and 1999, with the 'stable' cells highlighted. In these cells we find voters who made the same choice both times. The table reports panel data — that is the responses of the same people surveyed after both elections. This minimises errors of recall, but has the disadvantage of smaller numbers of respondents than the full post-election data set. (Note that those who chose the Green party in 1999 and the Alliance in 1996 are counted as 'stables', as the Green party was then a component party of the Alliance.) Reading across the rows, the percentages at the top of each cell indicate the 1996 sources of each party's 1999 votes.

Table 6.3: Flow of the Party Votes from 1996 to 1999

Row % *Cell %* (New voters) 1999	All	Lab	NZF	CC	1996 Nat	ACT	Oth	Non	N 99 total %
Green (7.0)	23.8 *1.0*	14.3 *0.6*	16.7 *0.7*	0.0 *0.0*	19.0 *0.8*	7.1 *0.3*	11.9 *0.5*	7.1 *0.3*	68 4.2
Alliance (6.8)	50.0 *3.2*	12.5 *0.8*	9.4 *0.6*	9.4 *0.6*	9.4 *0.6*	0.0 *0.0*	4.7 *0.3*	4.7 *0.3*	104 6.4
Labour (23.3)	8.1 *4.1*	59.1 *18.9*	12.8 *4.1*	1.6 *0.5*	10.0 *3.2*	1.6 *0.5*	2.5 *0.8*	4.4 *1.5*	519 32.0
NZ First (0.7)	0.0 *0.0*	5.7 *0.2*	77.1 *2.7*	0.0 *0.0*	8.6 *0.3*	2.9 *0.1*	0.0 *0.0*	5.7 *0.2*	57 3.5
CH (3.0)	0.0 *0.0*	4.8 *0.1*	9.5 *0.2*	76.2 *1.6*	9.5 *0.2*	0.0 *0.0*	0.0 *0.0*	0.0 *0.0*	33 4.2
National (15.4)	2.4 *0.6*	6.0 *1.6*	5.2 *1.3*	3.6 *0.9*	73.4 *18.5*	5.6 *1.4*	1.2 *0.3*	2.8 *0.7*	409 25.2
ACT (5.3)	0.0 *0.0*	1.7 *0.1*	1.7 *0.1*	3.4 *0.2*	50.0 *3.0*	39.7 *2.3*	3.4 *0.2*	0.0 *0.0*	94 5.8
Other (1.0)	13.3 *0.4*	10.0 *0.3*	10.0 *0.3*	3.3 *0.1*	23.3 *0.7*	10.0 *0.3*	23.3 *0.7*	6.7 *0.2*	48 3.0
Nonvote (37.5)	3.9 *0.7*	9.6 *1.7*	9.0 *1.6*	0.0 *0.0*	12.4 *2.2*	2.0 *0.4*	3.9 *0.7*	59.0 *10.5*	288 17.8
N 96 total	139	391	186	62	480	87	56	220	1621
% new voters N=130	8.6	24.1	11.5	3.8	29.6	5.4	3.5	13.6	

The reappearance of the Green party as an independent entity in 1999 provided the most significant change in the party choices available to voters between the two elections. While the cell sizes have small numbers, the indications are that the Greens garnered the greater part of their vote not from the Alliance, which contributed slightly less than a quarter of the Greens' 1999 vote, but from other sources across the political spectrum.[3] Labour, as expected, gained most of its new inflows from New Zealand First, but former National voters came second, just ahead of the Alliance. Despite its populist appeals, ACT appears to have made no significant inroads into other parties' 1996 support, with the exception of National. Half of those who chose ACT in 1999 had voted for National three years before. About 40 per cent of the Alliance's 1999 voting support was new, gained fairly equally from Labour, National, New Zealand First, and the former Christian Coalition.

The percentage of all respondents in the sample is given at the bottom of each cell. Reading down the columns, these percentages can be used to identify where parties lost votes. The Alliance, for example, appears to have lost more of its 1996 vote to Labour (amounting to 4.1 per cent of all respondents) than it kept (3.2 per cent of respondents). National lost mainly to Labour and to ACT, and picked up only small amounts of new support. New voters are not included in the main part of the table, but data from the small subsample of those aged 18–20 is provided in brackets in the 1999 label column. Nearly 40 per cent did not vote at all, but when they did, on this evidence they were more likely than the average voter to have chosen the Greens and the Alliance, and less likely to have voted for one of the larger parties. In all, one-quarter of new voters went to parties of the right, and the rest split evenly between the left and non-vote.

If, as suggested earlier, the transition to MMP is predicted to result in a return to more stable electoral patterns, there is some evidence of that occurring in Table 6.3, but the trend is only slight. Two estimates of stability and volatility are useful. Stable voters are those who have voted for the same party in two consecutive elections. They are estimated on a base of all those on the electoral rolls. Switchers are defined as those who voted for different parties in consecutive elections, but include only those who voted at the second election of the pair. On this basis, the table indicates a continued high level of vote volatility, with only a slight decline evident compared to 1996. Switchers formed 45 per cent of 1996 voters and 41 per cent of 1999 voters: a decline, but not a large one. Overall stability increased by only 1 per cent, because greater stability among voters was offset by an increase in non-voting. The persistence of volatility is coupled with late decision-making among electors. In a stabilising electoral environment, we would expect a growing proportion of electors to have made early voting decisions. In 1996, over half (52 per cent) of our respondents declared they had made their voting decision during the campaign. In 1999, this went down only slightly to 48 per cent — still a very high level.

Further evidence which counsels caution in accepting our stabilisation hypothesis is found in Table 6.4, reporting data for turnout and party membership. The decline in party membership is particularly significant, as it was already low in 1996. Declining membership indicates that political parties have fewer resources to call on for fund-raising and campaign activity. It also indicates that there are few people who wish to participate in the organisations that, in theory, provide the most opportunities for people to gain access to politicians and influence on their policies. A decline in party mobilisation of voters and a movement away from traditional parties have been linked to New Zealand's declining turnout (Vowles 1994). When New Zealand political parties had higher memberships, there was almost certainly significantly greater contact between voters and political parties face to face by means of party canvassing door to door, which also assisted the process of voter enrolment. We discuss these possible linkages more fully in Chapter 7, where we explore the tendencies and trends in turnout in detail.

Table 6.4: Turnout and Party Membership, 1990–1999

	Valid Votes as % of those enrolled	Age-eligible effective turnout	Party membership	Party membership as % adults
1990	82.8	76.0	–	–
1993	82.8	76.7	–	–
1996	85.6	78.4	153,000	5.8
1999	82.3	75.0	132,890	4.8

NOTE: Age-eligible turnout is measured as valid votes on a base of the population aged 18 and over, thus avoiding bias in the official figures due to differences in the electoral enrolment rate over time (Nagel 1988). Party membership is made up of the total figures for registered political parties released by the Electoral Commission for each election year since 1996.

As noted in Chapter 2, party identification is a stabiliser of voting behaviour and party systems. Party 'identifiers' are the most stable and predictable voters, while volatility is associated with weak or no party identifications. However, there is reason to expect that in time New Zealand's move to proportional representation may foster stronger identifications, because a wider choice of parties should mean that a larger number of voters can feel 'close' to one or another of the parties. Yet there was no sign of such a trend in 1999. Rather, along with the slump in turnout, there was a recurrence of declining party identification.

Figure 6.2 indicates that between 1996 and 1999 party identification in New Zealand dropped by eight percentage points (62 to 54 per cent), with the most committed group, the 'strong' or 'fairly strong' identifiers slipping from 48 to 41 per cent. Although on this indicator the proportion of the electorate with meaningful strong party identifications is greater than in 1990 (37 per cent), and the same as in 1993 (41 per cent), it is again below that of the first MMP election 1996. While the longer-term trend may be consistent with the international evidence of declining party identifications in most established democracies (Dalton, McAllister and Wattenberg 2000), it still suggests that the transition to MMP has done little yet to check the drift of citizens away from the political parties. From this analysis there are no grounds for expecting other than a continuation of the high level of voter volatility that marked the latter years of unstable plurality elections.

Figure 6.2: Party Identification Trends in New Zealand, 1975–1999

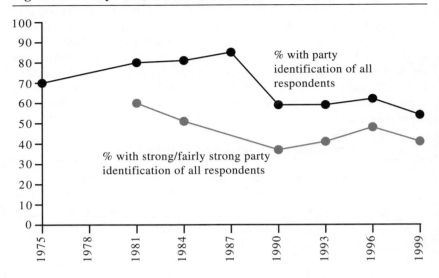

Party identification, being an emotional or psychological response to party politics, may itself be inherently changeable. A more solid foundation for the stability of party systems may derive from long-term patterns of socio-economic or ideological divisions. Of course such divisions may also be the seedbed of party identification, if they are closely associated with particular parties. In New Zealand our surveys have detected signs of a possible strengthening of the main cleavage that has underpinned the party system since the 1930s at least: the class or socio-economic divide between manual worker households, and other households. It is well known that the Labour party was originally formed by the New Zealand trade union movement, whereas National has traditionally drawn its core support from people living in farming and business households. By the mid-1980s, there were very few Labour MPs with a traditional union background, but from 1987 onwards people from union backgrounds became increasingly likely to become Labour MPs, and the post-1999 Labour-Alliance government's Cabinet contained a significant number of former unionists or union officials. Consistent with this development, the traditional alignment of the party system on left–right economic or distributional issues has revived slightly. Figure 6.3 shows the long-term decline of class-voting in New Zealand, and the recent somewhat unsteady recovery.

However, the historical roots of Labour in manual-worker trade unions have been weakened by the decline in manual employment and in trade unionism itself. Twenty-one per cent of households in our sample contained a trade unionist, and 30 per cent were 'headed' by a manual worker. In 1999 unionism in New Zealand was as much, if not more, a phenomenon of non-manual employment. Although manual-worker households still had a higher rate of union membership (27 per cent manual to 20 per cent non-manual), 60 per cent of union households contained a non-manual worker as head of household, and only 40 per cent a manual worker. However, people in manual-

Figure 6.3: Class Voting in New Zealand, 1963–1999

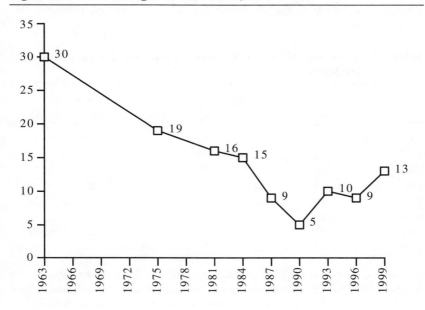

NOTE: The index of class voting is the Labour percentage of the manual household vote (including farmers) minus the Labour percentage of the non-manual household vote. This gives a scale that would read 0 where Labour voting was the same in manual and non-manual households, and could be 100 if Labour had 100 per cent of the manual vote and no non-manual votes at all. For this table, the household occupation is defined by the male in the household, unless there was no male with a reported occupation.

worker households were more likely to vote Labour than in non-manual union households (51 per cent to 41 per cent). Among both categories of unionists, Labour was well ahead of all the other parties. People in union households were also more likely to vote than non-unionists, offsetting to some degree the declining size of the union segment of the electorate. A slight recovery of historical alignments thus contributed to the 1999 election result. While most likely a response to Labour's growing political distance from its electorally disastrous years after 1987, it is also possible that with MMP and the presence of the Alliance, with its rhetoric of 'keeping Labour honest', potential Labour voters returned to Labour, more confident that it would henceforth keep in closer touch with its traditional electoral base.

Meanwhile, as Chapter 4 foreshadowed, in 1999 a newer alignment tendency was maintained and slightly strengthened: women were 9 per cent more likely to vote Labour than men. Given the slightly greater proportion of women in the electorate, this gender effect is likely to be as strong, if not stronger, than class. Over the years Labour has replaced National as the party more likely than the other to get the support of women. However, the deficit of female voters on the political right is not National's alone. In 1999 it was ACT that had the largest gender gap among its voters, with a 9 per cent vote among men but only 3 per cent among women. This is a gender imbalance that ACT has in common with ideologically similar parties in western Europe (Gidengil and Hennigar 2000).

Table 6.5: The National/Labour Gender Gap in New Zealand Elections, 1963–1999

	National			Labour		
	Female	Male	All	Female	Male	All
1963	51	44	48	43	45	44
1975	50	45	48	38	42	40
1981	40	38	39	39	39	39
1987	45	44	44	48	48	48
1990	48	49	48	36	34	35
1993	34	37	35	37	33	35
1996	33	35	34	32	24	28
1999	31	30	31	43	34	39

Although these potentially stabilising trends in the links between social structure and vote are still insubstantial, they are of some significance in that the shift to MMP had initially appeared to have the effect of weakening the foundations of party support in social structure (Vowles 1998a). It is premature, however, to see in this signs of a return to the stronger structural alignments of the 1960s and 1970s.

Another important indicator of the extent and stability of partisan support is the age profile of each party's voters. The most widely accepted theory of voting behaviour holds that young people may acquire a party attachment from their parents, but as new voters their attachment will be weak. They may either not vote at all, or vote for another party that appeals to them rationally or emotionally, thus departing from their parents' party alignments. As they age, however, their attachments, whether new or inherited, will tend to firm up and their likelihood of voting will increase. Of course, this theory leaves out those without party attachments and whose parents may not have communicated any political loyalties. Nonetheless, political parties take the theory seriously, and are particularly concerned to attract and retain young voters.

Yet this is a hard task, as Figures 6.4 to 6.9 show, for the most popular 'party' among the young is 'nonvote'.[4] It is not until most people reach their thirties that they begin to vote at an average rate for the parties in question, indicated by the horizontal lines across the figures. Among the youngest electors, the rate of non-voting is well over twice the average for all the age cohorts. As already indicated in Table 6.3, only the Alliance and Green parties managed to attract higher votes among the youngest voters than their average turnout levels, but the harvests were still meagre. ACT does better than average from people aged about 25 to 60, and National from those in their early thirties to mid-fifties, but it is not until about the fifties age group that Labour begins to do better than its average on an age basis (at which point both ACT and National are beginning to drop from their peak). National does much worse among the retired than Labour except among the very elderly.[5] Nonetheless, after nonvote, in absolute numbers Labour did win the battle for voters up to their early thirties.

Figures 6.4–6.9: Age, Non-Voting and Party Voting

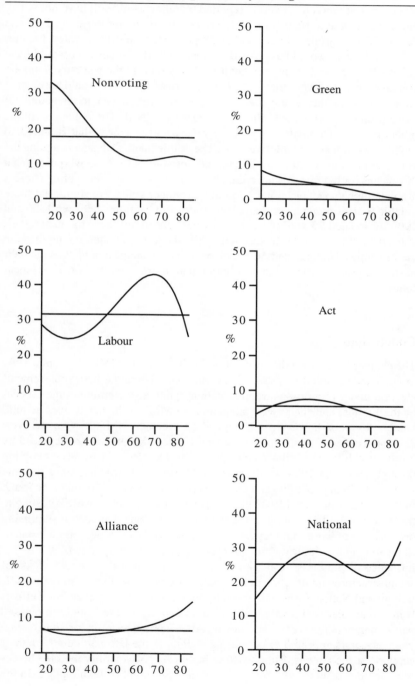

What do these age trends mean? It is hard to tell, because so many of the crucial younger voters did not vote, but can be expected to do so in greater numbers when they reach their mid-thirties. Respondents who reported not voting were asked how they would have voted had they been able to. Nearly 60 per cent of nonvoters over 35 reported that they would still have not voted, but the comparable figure was only about a third among those aged 35 and below. Of this group, about another 28 per cent would have voted Labour, twice those who would have voted National. Nearly 10 per cent would have voted Alliance, confirming the small tendency seen in the age curves among younger voters to favour that party. Only just over 1 per cent would have voted Green, but this indicates the effectiveness of the Green appeal to the young. Of those prone to vote Green, almost all were mobilised. The Alliance, on the other hand, had potential support among younger voters that it failed to mobilise as well as it could have done. The political left's advantage among the young applied as much to those who did not vote as to those who did. What this means for the future is uncertain, because, as we have seen, voting choices are volatile between elections. Moreover, younger voters are somewhat more volatile in their preferences than older voters. For example, between 1996 and 1999 those aged 35 and under were 10 per cent more likely to change their votes than those over 35. In addition, while the left did better among those in their twenties, National and ACT took over the advantage among those in their thirties, a group who are likely to participate more strongly in the very near future.

Conclusions

The chapter began with the speculation that the second MMP election in 1999 might stand in the future as a political landmark, being the first 'replacement' election under proportional representation, while also continuing the process of the parties' and the voters' adaptation to MMP. Whether it does acquire landmark status, however, will depend on whether MMP survives as New Zealand's electoral system. If in the near future MMP were to be replaced by a return to FPP or similar electoral system, the electoral patterns evolving through 1996 and 1999 would again be disrupted. It was hypothesised that signs of declining volatility and increased party system stability might be found in the 1999 result, as evidence that the parties and the voters were adjusting to the new electoral system. There are some indications that such a stabilising process was at work, but they are weak ones. Vote switching, reported potential campaign volatility, and split voting were slightly down, while the influence of the class cleavage increased slightly. Yet the overall effects of social structure on vote choices remained extremely low. Only voting for ACT, Labour and National was influenced by social structure, and even those effects were small.[6] Partisan loyalties remained at depressed levels, and turnout and party membership were both down. After taking account of non-voting, younger voters appeared to be shifting slightly to the left, particularly in their support for the Greens. But persisting high levels of volatility in vote choices provide no ground to infer that a long-term shift might be taking place. In the context of the collapse in support for one significant party in 1996, New Zealand First, and the reappearance of the Green party as an independent actor, a trend toward electoral stability and confirmation of the hypothesis was always less likely.

If MMP survives as New Zealand's electoral system into future elections, the verdict on the 1999 election is likely to be that it formed part of a transitional process that was still incomplete. The rise of the Greens and the near demise of New Zealand First are proof of that. By 1999, besides having damaged its reputation by entering into coalition with National after 1996, New Zealand First was something of an electoral anachronism in the MMP environment. Largely a product of ephemeral protest voting that pre-dated the advent of MMP, its challenge is to find and hold a distinctive constituency in the crowded centre ground of the electoral continuum. The Greens, however, emerged from the Alliance precisely in order to capitalise on the electoral opportunities presented by the new proportional system.

A fundamental question remains: why did National lose the 1999 election, and the parties of the centre-left 'win'? Taking a longer-term perspective, of the four periods of National government in New Zealand's history, only one (1960–72) covered more than an otherwise consistent three parliamentary terms. As governments tend to lose support at successive elections, and sometimes history is a guide to future expectations, all other things being equal the odds were low that National would win a fourth victory in a row in 1999. Moreover as the 1990s wore on, as Chapter 1 showed, National's victories were to some extent by default. Under MMP the centre-left would have won in 1993, and in 1996 centre-left votes bled to New Zealand First because many of those moving in that direction mistakenly believed New Zealand First would help expel National from government. Consequently, throughout most of the period since the 1996 election, Labour had led National in the opinion polls. The 'left–right' placings of voters and parties reported early in this chapter suggest that Labour was now closer to the crucial 'median voter' than National. While National sought to label Labour as a party of ideology, it was National that voters tended to place further from the ideological centre: only a whisker away from ACT, the party perhaps most clearly identified in that mould. While the advantages of government incumbency made it possible for National to be almost level with Labour in pre-campaign polling, Labour's campaign, risk-averse though it was, had the desired effect of reminding enough volatile voters of their dissatisfaction with National. Meanwhile National's more risky campaign tactics and New Zealand First's bungling of its list candidate selections gave the news media plenty of opportunity to dramatise the consequent trials and tribulations while Labour sailed on more smoothly.

Chapters 3 and 4 focus in depth on the importance of leadership, and how perceptions of leaders can be influenced by the ways that the media, and particularly television, cover political events. Incumbency gave Jenny Shipley an advantage, and she polled well as Prime Minister, but not strongly so for an incumbent. All governments and Prime Ministers face problems from time to time. Jenny Shipley was most effective at set-piece, planned events, or one-on-one in communication with individuals. But in an unexpected crisis, she was not fast on her feet, and often made matters worse rather than better. Her series of minor crises as Prime Minister were often not well-managed. Neither did she — or indeed, her predecessor, Jim Bolger — appear to have the government 'under control' in a way that projected confidence on a consistent basis. Problems were allowed to fester, rather than being dealt with decisively. Retrospectively, the contrast between Shipley and Clark as Prime Ministers is a sharp one. Helen Clark, once among the lowest-polling party leaders, has been transformed post-election into the most popular New Zealand Prime Minister since Sir Robert Muldoon. She has demonstrated considerable skill in managing her government, although few if any voters could have anticipated this evolution when they cast their votes in November 1999. However, Clark's strong but not outstanding performances in the 1999 debates were sufficient to recall her clearer victories over Bolger in the 1996 debates, and helped reinforce perceptions of her strength and trustworthiness.

Despite its historic importance, the electoral race between two women leaders showed no signs of distinctiveness. Gender stereotyping, except for Shipley's apparently unsuccessful attempt to gain momentum from 'motherhood', was absent, as was any significant emphasis on women's issues. Nevertheless, perceptions of leaders were influenced by media coverage. The traditional public broadcasting model of Radio New Zealand's coverage appealed more to voters thinking about issues, and less to those concerned with leaders than the two television channels, both of which are deeply influenced by commercial imperatives. The tone of coverage of leaders was almost entirely the result of the nature of the events covered, rather than the way they were covered, except insofar as journalists and editors sought to make the most out of them for the purpose of newsworthiness and impact. Despite sometimes strongly held belief to the contrary, media-commissioned polls had no effects on the election outcome, except for the Greens.

We return, therefore, to the electoral life cycle, and the degenerative effect on a government's support of an extended period in office as an explanation for the election outcome. The 1999 election would have been won by Labour regardless of the electoral system. But the change to MMP had made a difference, the consequences of which invite speculation. Under FPP, Labour almost certainly would have had a large majority. Would Jenny Shipley's leadership have survived such a defeat? In the light of the election outcome, complaints of Clark's decisive post-election leadership style and comparisons with that of Muldoon also pose an interesting question. A former supporter of FPP, Clark has blossomed as Prime Minister under MMP. Would her strength and decisiveness have been as popular without the constraints on her power imposed by the circumstance of her leading a minority government? Would she be as admired for her management skills in an FPP context that would not have so greatly demanded them?

CHAPTER 7

THE PUZZLE OF TURNOUT

Jack Vowles

New Zealand has a reputation as a country of high voting turnout. Since the 1960s, that reputation has become increasingly undeserved.[1] A smaller proportion of the eligible adult population 18 years and over cast valid votes in 1999 than at perhaps any other previous New Zealand election.[2] Part of the reason for misunderstandings about the state of voter turnout in New Zealand is confusion about measurement. The official figures are most frequently cited, and are on a denominator or base of those enrolled to vote. However, this excludes people who did not enrol: 8.94 per cent of those who should have, did not have their names on the rolls in 1999 (New Zealand Electoral Commission, 2000). The official figures also include as voters those who cast informal votes. Some of these may have spoiled their ballots on purpose, and therefore should not be counted as voting. Even more misleadingly, the official figures include as voters those who cast special votes that are disallowed, in most cases because their names were not on the published roll. Including in the numerator cases excluded from the denominator is bad mathematics. Valid votes that were actually counted provide a better estimate, and those eligible to be on the rolls constitute a better base than those actually on the rolls (Nagel 1988).[3]

Turnout tends to be higher in countries with proportional representation than in those with FPP systems. The cross-national evidence for this is consistent, although estimates of how much PR enhances turnout differ, ranging from 12 per cent and even higher to more conservative estimates of about 3 per cent (Franklin 1996; Norris forthcoming; Blais and Dobrzynska 1998). Anticipating some effects of electoral system change on turnout in New Zealand, the members of the Royal Commission on the electoral system took a cautious position, anticipating that the adoption of PR would 'provide for slightly more effective voter participation' and produce 'a turnout higher than plurality' (RCES 1986, 56–7). Cross-national evidence and the commission's predictions were both borne out when at the first MMP election in 1996 turnout increased from 85 per cent to 88 per cent of enrolled electors, or from 76.7 to 78.4 per cent of the population eligible by age to vote.

The shift to MMP was likely to attract a greater proportion of the electorate to the polls. This was one of the arguments in its favour, as turnout had been in decline since the 1950s, save for a recovery between 1975 and 1984 (Vowles 1994). The increase in 1996, although not large, was an encouraging start for

MMP, reversing a long-term trend. The upswing was notable also from a comparative perspective, as turnout has been declining in most OECD countries in the 1990s, including those with PR (Wattenberg 2000). But in 1999, the encouraging increase was halted when turnout as a percentage of the age-eligible population fell back again by 3.4 points to just under 75 per cent, or from 85.6 per cent to 82.3 per cent of the enrolled electorate.

Turnout decline in 1999 might be seen as New Zealand's reverting to a norm after the novelty and high stimulus of the first MMP election. This would suggest that the causes of the long-term decline counterbalanced the reasons for the higher turnout in PR systems. Or the 1999 result might simply be evidence that turnout fluctuates in PR countries as in any others in response to short-term influences on people's motivation to vote or not — for example, disillusion with the government's performance, and the quality of the opposition during the preceding three years. Nonetheless, in the context of the transition to a PR system, the 1999 decline in New Zealand is unexpected and merits closer analysis. Why it might have occurred is the problem we explore in this chapter.[4]

Various theories have been advanced to explain why some people vote and some do not. *Socio-economic* explanations assume that those with fewer resources (low educational qualifications, low income) are less aware of the relevance of politics to their lives, because they lack basic information and skills (Verba and Nie 1972; Verba, Schlozman and Brady 1995). *Demographic* explanations follow the same logic, assuming that those who are younger, unmarried and less integrated into society have less experience and less commitment to society in general (Converse and Niemi 1971). *Attitudinal* theories are rooted in the dominant tradition of research into electoral behaviour, the Michigan model, with roots in social psychology. This model focuses on how people feel, rather than what they think. A key variable is how much people identify with a particular political party. In this respect, confidence in politicians and the political process in general have become increasingly important (Pharr and Putnam 2000). *Economic* or *Rational Choice* theories of voting, on the other hand, are cognitive theories, based on the assumption that people do think and calculate what is in their best interest. These theories long ago identified a paradox. The influence of a person's vote is so small, the likelihood of benefits from it so low, and the costs in time and effort of casting a vote — particularly an informed vote — so relatively high that it is by no means clear why rational self-interested people should bother to go to the polls (Downs 1957).

Yet as critics of rational choice theories delight in pointing out, most people do vote — for reasons of civic duty and belief in the value of democracy, among others. Nonetheless, turnout is in decline in many of the older democracies, perhaps because people no longer feel a strong sense of civic duty and, maybe, are increasingly dissatisfied with the conduct of democracy. If those motives for turnout are no longer strong, and people have become less civic-minded and more self-centred, rational choice explanations may no longer be so easily dismissed. Rational choice theory may not explain all of the choices between voting and not voting, but it may explain a significant number of them (Blais 2000). Meanwhile, consistent with the rational choice perspective that voting has costs for individuals and may need encouragement, *mobilisation* theories suggest that political parties and social and political organisations can act to motivate people to vote who otherwise might not do so (Rosenstone and Hansen 1993; Gray and Caul 2000).

Incentives and Competitiveness

Rational choice theory is also helpful in suggesting some reasons why the difference between MMP and FPP could influence the decision to vote or not vote. The more effective people perceive their votes to be, the more likely they are to cast them. When an election outcome is close there is a greater chance that a person will believe that their single vote could make a difference. In FPP systems with single-member electorates, competitiveness is often confined to a relatively small number of electorates where parties concentrate most of their resources. In these electorates, parties are likely to mobilise voters, and voters are more likely to perceive their vote as making a difference. In the remaining electorates, where parties are often separated by wide margins, parties have less incentive to mobilise, and voters have less incentive to vote (Powell 1980). Evidence from the 1990 election in New Zealand supported this hypothesis. The highest rates of non-voting were found in electorates where National and Labour candidates were regarded as safely entrenched; while in competitive or marginal electorates the rate of non-voting decreased substantially (Vowles and Aimer 1993, 48–9). The lowest rates of participation were in the Maori electorates, which were also among the least competitive in the country (see Chapter 5).

Under MMP, however, it is the party vote, not the outcome in single electorates, that determines the partisan composition of Parliament. Parties therefore have a greater incentive to mobilise everywhere, and voters everywhere have equal incentives to cast a party vote (Denemark 1998). In the case of the electorate vote, voters may still care who their electorate MP is, and candidates may make more effort, the better the chance they have of winning. If so, turnout could still be a little higher where the contest between candidates is perceived to be close. But subject to this qualification, if the difference in turnout between safe and marginal electorates disappears under MMP, this change would be consistent with expectations raised by rational choice theory.

There are other reasons, also consistent with rational choice theory, for turnout to increase under MMP. The position of Maori and the politics of the Maori electorates have both changed dramatically under MMP (see Chapter 5). Previously fixed at four, the number of Maori electorates can now increase or decrease depending on the number of Maori who choose the Maori rather than the General roll. This is a change that could have happened under FPP — indeed, it was briefly introduced in 1975 but repealed before it could come into effect. While previously Maori have been less likely to vote for a combination of cultural, political, and socio-economic grounds, for two distinct reasons they have a greater incentive to participate under MMP. The number of Maori parliamentary seats increased from four to five in 1996 and to six in 1999, thus raising the value of votes cast from the Maori roll. Maori representation has also been increased by the introduction of party lists, where Maori and other under-represented groups are likely to be ranked high enough to win more seats than was possible for them under FPP. As a result, there was an increase in Maori turnout in 1996 (Karp and Banducci 1999, 375).

Supporters of small parties that had little chance of winning seats under FPP also have a greater incentive to vote under MMP, since the threshold for gaining representation was significantly reduced. The effect was evident from responses to the 1996 NZES, when, in the first MMP election, a greater percentage of people believed that their 'vote counts in elections' than under FPP, and the greatest changes occurred among small party supporters (Banducci, Donovan and Karp 1999). Along with these increases in efficacy, a greater percentage of the electorate expressed an interest in politics in 1996 than in 1993 under FPP, and fewer considered not voting than previously (Karp and Banducci 1999, 368). Those on the left of the ideological spectrum were also more likely to participate than previously. Although these changes were relatively modest, they nevertheless helped to stimulate turnout in 1996.

Given all this, we would have expected either a further increase in turnout in 1999, or at least some stabilisation around the increased 1996 figure. In the first MMP election, not all voters would have adjusted to the new system, and parties had still not fully adapted to the new geography of party competition under MMP (Denemark 1998). Across the whole country, the 1999 election was apparently more competitive than that of 1996. In 1996, National started out with a big lead in the polls and retained a comfortable lead at the end. In 1999, National and Labour were close rivals in the polls, and Labour drew away only toward the end of the campaign (see Chapter 2). Again, therefore, we would have expected higher turnout in 1999. However, perceptions of competitiveness at the time of voting are likely to be more decisive than judgements based on the election in general. By the last week of the 1996 campaign, because of Labour's ascent in the polls about half of the electors expected the party to be in government, indicating a high level of perceived competition (Vowles 1997). In 1999 that expectation was ten to twenty points higher over the same period (see Chapter 8). A comfortable Labour victory was widely predicted by election commentators just before election day, to the extent that party officials later expressed concern about possible turnout effects. Here is a possible partial answer to the puzzle.

The effect of the introduction of MMP on the relationship between turnout and competitiveness at the electorate level is shown in Figure 7.1, which compares the 1990 (FPP) and 1999 (MMP) elections. In 1990 there was a statistically significant relationship between electorate competitiveness and turnout (r=.79). The Maori electorates were major outliers, but even after removing them from the calculation, a statistically significant relationship remained among the general electorates (r=.54). Regression lines are shown in the tables for the calculations both with and without the Maori electorates. The steeper the lines, the stronger the relationship. Taking all electorates, for every 1 per cent increase in electorate safety, non-vote increased by about half a per cent. With the Maori electorates removed, the steepness of the slope of the 1990 regression line is halved, and the effect reduces to about a quarter of a percent.

Figure 7.1: Comparing Turnout by Electorate Safety/Marginality, 1990 and 1999 (Electorate Vote)

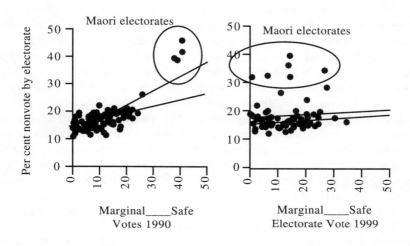

NOTE: The equations for 1990 are: for all including the Maori electorates, y=0.528x + 11.64 (r=0.79) and, for General electorates only, y=0.236x + 14.133 (r=0.54). For 1999: for all electorates they are y=0.055x + 17.505 (r=0.08), and for General only y=.055x + 15.914 (r=0.15).

The regression lines for the 1999 plot are far flatter. Indeed, under MMP, competition for the electorate vote hardly influences turnout at all, and the relationship is no longer statistically significant. Taking the Maori electorates out of the calculations, in 1990 the influence of electorate competitiveness on turnout was about four times that in 1999. Including the Maori electorates, the difference increases to tenfold. However, the Maori electorates in 1999 were outliers again. As the politics of the Maori electorates have changed for other reasons (see Chapter 5), it is probably not reasonable to ascribe all this difference to MMP. In 1999, the Maori electorates do not influence the slope of the probability estimate of the effects of competitiveness, but they reduce the strength of the correlation coefficient because of their greater distance from the regression line. The Maori electorates are still distinctive, but in a different way as compared to 1990. More generally, it seems clear that in their turnout behaviour, most voters have adapted to the national competition for the party vote under MMP, and this should enhance turnout.

If people need incentives or encouragement to vote, parties' mobilisation efforts may promote turnout. Parties can seek to mobilise the vote in at least two ways: by spending money, or by deploying volunteer workers. Logically, they will spend money where they think they can generate the best results. As candidates control some expenditure, we would still expect more spending in competitive electorates. Indeed, where there was closer competition for the electorate vote in 1999, taking all expenditures together in each electorate, candidates did spend more (r=0.19, b=0.29).[5] The same applied where party vote margins were close across the electorates, but this was an artefact of a high correlation between the party and electorate vote margins. Both theory and empirical analysis indicate that the electorate vote drives this relationship.[6] However, expenditure by electorate is only one part of total campaign expenditure and party mobilisation. Different political parties drawing on different sorts of supporters have different priorities in targeting their expenditures.

Table 7.1 displays official data reported to the Electoral Commission by the political parties, with figures in $000s. In the first column are the combined electorate expenditures of the various parties' candidates in the electorates, which are capped at $20,000 per candidate in each electorate. In the second column are the percentage changes since 1996. National failed to increase its expenditures for electorate contests in 1999, although it still spent more than Labour. Labour, however, increased its electorate-level expenditure by nearly 23 per cent, yet was the only party to do so. Total electorate-by-electorate expenditure by all parties in 1999 was 7 per cent lower than in 1996 (without adjusting for inflation).

In electorates where campaign expenditure was higher in 1996, turnout also appeared to be higher (r=0.30) — but not in 1999, when the relationship was not significant. Perhaps the lower level of 1999 expenditure in the electorates was partly responsible for the difference. But we need to be wary of over-simplifying possible causes and effects. There was a wide variation in the amounts spent in different electorates in 1999. Spending also appeared to be better targeted toward competitive electorates (r=0.19 in 1999, r=0.10 in 1996). This targeting was doubtless more difficult in 1996 given the change of electoral system. Nonetheless, electorate by electorate, variations in campaign expenditure had no association with turnout in 1999.

Table 7.1: Campaign Expenditures in 1999 and Percentage Changes from 1996

	Electorate		Central		Broadcasting		Total	
	$000	% change	$000	% change	$000	% change	$000	% change
National	937	–0.6	2140	50.1	597	10.5	3674	26.3
Labour	818	22.9	1039	23.1	606	38.8	2462	26.5
ACT	317	–10.2	656	–60.2	130	38.6	1104	–47.4
Alliance	284	–47.2	745	33.4	194	–22.6	1224	–9.2
NZ First	348	–37.1	108	–87.4	108	–56.7	565	–66.0
Green	95		236		43		374	
Others	424	1.1	313	–45.4	304	–37.0	1265	–14.2
Total	3223	–7.2	5238	–11.4	1983	–3.5	1044	–6.7

SOURCE: New Zealand Electoral Commission

The third and fourth columns in the table show party expenditure across the whole country. For electorate and national expenditure, the parties rely on funds they raise themselves or money they receive from private donations. The amount they have to spend, and how they allocate it between electorate and central campaigns, thus depends on the size of their war chests and their strategic priorities for that election. National spent close to the absolute maximum allowable for it under the Electoral Act, increasing its budget by 50 per cent over 1996.[7] Although Labour's central campaign expenditure was only half National's, it also increased by a healthy 23 per cent. ACT, however, went down heavily in the expenditure for its national campaign. It is tempting to suggest that many who donated heavily to ACT in 1996 may have channelled their funds to National in 1999. The Alliance, meanwhile, gave a greater priority to spending at the national level in 1999 than it had in 1996, no doubt in response to criticisms that in 1996 it had not campaigned as effectively as it should have done for the party vote. New Zealand First's drastic reduction of expenditure at both electorate and central levels reflects the party's split and dramatic electoral decline since 1996.

For the taxpayer-funded broadcasting funds allocated by the Electoral Commission to pay for campaign television presentations by the political parties (columns 5 and 6), Labour and ACT were the big winners, although National was also able to increase its expenditure slightly. Generally, small parties lost and the big two parties gained. Total party expenditure on the campaign was significantly down in 1999, the biggest decline being in the funds available for the national campaign for the party vote, even though National, Labour and the Alliance significantly increased their central campaign expenditures, a response that is consistent with the strategic importance of the overall party vote under MMP. But allowing for inflation, total party spending on the campaign was lower in 1999 by about 10 per cent in real terms, which could have influenced turnout.

What about other party activity that may help to mobilise voters? Even in the heyday of high voter turnout and more widespread and stronger party identification, political parties did not take for granted the voters' willingness to go to the polls. Because fewer voters were available for conversion in an age of stronger party loyalties, parties focused much of their campaigns on maximising the turnout of their supporters. In particular, for months before New Zealand elections, party volunteers would canvass street by street, identifying their party's supporters and the undecided, ensuring they were on the roll, and on election day, if necessary, encouraging and cajoling them to go out and vote.

In the 1990s, fewer people identify with a party, and fewer still express strong attachments (see Figure 6.2). If, as a consequence, people are less likely to vote, parties need to put even more effort into mobilising them to do so. Yet parties find it more difficult than in the past do this, because their memberships are lower, and they no longer have so many volunteer workers to canvass door to door (see Table 6.4). Instead, parties must rely on other means of contacting voters. Canvassing now takes place as much by telephone as door to door. Parties mail material to targeted groups of voters, or drop pamphlets in letterboxes and make less direct contact with householders. Contact by political parties enhances turnout (Kramer 1970; Rosenstone and Hansen 1993; Wielhouwer and Lockerbie 1994), and there is evidence that the more direct and frequent the contact between parties and voters, the more effective the mobilisation (Bochel and Denver 1971; 1972). Party organisational penetration into New Zealand communities can be associated with turnout (Vowles 1974).

A decline in such party contacts between elections and during the campaign could help to explain turnout decline.

Table 7.2: 1996 and 1999: Did Anyone from the Following Political Parties Contact You during the Campaign?

% Number contacts	1996	1999	1999 non-vote
0	8	17	25
1	8	11	18
2	11	13	21
3	12	16	12
4	15	10	10
5	27	21	13
6–7	14	9	8
8 or over	5	3	9
% all possible contacts	20	15	
N	2799	2924	2852

Table 7.2 compares the contacts between parties and voters reported by our respondents after the 1996 and 1999 election campaigns. The comparison is based on the same parties that contested both elections: National, Labour, New Zealand First, Alliance, and ACT. Green campaign contacts, included in the Alliance in 1996, were unfortunately not reported separately in the 1999 data. However, the Green contribution to the Alliance campaign in 1996 is likely to have been relatively minor. A substantial difference between the two elections quickly emerges: a larger proportion of the electorate received no contacts or only one or two, while a much smaller proportion recalled receiving multiple (more than four) contacts. From the five parties for which we have data, respondents could have been contacted in four different ways: by telephone at home, by a personal visit, being sent a letter, or given or sent a pamphlet. The maximum was therefore 20 contacts. Total campaign contacts as a percentage of all possible contacts were 20 per cent in 1996 and only 15 per cent in 1999.[8]

Table 7.3 compares the number of contacts of the five parties. In 1999, National's campaign contacts were down, but, to a lesser degree, so too were Labour's. New Zealand First was significantly down, the Alliance slightly so, and only ACT held its ground.[9]

Table 7.4 then breaks down the party contacts into four types — phone, visit, letter, and pamphlet. With only some exceptions, the table reveals a consistent decline across all parties and categories. National and Labour maintained their levels of personal visits, and the Alliance and ACT increased their reported contacts through personal letters. National dropped substantially in its reported phone contacts, Labour only slightly. The reasons for these differences almost certainly lie partly in the decline of party membership since 1996.

Does party contact enhance turnout? Looking back to Table 7.2, the cumulative effect of all types of party contacts shows a relatively strong influence. The last column in the table shows the rate of non-voting diminishing fairly

Table 7.3: Campaign Contacts, Percentage by Number, 1996 and 1999

		0	1	2	3	4	% all	N
National								
	1996	27	59	12	2	0	23	2861
	1999	38	55	7	1	0	18	2863
Labour								
	1996	21	61	16	2	0	25	2861
	1999	29	58	12	1	0	22	2863
Alliance								
	1996	31	62	6	1	0	19	2861
	1999	44	50	6	1	0	16	2863
ACT								
	1996	50	46	4	1	0	14	2861
	1999	54	42	5	0	0	13	2863
NZ First								
	1996	37	59	5	1	0	17	2861
	1999	67	32	2	0	0	9	2863

Table 7.4   Types of Contacts by Party, 1999 Election and (1996) Election, Percentages Contacted

	Phone	Visit	Letter	Pamphlet
National	2 (4)	3 (3)	17 (21)	49 (62)
Labour	3 (3)	4 (3)	24 (27)	55 (66)
Alliance	1 (1)	1 (4)	19 (8)	42 (63)
NZ First	1 (1)	1 (2)	5 (9)	29 (58)
ACT	1 (1)	1 (1)	13 (9)	37 (45)
Contacted by Any	6 (9)	8 (10)	42 (42)	68 (84)
Correlation of 1999				
non-vote by contact [r]	–0.00	–0.02	–0.05**	–0.12**

**significant at p=<.01

steadily as the number of reported contacts increased. What is surprising, and defies former findings, is the evidence in Table 7.4 that both kinds of personal contact — phone and visit — have minuscule effect, the correlation with non-vote not being statistically significant in either case. Letters and pamphlets, on the other hand, appear to be more effective. Perhaps the amount of personal contact is now so small that its effects are limited. Such contact may not be well targeted, as it requires electorate organisations with active members willing to do that work. Unless parties have adjusted to MMP and have built up organisations in safe seats, these organisations are likely to be weak in the very places where turnout was lower in the past and where such efforts might pay most dividends. On the other hand, the virtual absence of turnout differ-ences between competitive and non-competitive electorates under MMP indicates that if the parties have not yet sorted this out, most voters have. There are some indications of party adjustment. Personal contact seems well spread, and is only very slightly higher in competitive electorates. This is not unexpected. If parties' organisations were fully adapted to MMP, we would expect an even spread of total activity, with each party focusing more on their areas of concentrated support and little activity from others in those same areas. In competitive areas, we would expect activity to be more evenly balanced, but perhaps in total at least as high as elsewhere. And with motivated electorate candidates encouraging campaign contacts, one would expect slightly greater activity in the competitive electorates. This is indeed apparent, although only marginally so.

Deeper analysis of the campaign subsample in the 1999 data indicates that personal contact is more likely with people who said they were already intending to vote, and contact by letter or mail was even more likely to be with this group. Personal contact probably does influence a very small number of people to vote who might not otherwise have done so, but the numbers are too small to be statistically significant. The literature indicates that multiple personal contacts are most effective. We cannot test for this except by addition of different types of contact by party. For example, we do not know if someone who reported National party phone contact received one call or more than one. Only 15 per cent of those contacted by phone and 12 per cent of those visited were called or visited by more than one party (although multiple contacts go up to 21 per cent of personal contacts when visits and phone calls are put together). As for letters and pamphlets, there is reason for some scepticism about the effects found here. We might suspect that many less politically interested people receiving such material simply forget receiving it. Thus non-voters might simply be under-reporting such contact, and our findings would therefore be an artefact of this. However, when all of the potential explanations for turnout are put together, one can take account of the possible effects of respondents' interest in politics on their reporting of party contact (or lack of it).

One other source of political mobilisation remains, namely membership of organisations that, if not explicitly political, may become so. Trade unions, particularly those affiliated to the Labour party, often encourage their members and their families to vote, and provide organisational assistance to the Labour party. Internationally, union membership has been found to encourage turnout (Gray and Caul 2000). In the NZES samples people in households containing a union member declined from 25 per cent in 1996 to 20 per cent in 1999, indicating that declining union membership could be associated with turnout decline.

What about socio-economic and demographic changes? They are unlikely to have influenced turnout change greatly over a three-year period, unless their effects all run in the same direction. Maori and Pacific Island populations grew significantly, and each group has been shown to be less prone to vote in earlier studies. The population has only very slightly aged, which should enhance turnout. Moreover, young people entering the electorate are more highly educated than those leaving it, which should also enhance turnout. These small effects associated with a changing social structure therefore are likely to have offset each other, and are not likely to have significantly influenced turnout change.

Attitudes and Perceptions

Theory suggests that the effects of PR on attitudes can go in both directions. Jackman (1987) hypothesised and confirmed two potentially offsetting effects of PR on turnout. Turnout is probably encouraged by the equal value of all votes wherever they are cast, and by a greater sense of efficacy among those who favour small parties. However, if small parties capture a pivotal place in the party system, the formation of a government may be determined by negotiations between party leaders, not necessarily reflecting the preferences of a majority of voters. Where government formation is seen as lacking a popular mandate, turnout may be discouraged as voters — particularly those for disadvantaged major parties — may subsequently feel a lower sense of efficacy. As earlier chapters have shown, circumstances after the first PR election in New Zealand produced this situation. While most voters — including those for New Zealand First — expected the party to join with Labour in coalition, it eventually chose National (Miller 1998). The coalition collapsed in August 1998, and the subsequent fissure in New Zealand First meant that enough of its members defected to ensure a centre-right majority for the remainder of the parliamentary term. There was strong public disapproval of these developments (Karp and Bowler 2000).

Theory and evidence also indicate that economic adversity depresses turnout by inducing pessimism and passivity (Rosenstone 1982). One of the key election issues in New Zealand is the state of the economy. By the time of the 1999 election New Zealand's economic growth had recovered from the depths of the Asian crisis, and unemployment was little different from that at the time of the 1996 election. Moreover, despite the downturn in 1998, there had been some economic growth since 1996, more particularly in 1999, in the lead-up to the election (see Chapter 1). The first row in Table 7.5 indicates that there was more economic dissatisfaction in the air in 1999 than in 1996. In particular, most closely associated with non-voting were assessments of 'the state of the economy these days' and the 'financial situation of your household now compared to a year ago'. Put together, these form an index of economic dissatisfaction, which has a statistically significant association with turnout, albeit a small one.

Table 7.5 then sets out other indicators of attitudes and perceptions. Here we focus on the effects of people's perceptions of the political process under MMP. Between 1996 and 1999, if people developed lower expectations of government accountability because of coalition government, expressed less satisfaction with democracy, felt they were less effective in having their voices heard, and thus became less interested in politics, less attentive to the mass media, and less concerned about civic duty, we would surely expect them to be less inclined to bother voting. Such a response would also be consistent with aspects of rational choice theory. If people came to feel that their votes were less effective in determining the shape of post-election government, turnout would likely suffer. Finally, if people felt more alienated from political parties, and party identification declined, a drop in turnout would also follow.

Table 7.5: Attitudes, Perceptions and Non-voting

Scales between 0 and 10	1996	1999	Correlation with 1999 Non-vote	
Economic Dissatisfaction	4.6	5.1	0.06	**
Coalition Approval	6.1	5.3	0.01	
Satisfaction with Democracy	6.0	5.2	−0.08	**
Political Efficacy	4.0	4.2	−0.05	**
Interest in Politics	6.1	5.9	−0.20	**
Follow campaign in newspapers	5.8	6.1	−0.15	**
Civic Duty	8.1	8.1	−0.24	**
Strength Party Identification (0–10)	4.2	3.4	−0.10	**

* significant at >.05   **significant at >.01

NOTES: *Economic Dissatisfaction*: A scale 0–1, made up of responses to questions 'What do you think of the state of the economy these days in New Zealand?' (very good, good, neither, bad, or very bad) and 'How does the financial situation of your household now compare with what it was 12 months ago?' (a lot better, a little better, about the same, a little worse, a lot worse).
Coalition Approval: Responses to 'Do you think a government formed by one party or more than one party would be (1996) is (1999) better at doing the following things?', on four indicators: government stability, making tough decisions, keeping promises, and doing what the people want, scaled 0 to 1.
Satisfaction with Democracy: 'On the whole, are you very satisfied, fairly satisfied, not very satisfied, or not at all satisfied with the way democracy works in New Zealand?', scored 0 to 1.
Political Efficacy: made up of five-point agree or disagree responses as above to five questions: 'most members of Parliament are out of touch with the rest of the country'; 'people like me don't have any say about what the government does'; 'I don't think politicians and public servants care much about what people like me think'; 'you can trust the government to do what is right most of the time'; 'the New Zealand Government is largely run by a few big interests'. Scored 0 to 1.
Interest in Politics: 'Generally speaking, how much interest do you usually have in what's going on in politics?' (very, fairly, slightly, not at all), scored 0 to 1.
Attention to Newspapers: 'During the . . . campaign. How often did you follow political news, discussions, and advertising in newspapers?' (Often, sometimes, rarely, not at all), scored 0 to 1.
Civic Duty: Agreement or disagreement with 'It is a citizen's duty to vote', from strongly agree, agree, neutral, disagree, strongly disagree, scored 0 to 1.
Strength of Party Identification: Very strong partisans score 1, fairly strong .66, not very strong .33, and non-partisans 0.

As Table 7.5 shows, most but not all these expectations were met in reality. With the experience of the National–New Zealand First coalition in mind, people's approval of coalition compared to single-party government certainly declined between the two elections (see Chapter 11). The average score on a 10-point scale on this variable in 1996 was 6.1 per cent, giving a healthy edge to approval of coalitions. In 1999 the average score was closer to an even balance between approval and disapproval. However, preference for coalitions versus single party government had absolutely no influence on turnout in 1999, throwing doubt on the claim that disappointment with coalitions might be responsible for turnout decline.

Closer to expectations, but again with cross-cutting effects on turnout, there is evidence of a decline in satisfaction with the way democracy works, a perception that correlates with turnout decline. On the other hand, political efficacy slightly increased in 1999. While it is possible that as the survey was conducted after the election, efficacy levels may have been influenced by respondents' knowledge of the election result, nonetheless, people who felt greater political efficacy post-election were significantly more likely to have voted. However the relationship is a very weak one, and therefore unlikely to have substantive effects.

Interest in politics slightly declined between the two elections, consistent with a lower turnout, but against that people paid slightly more attention to following the campaign in newspapers in 1999 than they had in 1996, which would have the opposite effect of shoring up turnout. However, the largest correlation with vote or non-vote is generated by people's sense of civic duty, a variable based on agreement or disagreement with the statement 'it is a citizen's duty to vote'. While there was strong agreement with this assertion in 1999, it was no stronger than it had been in 1996. Thus one of the most important determinants of turnout was unchanged between the two elections, and cannot help us explain the turnout decline in 1999.

There is also a close association, well established in the literature on voting, between party identification and turnout. Indeed, recent comparative research suggests that this association might underpin the higher average turnout in countries having proportional representation compared to other voting systems. Under PR, voters usually have a wider choice of viable parties, possibly enabling a larger number of voters to feel more closely attuned to one or another party (Karp and Banducci 2000). Regardless of the electoral system, however, a decline in party identification can be expected to contribute to a decline in turnout. This has certainly been so in New Zealand up to the 1990s. At the first MMP election in 1996, the level of party identification rose, and most of all, the proportion of voters with 'strong' or 'fairly strong' identifications. Turnout also tracked upwards. But the trend was short-lived. Between 1996 and 1999, party identification declined again, those with 'strong' or 'fairly strong' identifications slipping back 7 per cent. The bottom row of Table 7.5 confirms this movement. Whatever contributed to the softening of partisanship between 1996 and 1999 also added momentum to the parallel decline of turnout.

Putting the Explanations Together

Changes between the 1996 and 1999 elections across a number of different dimensions indicate a number of likely influences on turnout decline. Because the samples include almost no people who were not on the rolls, valid votes on an enrolment basis have to be used to estimate the reasons for turnout decline. On an enrolment basis, turnout declined by about 3.4 percentage points between 1996 and 1999 — about the same as on an age-eligible base.

Figure 7.2 reports the results of a multivariate analysis of turnout decline (Vowles 2001a).[10] The addition of variables starts with social structure and demography and proceeds 'round the clock'. Social structure, demographic change, and union decline are all long-term effects, so they come first. Next comes economic dissatisfaction, which turns out to have a fairly significant effect. Dissatisfaction with MMP and coalitions, however, explains virtually no turnout decline. The biggest effects are declining party identification and campaign contact. These have been added last in this decomposition of the difference between non-vote in 1996 and 1999, so if anything underestimating their effects.

Figure 7.2. Accounting for Turnout Decline, 1996–1999

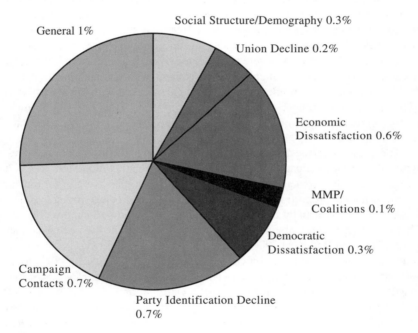

General 1%

Social Structure/Demography 0.3%

Union Decline 0.2%

Economic
Dissatisfaction 0.6%

MMP/
Coalitions 0.1%

Democratic
Dissatisfaction 0.3%

Campaign
Contacts 0.7%

Party Identification Decline
0.7%

SOURCE: Vowles 2001a.

Assuming the remaining 'unexplained' difference is real, and not an arte-fact of sampling error, what possible explanations are left to account for it? The model from which these findings are derived could not measure the effect of two variables: a decline in total campaign expenditure, and perceptions that the result of the election was no longer in doubt by the time of voting. However, examination of the campaign panel finds little evidence that rising expectations that Labour would form a government had any effect on the intention to vote at the campaign's end, or on the decision to vote itself. As for the effects of a decline in total campaign expenditure, or, for that matter, of a relatively un-exciting campaign, one can only speculate.

Net of the effects of all other variables, Maori were 9 per cent more likely not to vote, taking the 1996 and 1999 elections together. Taking each election separately, Maori became almost twice more likely not to vote in 1999 as they were in 1996 (by about 11 per cent to 7 per cent). Younger people also became less likely to vote in 1999, despite the strong appeal of the Greens to younger voters (see Chapter 6). Campaign contacts enhance turnout. Precisely, each type of campaign contact by party could improve the chance of an individual voting by 0.7 of a percentage point, net of the effects of all other variables (for example, the chance might increase from 15 per cent to 15.7 per cent). Location in a union household increased the probability of voting by about 3 per cent, again, all other things being equal. Declining union membership therefore had measurable effects on turnout that might be expected to reverse if union membership recovers in New Zealand, as it is likely to do as a consequence of changes in industrial law under the Labour–Alliance government. Economic dissatisfaction had some effects, bigger in 1999. Attention to newspapers, political interest, civic duty and party identification had substantial effects overall, although the effects of party identification weakened in 1999, so much so that it dropped out of statistical significance when controlling for the effects of all the other variables (Vowles 2001a).

Against the hypothesis that perceptions of lack of accountability in co-alition governments reduce turnout, approval or disapproval of coalitions or of MMP had no effect on turnout decline. More general dissatisfaction with democracy played some role, however, but in combination with other variables not necessarily linked to electoral system change. Contrary to expectations, disillusion with the effects of MMP, of which there was still a great deal in 1999, does not seem to have at all strongly influenced turnout decline. This leaves open the possibility that the move to PR might have staved off an otherwise more drastic continuation in 1999 of the long-term downward trend. There is some evidence of this in the increase in support for the Green party, only electorally viable under MMP, which drew heavily on young voters who otherwise might not have voted under FPP. More obviously, the most potent variables discovered in the quest to explain turnout decline — campaign contact, location in a union household, and party identification — represent features that can respond to organisational mobilisation: the recruitment of union members, and the revival of party organisations and of individual loyalties to political parties. Whether the key political actors and the broader public in New Zealand are together willing or able to bring about that re-mobilisation in the coming years is an open question.

CHAPTER 8

COALITION GOVERNMENT:
THE LABOUR–ALLIANCE PACT

Raymond Miller

With the advent of coalition government a major new fault line appeared beneath the surface of New Zealand politics. Almost from the moment of its formation in December 1996 the National–New Zealand First government was the object of public opprobrium and distrust. Throughout the coalition's eighteen-month tenure the brunt of the public's attack was borne by New Zealand First, a party troubled by weak management, poor internal discipline and little political experience. Of the party's seventeen MPs, only Winston Peters had a background in government, and thirteen were completely new to Parliament. The coalition's collapse in August 1998 was triggered by a seemingly minor skirmish over National's decision to sell the Crown's shares in Wellington Airport. Peters and three of his colleagues walked out of the weekly cabinet meeting in protest, the Prime Minister announced the New Zealand First leader's dismissal, and the first coalition of the new MMP era was at an end.

Between elections the Labour Opposition attempted to restore a measure of public confidence in coalition government by establishing the basis for a workable arrangement with the Alliance, the details of which were not finalised until after the 1999 votes had been cast. Although relations between the two centre-left parties remained strained, even acrimonious, both wished to avoid a repetition of the circumstances of 1996, when their failure to reach a pre-election agreement was compounded by the Alliance's steadfast refusal to negotiate after polling day. The resulting impasse had clearly frustrated the will of the voting public, the largest proportion of whom favoured a Labour–Alliance government over other available options. By the time of the 1999 election the seeds of a future centre-left coalition had begun to take root.

This chapter explores campaign attitudes toward coalition government. While the public's unfamiliarity with coalition government and the absence of any pre-election coalition agreements help to explain any significant variations in voter opinion in 1996, the emergence of centre-right and centre-left blocs might reasonably be expected to lead to more stable coalition preferences at the 1999 election. The chapter goes on to discuss the Labour–Alliance coalition's performance both in formation and in government. It has been said that coalition parties pursue three goals. In an attempt to maximise their *office-seeking* goals, prospective coalition partners negotiate for executive positions, both inside and outside of cabinet, that will both enhance their public profile and reap the material benefits that flow from political power. *Policy-seeking* behaviour, on the other hand, is directed toward maximising the party's policy objectives. Such behaviour is based on the assumption that coalition partners are prepared to look for common ground, even to the point of compromising important principles and policies. This may involve risks, including criticism that the party leaders have been out-manoeuvred by their counterparts, or worse, that they have betrayed the public's trust. The third, *vote-seeking*, goal is based on the assumption that there is a close correlation between the number of votes a party gets and its entitlement to the spoils of office, including the allocation of portfolios and policies (Muller and Ström 1999, 5–11). Because there is little likelihood that all three goals can be achieved at the same time, government formation typically involves compromises or trade-offs. If, for example, a party seeks to maximise the number of seats it holds in cabinet, it may have to sacrifice important policies. It may even be necessary for a party to withdraw from the government in order to win back lost party members or votes.

With a parliamentary review of the MMP system having begun in 2000, from the outset Labour and the Alliance were under pressure to demonstrate a capacity for effective and long-term government. As we will see, among the terms of their coalition negotiations were a commitment to a speedy negotiations process, a briefer and more open coalition document, allowing both parties room for disagreement under the terms of a more liberal interpretation of the principle of collective cabinet responsibility, and fair recognition of the relative strength of each partner when prioritising policies and allocating executive positions. This process and the resulting trade-offs left the Alliance with few substantive policy gains, an unwelcome situation for any small coalition partner, but especially one in competition for votes with a resurgent Labour party and the Greens.

Background to the Labour–Alliance pact

In contrast to the declining fortunes of National in partnership with New Zealand First, beginning in late 1996 Labour enjoyed its first significant revival of popular support in over a decade. At its peak, support for Labour reached 52 per cent (see Chapter 1). This led to speculation that, despite the intensely competitive electoral environment of MMP, Labour might conceivably expect to garner a sufficiently large share of the vote to be able to govern alone. Although refusing to dismiss the possibility, the Labour leader, Helen Clark, had come to see the Alliance in the same way as Tony Blair viewed the Liberal Democrats, that is, as Labour's best hope for a second, and perhaps third, term in government. Her guest appearance at the 1998 Alliance conference paved the way for joint meetings of the two parties' senior politicians, extra-parliamentary officials and advisers (Boston and Church 2000, 233–4). Opponents of this strategy warned that the Alliance's doctrinal inflexibility and political inexperience would lead to an attrition of votes on Labour's right flank. However compelling their argument was when Labour's popularity was at its peak, it became less relevant in the lead-up to the 1999 election, when the party's support began to slide back below 40 per cent (One Network News/Colmar Brunton, 10 August 1999).

Adding impetus to the Labour–Alliance initiative was a mutual desire to exploit the growing disarray among National's allies on the centre-right. Following Winston Peters' dismissal from cabinet in 1998 and the formation of a minority National government whose very survival depended on nine defections from the New Zealand First caucus, there appeared to be little prospect of a post-1999-election reconciliation between National and what remained of New Zealand First. To compound National's problems, ACT had made it clear that it would neither join nor support any coalition that included New Zealand First (*New Zealand Herald*, 2–3 October 1999). With the fledgling Mauri Pacific and United parties barely registering in opinion polls, the chances of another National-led government looked increasingly grim. Employing his trademark opaqueness, during the 1999 election campaign Peters both encouraged speculation that he might go into coalition with National and ridiculed the possibility when pressed by journalists. Such tactics simply compounded National's problems and encouraged the party's strategists, including its president, John Slater, to speculate about the possibility of a grand coalition with Labour (for example, *New Zealand Herald*, 26 September 1999).

Securing a pre-election compact with Labour provided the Alliance with at least two important benefits. First, there appeared to be strong public endorsement of the principle of prearranged coalition partnerships, mainly on the grounds that it would remove some of the unwanted doubt from the election contest and outcome. Indeed, a prearranged agreement might conceivably add some legitimacy to the Alliance's election campaign. Second, forging such an agreement reduced the risk that the Alliance might be outmanoeuvred in any post-election negotiations, particularly with New Zealand First, but also with the Greens. A slight resurgence in support for New Zealand First part-way through the campaign gave rise to media speculation that Winston Peters might once again be in a position to wield the balance of power (*New Zealand Herald*, 23–4 October 1999). To Anderton's consternation, Clark refused to rule out the possibility of dealing with Peters in the event that he stood between Labour and the Treasury benches. Compounding Anderton's concerns was the late surge in support for the Greens. The suggestion that the small environmental party might insist on being part of the coalition caused Anderton to respond dismissively: 'I want a strong stable government, and even the most casual glance at the Green candidate list gives no confidence that would be the result' (*New Zealand Herald*, 27 October 1999). As it eventuated, the coalition agreement was concluded quickly, and before the Green party's place in Parliament had been confirmed.

Even before the election, the Alliance was forced to review all major obstacles to a smooth working relationship with Labour. Whereas ACT and New Zealand First had a number of policies on which they refused to negotiate, the Alliance's approach was surprisingly flexible, as exemplified by the decision to flatten out its income tax rates to make them consistent with Labour's (*New Zealand Herald*, 28 September 1999). What this policy trade-off implied was a willingness to accept Labour's commitment to a free-market agenda, a major concession given the Alliance's long-standing opposition to economic liberalism. While the decision may have helped to assuage the fears of those Labour-leaning voters who believed that the Alliance was incapable of significant compromise, it failed to prevent the occasional spat with Labour. On one occasion, for example, the two party leaders crossed swords over Clark's claim that the Alliance's dismal poll ratings were due to its excessively ambitious policies, including the abolition of tertiary fees, free health care and an extra week's annual holiday for workers (*New Zealand Herald*, 19 October 1999). Yet throughout the campaign, as in government, Anderton demonstrated a capacity for ideological flexibility and moderation.

Public attitudes to coalition government and MMP

An important starting point for any investigation into attitudes toward coalition government is the level of public satisfaction with MMP. While the new electoral system enjoyed strong approval among Labour and Alliance voters in 1996, their enthusiasm was severely tested by the formation of a centre-right government. A vast majority of National voters, on the other hand, had always disliked MMP, largely on the grounds that it was unlikely to produce their preferred 'decisive' single-party government. The views of National voters were only marginally affected by their party's retention of power in 1996 (Vowles, Aimer, Banducci and Karp 1998, 207).

Since the 1996 election, support for MMP appears closely associated with changes in support for government parties: National and New Zealand First before August 1998, National alone until the election, and Labour and Alliance afterward. If a government becomes more popular, MMP becomes more popular too (UMR–Insight 2001). The effects turn out to be both qualitative and quantitative: that is, when the composition of a government changed, as in August 1998 and November 1999, the level of support for MMP changed substantially, but most of all after the 1999 election. Within each government period, support for MMP also varies. As a regression based on the data in Figure 8.1 shows, allowing for the effects of changes between government periods, between the 1996 election and June 2001, for every 1 per cent increase in support for the government, support for MMP rose by 0.19 per cent. At the collapse of the National–New Zealand First coalition in 1998 and after the general election of 1999, support for MMP tended to increase, with a rise of 1.6 per cent after the first event, and 7.3 per cent after the second.

While the lowest preference for coalition government was among National voters, the most significant results concern attitudes within Labour. With the party leadership having made a commitment to a coalition with the Alliance, one in two intending Labour voters had a preference for coalition government in the run-up to the election (see Table 8.1). Intending voters for small parties, including ACT, naturally had higher levels of support for coalition government. However, these figures conceal variations within the campaign. Figure 8.2

Figure 8.1: Support for MMP and Support for Government Parties

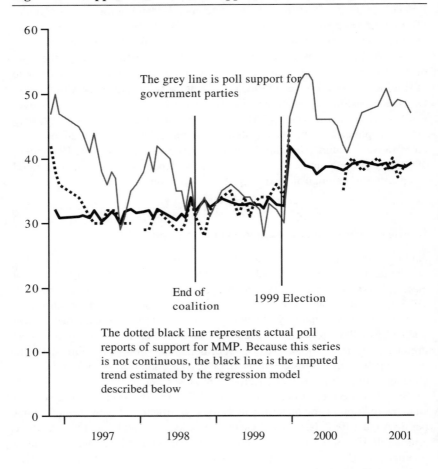

SOURCE: UMR–Insight polls, 1996–2001. Thanks are due to Stephen Mills for permission to use this data.

NOTE: The continuous black line shows support for MMP imputed from regression equation y=31.43 (.48)** + 0.19 *change in government support (0.08*) +7.25*LABALL (.81**) + 1.59*NATALONE (0.73*). The adjusted r-squared is 0.68. LABALL scores 1 after the 1999 election, 0 before it, NATALONE 0 before September 1998, 1 after it. Standard errors are indicated in brackets and ** indicates significance >.01, * >.05. Note that in the regression, although not in the figure, change in government support is a change variable, based on government support at time t minus support at time t-1. The intercept of the equation, 31.4, reflects baseline MMP support which is more concentrated among voters for parties of the left than the right. Change in government support therefore indicates movements among people volatile both in their voting behaviour and in their attitudes to MMP.

shows that, among Labour voters, single-party government preferences had a small lead over coalition government preferences early in the campaign, but then coalition government preferences began to move ahead. But this data also reveals movements among National voters. In particular, as Figure 8.2 shows, National voters appear to have responded to higher levels of support for small parties at the beginning of the campaign (see Chapter 2) by moving strongly against coalition government.

Table 8.1: Single-Party versus Coalition Government, 1999 Campaign, by Intending Voters

	Single-party	Coalition	Don't Know	N
Green	22	75	3	55
Alliance	22	74	5	138
Labour	48	50	2	581
National	62	35	3	489
ACT	38	61	1	110

Figure 8.2: Preference for Single-Party or Coalition Outcome: National and Labour Voters, 1999 Campaign

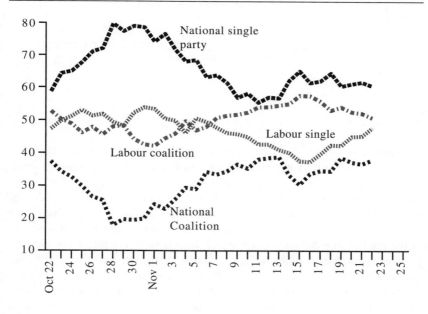

NOTE: 9-day rolling averages, campaign panel subsample.

Figure 8.3 shows that as the 1999 campaign progressed, the expectation of a centre-left coalition solidified. Early on, the two major parties were neck and neck in the polls (see Chapter 2), but drew apart toward election day. Expectations of a Labour-led government well exceeded Labour's poll margin until late in the campaign. This probably reflected Labour's more consistent poll lead for most of the period since the 1996 election and the message of more recent polls that, while the margin was small, Labour remained ahead. As polls indicated a wider lead, from about 18 November onward, Labour expectations drew well ahead of National's. Meanwhile expectations that New Zealand First would join the next government fell steadily as the campaign progressed.

Figure 8.3: Campaign Coalition Expectations

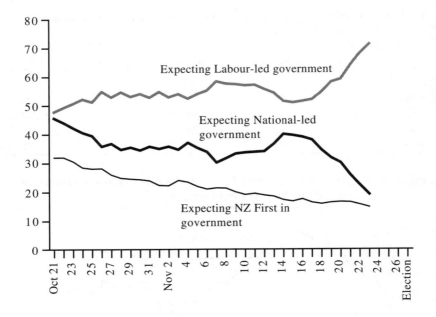

NOTE: 7-day rolling averages, campaign panel subsample.

Even more interesting than variations in voter expectations, however, were those concerned with voter preferences (see Figure 8.4). The possible sensitivity of public opinion to the prospect of inter-party disagreement can be illustrated with reference to two significant campaign events (Vowles 2000a, 154–5). On 10 November, Television New Zealand's One Network News, the most popular news source in the country, reported that 'cracks' had appeared in the relationship between Labour and the Alliance. Despite a pre-election pact not to attack each other during the campaign, the two had begun to 'bicker over a cabinet post and two billion dollars'. According to this, the top story in the 6 p.m. news bulletin, Labour's finance spokesman and deputy leader, Michael Cullen, had described the Alliance's $6.4 billion dollar spending promises over the following three years as being based on 'heroic assumptions'. He contrasted Labour's private-sector-driven economic development programme with the publicly administered Alliance proposal. According to Cullen, 'A central government bureaucracy in our view would not interrelate well with the New Zealand private sector'. Labour's deputy leader also denied that there were any plans to appoint Anderton to the cabinet position of Minister of Economic Development. Anderton rejected any suggestion that his party's spending proposal was 'heroic' and claimed that Helen Clark had already agreed to his request that he be given the Economic Development portfolio. Perhaps the most potentially damaging feature of the Network News story were the comments of the political editor, Linda Clark, who reminded viewers of past 'bitter' and 'nasty' fights between Anderton and Cullen, concluding that, if they were unable to agree on the campaign trail, 'Then voters will inevitably judge them down for it come election day'. Linda Clark added that National and ACT were of the view that this was a precursor to the sort of problems Labour and the Alliance would have working together after polling day. As Figure 8.4 shows, 10 November marked the high point in the level of public support for a Labour–Alliance coalition. Thereafter the preference of voters for a centre-left coalition tracked steadily downwards, albeit recovering somewhat as the election drew near.

Figure 8.4: Campaign Coalition Preferences

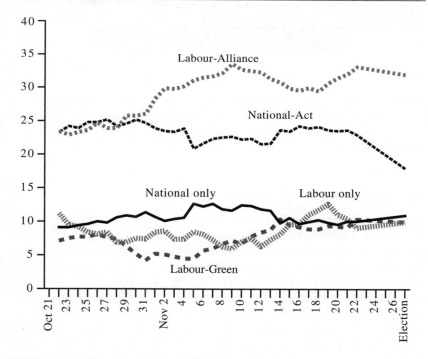

NOTE: 7-day rolling averages, campaign panel subsample.

A second campaign development that may have impacted on the coalition preferences of voters was an attack by National on ACT's economic policies. Largely motivated by concern that the National vote was being 'cannibalised' by ACT (*New Zealand Herald*, 16 November 1999), two of National's most prominent ministers, Bill English and Simon Upton, warned that the party's commitment to substantial tax cuts would lead to a $2.7 billion reduction in social spending (*New Zealand Herald*, 15 November 1999). They went even further in claiming that any substantial reduction in the top tax rate would have a similar effect on social services to that of Ruth Richardson's deeply unpopular 'Mother of all Budgets' of 1991. Despite assurances from Richard

Prebble that his party was not eating into the National vote, the disagreement resulted in an immediate and significant decline in support for a National–ACT government (see Figure 8.4). Prebble later acknowledged that the competition between National and ACT for the party vote in the final week of the campaign had damaged his party's chances of securing a better result (*New Zealand Herald*, 29 November 1999). As coalition preferences reveal (see Figure 8.5), Labour was the most warmly favoured party to form a government, followed by a combination of Labour and the Alliance and/or the late-rising Greens.

Figure 8.5: Labour–Alliance–Green Coalition Preferences

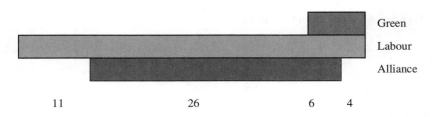

NOTE: This figure shows overlaps between the preferences for party-in-government for the centre-left parties (i.e. 11 per cent Labour alone, 26 per cent Labour–Alliance, 6 per cent Labour–Alliance–Green, 4 per cent Labour–Green).
SOURCE: Full post-election sample.

The role and efficacy of small parties

As agents of protest under FPP, the electoral support of small parties waxed and waned. Under MMP, their success has been more limited than many expected. In the unfamiliar role of junior coalition partner, both New Zealand First and the Alliance seem to have been required to shoulder the blame for the failures of coalition government, while apparently being denied any significant opportunity to share in its success. Although support for New Zealand First averaged 19 per cent in the twelve months leading up to the 1996 election, during its first year as a coalition partner its popularity plunged. The Alliance suffered also, dropping from an average of 6.7 per cent in the twelve months leading up to the 1999 election in One News/Colmar Brunton polls to 3.7 per cent during its first year in office. According to rival pollster UMR Insight, the Alliance may have been faring better, as an average of its polling for the Alliance over the same period is a more respectable 5.8 per cent. But even this was lower than the Alliance election-day vote of 7.8 per cent. Ironically, the Alliance's decline, whatever its extent, occurred even though the coalition as a whole was enjoying strong support.

New Zealand First provided a particularly negative experience of small-party coalition behaviour following the 1996 election. Only one of the party's eight new ministers had ever served on the executive (indeed, four were completely new to Parliament), there was little understanding of the importance of compromise or trade-offs in the party's dealings with its coalition partner, and by August 1998 it had suffered the defection of eight of its original 17-member caucus. Given these problems, it is hardly surprising that almost 60 per cent of intending National voters in 1999 were of the view that MMP gives small parties too much power, an opinion shared by followers of ACT. Labour voters were split between those who believe that small parties have excessive power (47 per cent) and those who do not (39 per cent).

Table 8.2: Campaign Opinion: MMP Gives Too Much Power to Small Parties

	Agree	Disagree	Neutral/ Don't know	N
All	47	39	14	1688
Labour	47	39	14	581
Alliance	35	54	11	138
National	59	30	12	489
ACT	53	40	8	110

The possibility that New Zealand First might again hold the balance of power was mooted frequently during the campaign. Jenny Shipley refused to rule out the possibility of conducting coalition talks with Peters (*NZ Herald*, 25 October 1999). For his part, the New Zealand First leader indicated that he might be prepared to talk to National, a prospect likely to have struck fear in the hearts of many National voters. Having declared his willingness to exploit any potential for influence with a centre-right government, Peters then targeted the centre-left. In particular, he threatened to block any plans by a Labour-led government to increase the tax rates for high-income earners. Labour's deputy leader, Michael Cullen, warned: 'We cannot afford to have a situation where Mr Peters tries to hold either potential government to ransom' (*New Zealand Herald*, 29 October 1999). Cullen's sentiments were echoed by respondents to a media poll, two-thirds of whom emphatically rejected any coalition involving New Zealand First (*New Zealand Herald*, 5–6 November 1999).

Halfway through the campaign, a One Network News/Colmar Brunton poll reported that Labour and National were running neck and neck and that Peters was set to become 'queenmaker' (One Network News, 12 November 1999). The report made the unambiguous claim that, with its seven seats, New Zealand First 'will hold the balance of power' and Peters 'will determine who governs'. This coincided with the resignation of New Zealand First's top-ranking party list candidate, Suzanne Bruce, amid reports that she was under investigation for tax fraud, and the allegation of a former New Zealand First minister, Robyn McDonald, that her relegation to twentieth place on the list simply confirmed that Peters was sexist and unworthy of the public's trust. While Shipley stated that 'I can work with anyone and any group of people who will put New Zealand's interests first', and Clark confirmed that she could 'work with anyone in the interests of the country', their prospective coalition partners disagreed. Prebble alleged that it was 'not possible to work with Mr Peters', and Anderton warned that 'having someone sitting across the way, sniping all the time and holding the country to ransom . . . is not a pretty look'. However, this media speculation about a future role in government for New Zealand First failed to stem the fall in intended votes for New Zealand First, or the steadily declining expectations that the party would form part of the next government.

Compatibility and Trust

Given the hostility between Labour and the Alliance during the early 1990s (see Miller and Catt 1993; Jesson 1997, 156–64), their mutual capacity for constructive government has always been an issue of public interest and concern. In response to the post-election survey question, 'Would you describe the Alliance as trustworthy or not trustworthy?', only one in three Labour voters deemed the Alliance to be trustworthy. Given that the coalition partnership had still to be tested, it is hardly surprising that a majority of Labour voters in the survey (51 per cent) reserved judgement on the matter. Sharing their caution were the former Alliance members, the Greens, only 27 per cent of whose voters found the Alliance to be trustworthy. But lack of trust is endemic to New Zealand politics (Karp and Banducci 1998, 155), as illustrated by the refusal of a significant 37 per cent of the Alliance's own voters to confirm that the Alliance was worthy of their trust, and 42 per cent of Labour voters to do the same for Labour. The attitudes of Alliance respondents toward Labour mirrored those of Labour voters with respect to the Alliance. In response to a separate question on their second most preferred party (after their own), half of all Alliance voters chose Labour and approximately the same proportion of Labour voters opted for the Alliance, followed by National (18 per cent) and the Greens (6 per cent).

One measure of compatibility is the extent to which preferences for one party's policies can be found among intending voters for another. Respondents were asked which party's views came closest to their own on a range of policies. Few Labour voters felt that the Alliance came closest to their position on the economy, taxes, health care and law and order: naturally enough most preferred Labour, the party for which they intended to vote. On the issue of taxation, for example, only 8 per cent of Labour voters agreed that the Alliance came closest to their views. But while Labour voters failed to choose Alliance policies, Alliance voters were more disposed to choose Labour's. For example, 38 per cent of Alliance voters favoured the tax policies being advanced by Labour, perhaps partly because, Labour being a major party, its policies were better known and more extensively covered by the media. Similarly on health, where the differences in policy between the two parties are relatively minor, only 12 per cent of Labour voters favoured the Alliance's policies. In contrast, over 45 per cent of Alliance voters identified with the policies of Labour (compared with only 40 per cent for their own party). On both taxation and the economy more intending Labour voters claimed a proximity to National than to the Alliance, indicating a larger number of Labour voters were closer to the centre than to the left.

Despite these examples of uneven policy overlap, with Alliance voters tending to favour Labour policies but not the reverse, an overriding desire to give the relationship time provided the most significant point of contrast with the centre-right coalition of 1996 to 1998. Any undercurrents of bitterness and distrust were much more subdued than they were between National and New Zealand First. The time taken to prepare the parties and voters for the Labour–Alliance union obviously helped, as did the measured language and modest ambitions of Anderton. Freed from the uncertainty, as well as the 'Peters-effect', of 1996, the voters were clearly of a mind to suspend judgement until the new coalition had been given a chance to establish its structures and priorities.

Political Response

In addition to the public response to coalition government, a multifaceted political accord was put in place within days of the 1999 election. As part of its plan to provide effective and long-term government, Labour promised initiatives designed to improve the formation, management and discipline of a centre-left coalition. Ironically, the main architects of these reforms, the party leader, Helen Clark, and deputy leader, Michael Cullen, had been leading critics of MMP. Although hardly constituting a rescue package for MMP, the reforms were intended to boost public confidence in coalition government. However, as the opinion polls soon revealed, while the resulting public optimism had positive spin-offs for Labour, the same could not be said for the Alliance.

Table 8.3: Parties Should Announce Their Coalition Intentions in Advance

	Agree	Disagree	Neutral/ Don't know	N
All	78	14	8	1685
Labour	83	11	5	581
Alliance	83	5	13	139
National	75	16	9	488
ACT	79	18	3	109

As we have seen, the time taken, secrecy, and unknown outcome of the 1996 coalition talks were major deterrents to public acceptance of coalition government. As the data in Table 8.3 show, there was overwhelming public endorsement across all four main parties for the principle of prearranged coalition partnerships.[1] New Zealand's two-party tradition led voters to expect clear-cut election results, with the winning party generally known on election night. During the two-month negotiating period in 1996 there had been growing concern over what some voters came to regard as a vacuum of power.

Given the lateness of the 1999 election, there was a speedy resolution of the talks by virtue of two events: the imminence of the Christmas break, and the prospect that the Alliance and Labour had the option of sharing power with the Greens. The Green party missed out on representation on election night, but a week later after the counting of special votes crossed the 5 per cent threshold and received seven seats, including the electorate of Coromandel, captured by Jeanette Fitzsimons. Clearly it was in neither Labour's nor the Alliance's interests to draw the negotiations out. As a result, they were able to announce the terms of the new government within a mere seven days.

While New Zealand First had made every effort to extract a range of policy concessions from National in their 1996 coalition negotiations, as exemplified by the 74-page Coalition Agreement,[2] the patience and guile shown by National's senior ministers gradually produced their rewards. As time passed, the junior partner was drawn into accepting policies that were both absent from the Agreement and at odds with the underlying principles and objectives of New Zealand First. Among the lessons learned from this unhappy experience was the importance of placing issues of process ahead of policy. As a result, the Labour–Alliance document focused on a commitment to 'consensus management and the avoidance of surprises'. In a document of little more than one page, the two parties formally acknowledged the principle of collective cabinet responsibility, with the proviso that the Cabinet Manual be revised to give the junior partner scope to adopt an independent position on matters it deemed to be important but which did not undermine the stability of the coalition (Boston 2001, 126–7). While it was thought to be unlikely that the safety-valve provision would be employed very often, it did offer the Alliance some freedom to distance itself from the policies of its senior partner, especially in the competitive environment immediately preceding an election.

One of the most controversial and popular of Labour's proposals was its anti-defection legislation, which was designed to ensure that MPs who defect from their parties immediately resign their seats. Had New Zealand First's ministers not defected under pressure from the Prime Minister, Jenny Shipley, in 1998, there is no reason to believe that the coalition would have survived. However, given the slim majorities enjoyed by recent governments, and bearing in mind the potential for embarrassment if any of the 59 members of the present minority coalition (together with the seven Green MPs who have agreed to support the government on key legislative initiatives) defect, the proposed legislation is seen to be a necessary prerequisite to stable government.

Despite opposition from National, ACT and the Greens (all on the grounds that it breaches individual freedom and gives unnecessary power to party elites), the Electoral (Integrity) Amendment Bill was introduced in December 1999. The Associate Minister of Justice, Margaret Wilson, conceded that 'Stability is one of the main reasons the new government is so keen to have this legislation passed'. She added: 'Not only do MPs who have defected from their parties undermine the proportionality of Parliament, they also undermine the credibility of government in New Zealand.' (*Dominion*, 23 December 1999.) An earlier version of the bill gave political parties the right to expel dissident members from the caucus, thereby triggering their inevitable expulsion from Parliament. Following criticism that it placed too much power in the hands of the parliamentary leadership, the bill was amended to put the onus on each disaffected member to tender his or her resignation from parliamentary party membership. Because the government expects the incidence of defections to drop once proportional representation has had time to bed in, the legislation was designed to last for a period of no more than six years. Due to opposition from other parties, including the Greens, further consideration of the anti-defection bill was deferred until after the report of the MMP Review Committee was released in mid-2001.

The stability and discipline of the coalition was tested sooner than expected. In the wake of a substantial decline in business confidence, partly fuelled by fears that the coalition's stance was anti-business, the Prime Minister either postponed or rejected a range of policy proposals, including several being promoted by senior Alliance ministers. Among those she vetoed were proposals for an extra week's annual leave, employer-funded parental leave, and an increase in the minimum youth rate (*New Zealand Herald*, 3–4 June 2000). However, she was not able to prevent Alliance members from opposing Labour's Singapore Free Trade Agreement (a measure that was passed with the support of National). In the words of Clark: 'What is the most fundamental fear of mainstream voters, is that the Alliance will drag Labour too far to the left' (*New Zealand Herald*, 11 June 2000). While her decision provoked an angry response from Alliance ministers and MPs, relations were not allowed to deteriorate to a point where they threatened to destabilise the coalition. However, by early 2001 the Alliance's lack of significant policy gains made it politically imperative that the cabinet accept Anderton's proposal for a 'Kiwi People's Bank', the misgivings of senior Labour ministers notwithstanding.

In the event that Labour withheld its support from any of the Alliance's policy initiatives, the junior partner had virtually no chance of securing a parliamentary majority (Boston 2000, 261). Whereas Labour (49 votes) could pitch for support from the Greens (7 votes), New Zealand First (5 votes), and perhaps even National (39 votes), the Alliance's only realistic source of parliamentary support lay with the Greens. Its credibility as a coalition partner was further weakened by opinion polls reporting its support well below that it received at the 1999 election. Tensions developed between Anderton and the party's left wing, notably the minister, Laila Harré, and president, Matt McCarten, over the leader's unwillingness to tolerate dissent over the direction of government policy. Anderton even used the threat of resignation as party leader to prevent Harré from addressing striking *New Zealand Herald* newspaper journalists. Significant setbacks for the Alliance included repeated delay of its paid parental leave proposal, as well as lingering doubts over the viability of the People's Bank. In June 2001, the Mana Motuhake party replaced its leader, Sandra Lee, with Willie Jackson, a move designed to lift the profile of the Alliance's Maori wing, and the following month the Democrats threatened that, in the event that their most prominent parliamentary candidates were relegated from the top few positions on the party list, the small monetary reform party might be forced to go it alone.

Conclusion

Apart from any lingering doubts over the future of MMP, the greatest un-certainty continues to be the question of the role, influence and political viability of small parties in government. The adverse public reaction to New Zealand First following its decision to coalesce with National cast a long shadow over negotiations between Labour and the Alliance. In an attempt to counter claims that small parties discourage constructive and stable govern-ment, the Alliance restricted its office-seeking demands to a pro rata allocation of cabinet posts and portfolios. The party's policy-seeking goals were even more modest, being limited to a mutually agreed declaration of intent. While helping to speed up the negotiations process, the Alliance's reluctance to bargain afforded Labour the luxury of being able to assess the merits of the third party's policies on a case-by-case basis. Successive policy defeats for the Alliance during the coalition's first year in office could be rationalised on the grounds that stable government was an essential prerequisite to a positive out-come from Parliament's MMP Review Committee. Thereafter, consistently poor poll ratings began to erode internal party confidence and morale. In failing to maximise its potential as a coalition partner, the Alliance was in danger of losing the bulk of its electoral support. To add insult to injury, the Greens announced that any future coalition with Labour would be conditional upon acceptance by the major party of a range of Green policy initiatives, as well as a generous allocation of ministries and portfolios.

Closely linked to the future of coalition government is the evolving nature of the party system. Peter Mair (1997, 207) has identified three factors that largely account for inter-party competition and governmental stability: the degree of alternation in government (that is, whether the change from govern-ment to government is complete, partial or non-existent); the extent to which government formation processes are familiar or new; and the number and range of parties holding the reins of power. In his view, New Zealand was developing the characteristics of a fragmented party system, a process that he saw as being 'accentuated by the recent adoption of a proportional electoral formula' (Mair 1997, 204). Contrary to this prediction, New Zealand appears to be avoiding the worst effects of fragmentation (Aimer 1997b, 186–95; Nagel 1994, 139–60; Vowles 1998a, 28–47). Despite New Zealand First's pivotal position in 1996 and the expectation of a recurring pattern of 'partial alter-nation' (Mair's term for a government which includes a party from the previous administration), a feature commonly associated with fragmented systems, recent developments suggest that the country is moving in the direction of 'wholesale alternation', with two quite distinct party blocs competing for the right to hold power. In other words, what is emerging is a modification of the familiar majoritarianism, with the promise of wholesale alternation between the centre-right and centre-left blocs.

The main minor party in each bloc can be seen as an offshoot of the dominant partner: ACT from National, and Alliance from Labour. If ACT and Alliance can maintain their support, each could potentially offer high levels of social and ideological homogeneity, which in time should help reduce the potential for policy disagreement (Budge and Keman 1990, 17). In addition, the more extreme ideological position occupied by the minor party relative to its senior partner largely eliminates the uncertainty that comes when one major party is played off against the other, as happened with New Zealand First in 1996. Indeed, if this process of wholesale alternation persists, the reputation of coalition government and small parties stands every chance of eventually being enhanced.

CHAPTER 9

MEMBERS OF PARLIAMENT
AND REPRESENTATION

Jeffrey Karp

... social representation ... refers to whether the
composition of legislatures reflects the society from which they
are drawn, in terms of politically salient cleavages like gender,
class, language, and ethnicity.
— Norris 1996

Democratic politics everywhere, regardless of the role of referendums (see
Chapter 10), are founded on representation. MPs elected to Parliament may
bring their personal attributes with them, but they are there to speak not for
themselves but as the representatives of various wider interests, some clear-cut,
others shifting or informal. Most obviously, they represent their respective
parties. The equally long tradition of geographical representation is present in
the country's 61 General electorates, while six separate Maori electorates in
1999 ensured the representation of New Zealand's indigenous population. The
process of group-interest representation is generally thought to be strengthened
when in the hands of an MP who is visibly of that group.

The Royal Commission which recommended MMP believed that the
introduction of proportional representation (PR) would improve the quality of
political representation in various ways (RCES 1986, 50–1, 63) Those campaigning for MMP in the lead-up to the 1993 referendum also made much of
this section of the commission's report. They maintained that among the
advantages of the new voting system was the expectation that there would be
a more diverse representation of interests in Parliament, which would then
better reflect New Zealand society. Aside from the enhanced representation of
small parties, groups such as Maori and women were likely to improve their
representation under MMP by means of the party lists. While improving
descriptive representation in this way and providing for proportional outcomes,
MMP would also retain some of the advantages of first past the post. Through
the preservation of single member districts, citizens would continue to choose
their individual representatives, and those MPs continue to have an incentive
to serve as local advocates. By diversifying representation, MMP was also
expected to promote greater policy responsiveness among politicians and
parties. Under FPP, parties had a strong incentive to appeal to the broadest

possible audience to win the most votes. The result was a system often characterised by two large parties sharing often very similar platforms. In a PR system, parties can maintain greater ideological purity and cater more specifically to their core supporters. This increases the number of parties competing for votes and offers clearer choices to voters. Such improvements in representation and policy articulation were in turn expected to strengthen satisfaction with the democratic process. Advocates of the new system argued further that PR would not only be fairer than FPP in the proportional allocation of parliamentary seats, but would also encourage a politics of consensus, requiring cooperation between several parties to achieve effective government, in contrast to the dominance in government of one party, and the resulting adversarial nature of politics under FPP. In this chapter we examine the extent to which MMP has met these expectations.

Attitudes toward Descriptive Representation

There is a growing expectation that Parliament and governments will mirror the diversity of society, that MPs collectively will not only represent this diversity in what they do, but in what they are. Peter Fraser's cabinet (1943–46) of fifteen men, with an average age of 58, the youngest being 43, would now evoke derision (Bassett and King 200, 259–60). After an election the proportions of women and Maori are promptly tallied, and notable newcomers identified in the media — an MP of Chinese descent (Pansy Wong, National, 1996), a Samoan (Taito Phillip Field, Labour, 1996), the first Rastafarian (Nandor Tanczos, Green party, 1999), and the first transsexual (Georgina Beyer, Labour, 1999). Heterogeneity has become, if not an end in itself, then at least a accepted attribute of the House of Representatives.

MMP delivered a more representative and a slightly more diverse Parliament. Following the first MMP election in 1996 the proportion of Maori in Parliament doubled from 6 to 13 per cent and the proportion of women increased from 21 to 29 per cent. In the second MMP election in 1999, women and Maori were able to maintain but not improve on their representation in Parliament. As comparative research has demonstrated, party lists enhance the representation of women (see e.g. Darcy, Welch and Clark 1994; Rule 1994). Whereas only 16 per cent of women entered Parliament by winning an electorate seat in 1996, 46 per cent entered via the party list. In 1999, a slightly lower percentage of women entered through the party list but 24 per cent won electorate contests. As for Maori MPs, similar proportions were elected in party list and electorate seats.

Improved representation for women and Maori is reflected in the electorate's changing attitude toward descriptive representation. In 1993 the unrepresentative nature of Parliament had been highlighted in the campaign for MMP, whereas it was a much less prominent issue in 1996 and 1999. In 1993, 60 per cent of the electorate believed that there should be more women MPs. Immediately following the 1996 election, the proportion holding this view was reduced by half. Similarly, the proportion believing that Maori representation should increase was reduced from 44 per cent in 1993 to just 17 per cent in

1996. This proportion was almost unchanged in 1998, while opposition to an increase doubled, possibly reflecting the fact that Maori were now represented in Parliament in almost exact proportion to their numbers in the 1991 census, and expressing also respondents' judgement of the erratic performance of some Maori MPs since the election. Yet when respondents were reminded in 1998 that women comprised about 30 per cent of the MPs in Parliament, more thought the number should be increased.[1] By the 1999 election, however, concern for the composition of Parliament appears to have fallen away again, especially among non-Maori respondents, a trend evident since 1993 (Table 9.1).

Greater representation of minorities has been shown in the United States to lead to greater trust in government and to higher levels of political interest and rates of participation in elections on the part of minority citizens (Bobo and Gilliam 1990; Vanderleeuw and Utter 1993; Lublin and Tate 1995). We do not know, however, how far these generalisations might apply to New Zealand, given that Maori have been guaranteed at least limited representation since 1867. As Tate (1991) suggests, once minority representation is achieved, interest and thus turnout decline, negating some of the gains expected from representation.

Maori have long been assured representation through the creation of separate Maori electorates that are defined territorially but overlap with the General electorates. While guaranteeing a Maori presence in Parliament, the creation of four separate Maori electorates also helped to preserve their under-representation. At the time the seats were created, the Maori population was around 50,000, compared to a European population of 250,000, represented by 72 MPs (Sorrenson 1986, B–21). The number of Maori electorates, and correspondingly of Maori Members of Parliament, remained unchanged from 1867 until the passage of the Electoral Act of 1993.

According to some scholars, descriptive representation has not resulted in substantive policy responsiveness to minority interests. Wide gaps remain between Maori and New Zealand Europeans in educational attainment, income, health and prison rates (Sullivan 1997). Disillusionment with Labour's perceived ineffectiveness in promoting Maori issues together with its mono-poly over the Maori electorates until the 1993 election may have contributed to growing alienation among Maori in the early 1990s (Sullivan and Vowles 1998). If we are to assume that the roots of Maori discontent lie in part in under-representation, then we may expect to see the recent gains in Maori representation leading to improvements in political support among Maori. The effects of under-representation on political cynicism may also be strong for Maori since they appear to place a greater emphasis on descriptive repre-sentation than other under-represented groups, such as women (see Banducci and Karp 1998).

As the data in Table 9.1 show, although fewer Maori than previously believe that their representation should be increased, a substantial proportion (44 per cent in 1999) continue to desire further representation. A majority of Maori also favour an increase in the proportion of women represented in Parliament, and the difference between Maori and non-Maori is greater on female representation than on Maori representation. These opinions have some influence on attitudes toward governmental responsiveness or external efficacy. Those who believe that Maori should be better represented are also more likely (77 per cent) than those who do not (67 per cent), to believe that MPs are out of touch. This suggests that attitudes toward responsiveness can be partly explained by the degree to which minorities feel properly represented.

As is evident from Table 9.1, Maori place a greater emphasis on descriptive representation than non-Maori. Not only are Maori consistently more likely to believe in furthering their own representation, they are also more likely to favour increased representation for women. Whereas the proportion of non-Maori who believed that there should be more women representatives in Parliament had declined to 20 per cent in 1999, a majority of Maori continued to believe that there should be more.

Table 9.1   Attitudes toward Descriptive Representation (1993–99)

	1993		1996		1998		1999	
Non-Maori	Yes	No	Yes	No	Yes	No	Yes	No
More Women MPs	59	19	23	13	41	35	20	15
More Maori MPs	41	31	11	30	16	57	6	32
Maori only								
More Women MPs	75	10	40	4	55	28	52	8
More Maori MPs	83	7	57	3	43	32	44	13
Total								
More Women MPs	60	18	30	15	42	32	22	14
More Maori MPs	44	29	14	28	18	55	10	29

NOTE: Row percentages do not add up to 100 because those who responded 'depends on candidate' or 'don't know' are not reported. The sample size in 1993 for Maori is 139, and for non-Maori is 2106; in 1996, Maori 390, non-Maori 3591; in 1999, Maori 1000, non-Maori 4461.

Attitudes toward descriptive representation are also manifested in support for the separate Maori electorates and appear to influence the decision on which roll to register — the Maori roll or the General roll. Despite its long history, separate Maori representation remains a controversial issue in New Zealand. As the data in Table 9.2 reveal, in 1993, 43 per cent of non-Maori wanted the seats abolished and just 11 per cent thought the number should be increased. Although this indicates strong resentment against the seats, many non-Maori also believed at the time that there should be more Maori MPs (see Table 9.1). This suggests that non-Maori respondents were often drawing a distinction between the means and the ends, the presence of separate and guaranteed representation being more contentious than the number of Maori MPs.

Consistent with this view, the Royal Commission had proposed that if MMP were adopted the separate Maori seats should be abolished, contending that they were no longer necessary to guarantee representation. Maori, however, expressed strong support for the preservation of the seats. As a compromise, the Electoral Act of 1993 allows the seats to be retained but their numbers may rise or fall depending on how many Maori choose to register on the Maori roll. After each five-year census, the drawing of the new electoral boundaries begins with a four-month Maori Electoral Option, during which time those who indicate on their enrolment forms that they are of Maori descent are sent letters asking them to choose between registering on the Maori or the General roll. Because the number of Maori seats is determined by enrolment, taking the Maori option is more important, at least in terms of descriptive representation, than voting. As Table 9.2 reveals, a majority of Maori who have opted to be on the Maori rolls desire further representation. In contrast, while Maori on the General rolls are more supportive of the seats than non-Maori they are about half as likely to want further representation than those taking the Maori option.

As of 1999, the electorate remained divided over the question of the Maori seats. Nevertheless there appears to be a consensus among Maori and non-Maori alike that whether or not the Maori seats are retained is a matter for all New Zealanders. While in 1999 a similar proportion of non-Maori as in 1993 believed they should be abolished, slightly more believe they should be retained. Among Maori, particularly those on the Maori rolls, the separate seats were still highly valued. Thus, at least for the foreseeable future, they will likely remain one of the unique features of the New Zealand electoral system.

Table 9.2: Opinions about Maori Seats over Time and by Enrolment Status

	Maori				Non-Maori	
		Roll Status				
	1993		1999		1993	1999
Future of Seats	All	Maori	General	All		
Have more Maori seats	74	51	25	38	11	4
Keep the six we have now	15	39	52	46	27	41
Get rid of Maori seats	6	5	15	10	43	43
Who Decides?						
Maori	54	34	18	27	26	20
All New Zealanders	38	63	79	70	62	75
N	123	514	405	1000	1885	4505

SOURCE: 1993, 1999 NZES; 1999 NZES Maori survey

Attitudes toward the Political Process

Recently, research has emphasised the importance that institutions have on influencing levels of popular support for the political system (see Lijphart 1999; Anderson and Guillory 1997). Specifically, in consensual systems based on proportional representation, winners and losers alike exhibit generally higher levels of satisfaction with democracy than under majoritarian systems. New Zealand's change from majoritarian FPP to consensus MMP thus forms an interesting test case of the hypothesis over time (almost all empirical studies being based on cross-national analysis).

The evidence in the NZES surveys appears to confirm these findings. Overall, the New Zealand electorate has become somewhat more satisfied with the political process after the introduction of MMP, indicating that the change of electoral system may have succeeded in generating more positive views toward the political process. As Table 9.3 shows, on most indicators the most substantial changes occurred between the last election held under FPP in 1993 and the first election held under MMP in 1996. In particular, more voters came to see that their votes really mattered, fewer thought that their MPs did not care or were out of touch, and fewer thought that government was run by a few big interests (see also Banducci, Donovan, and Karp 1999). Nearly three-quarters of the electorate expressed satisfaction with the democratic process. Although we have no similar measure of satisfaction prior to MMP, this level of support is high compared to many other advanced democracies (Karp and Bowler 2001).

These positive trends during the transition to proportional representation can be seen in part as a reflection of growing optimism about the new system. Yet such optimism appeared to be short-lived. Lengthy coalition talks followed by New Zealand First's decision to enter into a coalition with National were heavily criticised and surveys suggested a loss in confidence in both the government and the political process itself. When opinions were sampled in July 1998, dissatisfaction with the coalition government was high; half the electorate strongly disapproved of the way the coalition government was handling its job whereas just 15 per cent approved. When asked whether government could be trusted to do what is right, just 26 per cent agreed while two-thirds believed the government could not be trusted. Previously in 1996, New Zealanders were more reluctant to distrust government. While 30 per cent had said they could trust government, 44 per cent disagreed and 26 per cent were unsure. But the levels of discontent were not confined to the government. Satisfaction with democracy dropped from 73 per cent to 45 per cent. Close to a majority (42 per cent) agreed that MMP was a disaster and that the country should be rid of it as soon as possible. Three-quarters of the electorate believed that MPs were out of touch, an increase of 20 per cent. Such a substantive decline in support for the democratic system would pose a challenge, or even a crisis of democracy (see Fuchs and Klingemann 1995, 22).

The lack of experience with coalition politics together with the formation of a coalition that was neither expected nor desired may explain New Zealanders' reaction to MMP (see Chapter 11). As the experience of the National–New Zealand First coalition suggests, disillusionment with political processes in general may occur when a government is formed that is contrary to the expectations created by the election campaign. Such perceptions seem to have furthered the belief that politicians were out of touch and diminished the system's legitimacy. If such attitudes reflect dissatisfaction with the National–New Zealand First coalition, we might find greater levels of support for democratic processes over time as citizens in New Zealand experience elections that produce a more consensual (and expected) outcome. Unlike the previous election, in 1999 both Labour and the Alliance made their coalition intentions clear and pre-election surveys suggested (and later confirmed) that the centre-left would have enough support to govern.

During the 1999 campaign, pre-election surveys suggested that attitudes about the political process had recovered to levels comparable to 1996. At the beginning of the campaign, eight out of ten voters believed that their vote really counts in elections. With a number of parties and candidates courting their votes over the campaign, the percentage agreeing that their vote counts increased slightly to 85 per cent. We expect that this same courting would make MPs appear more responsive to voters. At the start of the 1999 campaign, about 75 per cent believed that MPs are out touch, almost the same proportion as measured in July 1998. But over the first five weeks of the campaign, the proportion of those believing that MPs are out of touch declined to a low of 57 per cent. Toward the latter part of the campaign, however, the trend reversed and reached 67 per cent in the last day of polling before the election. While there is some variation in satisfaction with democracy, the percentage satisfied at the beginning of the campaign is very similar to that at the end of the campaign just prior to the election.

After the election, there was a further increase in positive attitudes toward the process, indicating that election outcomes can make a difference. After increasing prior to the election, the evaluation of the responsiveness of MPs improved; the number agreeing that MPs are out of touch decreased to 52 per cent.[2] In particular, supporters of the new government experienced a greater change than those who supported parties that were defeated. Consistent with an increase in responsiveness, the percentage of people who are satisfied with democracy increased after the election to 57 per cent.[3] Nevertheless, compared to 1996, when MMP was first introduced, fewer were satisfied with the way democracy works in 1999. As for efficacy, between pre- and post-election surveys the proportion of those saying their vote counts dropped, indicating lower efficacy. This decline could be explained by a loss of efficacy among supporters of the parties that did not form part of the new government. Among those who did form the government, Labour voters experienced the greatest change, becoming significantly more satisfied with democracy than those who voted for other parties. It is clear that electoral outcomes continue to shape voter attitudes toward the political system, probably much as they always have done.

Opinions about Representatives

The belief that politicians are out of touch or do not care expresses diffuse attitudes toward politicians in general rather than toward specific individuals. As Table 9.4 shows, just half the electorate correctly recalled the name of their electorate MP, while list MPs have an even lower profile.[4] Just 19 per cent of respondents could give the name of any person when asked if they knew anything about a list MP. Within this group, 15 per cent named an existing list

Table 9.3: Changes in Political Attitudes over Time (% in agreement)

	1993	1996	1998	1999
MPs out of touch	61	53	76	52
People like me have no say	63	57	—	55
Politicians don't care what people think	66	57	—	55
Government is run by a few big interests	60	54	—	50
Satisfaction with democracy	—	73	45	57
Trust Government to do what is right	31	30	26	36
My vote really counts in elections*	75	85	66	77
N	2205	4086	535	5601

NOTE: All data are based on post-election surveys except for the survey conducted in July 1998.
* In 1996, the question was asked slightly differently: 'My party vote really counts in elections'.

MP and the other 4 per cent an electorate MP, usually in their area. Not surprisingly the list MPs that received a great deal of media scrutiny were those that New Zealanders remembered most. 'Party hoppers' had a higher profile among list MPs than their numbers deserved: they made up 25 per cent of those mentioned, and nearly four out of five of these respondents named one party hopper, Alamein Kopu (see Chapter 1). Knowledge of electorate MPs is considerably higher. About half of the respondents correctly recalled the name of their electorate MP, indicating that electorate MPs do indeed have a higher profile.

When our respondents were asked about the way in which the local electorate MP handled his or her job, about one-third approved, compared to only 18 per cent who approved of the way MPs in general handled their job. Even more significant is the difference between local electorate MPs and list MPs, with only 7 per cent approving of the latter group's performance. Yet, approval of both list and General electorate MPs is higher among those who correctly recalled the name of their electorate MP or any list MP. Among Maori, just 11 per cent approved of either Maori list MPs or Maori electorate MPs in general. About one in every four Maori could recall the name of a Maori list MP while a similar proportion of those on the Maori rolls recalled the name of their electorate MP. Whereas Maori were less likely to recall the name of their Maori electorate MP than non-Maori, they were more likely than non-Maori to recall the name of a Maori list MP.[5] The higher name recognition of Maori list MPs reflects the visibility of Alamein Kopu, whose name was recalled by 20 per cent of Maori. Approval among those who correctly recalled the name of a Maori list MP is about the same as those in the general election survey. There is evidence of greater dissatisfaction with the Maori electorate MPs, which helps to explain their resounding defeat in 1999 (see Chapter 5).

When the NZES questions moved from ascertaining people's superficial knowledge and evaluation of representatives to measuring the more demanding linkages that depend on the political involvement of respondents, rather than the behaviour of an MP, far fewer reported having any contact with either an electorate or list MP. Whereas almost half the electorate could recall the name of their electorate MP in 1999, only about a fifth reported having had some contact with an electorate MP over the previous twelve months (a similar proportion to that having reported contact in the past two elections). The proportion reporting contact with a list MP is about 3 per cent lower still. Contact is lower for both Maori electorate and list MPs. One in ten Maori reported having any contact with their Maori electorate MP, while just 6 per cent reported having contact with a Maori list MP. As Table 9.4 shows, approval of both electorate and list MPs is much higher among those who reported having contact with either representative.

Table 9.4   Opinions about Electorate and List MPs, 1999

	Percent who recall name correctly	Percent who approve regardless of name recall	Percent approval of those who recall name	Percent having contact	Percent approval of those having contact
General electorate MP	50	34	45	19	64
Specific list MP	16	—	43	16	72
List MPs in general	—	7	—	—	—
MPs in general	—	18	—	—	—
Maori electorate MP	27	19	34	11	36
Specific Maori list MP	28	—	42	6	76
Maori list MPs in general	—	11	—	—	—
Maori MPs in general	—	11	—	—	—

NOTE: Data on opinions about General electorate MPs, specific list MPs, list MPs in general and MPs in general are from the post-election survey (N=4816). The data on opinions about Maori MPs are from the Maori survey that includes only those who identify as Maori (N=1000). Evaluations of Maori electorate MPs are for those on the Maori rolls.

Evidence from Germany has long indicated that many people there find it difficult to distinguish between electorate and list MPs (Bawn 1999). In New Zealand, by contrast, the distinction is clear. In part this may be related to the introduction of MMP. New Zealanders had no experience with party lists to elect their representatives, and consequently their use raised questions of legitimacy and accountability. In the debates before the 1993 referendum which authorised the change to MMP, opponents of the new system attempted to discredit it by focusing on the use of closed lists, raising the spectre of MPs defeated in their electorates being returned to the House as list MPs, having secured a favourable place on their party's list by deferring to party 'bosses'. To whom were such representatives accountable? Such a question played on the long tradition of FPP elections in which MPs, no matter how small the plurality which had elected them, claimed a direct mandate from their constituents. Following the first MMP election, cartoons, TV political satire, and the print media contributed to a growing perception that there were two types of MPs and that list MPs were 'second-class' (see Ward 1998). In part, these perceptions may have been shaped by their perceived lack of legitimacy. But the behaviour of certain list MPs also helped to stimulate the criticism. List MPs rapidly became the focus of public concern, particularly with the departure of Alamein Kopu from the Alliance to become a government-aligned Independent, and the experience of other 'party hoppers'. While party hoppers included electorate as well as list MPs, the reputation of list MPs suffered most from that process. Post-election data in 1999 show that just over 80 per cent of respondents would approve of legislation to discourage party hopping. And those who support such legislation are more likely to disapprove of list MPs than those who do not.

While New Zealanders express fairly strong support for the principle of proportionality (see Chapter 11), there is far less support for the use of closed party lists to achieve that outcome, and a clear preference instead for open lists enabling voters to directly influence which candidates might be elected. When asked whether voters and not parties should decide which of the candidates on the party list should get seats in Parliament, 57 per cent agreed, compared to just 16 per cent who disagreed. Table 9.5 shows that opinions about the method for deciding the party list is influenced by approval of list MPs. Those who approve of the performance of list MPs are divided about whether voters or parties should decide the party list while two-thirds of those who disapprove believe that voters should decide the list. Opinions about the method for deciding the party lists also structure opinions toward MMP, suggesting that concerns about accountability are linked to opinions about the electoral system (see Chapter 11).

Table 9.5: Opinions about Open Lists and Approval of List MPs, 1999

Voters Should Decide the Party List	Approval of List MPs		
	Disapprove	Neutral	Approve
Agree	67	54	49
Neutral	15	19	18
Disagree	13	15	28

NOTE: Column percentages do not add up to a hundred because those who responded 'don't know' are not reported. The sample size is 4816.

Priorities of Electorate and List MPs

We have seen that a substantial gap exists in people's knowledge of list and electorate MPs. These differences can be attributed to the fact that electorate MPs have a strong incentive to respond to local interests, and are more generously funded for this purpose than their list colleagues, whereas list MPs have a stronger incentive to respond to party leaders, and develop expertise in issues that transcend local electorates. Indeed, one of the advantages of a mixed system like MMP is that it offers such countervailing electoral incentives (see also Bawn 1999). But differences in priorities between list and electorate MPs could also account for the lower visibility of list MPs. Data from the candidate survey confirms this.

Table 9.6 reveals substantial differences between list and electorate MPs in the importance they give to representative activities. While both electorate and list candidates attach great importance to committee work, they diverge when it comes to activities representing a specific constituency. Electorate candidates considered representing an electorate as the most important activity for an MP, whereas its importance for list MPs was ranked near the median. Electorate candidates are far more likely to attach importance to casework than list candidates; 52 per cent of electorate candidates believed helping with individual problems was a very important part of an MP's job, compared to just 21 per cent of list candidates. Similarly, nearly half the electorate candidates believed that attending local community functions was very important, compared to 14 per cent of list candidates. For list candidates, dealing with individual problems and attending community functions were the lowest among their priorities. Regional interests were also likely to be given much greater importance by electorate candidates than list candidates. In contrast, a somewhat larger proportion of list candidates believed that developing party policy was very important. Comparing the results from an identical survey conducted of candidates in the 1993 general election reveals that the priorities of electorate MPs have not changed dramatically with the advent of MMP with the exception that party voting is given more importance under MMP than under FPP.

Table 9.6: Importance of Representative Activities by Candidate Type

Type of Candidate	1999						1993	
	Electorate		List		Both		Electorate	
	% very imp.	Order	% very imp.	Order	% very imp.	Order	% very imp.	Order
Representing electorate	79	1	49	5	64	3	82	1
Select committee work	72	2	71	1	71	1	57	4
Holding regular electorate clinics	70	3	57	2	69	2	81	2
Representing regional interests	63	4	36	6	45	6	55	5
Voting with party	56	5	56	3	52	4	17	13
Helping with individual problems	52	6	21	12	43	8	62	3
Developing party policy	49	7	51	4	43	9	43	7
Attending local community functions	49	8	14	13	44	7	36	8
Supporting party leaders	44	9	34	7	31	11	20	12
Working with interest groups	44	10	29	10	41	10	32	9
Attend local party meetings	37	11	29	9	45	5	43	6
Speaking in Parliament	37	12	26	11	30	13	29	10
Being interviewed by media	30	13	32	8	31	12	21	11

SOURCE: NZ Candidate Study, 1999, 1993

Data from the candidate survey presented in Table 9.7 indicate that casework, as well as being given high priority by electorate representatives, is consuming an increasing amount of an MP's time. In 1993, 11 per cent of incumbents reported spending over 20 hours a week attending local functions. In 1999, the proportion has doubled. In 1993, 55 per cent of incumbents reported spending over 20 hours a week 'dealing with people's problems' and 28 per cent spent over 20 hours a week travelling. In 1999, 65 per cent reported spending over 20 hours a week on casework while 31 per cent reported spending as much time travelling. Aside from casework, more MPs are devoting time to party fund-raising. In 1993, just 6 per cent reported spending over ten hours a week on the activity. In 1999, three-quarters reported spending between 10 and 20 hours on raising funds for the party, while 15 per cent reported spending over 20 hours a week.

Table 9.7: Time Spent by Incumbent MPs

	1999 Hours Per Month			1993 Hours Per Month		
	<10	10 to 20	20+	<10	10 to 20	20+
Speaking at public meetings	54	41	5	87	11	2
Attending local functions	31	49	21	51	38	11
Party fundraising	8	77	15	94	4	2
Dealing with people's problems	8	28	64	15	30	55
Attending party meetings	49	41	10	83	13	4
Traveling	15	54	31	34	38	28
Attending national (non-party) meetings	69	23	7	—	—	—

NOTE: Number of MPs 1999=32; Number of MPs 1993=53
SOURCE: NZ Candidate Study, 1999, 1993

Constituents also appear to be demanding more of their electorate MPs. As Table 9.8 reveals, in an average week in 1993, 11 per cent of the MPs reported receiving at least 50 requests for help with constituents' problems compared to 54 per cent who received less than 25 requests. By 1999, almost half of the electorate MPs reported receiving at least 50 requests for help. The bulk of the increase appears to be handled by the electorate MPs; just one out of the thirteen list MPs in our sample reported receiving as many requests as half of the electorate MPs. These findings contrast with research in Germany which suggest that list MPs receive as much mail from constituents as constituency MPs (Burkett 1985). Our survey suggests that the list MPs are likely not to confine their casework to a single electorate. Of the former list MPs, just 17 per cent report having the most contact with the people they represent in a single electorate; almost half (47 per cent) reported representing people across a wider region including several electorates, and a third (37 per cent) across the whole of New Zealand.

To the extent that the processes of representation include assisting individual constituents, our evidence suggests that the introduction of MMP has had two effects. On the one hand the larger size of the single-member electorates under MMP has raised the case load of many MPs; on the other, however, list members are assuming a complementary service role extending beyond the boundaries of single electorates, a development of the process that may yet be incomplete.

Table 9.8: Number of Constituents' Problems per Week

Type of MP	1999		1993
	List	Electorate	Electorate
Less than 25	7	16	54
	(8)	(3)	(29)
Between 25–50	31	37	35
	(4)	(7)	(19)
More than 50	8	47	11
	(1)	(9)	(6)

NOTE: Sample size in parentheses
SOURCE: NZ Candidate Study, 1999, 1993

Policy Representation and Electoral System Change

Aside from improving the process of representation, the change in the electoral system was also intended to improve policy representation. In a plurality or FPP system, voters typically have an effective choice of only two political parties that often take similar positions on a range of issues. According to the proximity model of elections, which has been a predominant paradigm in election studies, parties are likely to adopt positions that are closest to their voters. When policy preferences are normally distributed, parties will thus converge to the median or 'average' voter, located in the crowded centre of the political population. Under PR, however, parties can gain representation without winning a plurality of the votes. Parties, therefore, have less of an incentive to widen their appeal to the largest group of voters, allowing them instead to maintain ideological purity. Thus, in a multi-party system, rather than converging toward the median voter, parties will strive to distinguish themselves on ideological and policy matters (Downs 1957, 126–7).[6] In multi-party systems, according to Downs (138), parties tend to 'narrow the spread of their policies, differentiate their platforms more sharply, and reduce ambiguity'. This strategy will have the effect of appealing to the full spectrum of interests in the electorate rather than simply the median voter. Proximity theory thus leads us to anticipate that a transition to PR will result in a more diverse offering of parties competing for representation. Under MMP we therefore expect to find parties distancing themselves more from each other on major issues, rather than converging toward the centre. To explore this tendency we have analysed party positions on seven major issues during the transition to MMP, comparing survey data from the last election under plurality rules in 1993 with the second MMP election in 1999.[7]

Figure 9.1 shows the parties' positions on each issue, derived from the responses in our candidate surveys, while the placement of the mean voter on each, calculated from the mass surveys, is also given. As anticipated, the party

Figure 9.1: Party Positions under FPP and MMP

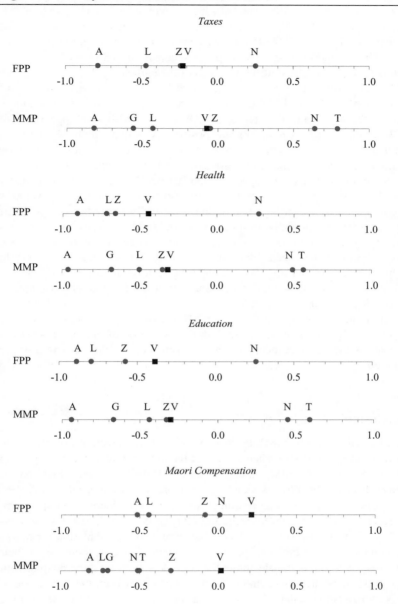

NOTE: A=Alliance, G=Green, L=Labour, N=National, T=ACT, Z=New Zealand First, V=Mean
voter. Note that ACT and the Greens do not appear under FPP rules because they did not
exist then.

SOURCE: NZES Candidate and Elector Surveys 1993, 1999.

positions have diverged under MMP, compared to their positions in 1993. The
movement has not been great, however, largely because the parties had not

clustered around the mean voter under FPP as much as theory might have led us to expect, except on the issues of superannuation and environment. Nevertheless, compared to 1993, the placement of parties on the issues, as perceived by their candidates in 1999, is more dispersed, partly owing to the emergence of the Greens and ACT as separate players, consistent with the advent of PR, and partly owing to the shifting positions of the parties.

For example, under MMP the distance has increased between the two largest parties, National and Labour, on taxes, National having moved more than twice as far from the centre, perhaps influenced by the appearance of ACT, which occupies a more extreme position. A similar pattern is evident on health and education, two of the most salient issues in both elections. There has been least divergence among the parties on the issue of superannuation, while on environment the Greens especially and less so ACT account for the greater spread of policy positions since 1993. The issue of compensation for Maori is unique, however, in that both before and since PR not only has the spread of party positions been relatively small, compared to other issues, but all parties have clustered on the side of compensation, and to one side of the mean voter. Although in 1999 the mean voter moved closer to a neutral position, the gap to the parties remains as they also have all become more committed to compensation. On overall ideology, the tendency toward a greater party spread under PR is confirmed, as, however, is the weakness of that tendency. As expected, the ACT party emerges under MMP as consistently least committed to government intervention, while with the exception of one issue — environment — the Alliance occupies the opposite pole of the new multi-party continuum.

Conclusion

After two elections under MMP, we are now in a better position to evaluate the impact of electoral system change. One of the most obvious changes has to do with the composition of Parliament. Under MMP, the New Zealand Parliament is more diverse than before, with a larger proportion of women and Maori MPs, along with more parties representing views across the ideological spectrum. These changes in descriptive representation have satisfied many New Zealanders. There is also some evidence that improved representation for Maori has helped increase the perception that government is responsive to their concerns. As a whole, the electorate has become somewhat more content with policy responsiveness and somewhat less cynical. However, the experience of the National–New Zealand First coalition showed that support for democratic processes can be rather fragile. While there have been some improvements over the longer term, most people in New Zealand continue to feel that politicians are unresponsive and unconcerned about the people they represent. In particular, most citizens strongly disapprove of the list MPs and prefer that they be held directly accountable through open lists. While MMP creates some incentives to enhance the responsiveness of MPs, the closed party list system would appear to create the opposite impression. It may also be difficult for list MPs to overcome these stereotypes. They are less well funded to carry out constituency service and they place a lower priority on such activities than electorate MPs. In addition, few list MPs place much importance on helping individuals with their problems. This may explain why they are less likely to have contact with constituents.

As for policy representation, the change to a PR system may have succeeded in promoting a more diverse representation of interests. Under the FPP system, parties in New Zealand appear to have taken more divergent positions than the proximity model would predict on a range of issues. But on average, parties operating under MMP took even more divergent positions than they had in the past. On such issues as taxes, health, and education, National and Labour have moved farther to the right along with the average voter. Yet other parties, such as the Alliance, have either remained where they were or moved slightly to the left. As a result, voters have greater representation and more choice than in the past. As Barker and McLeay (2000) observe, the larger number of parties under PR means that more voters' preferences are reflected in the policy process than under FPP, when one party was the sole significant source of policy.

In sum, MMP has delivered on its promise to provide greater diversity in Parliament and a greater choice. It is less clear how the change to PR has contributed to greater satisfaction with the democratic process. Most of the positive changes that we have observed in voter attitudes are rather subtle. In some cases, MMP appears to have contributed to voter cynicism by creating two types of MPs that may be held accountable in different ways. If, over the long term, voters develop different expectations for list and electorate MPs, the link between the representative and the represented may be strengthened and New Zealand may well be on its way toward a 'better democracy' — as the Royal Commission intended.

CHAPTER 10

DIRECT DEMOCRACY ON TRIAL:
THE CITIZENS-INITIATED
REFERENDUMS

Jeffrey Karp and Peter Aimer

An effective representative democracy with robust avenues
for public participation does not depend on the existence of
citizens-initiated referenda.
— Janet McLean 2000

. . . if the select committee had listened and had . . . made
some areas binding, ordinary and common New Zealanders
would have felt that at last they had some say in what happened
to them . . .
— Ian Peters, MP, Tongariro, 1993

When New Zealanders went to the polling booths on election day in 1999,
some were surprised to be issued with a bundle of papers. As well as their
general election ballots, voters also faced two citizens-initiated referendums
(CIRs). Citizens' initiatives were a relatively recent addition to the country's
democratic practices. The legislation enabling such initiatives was passed late
in 1993, only a few weeks before the referendum approving MMP. The timing
was not entirely fortuitous. Both CIR and MMP were nurtured by the same
widespread mood of disillusion, to which National politicians were tactically,
and in many cases reluctantly, responding (Jackson and McRobie 1998, 86–
92). Since 1993, however, only one initiative had proceeded to a referendum
vote.[1] In 1999, therefore, citizens-initiated referendums, like MMP, were on
trial.

One of the two 1999 initiatives, dealing with crime and punishment, arose
from the much-publicised callous bashing of an elderly woman in the context
of growing public concern over the incidence of violence in the community,
and particularly violence committed by intruders into people's homes. The
resulting referendum question asked: 'Should there be a reform of our justice
system placing greater emphasis on the needs of victims, providing restitution
and compensation for them and imposing minimum sentences and hard labour
for all serious violent offences?' Although three separate questions — greater

146

provision for victims, the imposition of minimum sentences, the introduction of hard labour — were woven into one, a format which defied the basic need to put to electors a simple, unambiguous question, the intent of the referendum was clear: get tougher on crimes of violence. The outcome, expressing the community's collective sympathy, indignation, fear of, and outrage at, such crimes, was an overwhelming 92 per cent 'yes' vote. That such a result was widely anticipated perhaps suggests that resort to a full-scale referendum was unnecessary to achieve a political response. It also raises questions about the extent of information on CIR issues available to the voting public. While the events preceding the referendum on violent crime were fully publicised in the media, the pros and cons of the various solutions embodied in the referendum question, such as 'minimum sentences' for violent crime, or the practicalities, even the meaning, of 'hard labour', received little or no attention. The substantive as distinct from the emotional basis for the huge 'yes' vote is thus open to question in a society that values informed action.

The second initiative asked: 'Should the size of the House of Representatives be reduced from 120 members to 99 members?' Simple, unambiguous, and on the surface dealing with a technical matter, the question nevertheless tapped into widespread feelings of distrust of politicians (Vowles, Aimer, Banducci, Karp 1998, 164). These had intensified with the experience of the radical reforms and broken promises associated with governments between 1984 and 1993. On top of this, the first MMP election in 1996 added a flood of negative perceptions of politicians' behaviour in Parliament, and of the competence and judgement of individual MPs. The advent of proportional representation and the increase in the size of Parliament to 120 MPs resulted in a more heterogeneous Parliament than before (Chapter 9), including an unusually high intake of inexperienced politicians, some of whom were plunged straight into taxing ministerial roles in the unfamiliar context of coalition government.

'Direct' versus 'Indirect' Democracy

Citizens-initiated referendums sit uneasily within the theory and practice of representative democracy. The essence of representative democracy is the election by voters of legislators, who then have the task of deciding the direction and details of public policy. In text-book language, representative democracy is therefore 'indirect democracy', since the citizens have largely delegated the responsibility of determining policy to others. The alternative, 'direct democracy', allows citizens to participate individually in the policy-making process by means of referendums; that is, by voting on specific policy options. Referendums are widely, but variously used among the world's major democracies (LeDuc, Niemi, and Norris 1996, 13–15). Most commonly, they are used to decide constitutional issues such as the question of European integration, the status of French Quebec in Canada, whether Australia should become a republic, and electoral reform, and the term of Parliament in New Zealand. Less frequently, 'direct democracy' has been extended to more general questions of public policy by means of the initiative, whereby citizens or groups outside the legislature directly propose public policies which are then voted on. Only in Switzerland and Italy is the initiative used frequently at the national level. Within the United States, about half the states have provisions for the initiative process, while some, such as California and Oregon, frequently use the initiative to decide public policy on a range of issues.

The merits of 'direct' and 'indirect' democratic practices are a matter of debate, both forms having their ardent advocates. Supporters of direct democracy claim that one of the virtues of the process is that it gives people the ability to enact reforms that representatives might be reluctant to consider. Direct democracy not only produces debate on issues that might otherwise be ignored, it also promotes government responsiveness and accountability by forcing public officials to adhere to the voice of the people. By enabling greater popular control of the policy agenda and outputs, referendums have strong normative appeal. What could be a more democratic way of determining policy than referendums — government 'by the people'? Accordingly, some have argued that the establishment of direct democracy legislation gives individuals a greater sense of involvement in politics, as well as reducing popular mistrust and alienation (Bowler, Donovan and Tolbert 1998; Mendelsohn and Cutler 2000).

Opposed to this is the belief that initiatives and referendums allow voters, many of whom are ill-informed, to exercise many of the powers normally reserved to Parliament. This view upholds a preference for laws to be made in a deliberative manner by representatives who have the time and expertise to grapple with the usually complex, often uncertain and always contestable nature of public policy. Critics of direct democracy also contend that it has the potential to threaten legitimate minority interests, resulting in the so-called 'tyranny of the majority' (see Gamble 1997). In New Zealand, the presence of an indigenous Maori minority has given these fears specific relevance. The Royal Commission on the Electoral System warned of the possible use of initiatives and referendums by larger groups 'to curb special programmes for disadvantaged minorities, or to enforce their own cultural dominance' (RCES 1986, 175). Lijphart (1999, 230–1), however, reverses the balance by finding the Swiss 'referendum-plus-initiative' procedure to be a way for minorities 'to challenge any laws passed by the majority of the elected representatives'. Critics of direct democracy also contend that the process has the potential to be undermined by the domination of special interests, especially those commanding superior resources. In the United States, virtually any initiative can qualify for the ballot if the backer has enough money, and voters may be manipulated by one-sided campaigns.

The Use of Direct Democracy in New Zealand

Although New Zealand (formerly a British colony) was constituted as a representative democracy, governments here, as in all democracies, have resorted to referendums from time to time. From 1911 to 1989 citizens voted every three years on questions about control of the liquor industry, and the location of 'licensed premises' (Hughes 1994, 156). Since 1949, New Zealand citizens have also voted in seven non-licensing referendums, four of which dealt with the constitutional questions of the term of Parliament and the voting system.[2] Historically, there has been periodical pressure to extend the practice of 'direct democracy'. Introducing the Citizens Initiated Referenda Bill in 1993, the Minister of Justice noted that the direct democracy debate had begun a century earlier (Hansard, 14 September 1993, 17951). Hughes (1994, 158) links the early twentieth-century impetus for using referendums and initiatives in New Zealand to the 'contemporary North American enthusiasms of the Populist and Progressive movements'. In New Zealand, the labour movement, first through the Social Democratic party, and after 1916 the Labour party (the nation's third party at the time), campaigned on promises to extend direct democracy by introducing such practices as the initiative, referendum and recall (Hughes 1994, 156). Yet by the time Labour was first elected to government in 1935, all these had been been dropped from its manifesto. New Zealand then entered a period of almost pure, Westminster-style, representative democracy (Lijphart 1999, 21–5).

Populist political instincts re-emerged after 1970. The growing perception that politicians were untrustworthy, and governments unresponsive, resulted in more strident advocacy of direct democracy. In 1984, the Social Credit MP, Garry Knapp, introduced a bill to Parliament in favour of citizens-initiated referendums. The Labour government referred the bill to the Royal Commission on the Electoral System. In 1986, the Royal Commission reported that they had 'received a wide range of suggestions on how there could be more opportunities for popular participation in Government through referenda', as well as other suggestions to enable the expression of 'the popular will' (*Report,* 171). The Commission, however, found little virtue in any provision for popular initiatives in the legislative process (173–5).

By 1988, the National party, still in opposition, had realised that political capital could be made by throwing its support behind the demand for citizens-initiated referendums (Church 2000, 185). They had read the mood accurately. At the time of the 1990 election, 78 per cent of respondents agreed with the proposition put to them in the NZES post-election survey that 'we should be able to make government hold a binding referendum if we want one on a particular issue'. Back in power after the election, National kept its word on the issue. Bending to the weight of demand (and hoping to deflect growing interest in electoral reform), the National government, unopposed by Labour, passed the Citizens Initiated Referenda Act establishing a CIR process. Even though the results of any referendum would not be binding on the government, the new procedure was a significant adjunct to the long-standing machinery of representative government.

For a CIR to take place, petitioners must secure signatures from 10 per cent of eligible voters in one year. If they succeed, government must hold a referendum within one year. Within two years of the Act's passage, close to twenty petitions had been approved for circulation on a wide variety of topics, such as the prohibition of egg production from battery hens, the ending of parole for murderers sentenced to life imprisonment, and an end to preference on the basis of ethnic origins (Catt 1996). Yet all of these petitions failed to gain the requisite number of signatures within the year (Catt 1996). Indeed, prior to 1999, only one CIR appeared before the voters (in December 1995). Sponsored by the Firefighters Union, the measure was intended to protect fire-fighter jobs by asking whether the number of employed full-time firefighters should be reduced. Consistent with the union's intent, voters decisively opposed reduction by 88 per cent (see note 1). The government refused to take notice of the result, citing low turnout, the general inappropriateness of using the CIR procedure to deal with a complex issue of industrial relations, and budgeting priorities (Mulgan 1997, 284).

Opinions about Direct Democracy

Since the introduction of the CIR procedure, public attitudes have remained strongly in favour of provision for referendums. In 1999, two-thirds of our respondents considered that 'referendums and citizen-initiated referendums' were 'good things', and only 1 per cent rejected them as 'bad things'. The remaining third in a sense shrugged their shoulders, either agreeing that referendums did not 'make much difference' or having no opinion on the matter at all. Yet while indicating strong approval of referendums in general, the data also hint at a waning of popular enthusiasm for them. Compared to 1990, when there was overwhelming support for the idea of forcing govern-ments to hold binding referendums, in 1999 slightly fewer than one-third of respondents agreed that the 'results of citizens initiated referendums should automatically become law'. While the wording of the two items differs, their sense is comparable, and the gap between 78 per cent and 32 per cent is too wide to be attributable solely to question wording.

Table 10.1: Mass Opinion about Direct Democracy (%)

	Agree	Disagree	Don't Know
Referendums and CIRs are good things	64	0	23
Referendums should become law	32	35	14
Referendums get attention	75	7	12
Referendums are too complicated	17	59	8
Parliament not voters should make final decisions on law and policy	50	32	8

SOURCE: NZES 1999 Post-election

Nevertheless, 32 per cent constitutes a substantial minority whose devotion to binding citizens-initiated referendums would, if implemented, amount to a significant diminution of Parliament's sovereignty. It would relocate New Zealand closer in constitutional practice to Switzerland, Italy and a number of states in the USA (Catt 1999, 57–61). Yet the data also show that populist enthusiasm for referendums is held in check by regard for Parliament's traditional role. Overall, 50 per cent of NZES respondents in 1999 agreed with the proposition that 'Parliament, not voters should make final decisions on law and policy'. Another 11 per cent expressed neutrality, while 32 per cent disagreed (the remaining 8 per cent confessing not to know). Agreement with this core principle of representative democracy rose to 61 per cent among those who were 'very interested' in politics, and even a third of the 31 per cent who advocated binding referendums, agreed.

Affirmation of Parliament's role also climbed steadily with the age of electors. For example, 65 per cent of respondents over 65 years of age agreed that Parliament should prevail over voters in determining law and policy, whereas only 32 per cent of those in the 18–23 age group did so. However, the gap between the age groups is more the result of uncertainty among the younger cohorts than their greater preference for direct democracy. While 34 per cent of respondents in the 18–23 age group disagreed that Parliament should prevail over voters, the proportion among the 55–64 group was only slightly less at 29 per cent. Meanwhile, the proportion who were neutral on the issue or could not say slumped from 35 per cent among the 18–23 age groups to 14 per cent for the 55–64 age group and further down again to 11 per cent among those over 65 years.

Aside from age-related attitudes, other factors might also incline people toward or away from the processes of direct democracy. For example, we might hypothesise that those who feel that politicians are out of touch or who are dissatisfied with democracy will want voters to make policy themselves. People's party preferences and ideology might also influence these attitudes. Because direct democracy is majoritarian in principle, and has the potential to threaten minority rights, particularly in small communities (see Donovan and Bowler 1998), we might expect minorities to be less supportive of the idea of direct democracy. We have used a basic regression model to explore such patterns of attitudes toward the role of Parliament versus voters in the policy process. The data in the table confirm that older citizens were far more sceptical of direct democracy than younger ones, but also show that women were more supportive than men. There is no evidence, however, that citizens view the process in either partisan or ideological terms, nor do we find any differences between minorities and New Zealand Europeans. On the other hand, people who believed MPs to be 'out of touch with the rest of the community', or who were dissatisfied with 'the way democracy works in New Zealand', were more likely to want to circumvent the legislature. This finding indicates that citizens may see direct democracy more as a vehicle for registering protest than as a means of influencing the policy-making process.

When the two sets of responses on referendums and the role of Parliament are combined, we find that the 'hard-line' populists — those who thought that citizens initiated referendums should automatically become law, and who also denied that Parliament, not voters, should make final decisions on law and policy — shrink to 17 per cent of electors, while their opposite number — the most ardent advocates of parliamentary supremacy ('no' to binding referendums, 'yes' to Parliament making the final decisions) — accounted for 27 per cent of electors. Discounting the 9 per cent who chose either the neutral or 'don't know' response for both items, it is clear that a majority of electors see some place for citizens initiated referendums within the more deliberative policy-making procedures of representative government, though the largest group do not want them to be binding. However, an unusually high proportion of respondents — 12 per cent — did not know whether or not referendums should be binding, and another unusually large group — 19 per cent — chose to be neutral on the matter. These replies from nearly one-third of our respondents suggest a high degree of uncertainty within the electorate over the place of referendums. This in turn is consistent with the evidence of a considerable shift in the balance of attitudes between 1990 and 1999. Such a shift may reflect any of a number of causes — the changed political climate, electoral turnover, the more inclusive and representative nature of MMP Parliaments, the extent to which governments have responded to the issues that prompted the referendum initiatives, and the mixed experience of citizens initiated referendums since 1993.

In practice, the CIR procedure in New Zealand has not so far been conspicuously successful. Critics have noted the difficulty of representing public policy issues in a form that is appropriate for a referendum, that is 'in neutral language in a simple question' (Palmer and Palmer 1997, 202). Perhaps because such referendums do not bind the government to any subsequent action, no provision has been made for an impartial public education programme on CIR issues. Electors thus risk casting their votes on inadequate or one-sided information, in an exercise the outcome of which is indeterminate. Yet even without the cost of a state-funded public education campaign, the expense of a referendum has been questioned. While two of the three referendums held so far were dovetailed with the general election in 1999, the 1995 referendum cost $9 million (Palmer and Palmer, 204). The purpose of non-binding referendums has also been questioned on the ground that they duplicate the less expensive practice by concerned citizens of petitioning Parliament in order to attract the politicians' attention to issues (McLean 2000, 366). While neither a non-binding citizen initiated referendum nor a well-supported petition guarantees a government response, both are equally capable of demonstrating public concern to which politicians may wish to respond. Having two overlapping procedures for this purpose is difficult to justify. Most contention, however, still surrounds the question of whether or not referendums should be binding. While a clear majority in 1999 thought that referendums, including citizens initiated referendums, were 'good things', not too complicated for the average voter, and very definitely a way of getting the politicians' attention, nevertheless, less than one-third wanted to see them become automatic tools of law-making.

Given the potentially antagonistic relationship between legislative institutions and CIRs, and the fact that CIRs might alter how legislatures operate, we should expect political elites to be more sceptical about direct democracy. Surveys in Canada and the United States have indicated greater resistance to CIRs among incumbents generally, the governing party in particular, and among respondents who placed themselves at the ends of the ideological spectrum (Bowler, Donovan and Karp 2001). Table 10.2 shows the responses of New Zealand candidates to a similar battery of questions. Overall, while support for CIRs is, as expected, somewhat lower among people aspiring to be policy decision-makers, there is still considerable sympathy for CIRs. Half the candidates agreed that referendums and CIRs are 'good things', most conceded that referendums get attention, and only a little more than a third believed that they are too complicated for voters. But there were far greater differences between electors and elites on the defining question of whether or not referendums should be binding. Only 9 per cent of the candidates thought that CIRs should 'automatically become law'. A similar distribution is evident on the question of whether Parliament or voters should make final decisions on law and policy. These results reveal support for the institutions of indirect democracy, and indicate that while elites may show some support for direct democracy in principle, they are nonetheless not very receptive to the idea of relinquishing their power to formulate policy to voters.

Table 10.2: Elite Opinion about Direct Democracy (%)

	Agree	Disagree	Don't Know
Referendums and CIRs are good things	50	13	34
Referendums should become law	9	81	10
Referendums get attention	87	8	5
Referendums are too complicated	37	44	19
Parliament not voters should make final decisions on law and policy	83	10	0
CIRs will make bad law	44	24	32
CIRs restrain parliament	44	31	24

SOURCE: NZES 1999 Candidate study

Voting on the 1999 CIRs

In politics, minor scandals make major headlines. After the 1996 election, the reputations of New Zealand First MPs, Tukoroirangi Morgan and Robyn McDonald, soon wilted under intense and deliberately destructive scrutiny by the Opposition and sections of the media. The performance of Alliance MP, Alamein Kopu, similarly drew scathing comment, rising to a chorus of public denigration when she left the Alliance and as an Independent MP switched support from the Opposition to the Government. A perception of MPs as being more self-interested than principled reached new heights with the collapse of the National–New Zealand First coalition in 1998 and the departure of a number of its MPs to other parties. Ironically, considering the tendency of many people to disparage politicians' blind adherence to party discipline, 'party hopping' brought more scorn on the heads of those who shifted their allegiance. Slighting politicians was by this time not merely rife, but even *de rigueur* in some walks of life.

Yet the resulting CIR seeking to cut the number of MPs was flawed in that its sponsor's aims were unlikely to be met by the means chosen to achieve them. The stated purpose of cutting the number of MPs was to improve their parliamentary behaviour. It was suggested that if there were fewer MPs they would have to work harder, which would reduce the time wasted in empty debate and partisan point-scoring. Yet such behaviour had been a feature of

New Zealand's adversarial style of politics well before the advent of the 120-member Parliament in 1996. Whatever the merit of the referendum's objective, reverting to 99 MPs would not solve the problem. But in addition to being ineffectual in achieving its prime objective, cutting back the number of MPs meant sacrificing significant gains in the practice of representative democracy. The move to MMP and the larger House of Representatives is too recent to allow a definitive assessment of the effects of the change. Nevertheless, it is clear that even after only one MMP election Parliament had become a more representative institution (Chapter 9), less overshadowed by the dominance of the Executive, and that its select committee system had been invigorated. Indeed, these were some of the benefits of a larger Parliament that had prompted the Royal Commission to recommend a minimum of 120 members, regardless of whether New Zealand adopted proportional representation or retained its traditional plurality electoral system (117–129).

Other possible benefits of the larger Parliament had yet to fully manifest themselves. For example, the quality of parliamentary debate was little improved, though the contribution of some members who owed their place to MMP and the larger Parliament provide exceptions. Other advantages were more evolutionary — for example, the effect of a larger 'pool of ministerial talent' promised by an expanded House. In this regard, normal recruitment paths favouring political experience within the two larger parties, and the lack of parliamentary expertise among most members of the smaller parties' caucuses, acted as delaying factors. Also requiring time to develop was the greater opportunity for MPs in a larger House to concentrate on, and develop special expertise in, particular policy areas. Nevertheless, at least one observer of the public policy process already saw portents of this during the first MMP Parliament (Easton 1999, 216).

While the stated aim of the CIR focused on the behaviour of MPs, the consequences of any reduction in their numbers were much wider. The reduction was almost certainly intended to be achieved by cutting the number of list seats to thirty-two. Indeed, the original wording of the petition had recommended this (Church 2000, 290). The alternative of reducing the number of electorate seats was not politically feasible, as it would have meant also increasing their geographical size to the detriment of effective local representation. A reduction in the number of list seats has consequences which the referendum's sponsors may or may not have intended. It is possible, though not inevitable, that a smaller ratio of list to electorate seats would put at risk the proportional allocation of seats intended by MMP. A second effect would be to greatly reduce the opportunity for larger parties to broaden their representation to perhaps include MPs from minority interests, or to achieve a better geographical spread of representation. For most of the larger parties' proportional share of parliamentary seats would be made up from the electorates they had won. In 1999, for example, because Labour did so well in the electorate contests, it would not have been eligible for any list seats in a hypothetical 99-seat House (see also Chapter 12). Even if no reduction were made in the present number of electorate seats, the effectiveness of local representation would be reduced. For the allocation of constituency duties to most list MPs, some of whom have set up offices in their home territories, has helped to compensate for the increase in size of electorates under MMP.

The proposed reduction in the size of the House was thus far from benign with respect to the functioning of MMP. Yet none of the possible wider consequences were adequately presented to the public in the lead-up to the referendum. While the advocates of reduction could rightly claim that a smaller Parliament would cost less in raw dollar terms, the estimated annual saving of $7.1 million is a mere drop in the bucket of public expenditure. Such a saving at the expense of a more effectively functioning Parliament would amount to false economy, as the Royal Commission had concluded (128–9).

Attempts to argue the case for more or fewer MPs on the basis of the ratio of MPs to populations are problematic because they are complicated by the presence or absence of state and local governments and of an upper house. Nevertheless, a comparison of the New Zealand Parliament with others shows that even with 120 MPs the New Zealand House is not disproportionately large (Electoral Commission 1999; NZES 2000, 59). Moreover, historically, even the present 120 MPs for 2.5 million registered voters compares unfavourably with the ratio a century earlier, when there were 70 MPs from European electorates to serve 303,000 registered electors (McRobie 1989).

There were clearly two sides to the proposal to cut the numbers of MPs, yet they were never adequately debated before the referendum. Rather, the objective of reducing the numbers was allowed to be subsumed within and borne along by anti-politician sentiment. There was virtually no official programme of public education on the issue.[3] Before the election campaign began, there was a certain amount of newspaper and magazine coverage of the issue, but this would have reached only a small fraction of eligible voters. During the campaign, the issue was almost completely crowded out, save for one very brief item on television news on each channel. When a group of academics opposed to the reduction moved to publicise and explain their case, they were castigated for their action by sections of the print media, and their analysis largely ignored.

Most, therefore, who cast votes for a reduction in the number of MPs may have done so sincerely, but only those who had gone to considerable personal effort would have made their choice on the basis of a balanced consideration of the arguments for and against such a cut. But the proportion of electors who made such an effort would be small. Indeed, during the campaign phase of the NZES voter survey, 35 per cent of those sampled said they had not even heard of the referendum, and they were about 6 per cent more likely than those who were aware of it to say they would vote for cutting the number of MPs.[4] Nevertheless, other research has demonstrated that even relatively uninformed voters can make effective decisions on initiatives and referendums (Lupia 1994).

To assess people's reasons for supporting the referendums we constructed a model that estimates the likelihood of voting for each of them. For the referendum on reducing the number of MPs, we included variables that measure evaluations of electorate and list MPs, along with a general measure of the degree to which citizens view politicians as responsive. If voters who supported the initiative were primarily venting their anger at politicians, we should expect to see stronger support among those who are dissatisfied with all

MPs and the political process. On the other hand, if voters reacted to the initiative in a rational way, then we should expect to see differences between voters depending on their policy preferences. Those disenchanted with list MPs specifically should be more likely to support the initiative while those who believe women's representation in Parliament should be increased, or those who value proportionality, should be less likely to support the initiative.

For the crime initiative, we include a measure of support for additional spending on police and law enforcement, and another assessing support for the death penalty. To determine whether voters who supported the initiatives believed they were participating in a meaningful policy-making process or simply engaging in a symbolic protest, we include two of the measures discussed earlier, measuring opinions about direct democracy. We have also controlled for ideology, preferred party, and socio-demographics (see Appendix C, Chapter 10 for more details). Figure 10.1 shows the relative impact of the five most important factors shaping support for the referendum to reduce the number of MPs, while Figure 10.2 shows the relative impact of three factors shaping support for the crime initiative.

In both cases, those with more political knowledge were significantly less likely to support the initiatives. Most likely this reflects the fact that people with more political knowledge are more likely to encounter some of the debate over the initiatives. For them, the issues were less clear-cut, and their voting patterns less skewed. This suggests that had there been a public education campaign, the size of the margin between the 'yes' and 'no' votes would probably have been much reduced.

The data also reveal some of the underlying attitudes and policy preferences steering electors toward their referendum choices. As Figure 10.1 shows, those who wanted more women in Parliament were far less likely to vote for the initiative, while those disapproving of the list MPs were more likely to vote in favour. This is consistent with evidence that the message about the consequences of reducing the number of MPs was getting through. Although not depicted in the figure, support for proportionality (in effect approval of MMP) is also significantly related to voting against the initiative to reduce the number of MPs. On the crime initiative, as Figure 10.2 shows, respondents who wanted more spending on police and law enforcement, or those who believed in the death penalty, were not surprisingly also more likely to vote in favour. In both initiatives those who believed that referendums should become law were more likely to vote in favour.

Although not shown in the figures, there was a detectable effect of ideology, with those on the left being far less likely to vote 'yes'. In this context, partisan differences also emerged, though these were more apparent on the initiative concerned with the size of Parliament. Labour, New Zealand First, and Green party voters were significantly less likely than National's (the comparison category) to support the initiative on MPs. The measures for the other parties, although statistically insignificant, were all negative, indicating lower support than National. In the crime initiative, however, only the Alliance and the Greens were significantly less supportive than National. In both initiatives, minority groups in the population were less supportive than New Zealand Europeans. The reason for this is not obvious for the crime initiative,

Figure 10.1: Factors Influencing Likelihood of Voting to Reduce the Number of MPs

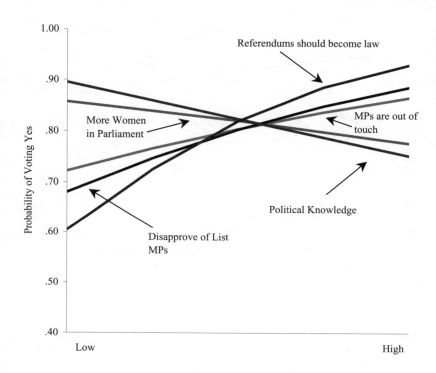

but the greater opportunities for minorities to achieve representation in a larger Parliament, especially by means of a favourable party list placing, would explain the response in the second case.

Conclusion

Two years before the election, the Palmers had written: 'Just what role citizens initiated referenda may play in the future is not easy to predict, but the portents are not favourable' (Palmer and Palmer 1997, 205). At that time, 20 of the 21 petitions launched since the CIR legislation had come into effect in 1994 had either lapsed or been withdrawn (Church 2000, 287–93). Only the initiative concerning the firefighters had been put to a vote, prompting a dismal 27 per cent turnout of enrolled electors. The referendums in 1999, in which 85 per cent of electors voted, were therefore the first serious test of the CIR experiment. They provided a comprehensive canvassing of electors' responses to two legitimate issues of public concern, which had aroused strong feelings across the community, and the distribution of votes was decisive.

Yet we are still left with a picture that is hardly clearer than the one the Palmers found. Ambiguity still surrounds the CIR process. The non-binding

158

Figure 10.2: Factors Influencing Likelihood of Voting to Get Tough on Crime

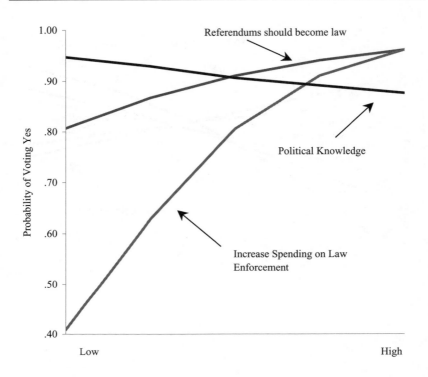

status of such referendums conflicts with the expectation of many citizens, especially those who have sponsored and supported a successful initiative, that action will automatically follow. In 1999, both initiatives received over-whelming endorsement from voters. Their moral mandates were therefore clear and powerful ones. Neither, however, bound the government to any action. Rather, the CIR process merely threw the issues back into the political arena. Subsequently, the government has acted in broad accordance with one of them, stiffening penalties for violent crime, but has taken no steps to reduce the size of Parliament (see Chapter 12). What had been a contentious issue before the CIR process remained one after. What had been achieved? At most, the initiative on the number of MPs had raised the salience of the issue, thus perhaps preparing it for another round of more deliberative assessment than has hitherto occurred.

In the avalanche of votes in favour of both initiatives, we can detect some elements of rationality in people's responses. In the circumstances of the election campaign, the issues at stake were given little attention, least of all attention that might have extended people's understanding of them. That on election day the voters expressed a collective judgement on the two refer-endum issues is not in doubt. That it was an informed judgement can be doubted. Rationality was given little chance. The result was two directives to the incoming government, neither of which could be said to represent a definitive expression of informed opinion, and neither of which obliged the government to do anything. Had the 1993 legislation made CIRs binding on governments, there might have been a more adequate (and expensive) programme of public education. But to move from indicative to binding CIRs would be a major constitutional step — a step forward, some would say, and others, a step backwards.

Our surveys have shown that there is wide popular support, extending even to the ranks of parliamentary candidates, for a measure of direct democracy in the country's governance. Yet on the evidence so far, the CIR process has failed to meet that demand. Rather, while offering much, it delivers too little. To resolve this by abandoning the process is politically untenable. So too at present is the alternative of making CIRs binding, an extension of direct democracy that is not yet widely supported by either electors or politicians. The Palmers' assessment therefore still stands. Citizens initiated referendums are still on trial.

CHAPTER 11

PUBLIC OPINION, PUBLIC KNOWLEDGE, AND THE ELECTORAL SYSTEM

Jack Vowles, Jeffrey Karp, Susan Banducci, Peter Aimer

Support for MMP between 1990 and 1993 was fuelled most by disillusion with the status quo. The vision of an alternative style of politics that might be expected to result from the shift to proportional representation, multi-party politics and coalition governments was less clear. For while the foundations of attitudes to FPP were based on experience, those for MMP were necessarily abstract and hypothetical. That changed after the first MMP election in 1996. From then on public opinion both for and against the new system would be shaped by experience. MMP, New Zealand's version of proportional representation, was on trial.

Foundations of Opinion

As they did in 1993, when they expressed a collective verdict on FPP, the jurors, the New Zealand people, could be expected to make their judgements of MMP on the basis of a mixture of considerations (Lamare and Vowles 1996). Among the first of these is partisanship — that is, what appears to be in the best strategic interest of a person's favoured party. People tend to make their assessments not necessarily on the basis of a sophisticated understanding of electoral systems, but more likely because they are cued by positions taken by party elites — the party's leaders, MPs and candidates. At first, Labour supporters were more likely to embrace the new electoral system than their National counterparts. Historically, National had benefited more than Labour from FPP. By 1993, Labour had held office for only twelve of the previous 44 years, and in 1978 and 1981 National succeeded in winning a majority of seats even though Labour had received more votes. As a result, Labour set up the Royal Commission that recommended MMP. Conversely, National's success in retaining government goes far to explain why there was little support for abandoning FPP within the National party and among its voters.

Supporters of small parties that would otherwise have difficulty gaining representation have been the most enthusiastic supporters of MMP. In 1990, parties such as NewLabour, Greens and Christian Heritage received 17.7 per cent of the vote, but garnered only 1 per cent of the seats in Parliament. In 1993, small parties received just over 30 per cent of the votes while gaining only 4 per cent of the seats. FPP thus enabled the country's two major parties to govern with alternating parliamentary majorities, despite their declining vote shares. However, in the first two elections under proportional representation, these smaller parties, as expected, fared much better, gaining 33 seats in a 120-seat Parliament in 1996, and 32 seats in 1999.

Considerations of partisanship colour many people's responses to day-to-day political issues, including their assessment of the performance of individual politicians, parties and the government. Such judgements also indirectly influence attitudes toward the electoral system, when they are projected on to it. Few issues put to the public are more complex than the evaluation of electoral systems. In 1992 and 1993, prior to each referendum, and particularly the first, substantial efforts were made to educate New Zealanders about electoral systems and their consequences. In those referendums, New Zealanders cast votes as informed about electoral systems as they were perhaps ever likely to be. Yet such complex information is often not retained when not needed in everyday life. Even the knowledge of the two votes and their respective importance under MMP tends to fade between elections as people put their minds to other things.

Independent of partisanship, a concern for abstract values such as fairness and democratic accountability is also likely to influence people's attitudes toward electoral systems. Within New Zealand's political culture there runs a strong vein of democratic populism. Expectations that parties make and keep election promises are high. To many people, the politicians and governments of the 1970s, 1980s, and early 1990s had failed to keep faith with the electorate. This negative reaction to recent political experiences under FPP was a major driving force behind the adoption of MMP (Lamare and Vowles 1996). A concern for fairness is also embedded in New Zealand culture and, indeed, evaluations of system fairness have been found to have had a strong impact on support for electoral system change in the 1993 referendum that mandated the switch to MMP (Banducci and Karp 1999).

The party elites who provide cues to the public also constitute a major interested group of persons in relation to the functioning of electoral systems. Once the process of transition from FPP is more or less complete, MMP makes incumbent MPs more secure, because it does not encourage such major changes in parliamentary representation as can occur under FPP. FPP elections tend to give more seats per vote to the largest parties, and where there is a large swing from one of two major parties to the other, the movement of seats will be even larger. Under MMP, seats' shares follow votes more closely, and being an MP is therefore a somewhat more secure and predictable position. Major parties losing elections also lose less heavily under MMP, as National discovered in 1999.

MMP also allows candidates to enter Parliament by either winning an electorate seat or via a party list. List MPs are able to enter Parliament without being directly elected by the voters. Moreover, defeated electorate MPs can still retain their positions in Parliament if they are placed high enough on the list. On rational assumptions, therefore, we might expect candidates and MPs, regardless of party, to be more supportive of a system that allows them two chances of winning a seat in Parliament, and a somewhat more secure future once having gained a seat. Elites from small parties should be the most enthusiastic supporters of a system that also guarantees proportional results, as opposed to candidates from large parties who would otherwise benefit under a system that offered no guarantees for small-party representation.

The Response to MMP

The NZES data from 1993 onwards, including election, mid-term, and candidate studies, enable us to probe more deeply into public attitudes and knowledge about MMP. Table 11.1 indicates the movement of public opinion from the 1993 referendum until July 2001. The form of the question that generated the data has changed somewhat over the years, and a little of the apparent movement of opinion may reflect this. In 1993, 1996, and July 2001 the data depict a straight choice between MMP and FPP. From July 1998, respondents were asked first whether MMP should be retained or replaced and, if replaced, by what alternative. Other options than MMP had been discussed and promoted over this period — in particular, a supplementary member system. Independently of the NZES surveys, however, public opinion polls continuing to ask respondents to make a straight choice between FPP and MMP provide findings consistent with our data, with estimates of FPP support falling close to those in the 'all alternative' column in our data. In other words, forced-choice questions asking for a straight choice between MMP and FPP measure the level of preference for MMP, but that for FPP is supplemented by supporters of alternative systems and those who, preferring any alternative to MMP, would vote for FPP in a 'straight fight'. On the other hand, asking for a forced choice gives a better estimate of core support for FPP, and an indication of any support for other options.

To clarify the trends from the 1993 referendum, those indicating a 'don't know' response have been removed. Otherwise in the telephone polls 'don't knows' tend to be lower than in our self-completion postal questionnaires, confusing the picture. From the most recent July 2001 study, we can also derive both straight choice and alternative electoral system formats.

Majority support for MMP remained fairly stable between the 1993 referendum and the first MMP election. Not long after the 1996 election, UMR-Insight polling that offered a straight choice between MMP and FPP showed that support for MMP had fallen well behind that for FPP. The composition of the coalition government was unexpected, and it had grown increasingly unpopular. The gap continued to widen through the first half of 1997, particularly among Labour voters (Vowles, Aimer, Banducci, Karp, 1998, 204–8). There was even greater dissatisfaction with the coalition's performance, as Figure 8.1 in Chapter 8 has already indicated (also see Karp and Bowler, 2001). Consistent with this polling, the NZES July 1998 mid-term survey, carried out just before the coalition broke up in August, indicated that

Table 11.1: Would You Vote to Retain or Replace MMP? (%)

	MMP	FPP	Other	STV	All Alter-native	Forced FPP	N
1993 referendum	54	–	–	–	–	46	
1996 election	57	–	–	–	–	43	4047
July 1998*	37	37	23	4	63	–	494
1999 Election	45	40	11	3	55	–	4765
Maori 1999 Election	54	25	21		46	–	759
Digipoll January 2001*	52				48	–	800
July 2001*	56	37	3	4	44	–	610
July 2001*	55	–	–	–	–	45	652

NOTE: The January 2001 poll was conducted for the *New Zealand Herald* by Digipoll (*New Zealand Herald*, 9 August 2001, A7)

* Telephone polls.

support for MMP was very low, having crashed twenty points to only 37 per cent of all those who would have been prepared to vote in a referendum.

Support for MMP had recovered somewhat by the time of the 1999 election, although it still lagged behind the forced-choice FPP option. The signs of slight recovery began after the coalition's collapse, but they seem to have intensified during the 1999 campaign. The campaign is likely to have reminded voters of some of the advantages of MMP, in particular the wider range of options presented by separate party and electorate votes. Some may also have relished the greater pressure put on politicians within the more competitive multi-party electoral framework under MMP, while for some others the anticipation of electoral success may have offset reservations about MMP. Additionally, the 1999 Maori election data indicates somewhat stronger support for MMP among Maori than among other New Zealanders, which has been a consistent feature since 1993.

After the election, support for MMP continued to recover, particularly as the new Labour–Alliance coalition remained popular, and as it appeared to be keeping more of its promises than other recent governments. By June–July 2001, the balance in overall public opinion appeared to have shifted once more in favour of MMP, much as it had been at the time of the 1993 referendum. But much of this support for MMP is almost certainly 'soft', as qualitative studies for the MMP review committee strongly suggest (UMR Insight, 2001). Given this, it is possible that the July 2001 data may represent a 'spike' rather than a consistent trend. UMR-Insight data up to its poll of June 2001 (47 per cent FPP, 39 per cent MMP) had not picked up the same improvement in support for MMP against FPP.

From Table 11.2 we can see that changes in support for retaining MMP were associated with changes in perceptions about MMP among the various groups of party voters or intending party voters. While the composition and strength of these groups have also changed over time, the largest partisan grouping in favour of MMP in 1993 were Labour voters, 68 per cent of whom reported choosing MMP in the referendum. But the outcome of the 1996 election was a disappointment for their party. MMP had not delivered the victory they had hoped for, and enthusiasm for the new electoral system began to flag, falling to 59 per cent immediately after the 1996 election and continuing to drop to below a majority between 1996 and 1999. After the 1999 election a majority of Labour voters still failed to express support for MMP. By the middle of the Labour–Alliance coalition's term, however, a majority of those intending to vote Labour were apparently supporting MMP once more.

Table 11.2: Vote to Retain MMP 1993–2001: Voters/Intending Voters and Party Candidates

		1993		1996		1999		2001	
		%	N	%	N	%	N	%	N
Labour	Voters	68	656	59	1301	44	2017	59	264
	Candidates	72	54	57	60	56	52		
National	Voters	24	742	25	1427	23	1608	30	219
	Candidates	15	39	18	44	22	41		
Alliance	Voters	82	400	75	416	56	406	81	41
	Candidates	100	79	96	48	82	54		
NZ First	Voters	69	168	6	669	58	222	71	16
	Candidates	95	43	88	34	69	26		
ACT	Voters			47	379	27	377	46	24
	Candidates			54	54	64	47		
Green	Voters					62	270	77	61
	Candidates					90	51		

1993, 1996, 2001: MMP versus FPP, base includes don't knows

1999: per cent who say they would vote to keep MMP if an election were being held today, base includes don't knows

Meanwhile National voters, the least enthusiastic toward MMP in 1993, discovered in 1996 that MMP had not prevented their party from governing. Yet National voters' support for MMP remained a little below a quarter in 1993, 1996 and just after the 1999 election. However July 1998 and campaign data suggest that support for MMP from prospective National voters may have risen above 30 per cent as National continued to govern under MMP, only to fall back immediately after the election to its earlier levels. In 1999 National voters, it seems, displaced their disappointment with the election outcome onto the electoral system, as Labour voters had done after 1996. Nonetheless, by 2001, even intending National voters were more supportive of MMP than they had been after the 1993, 1996 and 1999 elections. In all years, and consistent with partisan self-interest, people voting for the smaller parties exhibit the highest degree of support for MMP, though their levels of support also declined before recovering in 2001. ACT voters are the major exception.

As expected, given the additional element of rational self-interest in MPs' attitudes to MMP, support for MMP is higher among the candidates of all parties than among their voters. Only among National candidates did support fall short of a majority in 1999, reflecting accurately the low level of support among National voters. Yet among the elites too there has been a softening of commitment since 1993 in the Labour, Alliance and New Zealand First camps. Notable, however, is the conspicuous discrepancy in support for MMP between ACT voters and the party's candidates. In that respect, ACT voters are closer to National, suggesting that many of those who voted for ACT might nevertheless be National sympathisers.

Table 11.3 next reports the results from a question that directly put to respondents one of the key rhetorical claims of those opposed to MMP — that 'MMP must go' (Hunt 1998). In 1998 and 1999, that claim was put against two alternatives: that MMP has been a success and should be retained, or that it was 'too soon to tell'. The data show a consistent core of support for FPP at about a third of the electorate. Meanwhile the committed pro-MMP camp, though small, doubled in size after July 1998, and remained steady after the formation of the new government in 1999. Once more Maori prove to be significantly more supportive of MMP. In 1998 and 1999 by far the largest group of respondents preferred to withhold their judgements.

Table 11.3: MMP Disaster, Too Soon to Tell, or Success? Opinion 1998–2001

	Get Rid	Success	Too soon	Don't know	N
July 1998	40	6	49	5	478
Nov 1999	36	12	49	4	672
Post-election	29	12	51	8	5495
Maori post-election	14	17	60	9	726
July 2001	32	37	–	–	650

For 1998 and 1999, the question was: 'Some people say MMP has been a disaster and we should get rid of it as soon as possible. Others say MMP has been a success and we should keep it. Others say it is too soon to tell. Which is closer to your view?' For July 2001, respondents were asked to agree or disagree with each of the first two statements separately. The data exclude respondents who did not vote at the election or did not express an intention to vote for party during the intervening period.

While some people may have selected the 'too soon to tell' response category as an easy way of avoiding a more definitive stand, the consistent popularity of this response over time adds to the evidence that judgements of MMP were — and probably still are — in flux. For the 2001 study, we changed the question, asking respondents to agree or disagree with the first two statements in the question separately. This change is certainly partly responsible for much greater support for the view that MMP is a success, although clearly opinion has moved in that direction as well.

In sum, patterns and trends in support for MMP since 1993 are to a large extent consistent with perceptions of partisan advantage both for groups of electors and candidates alike. The main exception were ACT voters, who are strangely antagonistic toward MMP, compared to the voting groups of all other small parties. Candidates, with the exception of National, remained far more enthusiastic about MMP than their voters, especially after dissatisfaction with the outcome of the 1996 election, and the performance of the National–New Zealand First coalition had dampened voter enthusiasm for the new system. The NZES mid-term survey in July 1998 almost certainly captured public sentiment about MMP at its lowest ebb, during the most intense period of disillusion with the coalition government. MMP had become a label for a variety of ills associated with the government, including the 'party hopping' of a number of MPs, the increasing appearance of disunity within the coalition and of course its final collapse.

For candidates, however, the opportunities presented by MMP appear to have outweighed these concerns, and by 2001 the more favourable elite attitudes had become echoed among voters. It is tempting to interpret this as a lag effect between elite cues and mass responses, yet many ordinary people have almost certainly made their own judgements as the 1999 election was followed by a smooth transition to a new coalition government.

Coalitions or Single-Party Governments?

So far we have reported people's feelings about MMP in general, and noted that their attitudes often reflected political partisanship. They assessed MMP according to what they perceived as strategically beneficial to their party. We now shift the focus to two specific features of MMP that might influence people's evaluations of it, notably that it produces proportional outcomes, and, linked to that, it generates also a high probability of coalition governments. A liking or disliking of either or both of these might influence evaluations of MMP, independently of partisan considerations.

Given a long history of FPP elections and one-party rule in New Zealand, voters were not prepared for the process of coalition formation. In 1996 they were particularly not prepared for a process in which New Zealand First, a small pivotal party, took control of negotiations in a way that is unusual in most other countries having proportional electoral systems (Miller 1998; Boston 1998). Table 11.4, however, shows that the strong preference for single-party governments when concern about the National–New Zealand First coalition was at its height in 1998 has been replaced by more evenly balanced opinion, slightly to the advantage of coalitions.

Acceptance of coalitions did not, however, extend to the National party. Table 11.4 also shows that after the 1999 election National voters still yearned for the one-party governments that FPP had so frequently delivered them in the past half-century, and National candidates, unlike those of any other party, wholeheartedly agreed. Labour's major party status also found residual expression in a substantial minority of both voters and candidates who still preferred single-party government, although a narrow majority of both groups preferred coalition government by 1999. By July 2001 opinion had not changed markedly on this question, support for coalition government firming only very slightly at the expense of the 'don't know' category — a difference well within the possible range of sampling error.

Table 11.4: Preferences for Coalition or Single-Party Government, 1998–2001

		Single party	Coalition	Don't know	N
All NZ	July 1998	58	40	3	491
	1999 Election	44	47	10	5478
	Maori 1999 Election	32	58	10	1000
	July 2001	44	50	6	650
By party, post-election					
Labour	Voters	40	50	9	2012
	Candidates	42	55	4	53
National	Voters	64	28	7	1598
	Candidates	70	23	7	43
Alliance	Voters	20	72	6	406
	Candidates	6	91	4	55
NZ First	Voters	25	64	7	220
	Candidates	27	73		26
ACT	Voters	48	40	9	375
	Candidates	15	75	10	48
Green	Voters	16	73	11	268
	Candidates	2	94	4	51

The question was: 'After the coming election, what sort of government would you prefer (Generally speaking, do you prefer) – a government made up of a single party or a coalition government made up of more than one party?'
The top three rows of data exclude respondents who did not vote at the election or did not express an intention to vote for party during the intervening period.

Overall, support for governments made up of more than one party is greatest among the smaller parties that were most likely to benefit from coalitions. Once again, however, ACT voters as a group were closer to their National political cousins than their fellow small-party associates, more preferring single-party government than coalitions. With the exception of National, the candidates of all parties were more able to accept the prospect of coalitions than electors. It is clear from the shift of opinion between 1998 and 1999, however, that acceptance of the unfamiliar practice of coalition government is still contingent on the performance of such governments, and above all on the degree of stability they can achieve.

Coalition processes have still not yet been absorbed into the political culture in the way that single-party governments came to be regarded as the democratic norm in the 60 years between 1935 and 1995. On the other hand, the process by which the coalition was formed in late 1996 was extreme and unusual, even within the experience of most countries with PR. It was, in effect, about the worst example of the process one could have imagined, and the negative response of New Zealanders was easy to understand. The smoothness of government formation in late 1999 (Chapter 8) stands in acute contrast, and with that experience, New Zealanders' attitudes to coalitions have again become more favourable.

Table 11.5 indicates some of the grounds for people's changing assessments of coalition government. Even in 1993, when people were more optimistic about MMP, more thought one-party government would be better for stability. Immediately after the 1996 election, disillusion with the National–New Zealand First coalition had not yet set in. By 1999, after the collapse of that coalition, those seeing one-party government as better than coalitions for promoting stability were ten points up to a solid majority, with only a quarter still believing that multi-party governments were more stable. There was movement, too, on 'making tough decisions', but surprisingly people remained fairly evenly divided on that indicator even by 1999.

Ten-point changes against multi-party government also feature in the last two indicators, both of which refer to aspects of democratic accountability. Yet despite shifts of opinion, the largest group of respondents still saw multi-party governments as best for 'keeping promises', and thought them better for 'doing what the people want' than single-party governments. Had those questions been asked in July 1998, multi-party governments would have almost certainly come off worse. The more positive coalition experience after the 1999 election appears to have restored some confidence in coalition governments, particularly in their ability to deliver democratic accountability.

Table 11.5:   Generally speaking, do you think that a government formed by one party, or one formed by more than one party, is better at doing the following things?

	One party best	More than one best	Both the same	Don't know	N
Providing stability					
1993	45	34	8	13	1978
1996	46	35	10	10	3999
1999	57	25	11	8	4885
Making tough decisions					
1993	36	46	8	11	1959
1996	35	47	9	9	3961
1999	42	40	11	7	4851
Keeping promises					
1993	17	59	13	11	1969
1996	20	59	12	10	3996
1999	30	43	17	9	4861
Doing what the people want					
1993	13	64	12	12	1973
1996	10	63	15	12	3992
1999	19	51	19	11	4850

The Core Principle of Proportionality

The defining characteristic of MMP is that it is a means of achieving proportional representation. That is, it ensures that parties will win seats in Parliament much more closely and consistently in proportion to their voting strength than under FPP. A number of consequences flow from this — a multiparty Parliament, a more prominent parliamentary role for smaller parties, a greater diversity of MPs, and, as examined above, a greater likelihood of coalition governments. Attitudes toward proportionality are therefore fundamental to assessments of MMP. If the effects of proportionality are not valued, the supporting rationale for MMP will crumble.

But given the points made earlier about public knowledge of electoral systems, how well do voters understand the concept of proportionality, and, most particularly, its relevance to evaluations of MMP and FPP? For the July 2001 study, we read people two statements and, for each, asked them under which system, MMP or FPP, they thought they were more likely to be true. The two statements were:

*   'A party with 15 per cent of all the votes will get about 15 per cent of the seats in Parliament';
*   'A party that gets the most votes will get the most seats in Parliament'.

The correct answer was, in each case, MMP. MMP obviously favours small parties, and FPP does not. Fifty-five per cent agreed with this, but 22 per cent disagreed, and 23 per cent did not know, a significant slice of the electorate. At the 1978 and 1981 elections in New Zealand, held under FPP, the party with the most votes did not get the most seats. Such a scenario is much less likely under MMP, due to the 'top-up' role of the list seats assigned under the party vote. Yet a clear majority, 54 per cent, responded that FPP was more likely to deliver the most seats to the party with the most votes, only 32 per cent gave the right answer, MMP, and 14 per cent did not know.

Table 11.6 parcels out respondents into levels of support for the two electoral systems and levels of knowledge of their PR consequences. Only a quarter of respondents answered both PR knowledge questions correctly. Of those who correctly understood that MMP is a PR system, 55 per cent belong to the core MMP category. Among those who wrongly thought that FPP produces proportional results, 44 per cent belong to the core FPP category. Support for MMP is therefore enhanced by knowledge, and reduced by lack of knowledge of proportional representation. The rank order Spearman's r correlation between the two is 0.26. This lack of knowledge of the relations between proportionality and electoral systems is disturbing, as the concept is the main rationale behind MMP. If it is an accurate reflection of public knowledge, then current public opinion about electoral system issues is based on a great deal of misunderstanding.

Perhaps people misunderstood the questions. Yet interviewers were instructed to read them very carefully, repeating if necessary, and the idea is quite simple. Perhaps strong supporters of FPP were unwilling to concede the proportionality of MMP and admit that FPP can often produce disproportional election outcomes. Meanwhile more in-depth analysis of the 1999 post-election data confirms that a preference for PR leads people to believe MMP

Table 11.6: MMP versus FPP, Core and Soft Support by Knowledge of PR and Electoral Systems

| Column %s | Knowledge of PR Consequences | | | |
	0	1	2	MMP/ FPP all
Core FPP	44	32	18	33
Soft FPP	15	13	8	12
Soft MMP	18	17	18	18
Core MMP	24	38	55	38
Row %	32	43	25	
N	211	281	160	652

Knowledge of PR is defined by scoring one to each correct answer to the two PR knowledge questions, and adding them together. Core FPP support is made up of those who agreed 'MMP is a disaster' and for MMP those who agreed 'MMP is a success'.

SOURCE: 2001 NZES Midterm Study

is fairer, but does so much more among politically knowledgeable people. Therefore if more citizens knew that MMP fostered proportionality, its support would be greater (Vowles, Karp and Banducci 2000). Qualitative research backs up the inference that public knowledge about electoral systems, the differences between them, and their consequences is low.[1] It also suggests strongly that the problem is not simply understanding of MMP, but, perhaps even more important, a lack of understanding of FPP. A significant number of people simply do not understand that FPP elections do not necessarily generate proportional representation, and indeed frequently do not do so. Others are misled by the title, first-past-the-post, from which they take the inference that it means the most votes deliver the most seats.

Lack of understanding of the relationship between electoral systems and proportional representation therefore explains an apparent contradiction. In our successive surveys, and particularly since 1998, New Zealanders have consistently expressed support for the principle of proportional representation while, until our most recent work in the field, also expressing majority opposition to MMP. Table 11.7 provides more detail on various attitudes to proportionality compared to the opposing ideal and practice of the 'manufactured majority' aspect of FPP and related systems.

As the table shows, a substantial majority of about 60 per cent were favourable toward the principle of proportional representation, agreeing that we should 'Give each party a percentage of the seats in Parliament equal to its percent of the party vote'. A similar majority agreed with the ideal that governments should be grounded on the support of a majority, not just a plurality, of voters. On the other hand, slightly more oppose the principle of manufactured majority ('Ensure that only one party is needed to form the government') than support it.

The principle of proportionality is so fundamental to an understanding of

Table 11.7: Attitudes to Proportionality

An election should:	Agree	Disagree	Neutral/ DK	N
Provide a government at least half the people voted for	62	11	27	4600
Give each party a percentage of the seats in Parliament equal to its percent of the party vote	60	14	27	4663
Ensure that only one party is needed to form the Government	35	37	27	4639
Do you agree or disagree with the following:				
MMP is much fairer than the old first past the post system	42	27	31	4922
MMP gives too much power to small parties	36	32	26	4888
First past the post gave too much power to large parties	51	22	27	4870

MMP that in our 1999 questionnaire we probed our respondents' attitudes to it a second time, giving them a specific example: 'Imagine that one party wins the most votes in an election with about 40 per cent of the votes. Regardless of whether you liked that party or not, do you think that party should get about 40 per cent of the seats in Parliament, more than half the seats, so it can easily govern on its own, or somewhere between 40 per cent and half the seats?' In Table 11.8 this less abstract application of the principle of proportionality indicates lower (44 per cent compared to 60 per cent in Table 11.7) but still strong support for a proportional outcome. A significant number also indicate a preference for modifying proportionality so as to give a somewhat larger share of seats to the largest party without guaranteeing it a majority. In 2001, support for proportionality was at the same level as in Table 11.7. Acceptance of proportionality ahead of a manufactured majority runs across all party groups, and is stronger among candidates than voters. National's leaning toward FPP, however, is again evident in the size of the minorities of voters and candidates who agree with the idea of a manufactured majority, and of course, one-party government.

It is possible that those who expressed a preference for a proportional distribution of seats in Parliament also believed in one-party majority governments. For proportional representation does not prohibit a single party from governing alone on the basis of its own parliamentary majority. Yet in practice this is unlikely to happen except on rare occasions, and therefore a realistic assessment of preferences about PR must embody a trade-off between a preference for either proportional representation or one-party government. Accordingly, Table 11.9 displays the results of a question requiring respondents to balance their preferences for proportionality, if they have them, against those they might have for single-party government.

In our successive surveys, when thus forced to make this choice, a majority or near-majority of respondents have consistently supported proportionality,

Table 11.8: Attitudes toward Proportionality: Manufactured Majority

		About 40%	More than half	Between	Don't know	N
1999		44	19	19	18	5662
2001		61	27	3	9	650
Labour	Voters	42	18	22	17	2010
	Candidates	70	2	22	6	54
National	Voters	39	25	19	15	1594
	Candidates	44	29	20	7	41
Alliance	Voters	57	11	18	13	401
	Candidates	89		7	4	55
NZ First	Voters	45	17	17	18	222
	Candidates	80	12	8		25
ACT	Voters	54	19	15	10	374
	Candidates	83	6	8	2	48
Green	Voters	67	4	22	6	265
	Candidates	94		6		52

Table 11.9: Proportionality vs. Single-Party Governments, Voters and Candidates Post-Election 1999

		More than half	Same	Don't know	N
All NZ	July 1998	43	52	5	467
	Last week pre-election	38	55	7	632
	Post-election	39	49	11	5471
	July 2001	40	55	6	650
By party, post-election					
Labour	Voters	39	49	13	2008
	Candidates	9	89	2	53
National	Voters	53	36	11	1598
	Candidates	55	38	7	43
Alliance	Voters	21	68	11	405
	Candidates	2	98		55
NZ First	Voters	31	58	11	218
	Candidates	19	77	4	25
ACT	Voters	40	52	8	375
	Candidates	10	88	2	48
Green	Voters	10	83	7	267
	Candidates		100		52

The question was: 'Which of the following is most important to you? That one party has more than half the seats in Parliament so it can (easily) govern on its own? OR that parties have about the same percentage of seats in Parliament as their percent of the party vote?'. The top three rows of data exclude respondents who did not vote at the election or did not express an intention to vote for party during the intervening period.

even in July 1998 when MMP was most unpopular. Highest support came from those who voted for smaller parties and among candidates, the exception again being National voters and candidates. When compared to support for retaining MMP (Table 11.1), support for proportionality is higher. Lack of knowledge that MMP is a proportional system, and that FPP is not, almost certainly explains most of this difference. Many people fail to understand that MMP assures proportional electoral outcomes that increase the likelihood of coalition governments. Instead, MMP has become a label associated with lengthy coalition talks, failed coalitions, political scandal and party-hopping MPs. And as we saw in Chapter 8, evaluations of MMP are also strongly influenced by evaluations of the current government.

Conclusion

Our results indicate that elites express much stronger support for MMP than voters do. National elites and voters, however, contribute strongly to core support for FPP. Among elites and voters alike partisanship has significant effects, with self-interest an apparent added factor among candidates. While elites are more supportive of MMP, they also remain fairly close to their voters — probably because they provide significant cues to their voters and therefore influence them. ACT voters are an exception. They exhibit lower levels of support for MMP than ACT candidates and have a stronger preference for single-party government. As a result, their attitudes more closely resemble those held by National voters and candidates. There is some evidence that a large number of ACT voters are strategic voters with core National loyalties rather than sincere voters for ACT. This might help to explain the discrepancy.

By mid-2001, our data indicate that opinion about electoral systems appeared to have reverted to a pattern similar to that in 1993. But its stability remained dubious given that other independent polling on this issue has continued to show FPP ahead on a forced-choice basis, except for the occasional 'spike' in support for MMP. However, choice between MMP and FPP in a hypothetical referendum as proposed in surveys is primarily based on perceptions of politicians in general and of government performance more specifically. The level of understanding that MMP is a system of proportional representation and FPP is not appears to be low. Meanwhile our data indicate that New Zealanders continue to support the principle of proportional representation by margins of 10 to 15 per cent, even when it is traded off against a preference for the single-party governments fostered under FPP systems. Moreover, the more knowledge people possess that MMP is a proportional system and that FPP is not, the more likely they are to support MMP. We therefore conclude that 'hidden support' for MMP is higher than apparent support. If another electoral system referendum were held in conjunction with a comprehensive information campaign like those of 1992 and 1993, the odds are strong that MMP might once more prevail. That said, evaluations of MMP would still be shaped by other factors and by current events, and information campaigns can be crowded out by the more colourful efforts of strong advocacy by proponents and opponents alike.

During 2001 opponents of MMP, including National party leader Jenny Shipley, stepped up a campaign to have another electoral system referendum. Meanwhile Parliament's MMP review committee met, and released its report. In the next and final chapter, we consider the MMP review committee's work in more detail, explore the issues that it considered and speculate about what the future may hold for proportional representation in New Zealand.

CHAPTER 12

REVIEWING MMP

Jack Vowles, Jeffrey Karp, Susan Banducci, Peter Aimer, Raymond Miller

My view always was that if there was widespread discontent
with the system there would have to be another referendum.
But I don't see it, I don't hear it, I don't smell it. . . .
Under present conditions there's not the slightest prospect of a
referendum because nobody's saying the system is incurably
broken down. By and large they think it's working OK.
— Helen Clark, *Sunday Star-Times*, 26 November 2000.

In August 2001 a parliamentary committee set up to review MMP released its
report, somewhat oddly named as 'an inquiry into a review'. Made up of
representatives from all parties represented in Parliament except New Zealand
First, which had declined membership, the committee was unable to agree on
any action. The public reaction, such as it was, was critical. In particular, those
wishing to see the size of Parliament reduced and an immediate referendum on
MMP accused the members of the committee opposing those changes of
'arrogance'.

The work of the committee, if not the substance of its report, was a
requirement of the legislation that had set up the MMP system. Under section
264 of the Electoral Act 1993 (see Appendix D for the text), the House of
Representatives was required after April 2000 to appoint a select committee to
report specifically on (1) the manner in which the country was divided into
General electorates (sections 35 and 36 of the Act);[1] (2) the provisions for
Maori representation; (3) 'Whether there should be a further referendum on
changes to the electoral system', and if so what they should be, and when the
referendum should be held.

In 2000, Parliament added three further items to the original Act's list of
matters for the committee to consider, plus a general catch-all category. Its
terms of reference were now extended to include specifically the number of
MPs, the effect of party lists on the representation of women, and the 'effectiveness of the electoral system' for 'the representation of Maori and other
ethnic minorities' (Appendix D). Finally the committee was authorised to
consider 'any other matters'. It was required by the original Act to report to
Parliament before June 2002.

The Committee

As required under the law, the select committee of Parliament to review MMP was established in April 2000. Whereas most select committees operate on a majority basis, in order to minimise partisan divisions, the MMP review committee was modelled after Parliament's Business Committee. This required the review committee to reach unanimous or near-unanimous conclusions, 'having regard to the numbers in the House represented by each of the members of the committee' (MMP Review Committee 2001, 2). Following the model of the Business Committee, the government invited all parties represented in Parliament to contribute a member, and also proposed that the Speaker chair the committee. The task of the MMP committee was far more contentious, however, than the work of the Business Committee. Unanimity was never likely, and disagreement extended even to the form of the review committee.

National initially opposed the government's approach, arguing that the committee, like normal select committees, should reflect 'the proportionality of Parliament'. This would have given Labour and National MPs together a large majority. National also questioned the appointment of the Speaker, Jonathan Hunt, to chair the committee. Its spokesperson, Tony Ryall, who subsequently sat on the committee, predicted that it would end up in 'petty political squabbling', making it inappropriate for the Speaker to be involved. National eventually supported the motion to set up the committee on the 'unanimity' principle, but also argued for a guarantee of a referendum to endorse its findings — a position that effectively would have instructed the committee to take a position from the outset on a matter on which the Act obliged it to deliberate. Under the circumstances, consensus decisions did indeed seem an unlikely prospect. Meanwhile New Zealand First refused to take part in the committee, claiming that it was a 'jack-up' by Labour and National to get rid of MMP.

The government's approach and consequent composition of the committee did not support New Zealand First's interpretation. It contained three Labour MPs: Hunt, Georgina Beyer, and Chris Carter, and the government conceded that Hunt, as chair, would have no vote, although it would be his role to determine whether or not unanimity had been reached. The two National members were the leader, Jenny Shipley, and Tony Ryall (Marie Hasler replacing him from February 2001). This made up four voting members from the two major parties. Four others came from small parties: United's Peter Dunne, ACT's Stephen Franks, the Alliance's Grant Gillon, and the Greens' Rod Donald. Had New Zealand First accepted its place, the committee would have had a majority from the small parties. Yet even without New Zealand First, it was not likely that National and Labour would dominate its deliberations, nor that opponents of MMP would be in the driver's seat.

Few people either involved or observing from the sidelines expected radical recommendations. 'Near-unanimity' was defined as needing to include all parties except United.[2] Some members of the committee had gone on record with a variety of views on the issues before the committee. The Green member, Rod Donald, had been a campaigner for MMP before entering Parliament, and indicated that he would strongly defend MMP. The National leader, Jenny Shipley, an opponent of MMP, initially said that she had an open mind, and was not 'going in to throw out MMP'. However, her open advocacy of a referendum to pre-empt the work of the committee had the intended effect of adding strength to the cause of opposition to MMP. Meanwhile the chair of the committee, Jonathan Hunt, a former opponent of MMP, publicly expressed his belief that the committee 'was not going to be making a substantial change to our present electoral system' (*Sunday Star-Times*, 20 November 2000, C2).

The first submissions heard by the committee came from political parties. As it turned out, these were the most important, as those conducting the review almost invariably followed their party's position in committee. ACT, the only small party with ambivalent attitudes, effectively endorsed a 'too soon to tell' position, arguing for the retention of MMP for another two parliamentary terms, followed by a review. Labour, the Alliance and the Greens took the same position. National, as it had in the House when the committee was established, again argued for a referendum on the electoral system following the current review. United's Peter Dunne, while not opposing National's position, also favoured holding a referendum to enable the public to approve or reject any revisions to MMP recommended by the committee.

How many MPs? Proportionality and Representation

One of the most contentious issues before the committee was that of the number of MPs. The 1993 Electoral Act had set the size of the House under MMP at 120. Debate at the time indicated that those supporting the change to 120 members were made up of several distinct groups. Following the report of the Royal Commission on the Electoral System, one group sincerely believed that New Zealand needed a larger House, regardless of the electoral system. Others, however, wished to see MMP defeated by linking it with an increase to 120 MPs. For it was already clear that the proposed increase was widely unpopular, leading to the quip that MMP stood for 'many more politicians', whereas under FPP it was proposed that the House would remain at 99. This led to a third group, mostly advocates of MMP, who argued for 99 members in 1993 in order to have a fair contest between MMP and FPP, without the complicating factor of the size of Parliament.

The committee's deliberations on the number of MPs were clouded by the overwhelming result of the citizens initiated referendum on the issue, held at the same time as the election (Chapter 10). There was still some heat in the issue. Indeed, public discussion after the review committee released its report in July 2001 was largely dominated by it. It was an issue that fed on people's cynicism about politicians and politics, including a perception that public money was wasted on the activities and perquisites of MPs. For example, immediately after the first MMP election in 1996, a plan to modify and extend Parliament's buildings to accommodate the larger number of MPs was damned at the outset by the label 'parliamentary palace', amid a public outcry against the proposal. In 2001, the size of the House, while still a matter of great public concern, can also be said to have distracted attention away from the original purpose of the review.

Yet it is a serious issue for the future of MMP. NZES data shows strong support among electors for proportionality (Chapter 11). In this respect, a reduction of the size of the House to 99 members would almost certainly bring forward future problems for MMP, if that number were permanently fixed. This is on the assumption that a reduction in the number of MPs would be of list, not electorate, MPs. It is the list MPs who are allocated so as to maintain proportionality in party representation. Too few list MPs — some estimate less than 40 per cent — and there is a danger that electorate seat imbalances between parties may not be correctable by list seat allocation. Even if the House remained at its present size, the same problem would emerge, though in the more distant future. For under the 1993 Electoral Act, the size of the House is fixed at 120, and under sections 35 and 36 the number of electorate seats is pegged to a minimum of sixteen in the South Island. If the balance of population continues to shift to the North Island, as is likely, the number of electorate seats will continue to increase at the expense of list seats. Increases in the number of Maori electorates — which rise from six in 1999 to seven at the 2002 election — also take place at the expense of list seats. As a result, the number of list seats fell from 55 in 1996 to 53 in 1999, and will almost certainly fall at least as much again for the 2002 election. On the other side of the ledger, electorate seats rose from 65 to 67, and could be as many as 70 in 2002. Thus even with 120 MPs, list seats are likely to fall to about 42 per cent of the total in 2002, and perhaps below 40 per cent at the next election after that. This trend would be greatly accelerated, however, if the total number of MPs were to be reduced to 99. In that event, only 29 list seats would remain, or just under 30 per cent. As the list seats provide the proportional 'P' in MMP, the declining ratio of list to electorate seats is a concern, whether or not the current 120 seats are retained. The legal foundations of MMP as constituted in 1993 contain a self-destruct mechanism in the form of a steadily declining share of list MPs, an issue the review committee did not entirely ignore, but instead referred back to the government for further consideration.

Besides the effect on proportionality, there are other arguments for and against reducing the size of the House to 99 (see Chapter 10). Contrary to public opinion, the case for maintaining 120 members is a strong one, as the majority of the MMP review committee concluded, though the arguments were certainly not given much currency at the time of the 1999 referendum. While referendums may be a useful adjunct to parliamentary democracy, their value is conditional on the level of public information on the matter. If information is low, those voting may not be aware of the consequences of their choices. For the 1992 and 1993 referendums on MMP, substantial efforts were made to inform the public about the implications of the options before them (McRobie 1993). For the referendum on compulsory superannuation in 1997, there was a similarly well-funded information campaign.

By contrast, the referendum on the number of MPs took place in an information vacuum. In the 2001 mid-term survey, we asked two questions intended to measure the level of public knowledge of two issues relevant to judgement about the appropriate size of the House. It was frequently asserted by those supporting a reduction in the size of the House to 99 that New Zealand has a higher number of MPs per head of population than other countries. In fact, this is not the case, but only 7 per cent of our respondents knew this, 54 per cent wrongly indicating they thought this statement was true (New Zealand Electoral Commission, 1999; NZES 2000). Meanwhile, those who wished to maintain 120 MPs made the point that a reduction in the size of the House to 99 would give New Zealanders fewer MPs per head of population than ever before, a condition hardly likely to enhance the ability of voters to contact or influence their representatives and thus make them more responsive. Complaints that MPs are arrogant and out of touch are oddly paired with the advocacy of a reduction in their numbers, which would be likely to make them less accessible to individual voters. But only 29 per cent possessed this information. Table 12.1 indicates that only 3 per cent of respondents answered both knowledge statements correctly, a disconcertingly low level of public information given the importance of the issues at stake. Although the respondents whom we have classified as 'fully informed' were far less inclined than others to cut the numbers of MPs, because there were so few of them in our sample we can only speculate that greater information at the time of the referendum would have made a difference to the result.

Table 12.1: Knowledge by Opinion on the Size of the House

Column %	Knowledge			
	Both Wrong	One Correct	Both Correct	All
Reduce to 99	76	77	56	76
Stay at 120	15	19	42	17
Don't Know	9	4	2	7
Row % ( )	(67)	(30)	(3)	
N	487	216	25	727

NOTE: The two knowledge questions were: 'New Zealand has more MPs per person than most other countries' (correct answer 'false'), and 'If we reduced Parliament to 99 members, New Zealand would have fewer MPs per person than ever before' (correct answer 'true').

In the NZES submission to the review committee (NZES 2000), we advised retaining 120 MPs. However, aware of the strength of public opinion, we wished to make recommendations that also covered the contingency of reverting to a 99-member House, and the resulting potential threat to proportionality. Using the example of practices in some German states (*Länder*), we suggested the adoption of a mechanism to temporarily increase the size of the House by adding further list seats in conditions where, after an election, existing list seats might prove too few to compensate for electorate-seat disproportionality (often described as 'overhang'). While such temporary increases in list seats could resolve the proportionality problem for a 99-seat House, if the normal number of seats were permanently fixed at 99 the need for and extent of temporary increases would grow as the number of electorate seats increased. Indeed, simulation of the 1999 election result in a 99-member house indicates that Labour would have received no list seats, a situation already perilously close to an overhang.

A more satisfactory solution if the House were reduced to 99 members would be to allow the size of the House to gradually increase, as it had been until the 1993 Electoral Act. A fixed sixteen seats in the South Island could be maintained, as could an approximate 2:1 electorate seat to list seat ratio. This ratio would be likely to generate an occasional overhang, and for that reason a mechanism for making a temporary increase in the number of list seats would still be desirable, even though the need for it would probably be rare. In the review committee's report, National and United, the parties favouring reduction to 99 MPs, apparently accepted that, were the House to be reduced to 99 MPs, its size would also need to increase in response to population change (MMP Review Committee, 2001, 17).[3] Assuming the retention of the sixteen-electorate South Island minimum, a ratio of two electorates to one list seat, and a continuation of current population trends, the size of the House would increase more rapidly than it had been doing under FPP, because for every two electorate seats added another list seat would also be needed. At the last elections under FPP, two seats were normally added after every five-year census. Assuming the trend continued, the addition of three seats every five years could take the House back up to 120 in somewhat over 30 years. But it is by no means clear that New Zealanders campaigning for a 99-seat House would accept future increases beyond 99, however slow. It is an indication of the poverty of the debate that this issue has not been publicly discussed, at least to our knowledge, until raised in the review committee.[4]

With 120 MPs, however, significant overhangs would be unlikely for a little time to come. Nonetheless, adoption of a temporary increase mechanism would ensure proportionality in the medium term without a need for the size of the House to increase beyond 120, except on a temporary basis. The MMP review committee report made no reference to the proposal for temporary increases in the number of list seats. It did, however, refer to the government for consideration two other options canvassed by the NZES:

- To peg electorate seats at 60 per cent of the House (72), and 'unpeg' the South Island electorate requirement of sixteen, allowing South Island seats to fall below that figure if population movements decreed.
- To allow the size of the House to increase beyond 120 in order to maintain list seats at 40 per cent.

In the view of the NZES neither of these options is likely to find favour in the short term. South Islanders would strongly oppose the first, and in one of its few bursts of unanimity, the MMP review committee itself indicated that it favoured maintaining the South Island electorate seat minimum. This leaves an increase beyond 120 as the only option apparently recognised by the committee. Yet for the foreseeable future, New Zealanders in general seem unlikely to endorse further permanent expansion of the House beyond 120 members. Given the strength of public sentiment, no government would be likely to move in this direction. Therefore it should consider the provision to temporarily increase list seats when needed to prevent overhang. This would have the added advantage of experiencing the extent to which further list seats might be required as their fixed number declined, making it possible to consider an increase in the number of fixed seats at some time well into the future.

As well as being a mechanism for achieving a proportional allocation of seats, list seats contribute also to the representative nature of Parliament (Chapter 9). Table 12.2 indicates the influence of MMP, and list seats in particular, in increasing the proportion of women and minorities in Parliament. Assuming that the placing of candidates on the party lists had remained the same, the bottom row in the table provides an estimate of the effects had a 99-seat House been elected in 1999, with only 32 list MPs. The fall in the proportion of woman list MPs indicates the extent to which women tended to be placed lower on some lists than men. It also reflects the hypothetical failure of Labour to qualify for any list MPs, had the House been at 99. Labour tends to select woman candidates more than National.

Table 12.2: Women and Minorities in Parliament 1990, 1993, 1996 and 1999 Elections

	N	%	% elect	% list	N	%	N	%	N	%
		Women				Maori		Pacific		Asian
1990 FPP	16	16.2	16.2	–	6	6.1	1	1.0	0	0.0
1993 FPP	21	21.2	21.2	–	7	7.1	1	1.0	0	0.0
1996 MMP	35	29.2	15.4	45.5	16	13.3	3	2.5	1	0.8
1999 MMP	37	30.8	23.9	39.6	14	11.7	4	3.0	1	0.8
1999 (99 est)	26	26.3	23.9	31.3	11	11.1	2	2.0	0	0.0

SOURCE: MMP Review Committee 2001, 20. Note that the Electoral Commission (2000, 161) records Maori MPs in 1999 as 16 (13.3 per cent) and Pacific Islanders as 3 (2.5 per cent).

With shorter lists, parties might have made more effort to put women higher (see MMP Review Committee, 2001, 20). But even had party lists been adjusted to make women as likely to be allocated list seats as they were on the basis of a longer list, only another two women might have been elected, bringing the proportion up to 28.3 per cent. A smaller House would therefore probably slightly reduce the breadth of representation of women and minorities, albeit by perhaps not as much immediately as those using the argument have asserted. But if the proportion of list seats continued to fall, the effects would intensify.[5] Virtually all countries with higher levels of women's representation than New Zealand elect all of their legislators from party lists. The conclusion is therefore inescapable: reducing the proportion of list seats would make attaining higher women's representation more difficult. If the number of Maori electorates continues to grow, the effects would be less for Maori. But unless National were to give its Asian MP, Pansy Wong, a higher list placing in a 99-seat House, New Zealand's only Asian parliamentarian would lose her seat.

The question of Maori representation was another matter on which most correctly anticipated that the review would endorse the status quo. In recent years there has been agitation against the Maori electorates from ACT and from some within the National party. But National, seeking to gain greater support among Maori, agreed to the retention of Maori electorates in its submission to the MMP review. As we saw in Chapter 9, there appears to be a consensus among Maori and non-Maori alike that whether or not the Maori seats are retained is a matter for all New Zealanders. Maori strongly support their continuation, and many want more, but even among non-Maori there remains majority support for their persistence.

Closed or Open Lists?

List MPs have been a source of concern to many. They were identified by opponents of MMP as a vulnerable point in the system, even before the 1993 referendum. Some list MPs subsequently generated enough bad publicity during the first MMP Parliament to reinforce the worst predictions. As a result they rank low in public esteem, even though the NZES surveys show that people actually in contact with list MPs rate their performance no worse than those in contact with their electorate MPs (see also Chapter 9). However, list MPs are in contact with fewer voters than electorate MPs, although this may in part be because Parliament gives them less funding to maintain such contacts. Nevertheless, elected from a New Zealand-wide constituency, list MPs are portrayed as less directly accountable to voters than are electorate MPs. The line of accountability for list MPs runs in the first instance to their parties, which may rank them lower on the list if it considers that their performance has been inadequate, or that they have served long enough in politics and should move on. Parties may also rank list MPs low because they do not have the full support of the party's organisational or political leaders, perhaps because they are more attuned to public opinion than to that of the party establishment. Meanwhile MMP has made electorate MPs even more accountable as individuals, by allowing people to cast a separate vote for their MP regardless of their partisanship, something that was not possible under FPP.

To lessen the distinction between indirectly elected list MPs, and directly elected electorate members, some countries having list systems have made it possible for voters to indicate their choice of candidate from a party's list, thus influencing the order in which the party's candidates may be sent to Parliament. The German state of Bavaria, which has an MMP electoral system, and Finland, which has a pure list system of proportional representation, provide examples where party lists are 'open' in this way. Table 12.3 indicates majority support for open lists in New Zealand in June–July 2001 (as, indeed, did a similar question in the 1999 NZES). However, a significant minority still favours the parties' taking sole responsibility for the ordering of lists. Support for open lists is slightly higher among opponents of MMP, suggesting that such a change could persuade some opponents to become supporters.

All political parties, however, rejected the proposal for open lists except United, which has no list MPs. The review not only rejected open lists, it completely failed to address the arguments for and against them. Such an apparently unconsidered verdict does raise questions about the desirability of having such decisions made by representatives of organisations with interests at stake. Political parties jealously guard their control over candidate selection. Open lists would make the management of political parties' internal affairs

Table 12.3: Opinion on Changes to MMP, June–July 2001

	Yes	No	Don't Know/ Neutral
Voters should be able to decide which candidates on the party list get the seats a party has won	56	31	13
There are too many parties in the New Zealand Parliament	43	52	5
Parties should get seats in Parliament if they receive 4 per cent or more of the party vote	17	68	15
Prefers a government with more than half the seats in Parliament (all)	80	10	10
Prefers a government with more than half the seats in Parliament (among knowledgeable, N=185)	70	20	10
A party that wins one electorate and gets 3 per cent of the party voted should no longer get any list seats	47	31	22
The state should directly fund political parties and election campaigns	21	65	15

The questions were:

'Some people say that voters should be able to decide which candidates on the party list get the seats a party has won. Other people say that, as now, the party should decide which of the candidates on its list get seats. Which is your view?'

'Would you say that in the New Zealand Parliament there are too many political parties, about the right number of parties, or not enough parties?'

'Currently, parties may gain seats in Parliament if they receive 5 per cent or more of the party vote or they win an electorate seat. Do you think we should change MMP so that parties can get seats in Parliament if they receive 4 per cent or more of the party vote?'

'Which do you prefer: a government with more than half, or less than half the seats in Parliament?'

'Currently, parties winning an electorate but getting less than 5 per cent of the party vote may be allocated further list seats depending on their party vote. Think of a party that wins one electorate and gets, say, 3 per cent of the party vote. Should we change MMP so it no longer gets any list seats?'

'The state should directly fund political parties and election campaigns.'

SOURCE: NZES 2001 Midterm Study, N=733.

more complex, because they would provide some encouragement for candidates from the same party to compete against each other for public approval, particularly as elections drew near. Some experts on political parties argue that open lists reduce the effectiveness of political parties (Sartori 1976, chapter 4). In Italy, an open list system prior to reforms in 1990 encouraged party factionalism (Hine 1993, 130–2), and was further nourished by a political culture of clientelism (Marsh 1985, 371). But elsewhere there is only weak evidence that open lists are conducive to factionalism (Katz 1979, 31–4).

If lists were open in New Zealand, list MPs would have incentives to seek public support, and to increase their contacts with the public. On the other hand, existing spending limits on their campaign activity would discourage the worst effects of energetic self-promotion. Open lists, however, would have to be regionally based, rather than in the form of the present national list. If five or six regions were defined, they could return about ten MPs each. Voters would find it easier to evaluate the limited number of 'local' candidates presented by the various parties' list-makers than choose from much longer national lists. Research on open lists in Europe indicates that local candidates are favoured, which would have the desired effect of bringing list MPs closer to voters.

Critics of open lists on the other hand argue that they usually make very little difference to the ordering of candidates elected. This is particularly the case where parties indicate an ordering and voters may modify it but are not obliged to (Marsh 1985, 370). In those cases, most people either tend to vote for the highest-ranked candidates or, if they have the option, do not express list candidate preferences, thus endorsing the party's ranking by default. But European research in the 1980s indicated that more voters were using the possibilities of open lists with varied effects. As a result, turnover of incumbents is probably higher. Evidence from Finland, which has one of the most open systems, suggests that women there have similar chances of election as in other Scandinavian democracies that use closed lists (Marsh 1985, 373–5). Where voters are able to express their preferences in open lists, lower-ranked candidates can benefit, and the existence of open lists therefore encourages parties to take the public popularity of candidates more seriously when they prepare their lists. Other systematic study has revealed that there are differences in the design of open lists that determine whether they have significant or merely minimal effects (Katz 1986). But open lists with even minor effects are likely to act as a safety-valve, allowing voters to express preferences that may sometimes have influence in important cases. However, open lists for New Zealand would make the process of voting more complex, and in an MMP electoral system they could have the potential to confuse the crucial distinction between the roles of the party and electorate votes. Aware of the need to investigate this problem, the NZES offered to conduct research in Bavaria for the MMP review committee. The offer was not taken up.

Thresholds to Representation

Another important question relevant to the evaluation of MMP is the number of parties in Parliament and, in particular, the number of small parties. Opponents of MMP point to the danger that one or other small party may hold the balance of power, and determine the composition of a government in a way inconsistent with voters' preferences. Many people felt New Zealand First let down its supporters in 1996 by going into coalition with National, which most did not anticipate. A large number of small parties needing to be taken into account may also make forming governments difficult. After the 1999 election Labour and the Alliance formed a minority government with the Green party pledging to support the government on matters of confidence and supply —

those issues on which the government needs Parliamentary support to stay in power. At the same time as the MMP review concluded, this arrangement was still working well, but such arrangements can be unstable, and there have been times when the Greens have disapproved of proposed legislation, requiring the government to find support elsewhere in Parliament.

People's concerns over the effect of small parties suggest that the MMP review committee needed to consider ways of modifying MMP to give small parties less encouragement, without changing its fundamental principles. For example, New Zealand First received five seats in 1999 only because Winston Peters narrowly won his Tauranga electorate, and therefore put his party over the threshold for representation, even though it received only 4.3 per cent of the party vote. If it were slightly more difficult for small parties to get seats, majority two-party coalitions — or, occasionally, even single-party majority governments — might be more likely. For example, had New Zealand First got no seats in 1999, the Labour and Alliance parties would have had a majority in the House. When the mid-term sample of New Zealanders was asked in June–July 2001 if winning an electorate seat should no longer allow parties with less than 5 per cent of the party vote to cross the threshold, opinion was divided, with 47 per cent agreeing, 31 per cent in opposition, and a substantial 22 per cent unable to say (Table 12.3). The question used an example of 3 per cent to assist respondents to understand it. Public opinion on this question is difficult to estimate, however, because understanding about the details of MMP is low and few people have been exposed to particular proposals for change. Submissions to the committee on the subject were opposed to the one-seat threshold by about four to one, and support for change was hinted at in UMR-Insight's qualitative research. Among the parties, however, only ACT was prepared to consider it, and then only if the party vote threshold was lowered to 4 per cent. The committee unanimously rejected the proposal to end the electorate seat threshold.[6]

MMP has brought more parties into Parliament, and a lowering of the party vote threshold would be likely to increase the number over time. One of the proposals brought to the MMP review committee and supported by the Green party in particular was to lower the original 5 per cent party vote threshold to 4 per cent. Table 12.3 shows that a substantial majority of New Zealanders would oppose such a change. Although 52 per cent of respondents in the mid-term survey disagreed that there were too many parties in Parliament after the 1999 election (and a few even wanted more), a significant minority of 43 per cent thought there were already too many. There was little public tolerance of changes to MMP which might encourage further proliferation of political parties.

The number of parties in Parliament affects the likelihood of minority versus majority government. Limited public knowledge, however, makes opinions on this difficult to tap. Early in the mid-term questionnaire, respondents were asked what parties belonged to the government. Only 35 per cent correctly indicated Labour and Alliance. Another 29 per cent thought that the Labour–Alliance coalition also included the Greens. Respondents were subsequently informed of the correct answer. Later in the questionnaire, they were asked 'whether or not the current Labour–Alliance government has more than half or less than half of the seats in Parliament.' Fifty-one per cent wrongly believed that the two parties had more than half the seats, with only 26 per cent giving the correct answer. Given this level of misperception, it is impossible to estimate what people think of the experience of minority government. While 80 per cent preferred majority government, most also believed they had been experiencing it. The best estimate to hand is that, among those who knew the government was in the minority in the House, 70 per cent still preferred majority government.

A picture thus emerges of an electorate with a preference for moderate proportional representation, for majority governments, and wishing to discourage further party proliferation, and so also opposed to lowering the threshold for smaller parties polling below 5 per cent of the party vote. There was also considerable ambivalence among respondents over the merits of the one-electorate threshold for eligibility for list seats. Although the political parties represented on the review committee did not themselves support removing the electorate seat threshold, public opinion provided sufficient grounds for the committee to have recommended putting such a change to a referendum. This would have served several purposes. It would have provided an opportunity for some direct public input into the process of evaluation, with the object of reforming an aspect of MMP about which there were concerns, and it would have served to educate a public badly in need of more information about the electoral system.

Another Referendum on MMP?

Other than the number of MPs, the question of a referendum was perhaps the most difficult issue faced by the review committee, given National's demand for one, and indications that it had popular support. Even while participating in the review, National began a campaign for a referendum on MMP, and sponsored a Bill for a two-step referendum process much like that of 1992 and 1993: first, a vote on change versus the status quo, and another on possible alternatives; secondly, a straight fight between MMP and the most popular alternative. In May 2000, Shipley's Electoral Options Referenda Bill won the lottery for introduction to the House. Later, in February 2001 a 'Citizens' Majority Trust', with backing from notable individuals in the business community, began a petition under the CIR process to require a referendum on whether there should be a referendum on the electoral system, based on 99 MPs. The backers of the Trust, primarily opponents of MMP, were encouraged by the decisive result of the 1999 CIR on the number of MPs, by resentment at the government's failure to respond to that referendum in any other way than to add the issue to the review committee's agenda, and by a widespread expectation among the public that there would be another referendum on MMP.

In UMR-Insight research commissioned by the MMP review committee and conducted in November 2000, 52 per cent of New Zealanders said they believed there would be a future referendum on whether MMP should be kept or not, to 35 per cent who did not. The question did not apparently specify whether people thought there had been a legal or political commitment to a

Table 12.4: Referendums and Time to Decide, 2000–2001

	November 2000	June–July 2001
Wants Referendum	76	53
No Referendum	17	40
Don't know	7	7
Enough Time to Decide	57	48
Too Soon to Tell	38	46
Don't know	5	7
Referendum in 2001 or 2002	65	45
Referendum later	11	7
N	750	733

SOURCES: November 2000, UMR Insight 2001; June–July 2001, NZES Midterm.

further referendum, as some believed, or simply that people expected that there would be one — a crucial distinction. Because some people mistakenly thought a referendum was guaranteed, some argue that this creates a moral imperative to hold one. It is a false argument, for no one can reasonably claim an obligation on the basis of having a wrong belief that it exists. A current preference for a referendum is a better basis for proposing one, and, indeed, Table 12.4 indicates majority support for a referendum, most also wishing to have one sooner rather than later. However, opinion on this has shifted considerably in a short space of time. Between late 2000 and mid-2001 the majority wanting a referendum diminished markedly, and the earlier majority who considered there had been 'enough time to decide' changed to a more even balance with 'too soon to tell'. Poll data taken just before the release of the review thus suggests that the heat was dissipating from pro-referendum sentiment, though much still remained.

The Electoral Act did not specify that there would be a referendum, despite the perceptions of many that it had. While requiring the idea of a referendum to be considered by the review committee, the Act did not say what the specifics of such a referendum might be. The way was open, therefore, for a possible referendum on some key aspects of MMP, and not necessarily on the system itself. If the review recommended changes, it might have been appropriate to put them to referendum, as Peter Dunne's United party recommended. We have already suggested that the question of the one-seat electorate threshold was an appropriate matter to put to the public. While referendums are costly, education and debate about an aspect or aspects of MMP would not require as great an investment as a referendum pitting MMP against some other electoral system. And if such changes addressed issues of public concern about MMP, debate and decision on them might help generate a wider consensus of support for MMP as well as greater public awareness of its features.

Assessing MMP

Before the review committee could make a decision about the subject of any referendum it needed to hear and weigh the evidence about MMP. Had MMP fulfilled the goals its advocates hoped for it? Had the arguments of MMP's opponents been borne out by experience? And if MMP was not working as had been hoped by its advocates, did such problems indicate serious illness requiring major surgery, or more simply would a minor operation do? Table 12.5 outlines the main claims by advocates and opponents of MMP, with some very brief preliminary assessments.

Table 12.5   An MMP Scorecard

Advocates of MMP claimed as follows:

• MMP would significantly increase the odds of the party winning the most votes getting the most seats.	The design of MMP virtually guarantees this, unless the proportion of list seats falls below about 40%.
• MMP would facilitate a more competitive party system.	Yes.
• MMP would produce a more representative Parliament incorporating groups otherwise marginalised in policy debate, such as women and ethnic minorities.	Yes, although reducing the size of the House would weaken this tendency.
• MMP would reverse trends of declining turnout and political participation.	Yes for 1996, but not for 1999. The effects of MMP, if any, appear to have been offset by other factors.
• MMP would restore greater confidence in politicians and the political process.	No major improvement, but signs of minor shifts in the right direction.
• Small parties failing to act consistently with public expectations will be electorally vulnerable for punishment.	Applies well to New Zealand First. Experience since 1999 indicates small parties in government may be vulnerable regardless of their performance.

Opponents of change took a variety of alternative positions.

• Under MMP governments would be formed by bargaining between parties and therefore would not reflect voters' preferences.	Partly true, although both the major parties in the governments elected in 1996 and 1999 would have also been elected under FPP.
• By reducing accountability and dismissability of governments, MMP will not increase the influence of public opinion on government as its advocates hope.	As FPP would have returned National to power in 1996 and elected Labour in 1999, MMP has not so far prevented the dismissal of a government.

• Because it makes governments more responsive to public opinion, MMP will have bad consequences, because governments in an uncertain world sometimes have to make rapid policy changes without public consultation.	Partly inconsistent with the previous position, but probably as yet untested because there has been no major 'crisis'. On the other hand, governments since 1996 have made some unpopular decisions.
• MMP would promote instability and uncertainty in government.	Partly sustained in 1996–99, although such instability was not unknown under FPP: for example, Cabinet changes in the period 1987–1990. Not the case after 1999, and a reason for a turnaround in the trends of opinion about MMP.
• Under MMP small pivotal parties would exert excessive power in influencing policy.	This depends on what constitutes 'excessive'. Since the 1999 election it does not appear to be true for either the Alliance or the Greens.
• Under MMP small pivotal parties would exert excessive power in gaining Cabinet positions.	True for New Zealand First 1996–98, not for Alliance post 1999.
• MMP is a complex electoral system that voters would not understand.	With public education knowledge of the system rises to adequate levels. Voters also misunderstand aspects of FPP.
• MMP has perverse unintended consequences that might increase the size of Parliament and proliferate political parties formed for strategic reasons.	No, other than the survival of Peter Dunne's United Party, the days of which may be numbered.

From this list, one can conclude that the 'scorecard' is a mixed one on either side of the debate. Given the difficulties of transition from one system to another, the rocky path followed between 1996 and 1999 should not have been a surprise. However, the easier passage under the Labour–Alliance coalition since November 1999 should not blind observers to the likelihood of further trials and tribulations. The experience of two elections and two governments under MMP is simply not long enough for an informed decision, as the ACT party's submission wisely argued. In its submission to the review the NZES advised against another immediate referendum on electoral system alternatives. Revisiting the FPP/MMP debate would be divisive. Done properly, such a referendum would require a major investment in public education on the alternatives — particularly if opened up to consider again other electoral system alternatives. Whatever its content, any referendum should be held on a stand-alone basis, and not in conjunction with an election, so that both debate and education can take place without the distracting influences of a partisan election campaign. This would not only be costly at a time when government expenditures are highly constrained, but the 'scorecard' above, however tentative in places, provides no compelling grounds for such a drastic measure.

Conclusion

In not recommending a referendum on MMP, the committee acted appropriately. Overall, however, the committee's report was a disappointment. The adoption of the Business Committee model requiring unanimity among the MMP review committee members largely determined the outcome of the review. The upshot was endorsement of the status quo on all matters on which the committee agreed, and disagreement on all other issues, which included most that were significant. On all of those the committee's rules dictated that no action could be recommended, and so again the status quo prevailed.

In making no concessions to public opinion, most notably its refusal to support a reduction in the size of the House to 99 MPs, the committee ran the risk of public rejection of all of its recommendations. At the time of the report there was still a substantial gap in confidence between ordinary people and Parliament. Yet the government took the view that the electoral system and the number of MPs were no longer matters of major public concern in mid-2001. They may have been right, compared to 1998 and 1999. Nonetheless, there remained a deep-seated alienation from the political process, fed as much by lack of knowledge as by legitimate concerns about the behaviour of politicians and the policies of previous governments. For example, the demand for fewer MPs has not been adequately debated, and if implemented is likely to be self-defeating in its main object. If New Zealanders want politicians to be more responsive and accountable, reducing their number will have the opposite effect.

The committee should have made more concessions to public opinion on matters where change could be justified. Despite the unpopularity of list MPs, and evidence presented by the NZES that their level of contact with ordinary people was much lower than electorate MPs, the committee declined to address the issue of open lists. Despite continued public concern about the potential for small parties to play a pivotal role in the formation and business of governments, and an apparent preference for majority governments, the committee did not consider the option of a referendum to permit voters to decide whether or not to modify MMP by removing the one-electorate seat threshold.

When considering 'other matters', the committee spent some time on the question of state funding of political parties and election campaigns, a demand prominent in the Labour party submission, with support from the Alliance and Green parties. Again, the committee could not agree, because of opposition to any significant extension of state funding from National and ACT. There is already significant state funding for broadcasting expenses during election campaigns in New Zealand. Much less transparently, political parties represented in Parliament have significant indirect organisational support from the taxpayers that is allocated through Parliament to support MPs. Nevertheless, New Zealand does lag behind many other countries in the funding provided by taxpayers to support the ongoing activities of political parties. A need to clarify the process by which funds are allocated to parties and politicians through Parliament has recently been identified (Controller and Auditor-General, 2001). But any proposal to significantly increase taxpayer funds to political parties is unlikely to receive public approval, with nearly two-thirds of the mid-term sample opposed.

The decision to provide for a parliamentary review of MMP in 2000 and 2001 provoked little attention in 1993. Subsequently, many people developed an alternative expectation that a further referendum would be held (UMR-Insight 2001). Others argued that the Royal Commission on the Electoral System, or some other non-partisan body, should be called together to do the task. Others again took the view that after only two elections under MMP, a major review was premature. Given the unpopularity of MPs in New Zealand, it is surprising that objections to the parliamentary review were not stronger and more sustained. Yet a case could be made that MPs' experience of working within the new system made them uniquely qualified to evaluate it. Moreover, they were to do so after calling for submissions from the public, to which they might be expected to pay some attention. Yet the review allows sitting MPs to make judgements on an issue in which they have considerable self-interest. To many people this is sufficient ground for questioning the substance and even the legitimacy of the report.

The report of the MMP review committee confirms that important decisions about electoral arrangements should not be left to political parties and politicians alone: they have too much at stake. However, there must be a better alternative than referendums, the questions and options for which are determined by parties and politicians, or otherwise by loud, persistent, and single-minded campaigners who find it hard to tolerate any voices but their own. In 1986 the agenda for change was set, not by those means, but by a Royal Commission made up of intelligent and open-minded New Zealanders with no interests at stake and no prior commitments to electoral reform.[7] Unless the electoral system and the number of MPs are indeed no longer great matters of public concern, another independent body appointed on a similar basis to the Royal Commission will be needed to review and make recommendations on these important constitutional elements. Such an initiative could take the agenda out of the hands of political parties, politicians and crusading populists, identify the key issues rationally on the basis of further inquiry and deliberation, and return them to the people, at the appropriate time, for their ultimate decision.

THE 1999 NEW ZEALAND
ELECTION STUDY

Acknowledgements

The 1999 New Zealand Election Study (NZES) is funded primarily by the Foundation for Research, Science, and Technology (FRST), with supplementary funding from University of Waikato Internal funds, and the University of Waikato Faculty of Arts and Social Sciences Research Committee. Jack Vowles has been supported by a James Cook Research Fellowship for part of the project. Jeffrey Karp and Susan Banducci acknowledge Holli Semetko and the Amsterdam School of Communications Research (ASCoR), both for research support, and for time to revisit New Zealand in January 2001. More generally, research support for Susan Banducci has been provided by the European Union's Fifth Framework Programme. Research support for Jeffrey Karp has been provided by the Netherlands Organization of Scientific Research (NWO). Peter Aimer acknowledges with thanks the continued institutional support of the Political Studies Department, at the University of Auckland

Research Design and Implementation

(a) Samples

The 1999 NZES has four major components:

1. A 'New Sample'. This was randomly selected from the electoral rolls, proportionately from each of the 67 parliamentary electorates. Questionnaires were sent by post to arrive on Monday, 29 November onwards, followed by a reminder postcard ten days later, with a second questionnaire ten days after that to non-respondents. After the end of January, a month in which many people take holidays, about three weeks of shorter telephone interviews were conducted with non-respondents for whom telephone numbers could be found. The postal response rate was 58% (N=940), with the telephone interview adding another 6% (N=119), making a combined response rate of 64% (N=1059).

2. Election to Election Panels. These contained respondents from the 1990, 1993 and 1996 NZES (Vowles and Aimer 1990, Vowles, Aimer, Catt, Lamare, and Miller 1995; Vowles, Aimer, Banducci, and Karp 1998). The 1990 panel had an N of 960;

1993, 1128; 1996, 1770. Of all panel respondents, 2231 completed the postal questionnaire, and 149 were followed up by phone. The mailing and interview schedule followed that for the new sample. Respondents within each panel were subject to different levels of response rate attrition.

3. The Campaign Pre-election Sample N=3790 (54%). This was a random national sample from households with telephones numbers provided by Telecom. Respondents were randomly selected from within households. During the 5-week campaign, 3409 respondents agreed to a 15-minute interview and 381 to a shorter interview. The short interview was designed to enhance the response rate for the key voting variables. Respondents who gave long interviews were asked to participate post-election and were mailed the post-election questionnaire. Of these, 2060 responded again by post, 428 by phone, making for a final response rate for the pre- and post-election panel of 65 per cent. The mailing and interview schedule followed that for the new sample.

4. Maori Election Study. The Maori Election Study is a sample of 1000 based on personal interviews conducted on behalf of the NZES by A. C. Neilsen (NZ) Ltd. The method used was a fully national multi-stage stratified probability sample with clustering. A. C. Neilsen-defined area units containing less than 5 per cent Maori were excluded, but those covered only 2 per cent of the Maori population. Households were sampled and respondents chosen randomly within them. The sample is weighted by age and gender to reflect the Maori population. Personal interviews were chosen because of the high rate of residential mobility among Maori, especially younger Maori, plus factors such as lower access to telephones, a tendency to live in larger households than the general population, and the culturally more acceptable practice of interviewing kanohi ki kanohi (face to face). The interviews followed a structured format and lasted approximately 40 minutes. The response rate was 54%. Questions were adapted from the main post-election questionnaire, with some additions.

(b) Vote Validation

A researcher employed by the NZES inspected the marked rolls held at Electoral Offices throughout the country and identified whether or not identified respondents had cast a vote. Those who misreported a vote when they did not were subsequently redefined as non-voters.

(c) Non-Response Error and Weights

Response rates differed substantially across subsamples, raising issues of non-response bias. Response patterns to key questions were compared across the three subsamples directly administered by the NZES. In general, there was little evidence of an increase in obvious non-response error in the two subsamples subject to panel attrition. Given this, for most purposes the three subsamples were combined. All showed a slight bias toward Labour, consistent with a usual tendency of post-election samples toward the most popular party. They also had a bias toward people with higher education, and a slight over-representation of women. The total sample was therefore weighted to correct these biases, with weights for education, age and gender (household size for the campaign sample), and validated party vote. An over-representation of Maori electorates due to 1996 over-sampling of Maori electorates in the panel section of the data was also corrected.

At times, the between-election panel, the full pre-election campaign data, and the pre- and post-election panel have been used separately for particular purposes. Post-election analysis of the campaign pre-election sample indicated biases to Labour at particular points in the campaign. Where this bias is non-problematic, this pre-election data has simply been weighted by age, gender and household size. For the pre- and post-election panel, the data is weighted by the validated votes of respondents on election day for every day of the campaign. Over-representation of voters for the winning party is common in post-election surveys, but less so in pre-election surveys, and prolonged investigation of our data and methods can find no consistent explanation. However, we note that a similar study before the 2001 British election also appears to have encountered a similar Labour over-estimation problem. Some remaining differences between our findings and those of published polls may be due to question ordering. We asked questions which are the main predictors of vote before vote intention, contrary to other pollsters. Questions on the first debate, in which most observers agreed Alliance leader Jim Anderton did best, may have had the effect of shifting some of our respondents from a Labour to an Alliance intention in late October and early November. Similarly, there may have been a greater sensitivity in these estimates to issue effects which favoured National in mid-November.

Further details of variations in weights and use of subsamples may be found in individual chapters.

Candidate Survey:
The candidate survey provides data on the respondents' background, recruitment and selection, role as an MP (if relevant), and attitudes. Questions on issues and policies replicated those in the voter surveys, enabling comparison between the attitudes and behaviour of voters and those of political elites. Similar surveys were conducted in 1993 and 1996. The survey was administered by means of a post-election, self-completion questionnaire sent to all candidates nominated by the ACT, Alliance, Green, Labour, National and New Zealand First parties. Together these parties accounted for 93 per cent of the party votes, and 119 of the 120 MPs. All candidates in the sample received a follow-up letter and postcard. The overall response rate was 62 per cent (N=282), distributed among the parties as follows: ACT 68%, N=48; Alliance 77%, N=55; Green 72%, N=52; Labour 64%, N=56; National 52%, N=44; New Zealand First 40%, N=27. The response rate for the subset of candidates elected to Parliament was 50 per cent (N=60).

Television Content Analysis
For the first time as part of the NZES, we undertook to analyse the media content during the campaign. The results of the content analysis are reported in Chapter 3. In our case, we were interested in the content of media communication during the campaign, and within the general area of media communication we were specifically interested in the news coverage of the campaign. The purpose of our content analysis was threefold. First, we were interested in various questions about the amount, tone and focus of the campaign coverage on the news. Second, we were interested in a comparison between the two main news stations: Did TV3 cover the campaign differently than TV1? Third, by linking the campaign survey data and the content analysis, we were able to explore how the media influenced voter attitudes during the campaign.

We chose to focus on the coverage of the campaign on television. Close to 90 per cent of the sample in the post-election survey said they had watched some part of the campaign coverage on either TV1 or TV3. Therefore, a substantial portion of the electorate was exposed to the campaign via the news coverage on television. Our content analysis proceeded in two parts. First, we coded the entire content of the news coverage on TV1's One News 6.00 p.m. broadcast. Therefore, our analysis was not simply limited to stories that mentioned the upcoming election. This coding was completed by a single person who used a coding scheme developed by the NZES team (see below). Second, the first eight stories that covered New Zealand events or issues that aired on TV1's 6.00 p.m. news broadcast and TV3's 6.00 p.m. news broadcast were coded. Based on an analysis of the entire TV One broadcast, we found that 64 per cent of the election-related stories appeared within the first eight stories of the broadcast and 71 per cent of the time devoted to election news was in the first eight stories. Also, the top news stories occur in the first part of the broadcast and are more likely to be remembered by viewers. Therefore, we are fairly confident that in analysing the top eight stories we are capturing what a large share of the New Zealand electorate experienced in terms of campaign media coverage. This coding was completed by a group of coders who were also enrolled in a media and politics course. The coding scheme used by this group of coders was slightly different from the entire coding of TV1's news coverage (see below). In both cases of the content analysis, we coded only the early evening broadcast. The main stories and the formats are similar enough that our sample of the early broadcasts is a fairly accurate representation of what viewers would see on either broadcast.

Our sample of news broadcasts consists of the early evening news broadcasts on TV1 and TV3 that aired between 18 October and 26 November 1999. Within each of the news broadcasts, we coded the content of each story. Therefore, the unit of analysis is the news story. We defined a television news story as a segment introduced by the presenter and including interviews, footage and commentary. We selected stories focused on domestic events and issues to code fully. Therefore, we did not code sports or entertainment stories. We also did not code stories that focused on foreign events exclusively. We did code stories that mentioned New Zealand in the context of foreign events. For example, stories that mentioned New Zealand troops abroad were included in the analysis. Our reasoning in dropping foreign events stories was to exclude content that was produced overseas. In all, 626 stories were coded for the first part of the content analysis, focusing exclusively on TV1. For the second content analysis we focused on the first eight stories on both TV1's and TV3's 6.00 p.m. news broadcast, and used the same criteria in selecting the stories to code. Therefore, the first eight stories to cover domestic issues and events were coded. For the second part of the content analysis, 623 news stories were coded.

The 2001 Mid-Term Study

Interviews took place between 23 June and 22 July 2001 at the University of Waikato Faculty of Arts and Social Sciences CATI Facility, in the Department of Political Science and Public Policy. They were preceded by focus groups involving 20 former respondents of the NZES who had agreed to be re-interviewed. Financial support was from the University of Waikato Faculty of Arts and Social Sciences Research Committee. In all, 729 interviews were completed, with a response rate of 45 per cent. The data was weighted by household size, education and recalled vote in 1999. On this basis, the data set was reasonably representative of the population by age and gender.

QUESTIONNAIRES

(Questions common to both the Elector and Candidate post-election surveys were asked in exactly the same way.)

ELECTOR QUESTIONNAIRE

A: The Campaign and the Issues

A1.   Generally speaking, how much interest do you usually have in what's going on in politics?
Very interested
Fairly interested
Slightly interested
Not at all interested

A2.   During the election campaign, did you do any of the following things?
Discuss politics with others?
Talk to any people about how they should vote?
Go to any political meetings or rallies?
Do any work for a political party or candidate?
Contribute money to a political party or candidate?

A3.   During the election campaign, how often did you follow political news, discussions, and advertising on television, newspapers, and radio?
On TV One On TV3 Newspapers National Radio Talkback Radio
Often
Sometimes
Rarely
Not at all

A4.   Did you make use of the internet to get news or information about the 1999 election?
Don't have access
Have access but didn't use it
Yes, once or twice
Yes, on several occasions
Yes, many times

A5.   Did anyone from the following political parties contact you during the election campaign?
Labour, National, Alliance, New Zealand First, ACT
Telephoned at home
Personally visited
Sent letter
Gave or sent pamphlet

A6.   Here is a list of some important issues discussed during the election campaign. Which ONE of these parties' views — Labour, National, the Alliance, Act, or NZ First — would you say came closest to your own views on each of these issues? Which party is closest? (NOTE: Other response categories None, and Don't know)
The economy
Taxes
Health
Education
Race relations
Environment
Unemployment
Law and Order

A7.   Still thinking about the same issues, when you were deciding about how to vote, how important was each of these issues to you personally?
RESPONSE CATEGORIES: Extremely important, very important, moderately important, not very important, not at all important.
The economy
Taxes
Health
Education
Race relations
Environment
Unemployment
Law and Order

B: Democracy, Parties and the Political System

B1.   On the whole, are you very satisfied, fairly satisfied, not very satisfied, or not at all satisfied with the way democracy works in New Zealand?
Very satisfied
Fairly satisfied
Not very satisfied
Not at all satisfied
Don't know

B2.   Which of these opinions about different forms of government is closest to your own?
In any case, democracy is the best form of government, whatever the circumstances may be
In certain cases a dictatorship can be positive
For someone like me, it wouldn't make any difference whether we had a democracy or a dictatorship

B3.   We would like to know what you think about each of these political parties. Please rate each party on a scale from 0 to 10, where 0 means you strongly dislike that party and 10 means that you strongly like that party. If you haven't heard about that party or don't know enough about it, please tick 'don't know'.
Please tick one box in each row.
National
Labour
New Zealand First
Alliance
Act
United
Green Party

B4.   Which party do you like the most, and which party the second most?
      (NOTE; list of parties plus open-ended other category

B5.   Would you describe National as trustworthy or not trustworthy? And how about
      Labour, the Alliance, New Zealand First and Act?
      Please tick one box in each row.
      Trustworthy
      Not sure
      Untrustworthy
      Don't know

B6.   In politics, people sometimes talk about the 'left' and the 'right'. If you can,
      where would you place yourself on a scale from 0 to 10, where 0 means the most
      left and 10 means the most right?
      NOTE (Don't know category=99)

B7.   Using the same scale, where would you place each of these political parties?
      National
      Labour
      New Zealand First
      Alliance
      Act
      Green

B8.   Again using a scale from 0 to 10, or 'don't know', please show how much you
      like or dislike these party leaders.
      NOTE (Don't know category=99)
      Jenny Shipley
      Helen Clark
      Winston Peters
      Jim Anderton
      Richard Prebble
      Jeanette Fitzsimons

B9.   How well does 'provides strong leadership' describe the following party leaders?
      Very well
      Fairly well
      Not very well
      Not at all
      Don't know

      Jenny Shipley
      Helen Clark
      Winston Peters
      Jim Anderton
      Richard Prebble

B10. How well does 'trustworthy' describe the following party leaders? (as B9)

B11. How well does 'arrogant' describe the following party leaders? (as B9)

B12. How well does 'compassionate' describe the following party leaders? (as B9)

B13. How well does 'can really speak for women' describe the following party leaders?
      (as B9)

C: Policies

C1. Listed below are various areas of government spending. Please show whether you would like to see more or less government spending in each area. Remember that if you say 'more' or 'much more', it might require a tax increase to pay for it.
Much more
More
Same as now
Less
Much less
Don't know

Protecting the environment
Health
Police and law enforcement
Education
Military and Defence
Superannuation
Assisting low income families

C2. What do you think of the state of the economy these days in New Zealand? Would you say that it is —
Very good
Good
Neither good nor bad
Bad
Very bad
Don't know

C3. Here are some more questions about the economy, and how you think that affects your household and the country as a whole.

How does the financial situation of your household now compare with what it was 12 months ago? Is it —
A lot better
A little better
About the same
A little worse
A lot worse
Don't know

How do you think the general economic situation in the country now compares with a year ago? Is it —
(Response categories as above)

What do you think the general economic situation in this country will be in 12 months time compared to now? Is it —
(Response categories as above)

C4. Here are a number of policies which some people think might help solve New Zealand's economic problems. Please indicate whether you would support or oppose such a policy, and how strongly.

To solve New Zealand's economic problems, the government should —
Control wages by law
Control prices by law
Reduce taxes in general
Introduce import controls
Privatise more state assets

Strongly support
Support
Neutral
Oppose
Strongly oppose
Don't know

C5.   In particular, do you feel that the government should fully own, or partly own any
      of the following companies or industries? Should it not own them, but regulate
      their prices and how they provide services? Or should the government not own
      or regulate them at all?
      Please tick one box in each row.
      Telecom
      Bank of New Zealand
      Electricity
      Television New Zealand

      Fully own
      Partly own
      Not own but regulate
      Not own or regulate
      Don't know

C6.   This question asks how far we should go to protect the environment. ONE means
      that we should concentrate more on protecting the environment, even if it leads
      to considerably lower incomes, and SEVEN means that we should safeguard our
      income levels before we seek to protect the environment. Where would you place
      your view?
      (9=Don't know)

C7.   ONE represents the view that the government should reduce taxes, and SEVEN
      the view that there should be a tax increase so government can spend more
      money on health and education. Where would you place your view?
      (9=Don't know)

C8.   Do you strongly agree, agree, disagree, or strongly disagree with the following?
      (also neutral and don t know categories)

      Society would be better off if more women stayed home with their children.
      There should be a law to further reduce pay differences between women and men.
      The death penalty for murder should be reintroduced.

C9.   Where would you place your view at any number on this scale from 1 to 7?
      (9=Don't know)
      We should tax rich people more and redistribute income and wealth to ordinary
      people (1)
      Rich people should keep their own income and wealth because their taxes are too
      high now (7)

C10. Do you think the future of Maori seats in Parliament should be decided by Maori,
      or by all New Zealanders?
      Maori should decide
      All New Zealanders should decide
      Don't know

C11. What do you think should be the future of the Maori seats? Do you think we
      should get rid of the Maori seats, keep the six we have now, or have more Maori
      seats?
      Get rid of Maori seats
      Keep the six we have now
      Have more Maori seats
      Don't know

C12. Do you strongly agree, agree, disagree, or strongly disagree with the following? (also neutral and don t know categories)

References to the Treaty of Waitangi should be removed from the law.
Maori should be compensated for land confiscated in the past.

C13. Do you think the number of immigrants allowed into New Zealand nowadays should be —
Increased a lot
Increased a little
Remain about the same as it is
Reduced a little
Reduced a lot
Don't know

C14. Do you strongly agree, agree, disagree, or strongly disagree with the following? (also neutral and don t know categories)
The Employment Contracts Act should be scrapped.
Minimum wages reduce the creation of new jobs.
Trade unions are necessary to protect workers.
Big business in New Zealand has too much power.
People who are unemployed should have to work for their benefits.
Trade unions in New Zealand have too much power.

C15. Here is a list of four aims for New Zealand over the next ten years. If you had to choose among these aims, which would be your first and second choices? Please tick one box in each column.
Maintain order in the nation
Give the people more say in important government decisions
Fight rising prices
Protect freedom of speech

C16. Generally, do you think it should be or should not be the government's responsibility to provide or ensure —
Definitely should
Should
Shouldn't
Definitely shouldn't
Don't know

A job for everyone who wants one
A decent living standard for all old people
Decent living standards for the unemployed
Decent housing for those who can't afford it
Free health care for everyone
Free education from pre-school through polytechnic and university levels

D: Party Preferences and Voting

D1. Generally speaking, do you usually think of yourself as National, Labour, Alliance, New Zealand First, or some other, or don't you usually think of yourself in this way?
Don't usually think of myself in this way
Another party (open-ended option)
Labour
National
Alliance
NZ First
Act

If you don't usually think in this way:
Do you generally think of yourself as a little closer to one of the parties than the others?

No
Labour
National
Alliance
NZ First
Act
Another (open-ended option)

If you ticked a party box:
How strongly do you think of yourself as that party?

Very strongly
Fairly strongly
Not very strongly

D2.   With MMP New Zealanders now have two votes, one for a party, and one for a candidate in their electorate. Which do you think is the most important in deciding which party will get the largest number of seats in Parliament?
Party vote most important
Both equally important
Electorate vote most important
Don't know

D3.   Thinking now of the party vote, which party did you vote for in the 1999 election?
Did not vote for a party
Another party (open-ended option)
Labour
National
Alliance
NZ First
Act

D4.   If you didn't manage to cast a party vote in the 1999 election, which party would you have voted for if you had been able to?
I CHOSE not vote for a party
Another party (open-ended option)
Labour
National
Alliance
NZ First
Act

D5.   What about the electorate vote in 1999? Which party's candidate did you vote for?
Did not vote for a candidate
Another party candidate (open-ended option)
Labour
National
Alliance
NZ First
Act

D6.   Imagine that the 1999 election had been held under the old first past the post system, and you had only ONE vote for one of the candidates who stood in your electorate. Which party's candidate would you have voted for?
Another party (open-ended option)
Would not have voted
Labour
National
Alliance
NZ First
Act

D7.   Thinking about the 1999 election, how long ago did you decide definitely what party, and what electorate candidate, you would vote for?
Party Vote Electorate Vote
A long time ago
In 1999 but before the election campaign
During the campaign but before the last week
In the last week of the campaign before election day
On election day
Never did make up my mind
Don't know

D8.   Was there any time during the 1999 election campaign when you seriously thought you might vote for a different party than the one you voted for or not vote at all?
Yes
No
Thought of not voting
Don't know

Only some parties in parliament form a government, made up of a Prime Minister and Cabinet Ministers. The next two questions ask what parties you most wanted to be in government.

D9.   On election day, which of EITHER the National or Labour parties did you most prefer to form a government?
National
Labour
Neither
Both
Don't know

D10.   On election day, which OTHER party or parties did you want to be part of the government?
No other party
Labour
National
NZ First
Alliance
Act
Other (open-ended option)
Don't know

D11.   Regardless of the parties they were standing for, how did you feel about the candidates who stood in your electorate?
Please tick one box in each row.
How did you feel about the candidate for —
National
Labour
New Zealand First

Alliance
Act
Any other candidate (open-ended option)

Strongly dislike=0
Neutral=5
Strongly like=10
Don't know=99

D12. Which party's electorate candidate, if any, did you personally most like?
None of them
Labour
National
NZ First
Alliance
Act
Other (open-ended option)

D13. If you voted on the referendum about the number of MPs, which option did you choose?
Did not vote
Voted to reduce the number of MPs to 99
Voted to retain the current number at 120

D14. If you voted on the referendum about penalties for crimes of violence and more concern for victims, which option did you choose?

Did not vote
Voted for greater penalties and more concern for victims
Voted for same penalties and treatment of victims as now

D15. For what party did you cast your party vote in the 1996 election?
Did not vote
Labour
National
NZ First
Alliance
Act
Christian Coalition
Other (open-ended option)

E: Government and the Electoral System

E1. Which of the following statements about MMP is closest to your view?
MMP has been a disaster and we should get rid of it as soon as possible
MMP has been a success and we should keep it
It is too soon to tell about MMP
Don't know

E2. If there had been a referendum held on the electoral system at the same time as the election, how would you have voted?
To keep MMP
Return to the First Past the Post system (FPP)
For an alternative, neither MMP or FPP (open-ended option)
Don't know

E3. Did you vote in the electoral referendum held at the 1993 election? If so, for which option — First Past the Post (FPP) or Mixed Member Proportional (MMP)? Please tick one box.
Did not vote in referendum
FPP
MMP
Don't know

E4.   Generally speaking, do you prefer —
      A government made up of a single party
      A coalition government made up of more than one party
      Don't know

E5.   Imagine that a party wins the most votes in an election with about 40 per cent of
      the votes. Regardless of whether you liked that party or not, do you think that
      party should get:
      About 40 per cent of the seats in Parliament
      More than half of the seats, so it can easily govern on its own
      Somewhere between 40 per cent and half the seats
      Don't know

E6.   How much do you agree or disagree with these opinions about what elections
      should do?
      An election should —
      Provide a government at least half the people voted for
      Give each party a percentage of the seats in Parliament equal to its per cent of the
      party vote
      Ensure that only one party is needed to form a government

      Strongly agree
      Agree
      Neutral
      Disagree
      Strongly disagree
      Don't know

E7.   Which of the following is more important to you?
      One party has more than half the seats in Parliament, so it can easily govern on
      its own
      Parties have about the same percentage of seats as their per cent of the party vote
      Don't know

E8.   Sometimes one or more parties can govern with less than half the seats in Parlia-
      ment as a 'minority government'. In general, do you think that it is —
      Good that a government has more than half the seats in Parliament
      Not so good that a governments has more than half the seats
      Don't know

E9.   Do you agree or disagree with these statements?
      MMP is much fairer than the old First Past the Post system.
      Splitting your votes is always more effective than casting them both for the same
      party.
      I do not see the point of having two votes under MMP.
      Because National and Labour win so many electorate seats there is no point in
      giving either my party vote.
      MMP gives too much power to small parties.
      First past the post gave too much power to large parties.
      Voters, not parties, should decide which of the candidates on the party list get the
      seats the party has won.
      Parties should say before election day what other parties they would prefer to
      work with in a coalition government.
      Parties should put forward similar numbers of male and female candidates.

      Agree
      Neutral
      Disagree
      Don't know

E10. Here are some other statements about MMP. Do you think that they are true, or false?
Voting under MMP is like two separate elections, one for the electorate seats and one for the party list seats.
The party votes usually decide the total number of seats each party gets in Parliament.
A party that wins less than 5% of the party vote and wins no electorates at all cannot win any seats.

True
False
Don't know

E11. Generally speaking, do you think a government formed by one party, or one formed by more than one party, is better at doing the following things?
Providing stability
Making tough decisions
Keeping Promises
Doing what the people want

One party best
More than one party best
Both the same
Don't know

E12. Now, here is a quick quiz on New Zealand government. For each of the following statements, please say whether it is true or false. If you don't know the answer, put a tick under 'don't know' and try the next.
The term of Parliament is four years.
Cabinet Ministers must be MPs.
The New Zealand Parliament once had an Upper House.

True
False
Don't know

F: Representation and Participation

F1. There are various forms of political action that people take. For each one, have you actually done it, might you do it, or would you never? Please tick one box in each row.
Write to a newspaper
Go on a protest march, so long as it was legal
Phone a talkback radio show
Boycott a product or service
Occupying buildings, factories, or other property

Actually done it
Might do it
Would never
Don't know
Sign a petition

F2. Lately, there has been a lot of talk about changing Parliament and the way New Zealand is governed.
In New Zealand, do you think we should or shouldn't —
Give the Maori people more say in all government decisions?
Require that MPs resigning from their party must also resign from Parliament?

Have a law that limits the number of terms that MPs can serve in Parliament?
Make political parties fully disclose the sources of their finances?

Definitely yes
Yes
Neither yes or no
No
Definitely no
Don't know

F3. Do you or does anyone in your household belong to a trade union?
(Multiple responses possible)
Yes, I belong
Yes, my spouse or partner belongs
Yes, another person in the house belongs
No, no one
Don't know

F4. Are you a member of any of the organisations or associations listed below?
Trade union, farmers, employers, professional association
Political party, political organisation, or movement
Interest, pressure group, environmental group
Sports club or association
Cultural organisation
Church or religious organisation
Social Club
Youth Group
Community Service Group
Hobbies group or club

If so, how often have you attended any meetings in the past 12 months?
Are you a member?
No

If you are a member:
How many meetings in the last year?
None
Once or twice a year
About once every 2–3 months
Once or more per month
Once or more per week

F5. Overall do you think that referendums and citizen-initiated referendums are good
things, bad things, or don't you think they make much difference?
Good things
Bad things
No difference
No opinion

F6. Do you agree or disagree with these statements about referendums? Referendums
are too complicated for the average voter.
Citizens-initiated referendums enable citizens to get politicians' attention.
Results of citizens initiated referendums should automatically become law.
Parliament, not voters, should make final decisions on law and policy.

Strongly agree
Agree
Neither
Disagree
Strongly disagree
Don't know

F7.   Looking at the type of people who are MPs, do you think there should be more who are:
Maori
Women
Pacific Islanders
Asians
Independents

Yes
No
Depends on candidate
Don't know

F8.   How much do you agree or disagree with these opinions?
Most people would try to take advantage of others if they got the chance.
A few strong leaders could make this country better than all the laws and talk.
What young people need most of all is strict discipline by their parents.
Sometimes politics seems so complicated people like me can't understand what goes on.
I feel that I could do as good a job in public office as most people.
Generally speaking, most people can be trusted.
It is a citizen's duty to vote.

Strongly agree
Agree
Neither
Disagree
Strongly disagree
Don't know

With MMP we have two kinds of MPs: those who are elected from local electorates or constituencies, as before; and a new kind of MP, who are elected from lists supplied by political parties. First, here are some questions about your local electorate MP.

F9.   Before the election did you know the name of the electorate MP for your electorate since 1996, and their party affiliation when elected in 1996? (Write in name and party if you recall them, otherwise tick the don't recall boxes).

F10.   In the twelve months before the election, did you had any contact with your electorate or constituency MP in any way?
Yes
No
Don't know

F11.   Overall, did you approve or disapprove of the way in which your electorate MP was handling his or her job over the last three years?
Strongly approved
Approved
Neither approved nor disapproved
Disapproved
Strongly disapproved
Don't know

F12.   Overall, did you approve or disapprove of the way in which electorate MPs in general were handling their jobs over the last three years?
Strongly approved
Approved
Neither approved nor disapproved
Disapproved
Strongly disapproved
Don't know

F13. Before the 1999 election did you have personal knowledge about any LIST MP, and their party affiliation when elected? If you have personal knowledge about more than one, list MP, please write in the one with whom you had the most contact, if any.

FOR THOSE WHO HAVE PERSONAL KNOWLEDGE OF A LIST MP ONLY

F14. In the twelve months before the election, did you have any contact with that LIST MP in any way?
Yes
No
Don't know

F15. Overall, did you approve or disapprove of the way in which that LIST MP was handling his or her job over the last three years?
Strongly approved
Approved
Neither approved nor disapproved
Disapproved
Strongly disapproved
Don't know

F16. Overall, did you approve or disapprove of the way in which LIST MPs in general were handling their jobs over the last three years? Please tick one box.
Strongly approved
Approved
Neither approved nor disapproved
Disapproved
Strongly disapproved
Don't know

F17. How much do you agree or disagree with the following statements?
Most Members of Parliament are out of touch with the rest of the country
I feel I have a pretty good understanding of the issues facing New Zealand
People like me don't have any say about what the government does
The New Zealand government is largely run by a few big interests
My vote really counts in elections
You can trust the government to do what is right most of the time
I don't think politicians and public servants care much about what people like me think

Strongly agree
Agree
Neither
Disagree
Strongly disagree
Don't know

F18. ONE represents the opinion that parties ought to make specific promises and keep all those promises when they are in government, and SEVEN represents the opinion that parties shouldn't bother to make any specific promises at all about what they would do in government. Where would you place your view? (9=Don't know)

G: You and Your Background

Here are some questions about yourself and your background. Remember that the information you provide is strictly confidential. It won't be reported or released identifying you personally.

G1.   Are you
Male
Female

G2:   In what year were you born?

G3.   In what country were you born?
New Zealand
UK
Other Europe (open-ended option)
Pacific
Australia
Other (open-ended option)

If you were not born in New Zealand, please write in which year you came to live here

G4.   How many years have you lived in your district, town, or neighbourhood?

G5.   Would you say you now live in —
A rural area or settlement (under 10,000)
A country town (under 10,000)
A larger country town
A large town (over 25,000)
A major city (over 100,000)

G6.   Which one of the following indicates your highest formal educational qualification?
Incomplete primary education/ none
Primary School completed
Secondary education without UE or 6th form certificate
Complete Secondary Education
Non-degree professional, trade or technical tertiary qualification
University Degree

G7.   This question is about the work you are now doing. Which of the following best describes your present position? Please tick all that apply.
Working full-time for pay or other income (32 or more hours a week)
Working part-time for pay or other income (less than 32 hours a week)
Unemployed, laid off, looking for work
Retired
Temporarily or permanently disabled, unable to work
At school, university, or other educational institution
Unpaid work outside the home
Unpaid work within the home

The next few questions are about the work that you are now doing OR, if you are not working now, the work you did the last time you were in paid employment.

G8.   Who do you now work for or, if you are not working now, who did you work for in your last job in paid employment?

I am/was self-employed
I am/was paid a wage or salary by:
A private company or business
A state or Public agency or enterprise, central or local
A mixed public/private, or non-profit organisation
Never been in paid employment
Don't know

G9. In your present or last paid job do /did you directly employ or supervise any employee responsible to you?
Yes
No

G10a. What kind of paid work do you do, or did you do in your last paid job? Remember, if you are retired or otherwise not working for pay now, please describe your last regular paid job.

G10b. In what industry, profession, or business is or was your job ?

G11. Would you describe your present or last job (if you do not presently have one) as:
Managerial
Professional
Semi-professional or technical
Clerical
Service or Sales
Skilled Manual or Trade
Factory work
Manual or Labouring
Farming

G12. Did your father have any particular preference for a political party when you were young, say about 14 years old? And how about your mother? Please tick one box in each row.
Can't remember/ don't know
No, no preference
Yes, National
Yes, Labour
Yes, another (in New Zealand or overseas) (open-ended option)

G13. Do you:
Own your house or flat mortgage free
Own your house or flat with a mortgage
Rent your house privately as a family
Rent a house/flat from the Housing Corporation or a local authority
Board or live in a hotel, hostel, rest home, or temporary accommodation
Rent your house with a group of individuals
Live at your parents or other family members home

G14. Do you identify yourself as any of these? You can tick as many as apply.
A New Zealand European
A New Zealand Maori
As someone from a particular Pacific Island?
Or with some other ethnic group? (open-ended option)

If you ticked more than one box, with which ONE of them do you MOST identify?
Please tick only one box.
A New Zealand European
A New Zealand Maori
As someone from a particular Pacific Island?
Or with some other ethnic group? (open-ended option)

G15. Some people see themselves as middle class, and others as working class, while some don't see themselves as belonging to a class at all. Do you see yourself as:
Working class
Middle class
Belong to no class
Don't know

G16. Apart from weddings, funerals, and baptisms, about how often if at all do you attend religious services these days?
Never
Once a year
2–11 times a year
Once a month
2–3 times a month
At least once a week

G17. What is your religion, if you have one?
No religion
Latter Day Saints
Anglican
Ratana
Presbyterian
Independent–Fundamentalist Church
Catholic
Other Christian (open-ended option)
Methodist
Non-Christian (open-ended option)
Baptist

G18. Do you or anyone in your household receive any one or more of the following benefits?
Family support
Community wage job seeker/ unemployment benefit
Community wage sickness benefit
Invalid's benefit
Domestic Purposes Benefit
Youth or Student Allowance
Other (war, widow's, disability etc)

G19. Including yourself, please indicate how many adults (18 and older) and how many children (17 years and younger) live in your household.

G20. What was your personal income before tax between 1 April 1998 and 31 March 1999? What about the total income before tax of all members of your household in the same year?
Don't know
No income
Less than $13,900
$13,900–$19,899
$19,900–$31,399
$31,400–$48,099
$48,100–$71,599
$71,600–$93,099
Over $93,100

G21. At your level of personal income, do you think you should pay more tax, less tax, or about the same as you do now?
More tax
Less Tax
Same as now
Don't know

G22. Later on, we hope to do more research that will involve interviewing people who answer this questionnaire in person. Are you willing to be contacted for a personal interview?
Yes
No
Don't know

G23. What is your marital status? Please tick one box.
Married or living as married
Widowed
Divorced or separated
Single, never married

If you are married or living with a partner, please move on to the last few questions. Otherwise, you have completed the questionnaire.

H: Your Spouse or Partner

H1. This question is about the work your spouse or partner is now doing. Which of the following best describes his or her present position? Please tick all that apply. (options as G7)

The next few questions are about the work that your spouse or partner is now doing or, if s/he is not working now, the work they did the last time they were in paid employment.

H2. In their present or last paid job does or did you spouse or partner directly employ or supervise anyone responsible to them?
Yes
No

H3. Who does s/he now work for, or did s/he work for in their last paid employment? (options as G8)

H4a. What kind of paid work does your spouse or partner do, OR if now not working for pay, DID S/HE DO in their LAST PAID JOB? If they are retired or otherwise not working for pay now, please describe their last regular paid job.

H4b. In what industry, profession, or business is OR WAS their job?
Industry or business

H5. Would you describe your spouse or partner's present OR LAST job as:
(options as G11)

This is the end of the questionnaire. Please put the questionnaire in the pre-paid reply envelope and post it back to us. No stamp is required. Thank you again for your cooperation.

CAMPAIGN QUESTIONNAIRE

Good evening, I'm [interviewers name] and I'm calling from the University of Waikato's Department of Political Science in Hamilton.
May I talk to the adult in your household, someone 18 years or older, who most recently had a birthday over the last year?

Are you eligible to vote in New Zealand?
1   yes
2   no
88 refused to answer

Are you a New Zealand citizen?
1   yes
2   no
88 refused to answer

How long have you lived in New Zealand?

Are you on the electoral roll?
1   yes
2   no
88 refused to answer

Which roll are you on, the General or Maori roll?
1   general
2   Maori
99 don't know
88 refusal (no response)

(IF NOT ON ROLL) If you were to enrol, would you choose the general or Maori roll?
1   General roll
2   Maori roll
99 don't know
88 refused to answer

What is the most important issue to you personally in this election?

Which political party do you feel is closest to you on that issue?
1   Alliance
2   Labour
3   National
4   New Zealand First
5   Act
6   Christian Heritage
7   Green
8   McGillicuddy Serious
9   Mauri Pacific
10 United
99 Don't know/Don't care
88 Refused (no response)
77 None
11 Other party: (open-ended)

Of all the politicians in New Zealand, who would you most like to be Prime Minister?

Of all the politicians in New Zealand, who would you least like to be Prime Minister?

Did you see the debate among the party leaders on TV One?
(asked only in the days after the first debate)

In your opinion, which leader performed the BEST in that debate?
and which leader performed the WORST?

Generally speaking, do you usually think of yourself as Labour, National, NZ First, Alliance, Act or some other, or don't you think of yourself in this way?

How strongly do you feel about that party? Very strongly, fairly strongly, or not very strongly?

Do you generally think of yourself as a little closer to one of the parties than the others?

At the coming election you have two votes: one for a party, and one for a candidate in your electorate.

Which do you think will be the most important in deciding which party gets the largest number of seats in Parliament: the party vote, the electorate vote or would you say they are equally important?
1   Party vote most important
2   Equally important
3   Electorate vote most important
88 Refused (no response)
99 Don't know/Don't care

Taking the party vote first, if an election were held today, which party would you vote for?
(IF DON'T KNOW) Which party do you think you would be most likely to vote for?

Now turning to your electorate vote, if an election were held today, which party's candidate would get your electorate vote?
(IF DON'T KNOW) Which party's candidate do you think you would be most likely to vote for?

Were you eligible to vote in the 1996 election?
1   Yes
2   No
99 don't know
88 Refusal (no response)

Did you vote in that election?
1   Yes
2   No
3   No, because out of the country
99 don't remember
88 Refusal (no response)

Which party did you give your party vote to?

I'm now going to read out some statements about how MMP works.
For both statements, can you answer whether you think they are true or false.
1   true
2   false
99 don't know
88 refusal (no response)

Voting under MMP is like two separate elections, one for the electorate seats and one for the party list seats
The party vote usually decides the total number of seats each party gets in Parliament.

And for the following two statements, can you tell me whether you agree or disagree or are neutral.
Splitting your votes is always more effective than casting them both for the same party
Because National and Labour win so many electorate seats, there is never any point giving either my party vote.

Only some parties in Parliament form a government made up of a Prime Minister and Cabinet Ministers. The next questions ask what parties you most want to be in government.

If more than one party is needed to form a coalition government, which of EITHER the National or Labour parties would you most prefer to be in that government?

Which other party or parties would you prefer to be in that coalition government? (Can choose more than one).

Now we'd like to ask you what you EXPECT to happen at the coming election. There will probably be 120 members and seats in the new Parliament, which means that to become a government on its own, a party has to get over 60 seats.
(Add if necessary)
We need just a rough estimate, you don't have to add up your estimates to 120

How many seats out of 120 roughly, do you expect the Alliance to get in Parliament?

Repeated for National, NZ First, Labour, Act.

Do you expect any other parties to get seats?
(Can choose more than one) (NOT PROMPTED)

How many seats out of 120 roughly, do you expect (any other party mentioned) to get in Parliament?

Between National and Labour, which do you think is the party most likely to form the government after the election?

What other party or parties are most likely to be in the government, not just parliament, after the election?
(Can choose more than one)

Now lets talk about the chances the various party candidates have of winning in the electorate that you are voting in.
Which party's candidate, do you think, has the most chance of winning your electorate?

We are using a scale which runs from 0 to 100, where 0 represents no chance for the party, and 50 represents an even chance, and 100 means certain victory. What do you think (party respondent thinks is most likely to win) chances are of winning your electorate seat?

Which party's candidate is the one next most likely to win after (first party named)

Using the same scale from 0 to 100, where 0 represents no chance for the party, and 50 represents an even chance, and 100 means certain victory. What do you think (second party's) chances are of winning your electorate seat?

Do you think there is any other party's candidate who has a chance of winning?

Using the same scale from 0 to 100, where 0 represents no chance for the party, and 50 represents an even chance, and 100 means certain victory. What do you think (other party named)'s chances are of winning your electorate seat?

In the past week, have you read or heard any polls about how well the parties are doing?

Have any parties or candidates personally contacted you in the last five days?
Which party or parties?

At the 1996 election we changed our electoral system from First Past the Post to Mixed Member Proportional or MMP.

Some people say MMP has been a disaster and we should get rid of it as soon as possible. Others say MMP has been a success and we should keep it. Others say it is too soon to tell. Which is closer to your view?
1   MMP has been a disaster and we should get rid of it
2   MMP has been a success and we should keep it
3   Too soon to tell
99   Don't know
88   Refused (no response)

Have you seen, read or heard anything about a referendum on the number of MPs, to be held on election day?
1   yes
2   no
88 refused to answer

This referendum proposes to reduce the number of MPs from 120 to 99. How do you intend to vote on this referendum?
1   will vote to reduce the number to 99
2   will vote to retain the current number of 120.
3   will not vote
99 don't know
88 refused (no response)

There has been talk lately about the way democracy works in New Zealand. On the whole are you very satisfied, fairly satisfied, not very satisfied or not all satisfied with the way democracy works in New Zealand?
1   very satisfied
2   fairly satisfied
3   not very satisfied
4   not at all satisfied
99 don't know
88 refusal (no response)

What do you think of the state of the economy these days in New Zealand? Would you say it is very good, good, bad, very bad or neither good or bad.

How do you think the general economic situation in New Zealand now compares with a year ago? Is it the same, better or worse?

If a referendum were held today, would you vote to retain MMP or would you vote to replace it with an alternative electoral system?
1   vote to retain MMP
2   vote for an alternative system
3   would not vote
99 don't know
88 refused (no response)

What type of electoral system would that be?
1   first past the post (FPP)
2   STV
3   Supplementary member system (SM)
88 Refusal (no response)
99 Don't know
4   Other (open-ended)

After the coming election, what sort of government would you prefer — a government made up of a single party or a coalition government made up of more than one party.

Imagine that a party wins the most votes in an election with, say about 40 percent of the votes. Tell me, do you think it should get: about 40 per cent of the seats, more than half so it can govern on its own, or somewhere between 40 percent and half the seats?

Do you think in general, that parties should have about the same percentage of MPs in Parliament as their percent of party votes?
1   yes
2   no
99 don't know
88 refusal (no response)

Which of the following is most important to you?
That one party has more than half the seats in Parliament so it can govern on its own?

OR that parties have about the same percentage of seats in Parliament as their percent of the party vote.

I'm now going to read you some statements about elections and MP's. Can you tell me whether you agree, disagree or are neutral.

My vote really counts in elections:
Most Members of Parliament are out of touch with the rest of the country:
MMP is much fairer than the old first past the post system
Parties should say before election day what other parties they would prefer to work with in a coalition government
MMP gives too much power to small parties:

How well does 'can really speak for women' describe Jenny Shipley? Would you say: very well, fairly well, not very well or not at all?
How about Helen Clark?

How well does 'can really speak for men' describe Jenny Shipley?
How about Helen Clark?

How well does 'provides strong leadership' describe Jenny Shipley?
How about Helen Clark?

How well does 'trustworthy' describe Jenny Shipley?
How about Helen Clark?

How well does 'arrogant' describe Jenny Shipley?
How about Helen Clark?

How well does 'compassionate' describe Jenny Shipley?
How about Helen Clark?

Do you think New Zealand should become a republic with a New Zealand head of state, or should the Queen be retained as head of state?
1   NZ should become a republic with a NZ head of state
2   the Queen should be retained as head of state
99 don't know
88 refused to answer

Regardless of your opinion on this issue, when do you think New Zealand will become a republic — in less than five years, within five to ten years, more then ten years or never?
1   in less than five years
2   within five to ten years
3   more than ten years
4   never
99 don't know
88 refused to answer

Now we need some demographic statistics. We keep this information strictly confidential.
1   male
2   female

In what year were you born?

What is your highest formal education or qualification?
1   Incomplete primary education/no formal education
2   Primary School completed
3   Secondary education without
4   completed secondary education with
5   non-degree professional, trade or technical tertiary qualification

6 university degree
88 refused to answer

Do you identify yourself mainly as a New Zealand European or New Zealand Maori or some other?
(Can tick more than one box here)

How many people of voting age live in your household?

That concludes our survey.
The New Zealand Election Study thanks you for your cooperation.

APPENDIX C

STATISTICAL METHODS AND
SUPPLEMENTARY TABLES

What follows is a very brief discussion of the statistical methods employed in this book. Some of these statistical techniques are fairly sophisticated and based on assumptions and calculations that we do not have the space to provide. In these cases, we refer the reader to helpful texts.

The Nature of the Data

In social science analysis we usually speak in terms of dependent and independent variables. Dependent variables are the phenomenon we are trying to explain such as voting choice. Independent variables are the factors that explain variation in the dependent variable. For example, we hypothesise that issue positions explain vote choice. In this case issue position is the independent variable and vote choice is the dependent variable. In this book, variables are measured in one of three ways: nominal, ordinal, and interval.

Nominal data are divided into unordered categories. When numbers are assigned to the different values of a nominal variable, the numbers have no intrinsic meaning. We do not assume that higher values mean 'more' of something and lower numbers signify 'less'. An example of a nominal variable is voting choice which can take on a value of National, Labour, New Zealand First, etc. The categories are, in a sense, qualitative, for there is no obvious ordering or ranking of these choices.

Ordinal data, by contrast, can be ranked. For example, a respondent is asked whether or not he or she agrees with a statement. The possible responses given are 'strongly agree', 'somewhat agree', 'neutral', 'somewhat disagree' or 'strongly disagree'. In this case we can assume that someone who answers 'strongly disagree' disagrees more strongly than someone who responds 'somewhat disagree'. However, we are unsure of the exact distance between the values of, for example, 'somewhat' and 'strongly' and cannot say with certainty how much more one disagrees with another.

Interval data, however, clearly indicate the distance between each category so one can determine how much more or less one value is relative to another. Age measured in years is an example of interval level data. Most of the more powerful statistical techniques are properly applied only to interval-level data, but in practice it is possible to apply them to ordinal-level data by making an assumption that an ordinal ranking is close enough to interval-level to make little or no difference, or by combining ordinal variables into a scale or index. In fact it is still common for social scientists to employ statistical techniques appropriate for interval-level data when using nominal data, although in very specific ways.

Statistical Significance

A regression coefficient, parameter estimate or correlation coefficient is described as statistically significant when it can be demonstrated that the probability of obtaining such a result by chance only is relatively low. Customarily, we describe a finding as statistically significant when the obtained result is among those that (theoretically) would occur no more than 5 out of 100 times if the only factors operating are the chance variations due to using a random sample. In other words, when something is said to be statistically significant the probability is less than a .05 (p < .05) that the obtained result is due to chance. When the effect of an independent variable is statistically significant, we can then reject the null hypothesis that the variable made no difference on the dependent variable. Whether or not the effect of a variable is statistically significant depends on the size of the sample, the variation in the variables, and the size of the coefficient. Statistical significance is distinguishable from the strength of a relationship which is indicated by the size of a coefficient. In large samples, small effects can be statistically significant.

An example of a test of statistical significance is **chi-square** (χ^2) which is used in cross-tabulations of nominal or ordinal data and tests the difference between what one would expect if there were no relationship between the variables in the table and what one actually observes in the table based on the sample. If the difference is large enough, taking into account the size of the table, we can reject the hypothesis that there is no relationship between the variables.

Correlation is a simple and straightforward measurement of the strength of a bivariate relationship, that is, a relationship between two variables. Normally, one of these will be an explanatory or independent variable, and the other a dependent variable, the value of which we seek to explain. One of the most powerful indications of correlation is the **Pearson's R**, which strictly speaking should be used with interval data only, but may be cautiously employed with ordinal and nominal data, particularly if one can either assume or have some confidence that the ordinal ranking is not far off or approaches an interval-level scale. The values of Pearson's R can range between −1 and +1.

Regression

There are two kinds of regression used in this book: **ordinary least squares** (OLS), and **logistic**. Both are essentially predictive techniques, measuring to what extent knowing the values of a number of independent or causal variables can be used to predict the value of a dependent variable. Regression is a powerful technique of multivariate analysis, allowing us to analyse how a number of variables together explain or predict the value or nature of a dependent variable such as voting choice.

Ordinary least squares regression is the better known of the two, and strictly speaking should be used only when the dependent variable is interval-level. However, it does not normally provide misleading estimates when applied to a dichotomous or ordinal variable, and we use it at times in this way to allow for ease of interpretation. Regression coefficients indicate the amount of change that is predicted to occur in the dependent variable when the independent variable increases by one unit. These coefficients can either be unstandardised (b) or standardised (beta). For a more detailed discussion on regression see Achen (1982).

Logistic regression, however, is particularly useful for electoral studies, because it is designed for use with a dichotomous dependent variable: for example, we might estimate a model predicting Labour vote against other choices or, in a multinomial form, it can simultaneously model effects on more than two unordered categories. Logistic regression can be employed with nominal, ordinal, and interval-level data as independent variables. Since the dependent variable is usually dichotomous, the effect of an independent variable is expressed in terms of probabilities, e.g. the probability of voting for Labour. The strength of the relationship can be determined by interpreting the estimated parameters (logits) that express the effect of the explanatory variable on the logged odds of voting for a particular party. When the explanatory variable is dichotomous, converting the logged odds to probabilities is fairly straightforward.

To illustrate, assume the analyst uses a logistic model to test her hypothesis that Labour identifiers are more likely to vote for Labour than National. Labour identification is coded as a dummy variable where 1 indicates the respondent is a Labour identifier and 0 indicates the respondent identifies with another party. Her parameter estimate (measured in logged odds) for Labour identifier is .79. This positive coefficient indicates that persons in this category are 2.2 (natural log base of .79 [e.$^{.79}$]) times more likely to vote for Labour than National.

When interpreting the effect of non-dichotomous variables, a one-unit change in the explanatory variable changes the logged odds by the size of the parameter estimate. For example, if the parameter estimate for education is $-.16$, someone with a university degree (a value of 7) has a 33 percent chance (e$-.^{16*7}$)of voting for Labour while someone with an incomplete university education (a value of 6) has a 38 percent chance of voting for Labour (e$-.^{16*6}$), all other factors being equal. Therefore, moving from the low end of the education scale, no formal education, to the top of the scale, a university degree, decreases the probability of voting for Labour from .85 (e$-.^{16*1}$) to .33.

Multinomial logit estimates are interpreted in the same manner except k–1 equations are estimated where k equals the number of categories in the dependent variable. One category of the dependent variable is used as the comparison category and the estimates are the probability of being in a category different from the comparison category.

For a more detailed discussion of logistic regression see Aldrich and Nelson (1984) and Menard (1995). For multinomial logit see Hosmer and Lemeshow (1989) and Agresti (1990).

Goodness of fit

In OLS regression the R-squared (R^{s}) statistic gives an indication of the total explained variance by the combination of all the independent variables. This statistic ranges from 0 to 1, where 0 means the independent variables have no explanatory power, and 1, where they would explain all possible variance in the dependent variable. In practice, an R-squared above .5 is rare in analysis of survey data. The more variables in the model the greater the explained variance. The adjusted R-squared takes into account the number of independent variables. This statistic should be treated with caution, as the notion of 'total variance explained' does not necessarily capture the full explanatory power of a model (Achen 1982, 59). In logistic regression, a pseudo R-squared can be calculated to assess the fit of the model, although it is not exactly comparable to an r-square in OLS.

Another method of calculating a goodness of fit for a logistic regression or multinomial logit is to compare the predicted values of the dependent variable based on the model to the observed values in the sample. The per cent correctly classified, the measure of fit, is the number of cases correctly predicted over the total number of cases. Another useful indicator is a gamma, which indicates the proportion of fewer prediction errors one would be likely to make using the statistical model than one would make by chance alone (Demaris 1992, 54).

Both OLS and logistic regression have limitations. Regression assumes that relationships between the independent variables and the dependent variable are additive. For OLS regression, we must also assume that relationships are linear. For example, education in years could be used as an independent variable against vote, but the relationship between vote and education may be curvilinear: people with lower education tend to favour Labour, those with medium education favour National, and people with higher education favour Labour. This problem can be addressed in several ways. One method is to convert the categories of education into dichotomous variables. Another strength of logistic models is their ability to model non-linear effects.

Regression in itself provides no evidence about **causal** relationships between independent variables. Indeed, there is no guarantee that the independent variables chosen are a cause of the dependent variable — this is simply an assumption made by the analyst based on theoretical expectations. Ultimately it is the plausibility of the theory as much as its support in evidence which allows one to make a causal inference. Sometimes causal assumptions can be more easily justified, as when social structural determinants are seen as logically prior to social attitudes or opinions. Otherwise, there is considerable controversy among those who study electoral behaviour as to the status of rival models which assume different causal flows.

SUPPLEMENTARY TABLES

Chapter 3
Estimated coefficients used for Figure 3.2: Probability of Voting Labour: Logistic Regression Coefficients

	b	std.error
Clark Evaluation	2.80*	0.52
Attention to TV One	0.39	0.89
Attention to TV3	2.38*	0.82
Attention to Newspapers	−2.57*	0.80
Attention to National Radio	0.19	0.80
Attention to Talk Back Radio	−0.26	0.78
TV One*Clark Evaluation	−1.10	0.69
TV3*Clark Evaluation	−0.73	0.69
Newspapers*Clark Evaluation	2.92*	0.53
National Radio*Clark Evaluation	−1.59*	0.64
Talk Back*Clark Evaluation	0.24	0.65
Issue Scale	1.24	0.77
TV One*Issues	0.60	1.16
TV3*Issues	−2.57*	1.06
Newspapers*Issues	0.89	1.10
National Radio*Issues	0.99	1.05
Talk Back*Issues	0.11	1.02
Labour Party Identifier	4.27*	0.99
National Party Identifier	0.24	1.00
Alliance Identifier	0.61	1.03
NZ First Identifier	0.91	1.07
ACT Identifier	−0.73	1.48
No Party	2.32*	0.99
Education	−0.15*	0.04
Female	0.20*	0.09
Age (in 10's)	0.05	0.03
Constant	−5.00*	1.18
% Correctly Classified	81	
N=3634		

* Significant at p < .05.

Evaluations of Clark are based on the 10 point scale asking respondents to rate the leader (sclark). The issue scale is the mean score from responses to questions about desired spending on the environment (senvsp), health care (shealsp), education (seducsp), superannuation (supsp) and low income assistance (slowsp). The issues are coded so that high values indicate a preference for greater spending.

Estimated coefficients used in Figure 3.4: Media Tone, Gender and Preferred Prime Minister

	Clark as Preferred Prime Minister		Shipley as Preferred Prime Minister	
	b	std. errror	b	std. error
Leader Mentions	−0.02	(0.02)	0.00	(0.02)
Negative Tone Shipley	0.24*	(0.06)	−0.03	(0.08)
Negative Tone Clark	0.10	(0.07)	0.11*	(0.05)
Women	0.29*	(0.07)	0.00	(0.08)
Women*Leader Tone	−0.22*	(0.10)	−0.01	(0.12)
Intended Vote Labour	2.41*	(0.08)	−1.06*	(0.11)
Intended Vote National	−1.91*	(0.19)	2.57*	(0.08)
Constant	−2.20*	(0.10)	−1.61	(0.09)
Pseudo r-square	0.31		0.31	
% Correctly Classified	80.10		84.10	
N=2849				

Estimated change in probabilities:Prefer Clark as PMPrefer Shipley as PM

	Average Labour Voter		Average National Voter	
	min	max.	min	max
Negative Shipley Tone	0.46	0.69		
Negative Clark Tone			0.67	0.76

* Significant at p < .05

Chapter 4

Full model for Table 4.1: How Leadership Traits Affect Party Vote Choice: Change in Probability of Party Vote

	Labour		National		Alliance		ACT		NZ First	
	b	se	b	se	b	se	b	se	b	se
Female	0.24*	0.11	0.35*	0.12	0.04	0.18	−0.78	0.21	0.31*	0.27
Compassionate	0.32	0.27	0.56*	0.27	0.89*	0.45	0.21	0.45	0.85	0.56
Trustworthy	1.06*	0.29	1.87*	0.28	1.81*	0.50	2.19*	0.48	1.58*	0.54
Speaks for Women	−0.28	0.25	0.22	0.25	−0.51	0.35	0.05	0.47	0.35	0.56
Strong Leader	1.59*	0.28	0.67*	0.28	0.96*	0.44	0.99*	0.40	2.16*	0.51
Arrogant	−0.86*	0.23	−0.92*	0.21	−0.58	0.35	−0.62*	0.35	−1.65	0.42
Traditional Role	0.15	0.18	−0.29	0.20	0.13	0.29	−0.26	0.32	−0.01	0.45
Labour	4.36*	0.21	−5.16*	0.37	0.58	0.42	−1.46	0.48	−0.10*	0.47
Alliance	1.05*	0.35	−4.61*	1.07	4.18*	0.47	−5.41	11.92	−5.56	17.12
NZ First	0.55	0.55	−5.18*	1.44	−0.46	1.50	−5.25*	15.16	3.82	0.60
ACT	−0.88	1.13	−3.62*	0.47	−3.98	8.58	2.67	0.45	−5.61*	21.64
Other	0.49	0.56	−8.83	6.92	−0.10	1.12	−6.10	13.56	−1.77	1.72
No Party	2.56*	0.18	−2.27*	0.12	1.85*	0.38	0.04*	0.21	0.90	0.37
Education	−0.05	0.05	−0.01	0.05	−0.08	0.08	0.19	0.09	−0.16*	0.12
Manual	0.24	0.14	−0.21	0.17	−0.08	0.22	−0.76	0.34	−0.25*	0.33
Working	−0.39*	0.13	0.55*	0.15	−0.06	0.22	0.14	0.25	0.25	0.32
Public Employee	0.18	0.12	−0.12	0.14	0.04	0.20	−0.53	0.25	−0.29*	0.30
Union Member	0.29	0.16	−0.02	0.20	0.13	0.26	0.10	0.36	0.19	0.45
Maori	−0.07	0.17	−0.15	0.24	0.01	0.30	−0.54	0.48	0.41	0.36
Catholic	0.33*	0.15	0.41*	0.17	−0.11	0.26	−0.33	0.35	0.08	0.38
Religious	−0.62*	0.16	−0.08	0.18	0.02	0.26	−0.69	0.34	−0.12*	0.37
Age	0.00	0.00	0.00	0.00	0.01	0.01	0.00	0.01	0.02	0.01
Constant	−4.45*	0.47	−0.90	0.50	−5.95*	0.81	−3.56*	0.79	−5.43*	1.10
% Correctly Classified	0.821		0.866		0.932		0.935		0.972	

* Significant at p < .05

Full model for Table 4.2: How Traits Affected National and Labour Party Switches: Estimating Probability of Switching to Labour or National

	Switch to National		Switch to Labour	
	b	std. error	b	std .error
Female	0.61	0.24	0.34	0.21
Compassionate	−0.35	0.50	−0.69	0.56
Trustworthy	1.49*	0.51	0.57	0.56
Speaks for Women	0.21	0.46	−0.49	0.47
Strong Leader	1.11*	0.52	1.56*	0.49
Arrogant	−0.72	0.40	−0.49	0.47
Traditional Women's Role	0.21	0.35	0.53	0.34
Labour	−1.70*	0.57	0.32	0.36
Alliance	−1.04	1.22	−0.77	0.59
NZ First	−0.70	1.66	−0.16	1.02
ACT	−1.01	0.75		
Other	−6.09	10.29	−2.40*	1.03
No Party	−0.63*	0.23	0.54	0.34
Education	0.18	0.10	−0.03	0.09
Manual	0.02	0.33	−0.21	0.24
Working	0.68*	0.29	−0.31	0.25
Public Employee	−0.54	0.28	−0.05	0.23
Union Member	0.38	0.36	0.48	0.29
Maori	1.17*	0.45	0.11	0.32
Catholic	0.37	0.30	0.07	0.30
Religious	0.25	0.32	−0.06	0.31
Age	0.00	0.01	0.01	0.01
Constant	−3.66*	1.01	−0.70	0.92
N	658		731	
% Correctly Classified	75.5%		74.4%	

* Significant at p < .05

Full Model for Figure 4.4: The Impact of Trait Ratings on Preferred Prime Minister:

	Clark (vs. everyone else)		Shipley (vs. everyone else)		Clark vs. Shipley[1]	
Female	0.20	(.22)	−0.08	(.19)	0.24	(.51)
Day of Campaign	0.00	(.01)	−0.01*	(.01)	0.00	(.02)
University Degree	0.00	(.27)	0.56*	(.22)	−0.88	(.60)
Maori Ethnicity	0.32	(.38)	−0.05	(.44)	0.10	(.96)
Age	−0.08	(.07)	−0.08	(.06)	−0.11	(.16)
Labour Party Identifier	3.58**	(.48)	−2.05**	(.34)	4.26**	(.78)
Other Party Identifier	1.57*	(.62)	−1.09**	(.41)	1.36	(1.21)
Identify with No Party	2.11**	(.47)	−0.57**	(.22)	1.84**	(.69)
Economic Evaluations	−0.92a	(.49)	2.30**	(.49)	−2.89*	(1.22)
Compassionate	0.09	(.33)	0.65**	(.22)	−0.06	(.48)
Trustworthy	0.54	(.34)	1.01**	(.22)	2.20**	(.56)
Speaks for Women	1.58**	(.35)	0.42a	(.26)	1.79**	(.58)
Strong Leadership	1.35**	(.32)	1.25**	(.32)	1.57**	(.52)
Arrogant	−0.91**	(.26)	−0.53**	(.21)	−1.15*	(.48)
Speaks for Men	0.04	(.27)	0.35	(.24)	1.12a	(.65)
Constant	2.13	(6.40)	3.99	(5.63)	8.91	(15.37)
Nagelkerke Pseudo r-square	0.49		0.53		0.88	
N	862		920		436	

** Significant at p < .01 *p < .05 a p < .10

NOTE: The column entries are maximum likelihood estimates from logistic regression with standard errors shown in parentheses. For party identification, National party identifiers are the comparison category.

[1]Clark=1, Shipley=0 and traits are the difference between rating for Clark and Shipley (Clark Trait–Shipley Trait)

Chapter 6
Vote by Social Structure, 1999 Election (percentages)

	Grn	Allnce	Lab	NZF	Nat	ACT	Non-vt	%	N
All	4	6	31	3	24	6	17		5797
Gender									
Male	5	6	27	3	24	8	19	49	2838
Female	3	7	36	4	26	3	16	50	2923
Age									
18–24	8	6	26	1	18	4	31	10	579
25–34	6	6	26	1	23	6	27	22	1233
35–44	5	5	28	3	30	7	16	23	1276
45–54	3	6	35	4	27	8	12	18	1025
55–64	3	7	38	5	27	6	10	12	679
65 and over	2	9	42	8	23	3	10	16	890
Ethnicity									
European	4	7	31	3	28	6	15	83	4623
Maori	2	5	39	8	6	0	36	9	477
Pacific	3	2	57	0	10	1	25	1	74
Other	5	5	31	2	23	5	24	7	414
Occupation									
Manual	4	7	36	4	17	4	23	36	2068
Service	5	10	41	2	18	3	17	10	592
Non-manual	5	5	29	3	30	8	14	47	2708
Farmer	2	4	16	8	40	9	17	7	424
Work Status									
Self-employed	5	4	22	6	34	10	14	22	1231
Public sector	4	8	39	3	22	3	15	18	1044
Other	4	7	33	3	24	6	20	54	3063
Union 1235		5	8	41	3	19	4	17	23
Non-union	4	6	29	4	28	7	17	77	3221
Religion									
None	10	8	28	1	20	6	24	26	1436
Tradit. Christian	2	6	35	4	30	6	13	58	3186
Other Christian	2	5	28	5	17	4	19	14	756
Non-Christian	11	7	28	1	20	5	19	2	87
Education									
Incomplete	2	7	36	5	22	3	21	39	2158
Secondary	4	6	30	3	28	5	17	21	1185
Non-degree	6	7	27	3	28	7	15	27	1537
University degree	7	5	31	1	25	11	14	13	732
Benefit									
On benefit	6	8	41	5	13	2	18	24	1405
Not benefit	4	6	29	3	29	7	18	76	4391
Housing									
Mortgage-free	3	7	37	5	26	6	12	33	1877
Mortgage	4	6	30	3	31	7	14	27	2092
Private rent	4	6	31	3	19	5	27	11	630
Public rent	2	11	50	2	6	0	27	3	166

Vote by Social Structure, 1999 Election (percentages) (cont.)

	Grn	Allnce	Lab	NZF	Nat	ACT	Non-vt	%	N
Urban-Rural									
Rural	5	5	27	6	29	8	16	18	900
Small town	2	8	36	5	22	4	17	11	526
Larger town	4	6	40	4	23	4	15	9	464
Small city	4	6	35	3	22	5	18	23	1119
Large city	5	7	30	2	27	7	16	38	1919

NOTE: Occupation and Work Status refer to current or last occupation held, and are on a basis of the male in the household, unless the male has or had no occupation or work status. Benefit and Union are both on the basis of anyone in the household in receipt or a member, but benefits exclude New Zealand Superannuation.
Traditional Christian includes Catholics, Anglicans, Presbyterians, and Methodists.
Urban-Rural: Rural includes rural area or small settlement; Small town = less than 10,000; Larger town = 10,000–25,000; Small city = 25,000–100,000; Large city = 100,000 or more.

Social Structure and Voting Choices, 1999 (regression coefficients)

	ACT		Alliance		National		Labour		Green	
	b	beta	b	beta	b	beta	b	beta	b	beta
Occupation										
Manual	–3**	–5**	2	3	–9**	–9**	9**	8**	0	1
Farmer	3*	3*	–3	–3	15**	9**	–16**	–10**	–2	–2
Sector										
Public	0	1	1	1	–2	–2	–2	–2	1	2
Union household	–3**	–5**	3*	4*	–10**	–9**	15**	13**	–1	–1
Education										
University	5**	7**	–1	2	–4*	–3*	2	2*	3*	4*
School qualification	–3	–3	3	2	–14**	–7**	12**	6**	1	1
Maori	–5**	–5**	–0	–0	–14**	–8**	12**	7**	–2*	–4*
Age	–6**	–7**	4*	4**	–8**	–5**	18**	12**	–8**	–11**
Female	–7**	–13**	1	1	2	2	10**	10**	–2	–5
Adjusted r-square	4		0		4		6		2	

** Significant at >.01;   * Significant at > .05

OLS regression analyses showing unstandardised (b) and standardised (beta) coefficients, multiplied by 100 for easier interpretation, the bs predicting the percentage probability of vote for various parties for five separate models and the betas their relative predictive powers within the models. The dependent variable is each party's set of voters (1), against all other voters (0). Non-voters are excluded. For occupation, the residual category is non-manual households, and for education, those with qualifications beyond secondary school, excluding university. All variables are 1 for the category indicated, 0 for those not in the category, except for age. Age is a continuous linear variable where 0 is 18 and 70 is 1, therefore very roughly measuring the lesser or greater probability of a 70-year old voting for the party concerned compared to an 18-year old. As some age effects are non-linear, the model only measures the extent to which straight lines can be drawn over the curves and thus the effects of age are approximate only.

Chapter 10
Explaining Voting to Reduce the Number of MPs (Logistic Regression Coefficients)

	b	Std. Error
Age	0.00	(0.00)
Female	0.06	(0.09)
Minority	−0.44 **	(0.12)
MPs out of touch	0.23 **	(0.05)
Disapprove of List MPs	0.33 **	(0.07)
Disapprove of Electorate MPs	0.01	(0.06)
More Women in Parliament	−0.27 **	(0.08)
Labour	−0.38 **	(0.11)
NZ First	−0.47	(0.24)
Alliance	−0.25	(0.18)
ACT	−0.16	(0.19)
Green	−0.73 **	(0.22)
Left	−0.68 **	(0.13)
Right	−0.05	(0.13)
No ideology	0.01	(0.15)
Referendums should become law	0.54 **	(0.05)
Referendums get attention	0.19 **	(0.06)
Proportionality	−0.54 **	(0.09)
Education	−0.21 **	(0.04)
Political knowledge	−0.35 **	(0.06)
Constant	−0.56	(0.45)
Nagelkerke Pseudo r-square	0.23	
N	4276	

Dependent variable: If you voted on the referendum about the number of MPs, which option did you choose? 1=Voted to reduce the number of MPs to 99; 0=Voted to retain the current number at 120
** Significant at p<.01; * Significant at p<.01

Explaining Voting to Get Tough on Crime (Logistic Regression Coefficients)

	b	Std. Error
Age	0.00	(0.00)
Female	0.08	(0.13)
Minority	−0.35	(0.18)
MPs out of touch	0.19 **	(0.07)
Labour	−0.25	(0.16)
NZ First	−0.53	(0.37)
Alliance	−0.77 **	(0.25)
ACT	0.11	(0.34)
Green	−0.56 *	(0.28)
Left	−0.48 **	(0.17)
Right	0.59 *	(0.24)
No ideology	0.22	(0.25)
Referendums should become law	0.50 **	(0.08)
Referendums get attention	0.33 **	(0.09)
More Spending on police and law enforcement	0.92 **	(0.10)
Death penalty should be reintroduced	0.80 **	(0.06)
Constant	−5.66 **	(0.56)
Nagelkerke Pseudo r-square	0.37	
N	4512	

Dependent variable: If you voted on the referendum about penalties for crimes of violence and more concern for victims, which option did you choose?
1=Voted for greater penalties and more concern for victims; 0=Voted for same penalties and treatment of victims as now.
** Significant at p<.01; * Significant at p<.01

SECTION 264 OF
ELECTORAL ACT 1993

Review by Select Committee — (1) The House of Representatives shall, as soon as practicable after the 1st day of April 2000, appoint a select committee to consider the following matters:

(a) The effect of sections 35 and 36 of this Act on the electoral system:

(b) The provisions of this Act dealing with Maori representation:

(c) Whether there should be a further referendum on changes to the electoral system.

(2) The select committee appointed under subsection (1) of this section shall report to the House of Representatives before the first day of June 2002 and shall include in its Report a statement indicating —

(a) Whether, in its view, there should be changes to the sections 35 and 36 of this Act;

(b) Whether, in its view, there should be changes to the provisions of this Act dealing with Maori representation;

(c) Whether there should be a further referendum on changes to the electoral system, and if so, the nature of any proposals to be put to voters and the timing of the referendum.

Items added by Parliament in 2000:

(d) The appropriate number of members of Parliament, taking into account the results of the 1999 citizens initiated referendum on that issue;

(e) The extent to which party lists have resulted in a better representation of women;

(f) The effectiveness of the electoral system with respect to the representation of Maori and other ethnic minorities;

(g) Any other matters.

APPENDIX E

SUMMARY OF NZES
RECOMMENDATIONS
FOR THE MMP REVIEW, JULY 2000.

Term of reference c: **Whether there should be a further referendum on changes to the electoral system**.

1. We recommend a referendum if there are to be significant changes made to, or away from, MMP.
    a) In order to produce the optimal level of public information and consideration of the issues, we advise that such a referendum be held between elections, and accompanied by a substantial programme of public education, including equal public funding for those advocating each side of the question.
    b) We also advise that such a referendum would be best held either a year before or after the next election. The longer the delay, the more experience that would be accumulated of MMP as presently constituted, thus enhancing more informed and considered evaluations.

2. We advise that an electoral system for New Zealand should satisfy a base-line level of proportional representation that guarantees the largest number of seats in the House to the party with the largest number of votes. We believe that MMP is the best system on offer to promote this goal. If a referendum is held, we recommend that it should focus on modifications to MMP rather than proposing another radical change.

3. From our assessment of public opinion, we believe that a higher level of consensus on the electoral system is both desirable and possible, and might be achieved by changing MMP to –
    •   increase the odds of majority government,
    •   reduce the ability of small parties to play a pivotal role, and
    •   enhance the accountability of individual list MPs to voters.

4. With a view to introducing means of enhancing the accountability of individual list MPs to voters, we advise that close consideration should be given to open regional lists, with particular attention to the variation of MMP practised in Bavaria.

5. If open regional lists were established, we recommend that a small national top-up be retained to ensure proportionality on a national party vote threshold basis.

6.   To increase the odds of majority government, and reduce the ability of small parties to play a pivotal role, we recommend a referendum to determine whether the winning of an electorate or electorates by a party with less than 5 per cent of the party vote should, or should not, entitle that party to the allocation of further list seats.

Term of Reference d) **The appropriate number of members of Parliament, taking into account the results of the 1999 citizens initiated referendum on that issue.**

7.   If the size of the House is reduced to 99 members and reduction of the number of list seats is the means, a mechanism to compensate for electorate seat overhangs should be introduced allowing for extra compensatory list seats to be created on a temporary basis.

8.   As the referendum on the number of MPs was conducted in the absence of adequate information and debate on the matter, any reduction in the size of the House should only be given effect after a second binding referendum, accompanied by a substantial public information campaign.

9.   Notwithstanding recommendations 7 and 8, we recommend that the size of the house should remain at 120 at least, and that no action be taken on this matter except as indicated in recommendations 10, 11, and 12 below.

Term of reference a) **the Effect of sections 35 and 36 of the Electoral Act 1993**

10.   To safeguard proportionality, we advise that the proportion of list seats should not be allowed to fall below 40 per cent, unless a mechanism to compensate for electorate seat overhangs is introduced to enable extra compensatory list seats to be created on a temporary basis.

11.   We advise that, ideally, the South Island quota of 16 electorate seats should be retained, the electorate/list seat ratio be set at its present 67:53 and numbers of electorate and list seats should both expand, allowing the size of the House to gradually increase beyond 120. If this is judged to be politically unacceptable, the South Island quota should be abolished and the base number of MPs set at 120.

12.   Variation in the electoral populations of electorates should be increased to plus or minus 10 per cent, but only if there remain sufficient list seats to safeguard proportionality as specified in earlier recommendations.

Term of Reference e) **The extent to which party lists have resulted in a better representation of women** and Term of Reference f) **The effectiveness of the electoral system with respect to the representation of Maori and other ethnic minorities**.

13.   To enhance women's and minority representation, the present proportion of list seats should be at least maintained.

Term of reference b) **The provisions of the Electoral Act 1993 dealing with Maori representation.**

15.   Section 45 should become a reserved provision of the Electoral Act 1993.

16.   No other changes should be made to section 45 of the Electoral Act

NOTES

Chapter 2

1 The seven promises were: (1) to create jobs by promoting industries, with more support for exporters and small businesses; (2) to cut the costs to students of tertiary education, starting with 'a fairer loans scheme'; (3) to focus on patients, not profit, and cut waiting times for surgery in the public health system; reverse cuts to super-annuation rates and guarantee superannuation in future by putting a proportion of all income tax into a separate fund used for no other purpose; (4) restore income-related rents for state housing so that low income tenants paid no more than 25 percent of their income; (5) crack down on burglary and youth crime; (6) no rise in income tax for anyone earning under $60,000; (7) no increases in GST or company tax.

2 Preliminary data from the pre-election phase have already been published, but this data was not entirely consistent with the findings of the majority of other campaign polls, particularly in terms of the gap between National and Labour (Vowles 2000, 152). The data have therefore been re-weighed as explained in Appendix A.

3 This group includes those who did not express their intentions during the campaign (after probing), and who subsequently voted on election day.

4 The gap of two days between the last rolling average and election day is filled by figures assuming a smooth trend in intentions between the last cross-section and election day. The larger preliminary campaign data set is used for this figure because a larger N allows for more sensitive estimates of the day-to-day shifts, and the overall trend is virtually identical to that of our revised weighted estimates.

5 A useful way to evaluate one aspect of MMP is to compare the correlation between preferred party and party vote under MMP to that between preferred party and hypothetical FPP vote (see Chapter 6). The proportion of voters who cast party votes consistent with their party preference was nearly 79 per cent. Hypothetical FPP votes consistent with party preference were 75 per cent (see Vowles, Aimer, Banducci, Karp 1998, 197, for similar data from 1996).

6 See Vowles 2001c for the regression parameter estimates, standard errors, and full details of the models on which the table is based.

Chapter 3

1 Similar comparison of answers to our question on political interest shows no significant differences between levels of political interest after the two elections.

2 For a detailed qualitative analysis of the parties' television campaigns and the content of television coverage see Church 2000.

3 These conclusions, however, are generally based on studies of U.S. campaigns; we are not yet sure if they apply to New Zealand's coverage of the campaign.

4 Of all stories on the evening news, 46.6 per cent were domestic news stories, 16.4 were stories about countries other than New Zealand with no New Zealand content, 31 per cent were sports, and 6 per cent were entertainment or celebrities. We coded only the content of domestic stories.

5 While we acknowledge that making consistent coding decisions across three quite different kinds of discourse is somewhat prone to error and bias, nonetheless the larger differences between the distribution of One News television coverage and voters' most important issue concerns are very unlikely to be coding artefacts. Note also that our use of Spearman's rank coefficients is a conservative method of comparison.

6 Recent research from other countries indicates that the role of the media in setting the public agenda is overstated (Norris, Curtice, Sanders, Scammell, Semetko 1999). The state of knowledge about the agenda setting process lacks few definitive statements about what influences the public agenda except that the media may be more important in influencing what voters think about than how they think.

7 18 October was day 1, and the last day of the campaign, 26 November, was day 40. The correlation between the day and the tone of coverage for Clark is .14 and the correlation between the day of the campaign and tone of coverage of Shipley is −.15.

Chapter 5

1 Since 1867, New Zealand's electoral laws have provided for Maori representation by dividing the country into Maori electorates as well as General electorates. From 1867 to 1993, the Maori electorates were fixed at four. Since 1994, the criteria for the number of Maori electorates have been the five-yearly population census and the number of Maori who choose to be enrolled on the Maori electoral roll rather than the General roll. As a result, in 1996 there were five Maori electorates. This number rose to six for the 1999 election. At the 2002 election there will be seven Maori electorates.

2 Aggregate vote volatility refers to the amount of change in the electorate's party choices from one election to the next. It is calculated by adding up the differences in the percentage of the total vote received by each party and independents in each of the two elections — in our case, 1999 compared to 1996. This total is then divided by two, to avoid double counting, because all parties' increases are the result of other parties' losses. Aggregate volatility always underestimates the amount of individual volatility, because voters switching in opposite directions cancel each other out. For example, if out of 100 voters 10 switch to Labour and 10 switch to National, the statistics show an aggregate volatility rate of nil, yet the individual volatility rate is 20 per cent.

3 The lowest turnout was in the new electorate of Hauraki where only two thirds of eligible voters bothered to go to the polls. There are likely to be two reasons for this: disillusionment with New Zealand First coupled with belief that the high-profile Labour candidate John Tamihere was the only credible contender for the seat.

4 An October 2000 Marae-DigiPoll survey showed the prominent Mana Maori candidate, Tame Iti, to be polling around 11 per cent in Delamere's electorate. Iti withdrew from Waiariki and stood in the Auckland Central electorate (*New Zealand Herald*, 28 October 1999).

5 Just prior to the election he approved residency for 21 Chinese investors on condition that they invest around half a million dollars in Maori-owned land, businesses or specified provincial regions. He attempted to create new policy without consulting Cabinet. The Prime Minister fired him for his abuse of office (*New Zealand Herald*, 4 December 1999).

Chapter 6

1 It is computed by dividing 1 by the sum of the squares of the fractional shares of all parties votes or seats, as the case may be (Laakso and Taagepera 1979, 4).

2 The estimates from at least some cells of the data in this table can be validated from official data obtainable from the Chief Electoral Office. From this can be calculated the numbers and proportions of votes cast for the same party for both party and electorate votes, broken down by each party. Comparing this to the 'straight vote' cells, with the contrasts in brackets, the official figures are: Labour 77.9 per cent (+0.8), National 76.0 (–0.8), Alliance 37.0 (+2.6), New Zealand First 55.7 (–2.4), ACT 24.6 (+0.7), Christian Heritage 51.4 (+5.6), Green 30.7 (+8.0). Only in the case of the Greens is our data somewhat misleading. With an N of 261 for declared Green party voters we could have expected a margin of error of + or – 5.5 per cent, so the difference is somewhat outside it. All the other differences are trivial, and well within expected sampling error.

3 In the full sample, relying on recall data, the Alliance is shown as contributing an even lower proportion to the 1999 Green party vote.

4 The lines represented on the graphs are fourth-order polynomials drawn through the age by vote data, year by year. This method has the effect of smoothing out sampling error by date of birth, where the Ns are relatively small, and indicating where the trends are non-linear.

5 New Zealand First is not included in this series of figures for reasons of space, but also because the age profile of its support is the most linear. New voters were about 50 per cent less likely to vote New Zealand First than average, and 70-year olds about three times more likely.

6 For multivariate analysis of social structure and vote confirming this claim, and a full table of voting and social structure in 1999, see Appendix C.

Chapter 7

1 In the 1960s, New Zealand turnout on an age-eligible base averaged by decade has been estimated at tenth in a ranking of 19 countries; at eighth in the 1970s; and in the 1980s, at tenth once more (Jackman 1987; Jackman and Miller 1995).

2 Those doubting this claim are referred to the ratio of valid votes cast to age-eligible population found in Electoral Commission, 2000, 141, for the elections 1987 to 1999, and the figures back to 1928 estimated in Nagel, 1988. Unpublished preliminary estimates of age-eligible population back to the 1890s suggest that the proportion of valid votes cast on that base remained well above estimates for the 1990s.

3 Errors in estimating an age-eligible population are likely to be minor compared to those produced by differences in enrolment or registration over time. Where revision of electoral rolls or registers is inadequate, turnout may appear to decline without necessarily doing so because of the failure to remove the names of the deceased, or of those who have changed location and perhaps registered again elsewhere. In similar circumstances turnout is likely to decline because people fail to enrol or register when becoming eligible, or to re-enrol or re-register if this is necessary, but in these cases the official figures will fail to include them at all. Another problem may be that citizens of other countries currently resident in New Zealand may be counted in age-eligible population estimates. However, in New Zealand non-citizen permanent residents may enrol and vote after one year.

4 The data used in this chapter excludes the between-election panel component of the NZES for the most part of the analysis, relying on freshly sampled respondents to avoid the problem of partial self-selection by multiple respondents who may be likely to participate more in politics. This leaves over 3,000 respondents for both 1996 and 1999 elections. The data sets were re-weighted to ensure that both samples accurately reflected those on the electoral rolls, in terms of education, gender, age, vote choice, spatial distribution, and validated non-vote by electorate.

5 Safety and marginality is indicated by the two-party swing margins between the first- and second-placed party candidates in the same electorates at the previous election (on a base of the vote for those two parties only). Two-party swing is the generally accepted measure of competitiveness. It is calculated as follows: ((Votes for party or candidate coming first) minus (Votes for party or candidate coming

second)) divided by ((Votes for party or candidate coming first) plus (Votes for party or candidate coming second)) multiplied by (100 divided by 2). This simply estimates the proportion of votes cast for the two most popular parties or candidates that would need to shift from the first party to the second party to change the result. To take the 1990 and 1999 margins would be tautological, making the assumption that voters had perfect information about the margins that would be the as-yet-unknown result of the votes they and others were casting. The 1999 election was fought under different electorate boundaries than that of 1996. The safety and marginality estimates are therefore based on votes reallocated into the new boundaries (McRobie 1998).

6 A regression of the party and electorate vote margins against expenditures by electorate indicates this clearly.

7 The expenditure limits for parties' central campaign expenditure are $1 million plus $20,000 for every electorate candidate the party stands. As National stood candidates in 65 electorates, the maximum it could have spent in this part of its budget was $2.3 million.

8 Percentage possible contacts was calculated by summing the numbers of all contacts (nc) and dividing those by the maximum number of contacts (mc multiplied by the sample size (N): nc/(mc*N).

9 A higher response rate in the 1999 study could mean that these differences are an artefact of that difference. However, checking the 1600 respondents who answered the same questions in 1999 and 1996 indicates the same significant difference in National and Labour contacts, albeit slightly attenuated. The differences we find appear reasonably robust.

10 This study regressed a dummy variable for the 1999 election against non-vote versus vote in a pooled data set containing data from the 1996 and 1999 NZES. Successive blocks of controls were added to decompose the effects of turnout decline.

Chapter 8

1 Similar sentiments are apparent in Scotland, another political system that has recently adopted proportional representation. A poll conducted for the *Scotsman*, the ICM Monthly Poll on 3 March 1999, found that some 82 per cent of respondents thought that the Liberal Democrat party should announce before polling day whether it was intending to coalesce with Labour or the SNP.

2 The Scottish Labour–Liberal Democrat agreement, *Partnership for Scotland*, was similar to the National–New Zealand First one in giving considerable emphasis to a detailed policy programme in such areas as health, education, the environment and rural affairs. Unlike the recent Labour–Alliance coalition document in New Zealand, it said almost nothing about the process for resolving disputes. No amendment was made to the convention that the decisions made by cabinet are binding on all ministers.

Chapter 9

1 Before asking respondents for their opinion, they were reminded in 1998 of the proportions of women and Maori in Parliament, information which was not given in the three post-election surveys.

2 The pre-election study was conducted by phone, and respondents were only given an agree, disagree or neutral response option. In the post-election mail-back survey, respondents were given the options: agree strongly, agree, neutral, disagree or disagree strongly. We have collapsed the agree and strongly agree categories from the post-election to make the responses comparable between the pre- and post-election surveys.

3 The post-election version of this question differs slightly from the pre-election. In the pre-election survey no neutral category is offered. If the lack of the neutral

category in the pre-election poll was causing the change in responses, we would expect the percentage satisfied or very satisfied to decrease as respondents would spread themselves across five response categories rather than four, and the satisfied categories would have fewer respondents in them.

4 In 1993 under FPP, a larger proportion of the electorate (62 per cent) could recall the name of their local MP. The decline in awareness of electorate MPs possibly reflects confusion over the two types of MPs.

5 The lower recall of electorate MPs among Maori does not appear to be due to differences in the administration of the survey. Those Maori who were administered postal questionnaires were just as likely to recall the name of their electorate MP as those who were administered the survey face to face.

6 Some scholars, however, have criticised the proximity model, contending that such behaviour does not conform to reality. Instead of taking moderate positions on a range of issues, parties have been found to take more extreme positions in order to generate political support among an electorate that has diffuse policy interests (MacDonald, Listhaug and Rabinowitz 1991). The directional model, as developed by Rabinowitz and MacDonald (1989) differs from the proximity model by assuming that voters will support the party that advocates the direction of policy they prefer. For a comparison of the two models applied to the New Zealand case see Karp and Banducci (2002).

7 These issues were prominent in both the 1993 and 1999 campaigns and consequently were asked in both years, and in both the elector and party candidate surveys. The typical bipolar scale used for issue variables has the potential to confound intensity with extremity (see Maddens 1996). Four of the six issue variables specifically measure the intensity of preference and, therefore, overcome this limitation. For example, respondents are asked whether it should or should not be the government's responsibility to provide free education to polytechnic and university levels. They are also probed as to whether they think it should definitely be or not be the government's responsibility (for other issues see Appendix B). The remaining questions on taxes and the environment ask respondents to place themselves on a six-point scale. All issues are re-coded on a –1 to +1 scale so that 0 indicates a neutral or moderate position, –1 indicates an extreme left position and +1 an extreme right position.

Chapter 10

1 December 1995: 'Should the number of professional firefighters employed full-time in the New Zealand Fire Service be reduced below the number employed on 1 January 1995? ('No' — 87.8 per cent).

2 Off-course betting (March 1949); Compulsory military training (August 1949); Term of Parliament (September 1967); Term of Parliament (October 1990); Voting system (September 1992); Voting system (November 1993); Compulsory Retirement Savings Scheme (September 1997) (Electoral Commission 2000, 56–7).

3 The Electoral Commission produced an information leaflet relating to the referendum on the number of MPs, which was available on request, but not distributed to all households.

4 A pre-election survey conducted by the Political Change Project at Victoria University of Wellington a week before the election also found 35.9 per cent of those surveyed were unaware of the two referendums (Church 2000, 198).

Chapter 11

1 Prior to the 2001 Midterm Study, a series of focus groups were conducted at the University of Waikato on electoral system attitudes and opinion. Thanks are due to Jo Barnes who helped guide and facilitate these meetings.

Chapter 12

1 Section 35 defines the basis on which the country is divided into General electoral districts. Section 36 allows for a 5 per cent population tolerance in the drawing of electoral boundaries.

2 The United New Zealand party's sole MP is Peter Dunne, MP for Ohariu-Belmont (Wellington). At the 1999 election, the party won 0.54 per cent of the overall party vote.

3 One can make an approximate estimate of the increase in the size of the House for the 1999 election had FPP survived. Under FPP, the formula was based on 25 electorates in the South Island. However, the estimate is complicated by changes to the definition of the Maori electorates, which has allowed them to increase above four since 1995. Because as a response to this change more Maori have registered on the Maori roll, it is impossible to estimate exactly what the size of the House might have been had Maori seats been held at four. Including an expansion of the number of Maori seats, the size of the House would have probably risen to 104 seats in 1999 under FPP.

4 As it did under FPP, this process would peg change in the size of the House almost solely to the ratio between the South and North Island populations. On reflection, it seems odd that this one consideration should determine the size of Parliament. Is the ability of South Island electorate MPs to service their constituents the only thing that matters?

5 Those promoting reduction in seats to 99 argue that a lower number of women and minorities in a smaller House could be prevented by parties simply working to select and elect enough women and other minorities to maintain their representation. While this is true, it puts remarkable faith in political parties' willingness and ability to put that goal above other considerations more than is currently the case. But those wishing to reduce the size of the House also argue that this would improve parliamentary behaviour. Yet on their own logic, one could also argue that MPs could simply work to improve their behaviour, and therefore no change in the size of the House is necessary. In fact, even those members of the committee supporting a smaller House did not believe that it would make any difference to the behaviour of MPs. Meanwhile there is no doubt that the lower the proportion of list seats, the harder it will be to elect women to Parliament.

6 In its submission to the review committee, the NZES identified the one-electorate threshold as an appropriate item for inclusion in a referendum (see Appendix E, 6).

7 Claims that the Royal Commission was appointed on any other basis (see Hunt, 1998, 3) have been rebutted (Chou, 2001, 54–55).

REFERENCES

Achen, C. H. (1982) *Interpreting and Using Regression*, Beverly Hills, Sage.

Agresti, A. (1990) *Categorical Data Analysis*, New York, John Wiley and Sons.

Aimer, P. (1997a) 'Leaders and Outcomes: The Clark Factor in 1996', in J. Boston, S. Levine, E. McLeay, N. S. Roberts (eds), *From Campaign to Coalition: New Zealand's First General Election Under Proportional Representation*, Palmerston North, Dunmore Press.

Aimer, P. (1997b) 'The Future of the Party System', in R. Miller (ed.), *New Zealand Politics in Transition*, Auckland, Oxford University Press.

Aimer, P. (2001) 'The Changing Party System', in R. Miller (ed.), *New Zealand Government and Politics*, Auckland, Oxford University Press.

Aldrich, J. H., and Nelson, F. D. (1984) *Linear Probability, Logit, and Probit Models*, No. 45, Beverly Hills, Sage.

Anderson, C. J. and Guillory, C. A. (1997) 'Political Institutions and Satisfaction with Democracy: A Cross-National Analysis of Consensus and Majoritarian Systems', *American Political Science Review*, 91:66–81.

Banducci, S., and Karp, J. (1998) 'Representation under a Proportional System', in J. Vowles, P. Aimer, S. Banducci, J. Karp (eds), *Voters' Victory? New Zealand's First Election under Proportional Representation*, Auckland, Auckland University Press.

Banducci, S., and Karp, J. (1999) 'Perceptions of Fairness and Support for Proportional Representation', *Political Behavior*, 21:217–38.

Banducci, S. and Karp, J. (2000) 'Gender, Leadership and Choice in Multiparty Systems', *Political Research Quarterly*, 53:815–48.

Banducci, S., Donovan, T., Karp, J. (1999) 'Proportional Representation and Attitudes About Politics: Results from New Zealand', *Electoral Studies*, 18:533–55.

Barker, F., and McLeay, E. (2000) 'How Much Change? An Analysis of the Initial Impact of Proportional Representation on the New Zealand Parliamentary Party System', *Party Politics*, 6:131–54.

Bartolini, S., and Mair, P. (1990) *Identity, Competition, and Electoral Availability: The Stabilization of European Electorates, 1885–1985*, Cambridge, Cambridge University Press.

Bassett, M., and King, M. (2000) *Tomorrow Comes the Song: A Life of Peter Fraser*, Auckland, Penguin Books.

Bawn, K. (1999) 'Voter Responses to Electoral Complexity: Ticket-Splitting, Rational Voters, and Representation in the Federal Republic of Germany', *British Journal of Political Science*, 29:487–505.

Bean, C. (1992) 'Party Leaders and Local Candidates', in M. Holland (ed.), *Electoral Behaviour in New Zealand*, Auckland, Oxford University Press.

Blais, A. (2000) *To Vote or Not to Vote: The Merits and Limits of Rational Choice Theory*, Pittsburg, University of Pittsburg Press.

Blais, A., and Carty, R. K. (1990) 'Does Proportional Representation Foster Voter Turnout?', *European Journal of Political Research*, 18:167–82.

Blais, A., and Dobrzynska, A. (1998) 'Turnout in Electoral Democracies', *European Journal of Political Research*, 33:239–61.

Blais, A., Gidengil, E., and Nevitte, N. (1997) 'Do Polls Influence the Vote?', paper presented at the Campaign Colloquium, 21–2 June, University of British Columbia.

Bobo, L., and Gilliam, F. D. Jr. (1990) 'Race, Sociopolitical Participation and Black Empowerment', *American Political Science Review*, 84:377–94.

Bochel, J. M., and Denver, D. (1971) 'Canvassing, Turnout, and Party Support: An Experiment', *British Journal of Political Science*, 1:257–69.

Bochel, J. M., and Denver, D. (1972) 'The Impact of the Campaign on the Results of Local Government Elections', *British Journal of Political Science*, 2:239–44.

Boston, J. (1998) *Governing under Proportional Representation: Lessons From Europe*, Wellington, Institute of Policy Studies.

Boston, J. (2000) 'Forming the Coalition Between Labour and the Alliance', in J. Boston, S. Church, S. Levine, E. McLeay and N. S. Roberts (eds), *Left Turn: The New Zealand General Election of 1999*, Wellington, Victoria University Press.

Boston, J. (2001) 'Forming a Government', in R. Miller (ed.), *New Zealand Government and Politics*, Auckland, Oxford University Press.

Boston, J., and Church, S. (2000) 'Pre-Election Wheeling and Dealing: The New Zealand Experience', in J. Boston, S. Church, S. Levine, E. McLeay and N. S. Roberts (eds), *Left Turn: The New Zealand General Election of 1999*, Wellington, Victoria University Press.

Boston, J., and McLeay, E. (1997) 'Forming the First MMP Government: Theory, Practice and Prospects', in J. Boston, S. Levine, E. McLeay, N. S. Roberts (eds), *From Campaign to Coalition: New Zealand's First General Election Under Proportional Representation*, Palmerston North, Dunmore Press.

Boston, J., Levine, S., McLeay, E., and Roberts, N. S. (eds). (1996) *New Zealand under MMP: A New Politics?*, Auckland, Auckland University Press/Bridget Williams Books.

Bowler, S., Donovan, T., and Karp, J. (2000) 'When Might Institutions Change? Elite Support for Direct Democracy in Three Nations'. Paper prepared for XVIII World Congress of the International Political Science Association, Quebec City, 1–5 August.

Bowler, S., Donovan, T., and Tolbert C. J. (1998) *Citizens as Legislators: Direct Democracy in the United States*, Ohio University Press.

Budge, I., and Keman, H. (1990) *Parties and Democracy: Coalition Formation and Government Functioning in Twenty States*, Oxford, Oxford University Press.

Burkett, T. (1985) 'The West German Deputy', in V. Bogdanor (ed.), *Representatives of the People? Parliamentarians and Constituents in Western Democracies*, Aldershot, Gower.

Butler, D., and Ranney, A. (eds). (1992) *Electioneering: A Comparative Study of Continuity and Change*, Oxford, Oxford University Press.

Catt, H. (1996) 'The Other Democratic Experiment: New Zealand's Experience with Citizens' Initiated Referendum' *Political Science*, 48:29–47.

Catt, H. (1999) *Democracy in Practice*, London, Routledge.

Chapman, R. (1986) 'Voting in the Maori Political Sub-System, 1935–1984', in Report of the Royal Commission on the Electoral System: *Towards a Better Democracy*, Wellington, Government Printer.

Chou, R. (2001) 'The New Zealand Parliament under MMP: A New Policy Process?' MPhil thesis, University of Oxford.

Church, S. (2000) 'Lights, Camera, Election: The Television Campaign', in J. Boston, S. Church, S. Levine, E. McLeay and N. S. Roberts (eds), *Left Turn: The New Zealand General Election of 1999*, Wellington, Victoria University Press.

Cohen, D. (1997) 'New Zealand Politics: A Woman's Place', *Christian Science Monitor*, 7 November.

Controller and Auditor-General (2001) *Report of the Controller and Auditor-General, Parliamentary Salaries, Allowances and Other Entitlements: Final Report,* Office of the Controller and Auditor-General, July 2001, Wellington.

Converse, P., and Niemi, R. (1971) 'Non-Voting Among Young Adults in the United States', in W. Crotty, D. Freeman, and D. Gatlin (eds), *Political Parties and Political Behavior*, 2nd edn, Boston, Allyn and Bacon.

Dalton, R., McAllister, I., and Wattenberg, M. (2000) 'The Decline in Party Identification and the Consequences of Dealignment: The Evidence from 20 OECD Nations', in R. Dalton, R. and M. Wattenberg (eds), *Parties without Partisans: Political Change in Advanced Industrial Democracies*, Oxford, Oxford University Press.

Dalziel, P., and Fox, M. (1996) 'Ethnic Disparities in Economic Attainment: A survey of economic literature.' Paper prepared for Te Puni Kokiri/Ministry of Maori Development.

Darcy, R., Welch, S., and Clark, J. (1994) *Women, Elections, and Representation*, 2nd edn, University of Nebraska Press.

Demaris, A. (1992) *Logit Modelling: Practical Applications*, Newbury Park, Sage.

Denemark, D. (1998) 'Campaign Activities and Marginality', in J. Vowles, P. Aimer, S. Banducci, and J. Karp (eds), *Voters Victory? New Zealand's First Election under MMP*, Auckland, Auckland University Press.

Donovan, T., and Bowler, S. (1998) 'Direct Democracy and Minority Rights: An Extension', *American Journal of Political Science,* 42:1020–4.

Downs, A. (1957) *An Economic Theory of Democracy*, New York, Harper and Row.

Easton, B. (1999) *The Whimpering of the State. Policy after MMP,* Auckland University Press, Auckland.

Farrell, D. (1996) 'Campaign Strategies and Tactics', in L. LeDuc, R. Niemi, and P. Norris (eds), *Comparing Democracies: Elections and Voting in Global Perspective*, Thousand Oaks, Ca,. Sage.

Fenno, R. F. Jr. (1978) *Home Style: House Members in their Districts*, Boston, Little, Brown.

Fiorina, M. P. (1981) *Congress: Keystone of the Washington Establishment*, New Haven, Yale University Press.

Franklin, M. (1996) 'Electoral Participation', in L. LeDuc, R. Niemi, and P. Norris (eds), *Comparing Democracies: Elections and Voting in Global Perspective*, Thousand Oaks, Ca., Sage.

Fuchs, D., and Klingemann H. D. (1995) 'Citizens and the State: A Changing Relationship?', in H. D. Klingemann and D. Fuchs (eds), *Citizens and the State*, New York, Oxford University Press.

Gamble, B. S. (1997) 'Putting Civil Rights to a Popular Vote', *American Journal of Political Science*, 41:245–69.

Gelman, A., and King, G. (1993) 'Why Are American Presidential Campaign Polls so Variable When Votes Are So Predictable?', *British Journal of Political Science*, 23:409–51.

Gidengil, E., and Everitt, J. (n.d.) 'Gender, Media Coverage and the Dynamics of Leader Evaluations: The Case of the 1993 Canadian Election', in H. E. Brady, and R. Johnston (eds), *Capturing Campaign Effects*, Ann Arbor, University of Michigan Press (forthcoming).

Gidengil, E., and Hennigar, M. (2000) 'The Gender Gap in Support for the Radical Right in Western Europe', paper presented at the Annual Meetings of the American Political Science Association, Washington DC, 31 August–3 September.

Gray, M., and Caul, M. (2000) 'Declining Voter Turnout in Advanced Industrialized Democracies', *Comparative Political Studies*, 33:1091–122.

Harcourt, G. (2000) 'Public Broadcasting — the Tasmanian Tiger of New Zealand', *ABCzINE* ,Winter:18–20.

Harris, S. (2000) 'Following the Leaders', in J. Boston, S. Church, S. Levine, E. McLeay and N. S. Roberts (eds), *Left Turn: The New Zealand General Election of 1999*, Wellington, Victoria University Press.

Hayward, J., and Rudd, C. (2000) 'Metropolitan Newspapers and the Election', in J. Boston, S. Church, S. Levine, E. McLeay and N. S. Roberts (eds), *Left Turn: The New Zealand General Election of 1999*, Wellington, Victoria University Press.

Hellweg, S. (1979) 'An Examination of Voter Conceptualizations of the Ideal Political Candidate', *Southern Speech Communication Journal*, 44:373–85.

Hine, D. (1993) *Governing Italy: The Politics of Bargained Pluralism,* Oxford, Clarendon.

Holtz-Bacha, C., and Norris, P. (2001) 'To Entertain, Inform and Educate. Still the Role of Public Television in the 1990s?', *Political Communication*, Summer.

Hosmer, D. W., and Lemeshow, S. (1989) *Applied Logistic Regression*, New York, John Wiley and Sons.

Hughes, C. (1994) 'Australia and New Zealand', in D. Butler and A. Ranney (eds), *Referendums Around the World. The Growing Use of Direct Democracy*, Washington DC, AEI Press

Hunt, G. (1998) *Why MMP Must Go*, Auckland, Waddington Press.

International Idea (1997) *Voter Turnout from 1945 to 1997: A Global Report*, Stockholm, Institute for Democracy and Electoral Assistance.

Iyengar, S., Peters, M. D., and Kinder, D. A. (1982) 'Experimental Demonstrations of the "Not-So-Minimal" Consequences of Television News Programs', *American Political Science Review*, 76:848–58.

Jackman, R. (1987) 'Political Institutions and Voter Turnout in Industrial Democracies', *American Political Science Review*, 81:405–23.

Jackman, R., and Miller, R. (1995) 'Voter Turnout in the Industrial Democracies during the 1980s', *Comparative Political Studies*, 27:467–92.

Jackson, K., and McRobie, A. (1998) *New Zealand Adopts Proportional Representation*, Aldershot, Ashgate.

Jesson, B. (1997) 'The Alliance', in R. Miller (ed.), *New Zealand Politics in Transition*, Auckland, Oxford University Press.

Johnston, R. (1998) ' Issues, Leaders and the Campaign', in J. Vowles, P. Aimer, S. Banducci, and J. Karp (eds), *Voters' Victory? New Zealand's First Election under Proportional Representation*, Auckland University Press, Auckland.

Johnston, R., and Vowles, J. (1997) 'The New Rules and the New Game in New Zealand Elections: Implications for the Campaign', paper presented at the American Political Science Association Meetings, Washington DC, 27–31 August 1997.

Kahn, K. (1994) 'Does Gender Make a Difference? An Experimental Examination of Sex Stereotypes and Press Patterns in Statewide Campaigns', *American Journal of Political Science*, 38:162–95.

Kaiser, A., and Brechtel, T. (1999) 'Party System, Bargaining Power and Coalition Formation after the 1999 New Zealand General Election', *Political Science* 51:182–7.

Karp, J., and Banducci, S. (1998) 'Voter Satisfaction after Electoral System Change', in J. Vowles, P. Aimer, S. Banducci, and J. Karp (eds), *Voters' Victory? New Zealand's First Election under Proportional Representation*, Auckland, Auckland University Press.

Karp, J., and Banducci, S. (1999) 'The Impact of Proportional Representation on Turnout: Evidence from New Zealand', *Australian Journal of Political Science*, 34:363–77.

Karp, J., and Banducci, S. (2000) 'Political Efficacy and Participation in Eighteen Democracies: How Electoral Rules Shape Political Behaviour'. Paper prepared for presentation at XVII World Congress of the International Political Science Association in Quebec City, Quebec, 1–5 August.

Karp, J., and Banducci, S. (2002) 'Issues and Party Competition under Alternative Electoral Systems', *Party Politics*, 8:123–41.

Karp, J., and Bowler, S. (2001) ' Coalition Government and Satisfaction with

Democracy: An Analysis of New Zealand's Reaction to Proportional Representation', *European Journal of Political Research*, 57–79.

Karp, J., Vowles, J., Banducci, S., and Donovan, T. (2002) 'Strategic Voting, Party Activity, and Candidate Effects: Testing Explanations for Split Voting in New Zealand's New Mixed System', *Electoral Studies*, 21:1–22.

Katz, R. (1979) *A Theory of Parties and Electoral Systems*, London, Johns Hopkins University Press.

Katz, R. (1986) 'Intra-Party Preference Voting', in B. Grofman, and A. Lijphart (eds), *Electoral Laws and Their Political Consequences*, New York, Agathon.

Katz, R., and Mair, P. (1994) *How Parties Organize: Change and Adaptation in Party Organizations in Western Democracies*, London, Sage.

Kim, J., and Mueller, C. W. (1978) *Introduction to Factor Analysis*, Beverley Hills, Sage.

Kinder, D., Peters, M., Abelson, R., and Fiske, S. (1980) 'Presidential Prototypes', *Political Behavior*, 2:315–37.

Kramer, G. (1970) 'The Effects of Precinct-Level Canvassing on Voting Behaviour', *Public Opinion Quarterly*, 34:560–72.

Laakso, M., and Taagepera, R. (1979) 'Effective Number of Parties: A Measure with Application to West Europe', *Comparative Political Studies*, 12:3–27.

Lamare, J., and Vowles, J. (1996) 'Party Interests, Public Opinion, and Institutional Preferences: Electoral System Change in New Zealand', *Australian Journal of Political Science*, 31:321–46.

LeDuc, L., Niemi, R., and Norris P. (eds) (1996) *Comparing Democracies: Elections and Voting in Global Perspective*, Thousand Oaks, Ca., Sage.

Leithner, C., (1997) 'Of Time and Partisan Stability Revisited: Australia and New Zealand 1905–1993', *American Journal of Political Science*, 41:1104–28.

Leithner, C., and Vowles, J. (1997) 'Back to Instability? The Rise and Decline of Party Loyalty in the New Zealand Electorate, 1905–1993'. Paper presented to the Annual Meetings of the American Political Science Association, San Francisco, 31 August–2 September 1996.

Levine, S., and Roberts, N. S. (1997) 'The 1996 Election,' in R. Miller (ed.), *New Zealand Politics in Transition*, Auckland, Oxford University Press.

Lijphart, A. (1987) 'The Demise of the Last Westminster System? Comments on the Report of New Zealand's Royal Commission on the Electoral System', *Electoral Studies*, 6:97–103.

Lijphart, A. (1994) *Electoral Systems and Party Systems*, Oxford, Oxford University Press.

Lijphart, A. (1999) *Patterns of Democracy. Government Forms and Performance in Thirty-Six Countries*, New Haven, Yale University Press.

Lublin, D., and Tate, K. (1995) 'Racial Group Competition in Urban Elections', in P. Peterson (ed.), *Classifying by Race*, Princeton, N.J., Princeton University Press

Lupia, A. (1994) 'Shortcuts versus Encyclopedias: Information and Voting Behavior in California Insurance Reform Elections', *American Political Science Review*, 88:63–76.

MacDonald, S. E., Listhaug, O., and Rabinowitz, G. (1991) ' Issues and Party

Support in Multiparty Systems', *American Political Science Review*, 85:1107–31.

Maddens, B. (1996) 'Directional Theory of Issue Voting: The Case of the 1991 Parliamentary Elections in Flanders', *Electoral Studies*, 15:53–70.

Mair, P. (1997) *Party System Change: Approaches and Interpretations*, Clarendon Press, Oxford.

Marsh, M. (1985) 'The Voters Decide? Preferential Voting in European List Systems', *European Journal of Political Research*, 13:365–78.

McAllister, I. (1996) 'Leaders', in L. LeDuc, R. G. Niemi, and P. Norris (eds), *Comparing Democracies: Elections and Voting in Global Perspective*, Thousand Oaks, Calif., Sage.

McCombs, M., and Shaw, D. (1972) 'The Agenda-Setting Function of the Mass Media', *Public Opinion Quarterly*, 36:176–87.

McLean, J. (2000) 'Making More (or Less) of Binding Referenda and Citizens-initiated Referenda', in C. James (ed.), *Building the Constitution*, Wellington, Institute of Policy Studies.

McQuail, D. (1994) *Mass Communication Theory: An Introduction*, London, Sage.

McRobie, A. (1989) *New Zealand Electoral Atlas*, Wellington, GP Books.

McRobie, A. (1993) 'Educating the Public', in A. McRobie (ed.), *Taking It To The People: The New Zealand Electoral Referendum Debate*, Christchurch, Hazard Press.

McRobie, A. (1996) *The 1995 Electoral Redistribution*, Christchurch, Alan McRobie.

McRobie, A. (1998) *New Zealand's 1998 Electoral Redistribution*, Christchurch, MC Enterprises.

Menard, S. (1995) *Applied Logistic Regression Analysis*, No. 106, Beverly Hills, Sage.

Mendelsohn, M. (1996) 'The Media and Interpersonal Communications: The Priming of Issues, Leaders, and Party Identification', *Journal of Politics*, 58:112–25.

Mendelsohn, M., and Cutler, F. (2000) 'The Effect of Referendums on Democratic Citizens: Information, Politicization, Efficacy, and Tolerance', *British Journal of Political Science* 30:669–98.

Miller, R. (1998) 'Coalition Government: The People's Choice?', in J. Vowles, P. Aimer, S. Banducci, and J. Karp (eds), *Voters' Victory? New Zealand's First Election under Proportional Representation*, Auckland, Auckland University Press, .

Miller, R., and Catt, H. (1993) *Season of Discontent: Byelections and the Bolger Government*, Palmerston North, Dunmore Press.

MMP Review Committee (2001) 'Inquiry into the Review of MMP', Wellington, New Zealand Parliament.

Mughan, A. (1995) 'Television and Presidentialism: Australian and U.S. Legislative Elections Compared', *Political Communication*, 12:327–42.

Mulgan, R. (1997) *Politics in New Zealand*, 2nd edn, Auckland, Auckland University Press.

Muller, W. C., and Ström, K. (eds) (1999) *Policy, Office, or Votes? How*

Political Parties in Western Europe Make Hard Decisions, Cambridge, Cambridge University Press.

Nagel, J. (1988) 'Voter Turnout in New Zealand General Elections 1928–1988', *Political Science*, 40:16–38.

Nagel, J. (1994) 'How Many Parties Will New Zealand Have under MMP?', *Political Science*, 46:139–60.

New Zealand Election Study (NZES) (2000) 'Submission to the MMP Review Committee'.

New Zealand Electoral Commission (1997) *The New Zealand Electoral Compendium*, Wellington, New Zealand Electoral Commission.

New Zealand Electoral Commission (1999) 'Information for Voters Relating to the Citizens Initiated Referendum on Whether the Number of MPs Should Be Reduced from 120 to 99', Wellington, New Zealand Electoral Commission.

New Zealand Electoral Commission (2000) *The New Zealand Electoral Compendium*, 2nd edn., Wellington, New Zealand Electoral Commission.

Norris, P. (1996) 'Legislative Recruitment', in L. LeDuc, R. G. Niemi, P. Norris (eds), *Comparing Democracies: Elections and Voting in Global Perspective*, Thousand Oaks, Ca., Sage.

Norris, P. (2000) *A Virtuous Circle: Political Communications in Post-industrial Societies*, Cambridge, Cambridge University Press

Norris, P. (2002) *Count Every Voice*, Cambridge, Cambridge University Press (forthcoming).

Norris, P., Curtice, J., Sanders, D., Scammell, M., and Semetko, H. (1999) *On Message: Communicating the Campaign*, London, Sage.

Palmer, G., and Palmer, M. (1997) *Bridled Power. New Zealand Government under MMP*, Auckland, Oxford University Press.

Patterson, T. E. (1993) *Out of Order*, New York, Random House.

Pharr, S., and Putnam, R. D. (eds) (2000) *Disaffected Democracies: What's Troubling the Trilateral Countries?* Princeton, Princeton University Press.

Pinto-Duschinsky, M. (1999) 'Sending the Rascals Packing: Defects of Proportional Representation and the Virtues of the Westminster Model', *Representation*, 36:117–26.

Powell, G. B. (1980) 'Voting Turnout in Thirty Democracies', in R. Rose (ed.), *Electoral Participation*, Beverly Hills, Sage.

Powell, G. B. (1982) *Contemporary Democracies: Participation, Stability, and Violence*, Cambridge, Cambridge University Press.

Rabinowitz, G., and MacDonald, S. E. (1989) 'A Directional Theory of Issue Voting', *American Political Science Review'*, 83:93–121.

Rosenstone, S. (1982) 'Economic Adversity and Voter Turnout', *American Journal of Political Science*, 26:25–46.

Rosenstone, S., and Hansen, J. (1993) *Mobilization, Participation and Democracy in America*, Macmillan, New York.

Royal Commission on the Electoral System, (1986) Report of the Royal Commission on the Electoral System: *Towards a Better Democracy*, Wellington, Government Printer.

Rule, W. (1994) 'Women's Representation and Electoral Systems', *PS: Political Science & Politics*, 27:689–92.

Sartori, G. (1976) *Parties and Party Systems*, Cambridge, Cambridge University Press.

Sorrenson, M. P. K. (1986) 'A History of Maori Representation in Parliament,' Appendix B in Report of the Royal Commission on the Electoral System: *Towards a Better Democracy*.

Statistics New Zealand (1997) *New Zealand Official Yearbook*, Statistics New Zealand , Wellington.

Stevenson, R. T., and Vavreck, L. (2000) 'Does Campaign Length Matter? Testing for Cross-National Effects', *British Journal of Political Science*, 30:215–35.

Sullivan, A. (1997) 'Maori Politics and Government Policies', in R. Miller (ed.), *New Zealand Politics in Transition*, Auckland, Oxford University Press.

Sullivan, A., and Margaritis, D. (2000) 'Maori Voting Patterns in 1999', in J. Boston, S. Church, S. Levine, E. McLeay and N. S. Roberts (eds), *Left Turn. The New Zealand General Election of 1999*, Wellington, Victoria University Press.

Sullivan, A., and Vowles, J. (1998) 'Realignment? Maori and the 1996 Election', in J. Vowles, P. Aimer, S. Banducci, and J. Karp (eds), *Voters' Victory? New Zealand's First Election under Proportional Representation*, Auckland, Auckland University Press.

Tate, K. (1991) 'Black Political Participation in the 1984 and 1988 Presidential Elections', *American Political Science Review*, 85:1159–76.

Trotter, C. (1999) *The Independent*, 12 May 1999.

UMR-Insight (2001) 'MMP: A Study of Public Attitudes', Report to the MMP Review Select Committee, UMR Insight Ltd., Wellington.

Vanderleeuw, J., and Utter, G. (1993) 'Voter Roll-off and the Electoral Context: A Test of Two Theses,' *Social Science Quarterly*, 74:664–73.

Verba, S., and Nie, N. H. (1972) *Participation in America*, New York, Harper and Row.

Verba, S., Schlozman., K., and Brady, H. (1995) *Voice and Equality: Civic Voluntarism and American Politics*, Cambridge, Mass., Harvard University Press.

Vowles, J. (1974) 'Community and Organisation', MA thesis, University of Auckland.

Vowles, J. (1993) 'Gender and Electoral Behaviour in New Zealand: Findings From the Present and the Past,' *Political Science*, 45:122–38.

Vowles, J. (1994) 'Dealignment and Demobilisation? Nonvoting in New Zealand 1938–1990', *Australian Journal of Political Science*, 29:96–114.

Vowles, J. (1997) 'Waiting for the Realignment: The New Zealand Party System 1972–1993', *Political Science*, 48:184–209.

Vowles, J. (1998a) 'A New Post-MMP Party System?' in J. Vowles, P. Aimer, S. Banducci, and J. Karp (eds), *Voters' Victory? New Zealand's First Election under Proportional Representation*, Auckland, Auckland University Press.

Vowles, J. (1998b) 'Countdown to MMP', in J. Vowles, P. Aimer, S. Banducci, and J. Karp (eds), *Voters' Victory? New Zealand's First Election under Proportional Representation*, Auckland, Auckland University Press.

Vowles, J. (2000a) 'The Impact of the 1999 Campaign', in J. Boston, S. Church, S. Levine, E. McLeay and N. S. Roberts (eds), *Left Turn: The New Zealand General Election of 1999*, Wellington, Victoria University Press.

Vowles, J. (2000b) 'Introducing Proportional Representation: The New Zealand Experience', *Parliamentary Affairs*, 53:680–96.

Vowles, J. (2001a) 'If PR Enhances Turnout, Why Not in New Zealand? The Puzzle of the 1999 Election'. Paper prepared for delivery at the Annual Meetings of the American Political Science Association, San Francisco, 30 August–2 September.

Vowles, J. (2001b) 'Submission to the Justice and Electoral Committee on the Electoral Amendment Bill No 2.'

Vowles J. (2001c) 'Did the Polls Influence the Vote? A Case Study of the 1999 New Zealand Election'. Paper presented to the New Zealand Political Studies Association Conference, Massey University, 7–9 December.

Vowles, J., and Aimer, P. (1993) *Voters' Vengeance: The 1990 Election in New Zealand and the Fate of the Fourth Labour Government,* Auckland, Auckland University Press.

Vowles, J., Aimer, P., Catt, H., Lamare, J., and Miller, R. (1995) *Towards Consensus? The 1993 General Election and Referendum in New Zealand and the Transition to Proportional Representation*, Auckland University Press, Auckland.

Vowles, J., Aimer, P., Banducci, S., and Karp, J. (1998) 'Voter Rationality and the Advent of MMP', in J. Vowles, P. Aimer, S. Banducci, and J. Karp (eds), *Voters' Victory? New Zealand's First Election under Proportional Representation*, Auckland, Auckland University Press.

Vowles, J., Aimer, P., Banducci, S., and Karp, J. (eds) (1998) *Voters' Victory? New Zealand's First Election under Proportional Representation*, Auckland, Auckland University Press.

Vowles, J., Banducci, S., and Karp, J. (2000) 'Proportional Representation on Trial: Elite vs. Mass Opinion on Electoral System Change in New Zealand'. Paper prepared for presentation at the Annual Conference of the American Political Science Association, Washington DC, 30 August – 3 September.

Vowles, J., Karp, J., and Banducci, S. (2000) 'Proportional Representation on Trial: Electoral System Opinion and Knowledge in New Zealand'. Paper presented at the American Political Science Association Meetings, Washington DC, September 1–5.

Ward, L. (1998) 'Second-Class MPs? New Zealand's Adaptation to Mixed-Member Parliamentary Representation', *Political Science*, 49:125–52.

Ware, A. (1996) *Political Parties and Party Systems*, Oxford University Press, Oxford.

Wattenberg, M. (2000) 'The Decline of Party Mobilisation', in R. Dalton and M. Wattenberg (eds), *Parties without Partisans: Political Change in Advanced Industrial Democracies*, Oxford, Oxford University Press.

Wielhouwer, P. W., and Lockerbie, B. (1994) 'Party Contacting and Political Participation 1952–90, *American Journal of Political Science*, 38:211–29.

Zaller, J. (1992) *The Nature and Origins of Mass Opinion*, Cambridge, Cambridge University Press.

NOTES ON AUTHORS

Peter Aimer is an honorary research fellow in the Department of Political Studies, University of Auckland. He has been associated with the New Zealand Election Studies programme, now funded by the Foundation for Research, Science, and Technology, since its beginning, and has been co-author or co-editor of the resulting books on the 1990, 1993, and 1996 elections. He is also author of *Wings of the Nation* (2000), a history of New Zealand's state-owned domestic airline.

Susan Banducci is currently a research fellow at the Amsterdam School of Communications Research, University of Amsterdam, where she is researching media effects, public opinion toward European integration, and turnout in European parliamentary elections. Prior to her current appointment, she spent three years with the New Zealand Election Study, and was a co-editor of *Voters' Victory?,* the 1996 election study. She has also published articles on New Zealand electoral politics, public opinion, gender and politics, and campaigns and elections in international journals including *Party Politics, Political Behavior, Australian Journal of Political Science, Electoral Studies, Political Research Quarterly, British Journal of Political Science, Comparative Political Studies,* and *American Politics Research.*

Jeffrey Karp is a postdoctoral fellow in the Amsterdam School of Communications Research, University of Amsterdam. Prior to his appointment in Amsterdam, he was a postdoctoral fellow at the University of Waikato where he helped plan and implement the 1999 New Zealand Election Study. He was a co-editor of the 1996 election study, *Voters' Victory?*. His research interests focus on public opinion and electoral behaviour, resulting in published articles in *British Journal of Political Science, Comparative Political Studies, Party Politics, European Journal of Political Research, Political Research Quarterly, Electoral Studies, Political Behavior, Australian Journal of Political Science, Public Opinion Quarterly,* and *American Politics Quarterly.*

Dimitri Margaritis is an associate professor in economics at the University of Waikato. He previously taught at the University of British Columbia, Southern Illinois University, and the State University of New York at Buffalo.

His research interests are in quantitative aspects of micro and macro-economics, with particular emphasis on policy-related issues. His recent publications include work on the efficiency of the US health service industry, measures of total factor productivity, and real time rules for monetary policy.

Raymond Miller is a senior lecturer and specialist in New Zealand and comparative politics in the Department of Political Studies, University of Auckland. His publications include *New Zealand Politics in Transition* (1997) and *New Zealand Government and Politics* (2001). He has been either a co-author or contributor to several books on New Zealand elections, including *Towards Consensus?* and *Voters' Victory?*, and is currently completing a book on political parties.

Ann Sullivan is Nga Puhi and a senior lecturer in the Department of Political Science and Public Policy at the University of Waikato. Her research and writing are in the areas of Maori politics, ethnic politics, and public policy, and as a member of the New Zealand Election Study team, she has analysed and reported the trends in Maori voting behaviour in *Voters' Victory?* and the present study.

Jack Vowles, until recently associate professor in the Department of Political Science and Public Policy at the University of Waikato, is a professor of Political Studies at the University of Auckland. He leads the New Zealand Election Study research programme funded by the Foundation for Research, Science, and Technology. His current research interests are in New Zealand politics, elections, and the consequences of electoral systems. He has published widely on these areas in New Zealand and international journals, and is co-author or co-editor of all four books arising from the NZES research programme.

INDEX

Note: references to parties and party leaders have been selectively indexed, as they occur frequently in most chapters.

ACT New Zealand, 6, 8, 36, 116, 121, 185; formation of, 4; electoral trends, 9, 17–18, 89; and strategic voting, 30–1; issue priorities, 43–4; gender gap, 56, 93–4; and Maori, 79; place on 'left–right' scale, 85, 86, 128; and split voting, 87, 88; campaign expenditure, 104–5; vs. National, 121–2; attitudes to MMP, 165, 173

age, *see* voting behaviour

'agenda setting', 36, 43, 44, 48. *See also* issues

Alliance, 5; formation of, 4; relations with Labour, 12–13, 93, 114, 115–7, 120–1, 124–5, 127; electoral trends, 9, 17–18, 90, 122; issue priorities, 43–4; voters, 30; gender gap, 56; and Maori, 69; place on 'left–right' scale, 86, 128; and split voting, 87, 88; and young voters, 94, 95; campaign expenditure, 104–5; coalition with Labour, 114–7, 125–7, 128; internal strains, 127

Anderton, Jim, 1, 5, 12, 22, 32, 36, 88, 116, 120, 123, 126; and campaign, 53; voters' evaluations of, 45; traits, 61, 62–3

APEC conference, 13, 50

attitudes, trust in parties, 2; trust in government, 135; to MMP (among voters), 8–9, 117, 123, 135–6, 160–6, 173; (among candidates), 161–2, 164–6, 173; to coalition government, 117–22, 124–5, 166–8; to descriptive representation, 131–3; to MPs, 136–42; to party lists, 139, 182–4; to direct democracy (among voters), 150–2, (among candidates), 152–3; to electoral systems, 161; to proportionality, 169–73; to one-seat threshold, 185; to 5 per cent threshold, 185; to minor parties, 185; to state funding, 190; of Maori voters, 79–81, 132–3. *See also* opinions

Banks, John, 8

Batten, Ann, 11, 75

Bavaria, 182

Beyer, Georgina, 131, 176

Birch, Bill, 3

Blair, Tony, 115

Bolger, Jim, 1, 3, 5, 7, 98; loses leadership, 10

Bruce, Suzanne, 123

Cabinet manual, 126

campaign expenditure, *see party entries*

canvassing, 105–6; effectiveness of, 106–7
CanWest, 37
Carter, Chris, 176
Christian Coalition, 4, 24
Christian Democrats, 4
Christian Heritage, 4
Citizens Initiated Referenda Bill (1993), 149
Citizens' Majority Trust, 186
Clark, Helen, 5, 10, 12, 13, 36, 54, 98, 115, 116, 120, 125; as preferred PM, 21–2, 32, 33, 46, 47, 52–3; and 1999 campaign, 50, 51, 53ff; voters' evaluations of, 45–7; and gender gap, 54–5; as feminist, 51; traits compared to Shipley, 57–65
Clark, Linda, 121
class voting, 93
coalitions, goals of, 115; National–New Zealand First, formation of, 6–7, difficulties, 7–8, 10, collapse, 11, 75, 114, 116, 153, attitudes to, 110–1, 135; Labour–Alliance, 114–7, 125–7, 128, 163, 184, 189, preliminary moves, 12–13, 115–7
communications, political, *see* media
Coromandel electorate, 17, 26–7, 32–3, 46, 48, 49, 52, 126
credit card, *see* Labour

Delamere, Tuariki, 11, 76
direct democracy, 147. *See also* attitudes
Donald, Rod, 176
Douglas, Roger, 3, 4
Dunne, Peter, 5, 6, 11, 176, 177, 187

economy, 14, 109; *see also* issues
'effective' parties, 87, 234
efficacy, 111, 136
Elder, Jack, 5, 11, 75
elections, 1990, 1; 1993, 3; 1996, 5, 6; 1999, 14–15, as 'replacement' election, 83, 96, assessment of, 97, turnout in, 102–113

Electoral Act (1993), 175, 178, 180
Electoral (Integrity) Amendment Bill, 126
Electoral Options Referenda Bill, 186
Electoral Reform Coalition, 2
electoral systems, *see* FPP, MMP
electorate MPs, 136–42; roles of, 139–42
electorates, *see under electorate names*
Employment Contracts Act, 16
English, Bill, 8, 36, 121

Field, Taito Phillip, 131
Finland, 182, 184
Firefighters Union, 150
Fitzsimons, Jeanette, 22, 26, 32, 88, 126; voters' evaluations of, 45, 46, 49
Fox, Derek, 72, 74, 75
FPP (first-past-the-post), effects of, 3, 82, 130–1; hypothetical vote, 84; knowledge of, 170
Franks, Stephen, 176
Fraser, Peter, 131

gender gap, 53–6, 93–4. *See also party entries*
Gillon, Grant, 176
Greens, 1, 45, 48, 49, 86–7, 97, 113, 116, 121, 126, 235; electoral trends, 9, 17–18, 19, 20, 22, 24–7, 29–30, 32, 46; gender gap, 56; and Maori, 79, 82; place on 'left–right' scale, 86; and split voting, 87–8; and young voters, 94, 95, 96; as support party, 184–5

Harré, Laila, 13, 51, 127
Hasler, Marie, 176
Hauraki electorate, 72, 74, 234
Hawkesby, John, 13
Henare, Tau, 5, 10, 11, 13, 66, 75
Hunt, Jonathan, 176, 177

Ikaroa-Rawhiti electorate, 72, 74, 75, 76, 82

International Institute for Democracy
and Electoral Assistance, 50
interest in politics, 111
issues, electoral reform, 2; health,
22–4, 44; education, 22–4, 44;
economy and taxes, 23–4, 44;
student loans, 44; electoral effect
of, 32, 40–1; party priorities, 43–
4; Maori issues, 44; women's
issues, 51; party positions on,
142–4, 145. *See also* 'agenda
setting'
Italy, 183
Iti, Tame, 234

Jackson, Willie, 127

Kirton, Neil, 8
Knapp, Garry, 149
knowledge, political, *see* FPP, MMP
Kopu, Alamein, 9, 11, 76, 137, 139,
153

Labour party, and electoral reform,
2, 160; and transition to MMP, 5;
1999 campaign, 16, 97; electoral
trends, 9, 17–18, 24–6, 90, 115;
issue priorities, 43–4; gender gap,
56, 93, 94; and Maori, 66, 68, 72,
74, 77, 80–1, 82; place on 'left–
right' scale, 85, 86; and split
voting, 87, 88; and trade unions,
92–3; campaign expenditure,
104–5; coalition with Alliance,
114–7, 125–5, *see also* coalitions;
relations with Alliance, 115–7,
120–1, 124–5, 127; attitudes to
MMP, 160, 163–4; credit card
promises, 233
Latter Day Saints, and Maori, 77, 78
Laws, Michael, 5
leaders, electoral effects of, 10, 32,
40, 42; and campaigns, 46, 50–1,
65; debates, 51. *See also* traits
Lee, Graeme, 4
Lee, Sandra, 127
'left–right' scale, 84–5, 97. *See also*
party entries

Liberal Democrat party, 115
list MPs, 9–10, 136–42, 190; in
Germany, 138, 141; roles of, 139–
42. *See also* attitudes, list seats
list seats, 154; number of, 178, 179;
effect of, 178, 180–1; open and
closed lists, 182–4

Mahuta, Nanaia, 72
Mana Maori party, 69, 76, 82
Mana Motuhake party, 75, 127
Mana Wahine Te Ira Tangata party,
76
Maori, and Labour, 66, 68, 72, 74,
77, 80–1, 82; electorates, 66, 101,
102, 103, 130, 132, 133–4, 178,
181–2, 234; and New Zealand
First, 66, 67–72, 74, 76, 78, 82;
voting, 67–72; split voting, 72–5;
voters, 77–8; and National 77, 79;
in Parliament, 131, 181; attitudes
to representation, 132–3; electoral
option, 134; attitudes to MPs,
137; contact with MPs, 138
Mauri Pacific party, 13, 69, 74, 75,
82, 116
McCardle, Peter, 5, 11
McCarten, Matt, 127
McDonald, Robyn, 8, 123, 153
McKinnon, Don, 8
media, voters' attention to, 35, 41,
42; news content of, 38, 39, 42;
effect of, 34, 42, 45–7, 48
median voter, 85, 142
MMP, introduction of, 1; transition
to, 4; first election, 6–7; effects
of, 16, 33, 51, 83, 85, 99, 101,
102, 109, 130–1, 135, 141–2, 144,
145, 161; review committee, 127,
128, 175–7, 190, 191; knowledge
of, 169, 178–9, 185–6; assessment of, 188–9. *See also* attitudes
mobilisation, 103
Moore, Mike, 5
Morgan, Tukoroirangi, 7, 75, 76, 153
Mormon church, *see* Latter Day
Saints
Morris, Deborah, 11

MPs, *see* electorate MPs, list MPs
Muldoon, Sir Robert, 98

National party, in government, 1, 11, 13; and 1993 election, 3; and transition to MMP, 5; coalition with New Zealand First, *see* New Zealand First; and electoral reform, 2, 160; 1999 campaign, 16, 36, 97; electoral trends, 9, 17–18, 24–6, 30, 90; issue priorities, 43–4; gender gap, 56, 93, 94; and Maori, 77, 79; place on 'left–right' scale, 85, 86, 97; and split voting, 87, 88; reasons for defeat, 97; campaign expenditure, 104–5; vs. ACT, 121–2; attitudes to MMP, 160, 164, 186
NewLabour, 1, 12
newspapers, 35, 40, 42
New Zealand First party, formation, 4; and 1993 election, 5; and 1996 election, 6; coalition with National, 7–8, 97, 109, 114, 122–3, 125, 128, 135, 144, 153, 184; party split, 11; electoral trends, 9, 17–18, 24–6, 32, 116, 122; list candidates, 36, 97, 123; gender gap, 56; and Maori, 66, 67–72, 74, 76, 78, 82; place on 'left–right' scale, 85, 86; campaign expenditure, 104; and MMP review committee, 176
New Zealand on Air, 37
non-vote, 20, 94–6, 112–3; among Maori, 68, 69, 72, 112–3, 234; theoretical explanations for, 100–1. *See also* turnout

opinions, formation and change, 44; of Clark and Shipley, 45–7
opinion polls, 37, 52; influence of, 24–8, 32–3, 36–7; in Canada, 33
O'Regan, Katherine, 26
'overhang' seats, 179, 180

paid parental leave, 51
Parliament, number of MPs, 177–81. *See also* referendums

'party hoppers', 137, 139, 153. *See also* Electoral (Integrity) Amendment Bill
party identification, 21, 29, 91–2, 105; effect of, 30–2; and turnout, 111
party lists, *see* list seats
party membership, 91
'People's Bank', 127
Peters, Winston, 5, 7, 8, 10, 11, 26, 32, 66, 88, 114, 116, 123, 185; voters' evaluations of, 45–6; traits, 62–3, 65
Piri Wiri Tua Movement, 76
political knowledge, *see* FPP, MMP
polls, *see* opinion polls
Prebble, Richard, 13, 22, 122, 123; voters' evaluations of, 45, 46; traits, 62, 65
'priming', 40, 42
proportional representation, *see* MMP

radio, 40–1
Ratana, and Maori voters, 77
referendums, on electoral system, 2, 3, 161; on crime and punishment, 146–7, 156–8; on number of MPs, 147, 153–7, 177; on MMP, 186–7, 189, 191; citizen-initiated referendums (CIR), 149–50; use of abroad, 147–8; use of in New Zealand, 148–9, 152, 237; pros and cons of, 148, 157–8, 178
representative democracy, 147
Retirement Savings Scheme, 8
review committee, *see* MMP
Richardson, Ruth, 3, 121
Ringatu church voters, 76
Royal Commission on electoral system, 2, 99, 130, 133, 145, 148, 149, 160, 177, 191
Ryall, Tony, 176

Scandinavia, 184
Shipley, Jenny, 36, 97–8, 123, 173, 176, 177; becomes PM, 10; as preferred PM, 13–14, 21–2, 32,

46, 52–3, 97; and 1999 campaign, 50, 51, 53ff; voters' evaluations of, 45–7; and gender gap, 54–5; as feminist, 51–2; traits compared to Clark, 57–65
Singapore Free Trade Agreement, 127
Slater, John, 116
split voting, *see* voting behaviour, *party entries*
state funding, of parties, 190
strategic voting, *see* voting behaviour
swing, 235

Tamihere, John, 72
Tanczos, Nandor, 131
Tauranga electorate, 26, 32, 185
television, 34ff
Te Tai Hauauru electorate, 72, 76
Te Tai Tokerau electorate, 66, 75
Te Tai Tonga electorate, 71, 73, 75
Te Tawharau party, 76
Thatcher, Margaret, 52
thresholds, of representation, 184–5, 186
Tourism Board, 13
trade unions, 92–3; and turnout, 108
traits, 56–7; Clarke and Shipley compared, 57–64; electoral effects of, 61–4
Treaty of Waitangi, 66, 81
Treaty of Waitangi Act, 66
trust, *see* attitudes
turnout, 99–113, 234; decline of, 99, 100, 111–3; increase in 1996, 99, 102; rates in 1990, 101; and electorate competition, 102–3; and party expenditure, 104–5; and party contacts, 106–8; and

attitudes, 109–11. *See also* non-vote
TV One, 34ff, 120
Television New Zealand (TVNZ), 37
TV 3, 34ff

unemployment, 109
United New Zealand party, 116, 238; formation of 5; place on 'left–right' scale, 85, 86
Upton, Simon, 121

Values party, 86
voting behaviour, volatility, 2, 20–1, 28, 83, 89–90, 91, 96, 234; vote stability, 84, 89–90; vote 'switchers', 90; campaign vote intentions, 17–20, 29–30; strategic voting, 27–9; preference voting, 28–9; Maori voting, 67–76; split voting, 87–8, among Maori, 72–5; voting theories, 83–4; age and voting, 94–6; models of, 237. *See also* FPP, MMP, non-voters, party identification

Waiariki electorate, 74, 76
Waipareira Trust, 74
Waitai, Rana, 75, 76
Wilson, Margaret, 126
women's suffrage, 50
women, as party leaders, 50; as voters, *see* gender gap; and evaluation of party leaders, 47–8; in Parliament, 131, 181
Wong, Pansy, 131, 181
Work and Income New Zealand, 13
Wylie, Tutekawa, 71